NELSON'S YANKEE CAPTAIN

THE LIFE OF BOSTON LOYALIST
SIR BENJAMIN HALLOWELL

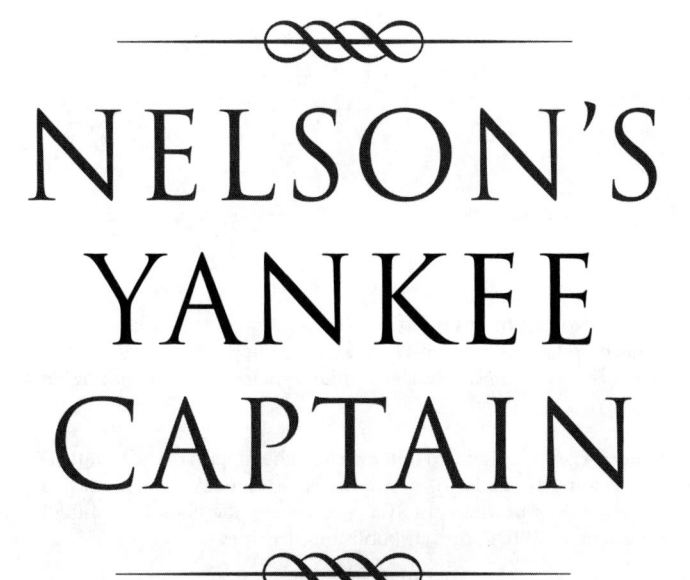

NELSON'S YANKEE CAPTAIN

BRYAN ELSON

FORMAC PUBLISHING COMPANY LIMITED
HALIFAX

For Maxine and Christopher, with love

Copyright © 2008 Bryan Elson

All rights reserved. No part of this book may be reproduced or transmitted in any form or by any means, electronic or mechanical, including photocopying, or by any information storage or retrieval system, without permission in writing from the publisher.

Formac Publishing Company Limited acknowledges the support of the Culture Division, Nova Scotia Department of Tourism, Culture and Heritage. We acknowledge the financial support of the Government of Canada through the Book Publishing Industry Development Program (BPIDP) for our publishing activities.

We acknowledge the support of the Canada Council for the Arts for our publishing program.

Library and Archives Canada Cataloguing in Publication

Elson, Bryan
    Nelson's Yankee captain : the life of Boston loyalist Sir Benjamin Hallowell / Bryan Elson.

ISBN 978-0-88780-751-0

    1. Carew, Benjamin Hallowell, 1760-1834. 2. Admirals—Great Britain—Biography. 3. Great Britain. Royal Navy—Officers—Biography. 4. Hallowell family. 5. American loyalists--Biography. 6. Great Britain—History, Naval—18th century. 7. Great Britain—History, Naval—19th century. I. Title.

DA87.1.H15E48 2008   359.0092   C2008-903849-5

Formac Publishing Company Limited
5502 Atlantic Street
Halifax, Nova Scotia B3H 1G4
www.formac.ca

First published in the United States in 2009
Distributed in the United States by:
Casemate
2114 Darby Road, 2nd Floor
Havertown, PA 19083

Printed and bound in Canada

CONTENTS

	ACKNOWLEDGEMENTS	7
	INTRODUCTION	9
1.	EXPELLED	13
2.	THE WOODEN WALLS	33
3.	THE WORLD TURNED UPSIDE DOWN	58
4.	ON THE BEACH	83
5.	PROMOTION	102
6.	COURAGEUX	130
7.	THE NILE	158
8.	SURRENDER	187
9.	TAKING STOCK	216
10.	ARGO	232
11.	ENDURANCE	256
12.	LOST FRIENDS	285
13.	REAR ADMIRAL OF THE BLUE	311
14.	AT ANCHOR	333
15.	THE LEGACY	358
	EPILOGUE	371
	APPENDIX	376
	NOTES	390
	BIBLIOGRAPHY	402

PHOTO CREDITS

Archives and Collections Society, Ontario: 374B, 375; Archives of Ontario: 222; Arrowsmith: 280; Beresford, 185; *Boston Daily Globe*, 29 Dec. 1901: 29; Cambridge Military Library: 326; Captain A. T. Mahan: 76, 155, 180; Cooper Willyams: 189, 193; Courtesy of the Massachusetts Historical Society: 19; Dave Ley: 113; E.T. Compton: 127; Ellison Fine Art, miniature now privately owned in the UK: 269; Ernest Prater: 153; Gordon C. Bond: 286; Henry Hoppner Meyer: 260; Howard Henry: 291; Hulton Getty: 218; Imperial War Museum: 374T; J. Cruickshank: 45; James Northcote: 59; John Hatch: 235; John Hayter: 361; John Singleton Copley: 85; L. Guzzardi: 202; London Borough of Sutton Local Studies Centre: 363; Messrs T.H. Parker Bros.: 157; *Port Mahon, the Harbour at Minorca*: 306; Sir Joshua Reynolds: 343; *The landing in Egypt*, 8 March 1801: 319; The National Archives of the UK: 145; Thomas Buttersworth: 168; Thomas Luny: 183.

Map and Family Tree Credits: Peggy McCalla: 14, 46, 70, 98-99, 124, 171, 315.

ACKNOWLEDGEMENTS

I could not have started, continued or finished this biography without the assistance and support of more people than I can properly acknowledge, in three countries.

In the United Kingdom I am grateful to Roger Nixon for his expert research at the National Archives when I was unable to visit in person. Claude and Patricia Charron navigated me through the back lanes of Surrey in search of locations that were important to my subject, and Kathleen Shawcross in the local studies section of the Sutton Library gave me a great deal of help with the history of Beddington Manor.

Mr. Danny D. Smith, AB, is the Chair of the Special Collections Committee, Gardiner Library Association, Curator of the Yellow House papers, and historian of the Gardiner-Hallowell area of Maine. Sandra Webber of Williamstown, Massachusetts is currently working on a biography of my subject's father, Benjamin Hallowell Sr. They could not have been more generous with their time and advice, and the American thread of my story owes much to their guidance. Mr Harris Hollin generously gave me access to Chaplain Willyams' unique Journey up the Mediterranean in his collection of rare books, a priceless eyewitness source. The library staff at the Massachusetts Historical Society were of great assistance in my research of another critical resource, the Boylston family papers.

Paul Adamthwaite of the Archives and Collections Society, Picton, Ontario was very forthcoming with information concerning Hallowell Township and HMCS *Hallowell*. In Halifax my thanks are due to the staff of the Provincial Archives of Nova Scotia, the Maritime Museum of the Atlantic, the Killam Library at the University of Dalhousie, and especially to Marilyn Gurney Smith, curator of the Maritime Command Museum, who provided critical assistance and a work space very appropriate to my subject. Tinker Pullen Mackie helped with early Halifax records, and I am indebted to Julian Gwyn for his interest and frank comments.

Assisted by Jean Chard, Nancy Roberts edited the first version of the manuscript with patience and discernment and eliminated many shortcomings. I am most grateful to James Lorimer for taking on an unknown author, and to the staff of Formac Publishing for making the book a reality. I owe a particular debt to Christen Thomas for her patient guidance and assistance throughout the publishing process.

In thanking these and many others for their contributions I naturally accept the entire responsibility for any deficiencies that survive.

INTRODUCTION

The subject of this story died Admiral Sir Benjamin Hallowell-Carew, but the 'Carew' was only added late in life through a very strange chain of circumstances. For most of his life he was simply Benjamin Hallowell.

As an amateur student of naval history I first noticed references to Hallowell as a Canadian and as one of Nelson's famous 'Band of Brothers'. No less an authority than the latest edition of the *Dictionary of National Biography* gives him a Canadian birthplace. How was it that I, as a former officer of the Royal Canadian Navy, had never heard of him, and how was it that some Canadian town was not proud to claim him as a native son?

The answer is that Hallowell was *not* born in Canada. There seems no doubt that he was actually born in Boston at a time when Massachusetts was still a colony of Great Britain.

The mistake was first made in one of the two obituaries published immediately after Hallowell's death. (The second does not refer to any place of birth.) The name of the author has been lost, making it impossible to assess his credibility. On the basis of internal references, I believe him to have been Hallowell's brother-in-law, Captain Samuel Hood Inglefield. If so, he might have been expected to know the truth, but nevertheless seems to have committed the initial error either out of ignorance or from some unknown motive.

Not only was Hallowell not born in Canada, but he seems never to have set foot on what is now Canadian territory. On the other hand, his Loyalist family had significant land holdings in both Nova Scotia and Ontario, and the family name has been perpetuated not only in those provinces but also in Nunavut and British Columbia, and in the name of a Second World War ship of the Royal Canadian Navy.

Born in what became the United States, and with enduring Canadian links, he served a lifetime in the navy of Great Britain, in which country he died on an estate that meant virtually nothing to him. He had near relatives and property interests in all three countries. Rootless for most of his life, he may in the end have been psychologically positioned somewhere in mid-Atlantic, carried there by the tides of the American and French revolutions that convulsed the world between 1775 and 1815. His life spanned the tumultuous first stages of the working out of new relationships among the British mother country and the two new North American nations, a process that in a naval sense culminated in their joint victory in the Second World War Battle of the Atlantic, a struggle in which the Hallowell name was to find an echo.

This impression of Hallowell as a casualty of history in the making was one of the two major factors influencing my decision to share the results of my research with a wider audience. The second was my fascination with Hallowell as an individual. I discovered a dedicated professional of great physical and moral courage, sometimes eccentric, intolerant of injustice, a valued friend to many and a dutiful family man, as devoted as a largely absent father could be, who nevertheless maintained an intense lifelong friendship with another woman. He was a close friend of Admiral Nelson; in spite of their very different personalities, their tactical instincts were very similar.

By the time Hallowell reached high rank, peace closed off opportunities for distinction at the strategic level, but his grasp of political and military affairs suggests that he had much to offer if a wider sphere had ever been open to him. Sailors of any navy will find themselves nodding in recognition at elements of Hallowell's service life that strike a chord after more than two hundred years, a remarkable continuity of tradition and professional ethos.

I have relied as much as possible on primary sources for information of direct relevance to Hallowell's career and personal life. Occasionally, I have attributed to him thoughts and emotions for which there is no direct evidence, but which are entirely consistent with his character and the given situation. Otherwise, the account is strictly factual and evidence based, and emphatically not a work of historical fiction. His true story needs no embellishment.

The bibliography lists numerous scholarly works, both traditional and modern. From them I have drawn much of the historical background and the sociological and material context of the complex fighting system that was the Royal Navy in which Hallowell spent his life. The Appendix contains basic information on seamanship, tactics, and personnel that readers new to the subject may find useful.

To maintain the narrative flow I have avoided the use of footnotes. Scholars and others interested in further research will find references to the sources in the Notes at the end of the volume.

To the best of my knowledge there has been no previous serious biography of Benjamin Hallowell. I am aware of three works of historical fiction in which he appears, in two of them very briefly. Patrick O'Brian's *Desolation Island* depicts him as a dinner guest of Jack Aubrey's, refighting the battle of Cape St. Vincent as the gentlemen lingered over their port, using nutshells to form the lines of battle. He is not described nor does he utter a word. In *Ramage and the Drumbeat* Dudley Pope places Hallowell on board Admiral Jervis's flagship on the eve of the same battle. This is historically accurate, and Hallowell is presented as being sympathetic to Pope's hero, in contrast to the shabby treatment of Ramage by Captain Calder, Jervis's chief of staff.

It is only in Showell Styles's *The Admiral's Fancy* that Hallowell is the principal character. The author postulates an early acquaintance between Hallowell and the future Lady Hamilton on the basis of which Hallowell identifies her as an unprincipled schemer. He is later cast in the role of attempting to protect his friend Horatio Nelson from the wiles of this unworthy temptress. Some of the other characters and a few events are real, but essentially the work is a fantasy. Read as such it is mildly interesting but heavily dependent on coincidence, and the real Hallowell is nowhere to be found.

My interest was sparked by a mistake, but even as I learned the truth I found much that was interesting about the man and the navy in which he served, set in the context of history-shaping events. It was in the hope that others would find his story as fascinating as I do that I decided to record it.

1

EXPELLED
1768–1777

If the boy has understanding he keeps it to himself, neither your mother or myself can discover the least of the Character by which he has been recommended to us.

Benjamin Hallowell Sr.,
letter to his son Ward, 1776

Benjamin Hallowell, the fourth to bear the name, was born on 1 January 1761, not in Canada, as the *Dictionary of National Biography* incorrectly states, but in the thriving seaport of Boston in the British province of Massachusetts. The first Hallowells had emigrated from Devonshire in 1643, seeking freedom to practice their Dissenter beliefs in the New World. By the 1760s they had become a family of substance, although not of the elite whose sons were educated at Harvard and provided the clergy, lawyers, and officials of the colony. Our Benjamin's Grandfather Hallowell possessed extensive property in the city, including water frontage and a shipyard on Batterymarch. He traded with the West Indies, was involved in the Newfoundland fishery, and became a shareholder in a tract of land along the Kennebec River, including most of the present town of Hallowell, Maine.

We shall continue with the career of the boy's father, Benjamin Hallowell Sr., in order to explain the circumstances of young Benjamin's childhood.

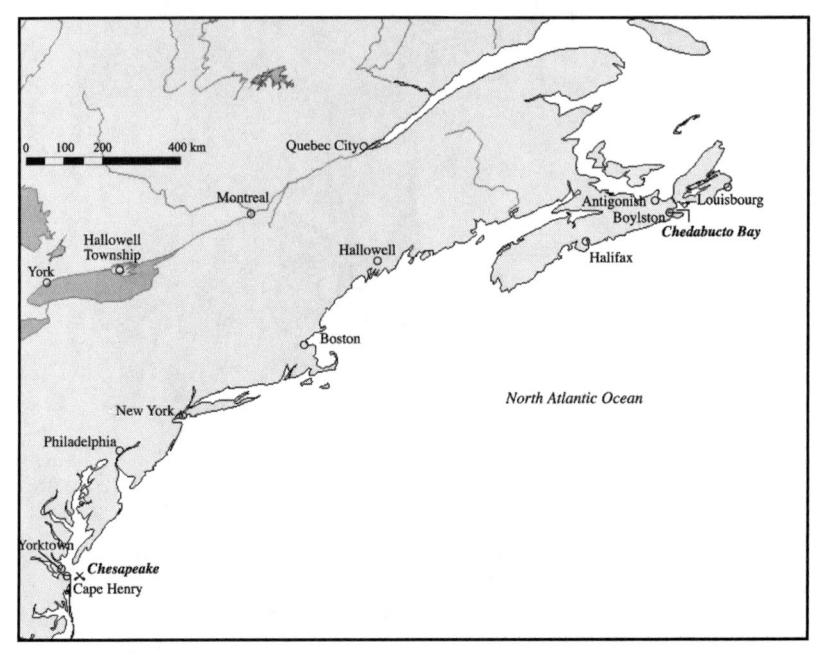

Eastern Seaboard of North America

When the boy was born, his father, also named Benjamin, was captain of the *King George*, a 20-gun brig belonging to the province. War between Britain and France had been raging for six years. Each year the *King George* had patrolled the waters between Boston and Halifax, protecting the trade against French privateers, or, as his orders stated, 'cleansing the sea of those vermin from Louisbourg.' After Louisbourg fell in 1758 he carried dispatches and troops between there and Halifax, and in 1762 he served under Admiral Colville in the expedition that retook St. John's, Newfoundland, from the French.

When the war ended in 1763 his services were rewarded by a grant of 20,000 acres in a location of his choice. In the autumn of 1759 he had unsuccessfully chased a privateer into a broad inlet in northeastern Nova Scotia — Chedabucto Bay, whose forested and deserted shores gradually narrowed to a sheltered harbour at its western head. The sight had remained with him, and when the opportunity arose he chose 'a Tract of land, situate, lying and being on the east side of Chedabucto Harbour, just entering into the Second Basin.' At the time the undeveloped land in a virtually empty colony was practically valueless.

In 1746, aged twenty-two, Benjamin Sr. had married Mary Boylston, daughter of another substantial Boston family. Their first child, christened Ward Nicholas, was born in 1749. Six others were born, but only Lucy survived infancy. Mary Hallowell became unusually attached to her firstborn. Ward Nicholas would be his mother's favourite for the rest of her life, and at her death he received half of her personal estate, while each of his younger siblings received one-quarter.

With the end of the war the *King George* was paid off. Rather than returning to his mercantile life in Boston her former captain travelled to London to lobby for a position in colonial administration. Such appointments were routinely awarded through influence and patronage. With the help of Admiral Colville, Hallowell Sr. gained access to Lord North, the dominant figure in the British government, and a suitable position was soon identified. Patronage indeed, but as a former merchant captain Hallowell also possessed excellent qualifications for his new post, Comptroller of Customs for the Port of Boston. He was sworn in on 18 July 1764, when young Benjamin was three years old.

The elder Hallowell's future in the empire seemed assured. He was financially secure, his own father was a man of substance, and he was a war hero who possessed unusually strong connections and affinities with the mother country. His association with the British forces through seven years of war further reinforced the links with colonial officialdom. John Adams, the future American president, knew him well, and their wives were cousins. Adams described Hallowell Sr. at this time as 'high flying, high church, and high state.'

No one could have predicted that Benjamin Hallowell's sought-after appointment was to place him at the eye of a storm that was already gathering and would lead within a dozen years to the revolt of the colonies and the exile of his family.

Initially, at least, the issue was monetary: who should pay for the defense of the colonies, for the salaries of their governors and other crown officials, and for the general costs of administration?

As a new device to extract revenue from the colonies the British Parliament enacted the Stamp Act, which became law 22 March 1765.

The act required an official stamp to be affixed to every governmental and commercial transaction, including contracts, ship's clearance papers, licenses, land grants, and even newspapers and playing cards and calendars. The stamped paper had to be purchased from designated distributors working on commission.

The papers arrived in Boston on August 14. Rioting mobs burned in effigy Andrew Oliver, the Boston Collector for the Stamp Act, and his house was put to the torch. The next day Oliver resigned. On August 26 the mob burned the house of Governor Hutchinson and ransacked the residences of a number of unpopular officials including that of Benjamin Hallowell. He had nothing directly to do with the Stamp Act but was already making enemies as Comptroller of Customs. There is no record of any personal injury to the Hallowells, including four-year-old Ben and one-year-old Mary. In all probability Mrs. Hallowell and the children had prudently retired to their country property at Roxbury.

Except in Nova Scotia, the colonists generally continued to conduct business without stamps. Recognizing that the Stamp Act was unenforceable, Parliament repealed it in March 1766. At the same time it passed the Declaratory Act, reaffirming Parliament's right to legislate for the colonies, notwithstanding the failure of the Stamp Act.

In June 1767 Parliament passed the Townshend Acts 'for making a more certain and adequate provision for the charge of the administration of justice, and the support of the civil government, and defraying the expenses of defending, protecting and securing the said colonies....' The American Board of Customs Commissioners, a new body, became responsible for enforcement in the whole of North America. Boston was chosen as the headquarters.

In the past, not least in Boston, customs officials had been open to bribery and had habitually winked at evasion of the duties. Even reputable merchants were deeply involved in a culture of condoned smuggling that had the full support of the population. As Comptroller of Customs, Benjamin Hallowell Sr. was thrust — not unwillingly — to the centre of events. Stubborn by nature and a loyal public servant, he was determined to enforce the regulations to the best of his ability. Others might be intimidated into casting a blind eye, but he would do his job as he saw it, whatever the cost in personal popularity. His equally conscientious and determined brother Robert had joined him as Deputy Comptroller. Thus, Boston, the heart of resistance to the new customs regime, became at the same time the city in which that regime would be most strictly applied. The opposing forces fed on each other in a spiral of escalating conflict that contributed much to the final rupture between the colonies and the mother country.

Ships of the Royal Navy had the duty of seizing suspected smugglers. Cases were then adjudicated in the Crown Courts of Vice-Admiralty. As usual in a time of peace, the strength of the Royal Navy had been allowed to decline — only ten ships were stationed in the whole of North America. The Board of Customs requested naval reinforcements for Boston. In response, Commodore Samuel Hood, the Halifax-based Commander in Chief, dispatched the 50-gun *Romney* and two sloops, and later followed in person.

On 10 June 1768, emboldened by this reinforcement, Benjamin Hallowell Sr. ordered the seizure of John Hancock's ship *Liberty* for suspected customs infractions and had her brought under the guns of the *Romney*. While returning home Hallowell and his assistant Acklom Harrison were surrounded by a mob and pelted with dirt and stones. Hallowell might well have been murdered had some passersby not come to his aid. That night the mob surrounded his house but withdrew after breaking a few windows.

Rioting continued, forcing the members of the Board of Customs to flee to Castle William. Virtual prisoners and quite unable to carry out their duties, they decided to send an emissary to London to report on the situation and seek guidance. A trustworthy, knowledgeable, and credible go-between was essential, and the choice fell on Hallowell, partly no doubt to remove him from the situation of personal danger his diligence had created.

He decided to take his younger son with him. Given the excellent standard of education in Massachusetts, we can rule out the idea that young Ben was sent in order to obtain more advanced schooling. A very important consideration was probably fear for Benjamin's welfare at a Boston school. Adult opinion would no doubt be reflected in bullying by his son's schoolmates, perhaps carried to the point of physical or emotional harm to the boy. The senior Benjamin may have wished the boy to acquire the outlook of an English gentleman, as opposed to that of the colonial bourgeoisie. As a bonus, the boy might form friendships that would stand him in good stead in the Anglo-colonial official world.

When he was not yet two years old the birth of his sister Mary had ended young Benjamin's status as the baby of the family. Thereafter he was to occupy an ambiguous position between the beloved elder brother Ward, elder sister Lucy, and infant sister Mary. In later life Ben showed a strong streak of mischief, a penchant for the unorthodox, and a lack of respect for authority. At seven he was perhaps already becoming a problem. The father's absence from the household would place an added burden on the mother. Mary Hallowell may not have found it difficult to reconcile herself to the temporary loss of her second son.

If the Hallowells had felt any serious doubt about their future it would have been quite possible for the entire family to leave Boston in 1768. They must have judged that Benjamin was the only one at serious risk and that the irritating political difficulties of the moment would soon be settled. When things returned to normal the boy could resume the life of a scion of the Boston middle class. They were wrong on all counts.

On their arrival in England father and son were welcomed into the home of Samuel Vaughan and his wife Sarah, the elder Hallowell's sister. Samuel Vaughan had prospered in the three-way trade between Britain, the West Indies, and the Thirteen Colonies, and had built a large residence at Wanstead near London. The couple had seven children ranging in age from seventeen-year-old Benjamin to two-year-old Rebecca. Three of the cousins — Charles, Sarah, and Samuel Jr. — were near young Ben's age, ideal playmates to help him adjust to his new surroundings now that the excitement of the voyage was over and his father was becoming fully involved in his mission. In the ensuing years the Vaughans were to treat Benjamin as one of their own, and their home was to offer the nearest approach to a family circle that he was to know as a child.

Ben became a student at the school of Mr. John Morrice in what was then the country village of Cheshunt about fifteen miles north of London. Thanks to Britain's prosperity its middle class was growing rapidly. The long-standing church and grammar school system offered a classics-based curriculum ill-suited to the evolving economic and social environment. The result was a proliferation of new-model schools operated as private enterprises by masters who provided boys with board and lodging, clothed them, and taught them according to the master's idea of the new model. These so-called public schools were unregulated, designed their own courses of study, and prospered according to their reputation and the social level of the students they were able to attract. Some famous ones, such as Eton and Harrow, survive to this day; many have vanished without trace.

The curriculum illustrates the general education considered appropriate for a gentleman of the time.

Mr. Morrice's school has left no records, but Ben's experience can be traced through the itemized bills presented to his father every six months. Benjamin Hallowell paid Mr. Morrice £21 a year for his son's board and instruction, approximately half the amount charged at top-ranked Eton. In addition to the basic rate there were supplementary charges for books and other supplies, clothing, coach hire for vacation travel, and extracurricular activities such as drawing and dancing.

The core subjects were mathematics (ciphering), French, and Latin, and of course English literature and composition. Two years later Ben was also taking classical Greek. In essence he received a 'modern' education, based on the addition of the more practical subjects of French, drawing, and mathematics to the traditional classics. Ben learned to write an almost copperplate script, and his later official letters are models of clear and concise expression. He must have acquired a skill in mathematics adequate for the study of navigation, though no one could have foreseen his naval career during his Morrice years. Still less could he have foreseen the value of French to one who would later be a prisoner of war of France.

In most public schools life was hard and brutal, flogging was common for infractions of discipline, and drinking and fisticuffs among the pupils were not uncommon. A few years at such an institution was good, if unintentional, preparation for the navy.

When Benjamin Hallowell Sr. returned to Boston in September 1770, he found the atmosphere even more threatening than when he had left. Indeed, in his later submission to the Loyalist Claims Commission he asserted that in his absence the family had suffered repeated insults and abuse, indirectly leading to the death of fourteen-year-old Lucy, who 'was deprived of her reason, and after languishing more than a year, died.'

Hallowell Sr. was now to play a prominent role in the developing conflict. The British government rewarded his work in London by making him one of the five Commissioners of the American Board of Customs at a salary of £500 a year. His brother Robert succeeded him as Comptroller of Customs.

Over the next six years each new British measure of control provoked a corresponding reaction in the direction of independence. Spearheaded by the radical Sons of Freedom, opposition to the Tea Duties became increasingly violent. In June 1772 the cutter HMS *Gaspée* was boarded by surprise and burnt while at anchor off Rhode Island. The suspected perpetrators escaped arrest, evidence of a virtual breakdown in public order. In December 1773 two of the customs commissioners were shut up in Castle William and a mob under the influence of wealthy smugglers disguised themselves as Indians and jettisoned a cargo of tea from a merchant vessel alongside the wharves — the famous Boston Tea Party.

In response the British Parliament passed the Boston Ports Bill, effectively prohibiting all seaborne trade. The Massachusetts legislature then passed a series of resolves that constituted a direct challenge to British rule. A new governor, General Gage, thereupon dissolved the General Court, and proceeded to govern with the advice of an appointed body, the Mandamus Councilors.

Many of these appointees resigned under threat, and Benjamin Hallowell, not a Mandamus Councilor, was mobbed and escaped only after threatening to use his pistols on his pursuers. Anyone opposing the mob risked tarring and feathering and having his house pulled down.

General Gage was married to an American and had a lot of American experience. He and Hallowell Sr. shared the opinion that above all a strong hand was needed. Hallowell found the inaction of the troops under Colonel Dalrymple 'shameful' and an encouragement to mob rule. 'If government does not assert itself this country will certainly be independent of the mother country. They talk as freely of throwing off their dependency as you can possibly conceive, but if they once could but see that the lion was aroused they would tremble, they at present are mighty valiant there being nobody to oppose.'

Again and again the authorities took measures that were bound to inflame the colonists, while at the same time lacking the will or the force to ensure compliance. Retreats under duress over the Stamp Act, the Townshend Duties or the maintenance of local order did nothing to earn the goodwill of the more extreme Americans. They saw themselves as simply asserting their claim to representative government on the British model, in opposition to Parliament's insistence on its own right to tax the colonies. On this question of principle the patriot party would not compromise.

As the political and security situation spiralled toward disaster, significant events took place within the Hallowell family. In 1774 Young Benjamin's grandfather, the prosperous shipwright, died bewildered by the collapse of the ordered colonial world he had known for most of his seventy-five years. Three years earlier, Ben's mother and brother Ward had enjoyed a stroke of good fortune when Mary's brother Nicholas Boylston bequeathed £3000 to her and £4000 to Ward. In order to inherit, Ward had to change his surname from Hallowell to Boylston. He duly took the necessary legal action, entered into his inheritance as Ward Nicholas Boylston, and embarked on a mercantile career in which he enjoyed increasing prosperity.

Shortly after coming into his inheritance he had married Anne Molineaux, who in 1771 had presented him with a son, also christened Nicholas, but usually referred to as Nicky. Almost from the first the marriage was in trouble. Anne appears to have been a disturbed personality and suffered from increasingly violent fits that may have been epileptic. In late 1773 Ward escaped by embarking on a foreign tour, leaving Anne and Nicky in Boston.

Apart from connections with the hated customs service, other links helped to identify the Hallowells with British 'tyranny.' Benjamin's aunt, Anne Hallowell, had married Captain Paston Gould of the British Army. The Goulds had since returned to England, but another aunt, Rebecca, had married Captain Thomas Bishop, of the 20-gun frigate *Lively*, stationed at Boston. The *Lively* had protected the arrival of the detested stamp papers and was of course involved in customs enforcement. The Hallowells numbered among the most unpopular Tories, and the family must have been grateful that young Ben at least was not at risk.

The absent son tried to follow family events through parental letters, probably not very numerous and always taking several weeks to cross the Atlantic. His main source of information would have been his visits to the Vaughans. Like many Englishmen, Samuel Vaughan was sympathetic to the ideas of Thomas Jefferson and Benjamin Franklin and strongly disagreed with his own government's policy. Ben must often have listened uncomfortably to conversations that inevitably placed his father on the wrong side of the quarrel, thanks to his loyal execution of what Samuel Vaughan would have seen as oppressive and unreasonable measures.

In July of 1775 Ward and the fourteen-year-old Benjamin were reunited for the first time in seven years at the Vaughans' London home. Ward had voyaged via Newfoundland to Naples, and thence first to the Holy Land and then to Egypt, at that time almost unknown to westerners. He purchased a mummy to which he became so attached that he carried it with him on his journey through Italy to England and later dispatched it to Halifax. In November 1780 his agent there was to report, 'The long case containing ye mummy remains in store and appears to be undamaged.' It eventually found its way to Boston, where Ward presented it to Harvard University.

In time to come Ben Hallowell would be deeply involved in the Franco-British struggles for Egypt. It is tempting to believe that the first-hand information acquired from Ward as a teenager contributed to his later successes in the morass of Egyptian politics.

Shortly after the reunion Ward became aware that an atmosphere bordering on the sinister prevailed at his brother's school. Writing to Ward from Cheshunt and thanking him for 'the many kind Favors I received of you while in Town,' young Benjamin goes on to assure his brother that 'it shall be my constant Endeavour to conduct myself in such a manner as to continue deserving of them.' Perhaps his behaviour had already attracted unfavourable notice. The letter concludes:

> *If you hear from Boston should be glad if you would write me word at any convenient Time, and put your Letters in a Sheet of Paper and counterfeiting your Hand Please to Direct to Mr. Wagner at Mr. Morrice's Cheshunt Herts, and he will deliver them to*
>
> *Your affectionate Brother*
> *Benjamin Hallowell*

The plea for news is revealing. By this time the boy had been separated from his mother for seven years and his father for five. Their failure to communicate regularly must have reinforced his feelings of isolation and insecurity in the hands of Mr. Morrice. Ward's arrival was a godsend and he hastened to seek the help of this surrogate parent.

Ward's prompt reply was successfully smuggled through to Ben, who replied on August 7:

My Dear Brother

It gave me great pleasure to hear by your letter which I received on Friday that my Father, Mother, Sister and all Friends at Boston were well, hope this will find you well, as I am at present. I have been very careful of my health and have used no violent Exercise since I have been down. I should be glad if you would favour me with a Letter at first Opportunity informing me if you can conveniently come down here next Sunday when I shall be exceedingly glad to see you well. Please give my duty to my Aunts Vaughan and Gould when you have the pleasure of seeing them with love to Cousins and accept the same yourself from Your

Affectionate Brother B. Hallowell

In one of his adult portraits Hallowell is pictured with a very marked broken nose, more typical of a prizefighter than a naval officer, quite possibly a souvenir of 'violent Exercise' as a schoolboy.

The August 7 letter refers for the first time to an Aunt Gould. It was his aunt Anne Hallowell who had married Captain Paston Gould of the British Army. The Goulds had a son James, and a daughter, another Anne, then only five years old but later to become perhaps the most important woman in Benjamin Hallowell's life.

Ward's Sunday visit does not seem to have relieved the pressure. His next letter again warns Ward to route his reply through the invaluable Mr. Wagner and concludes:

> *I have for some Days past been expecting to see my Mother, who I hear has arrived at Portsmouth, but my Expectations have proved vain therefore I take this Opportunity of writing to you to enquire if you have seen her and if you know when I shall have that pleasure. I should take it as a particular Favor if you would write me an answer by return of Post. Please remember me to my aunts Vaughan and Gould.*

Ward soon acquainted Ben with the truth: his mother had not arrived at Portsmouth or anywhere else in England. She was still in Boston.

This is very puzzling. Some unknown person in England, obviously not Ward, had given Ben specific but absolutely false information that Ben felt was reliable. His eagerness to see his mother for the first time in seven years is apparent, as is his ignorance of what was really happening in the family. Pathetically, he assumes that it will be Ward rather than his mother who will let him know of her plans to visit Cheshunt. Ben sensed that he was far from uppermost in his mother's thoughts and the evidence certainly points in that direction. At a critical stage of his adolescence events had conspired to distance him geographically and emotionally from the rest of the family.

Young Ben did not return to Mr. Morrice's school after the Christmas break of 1775, perhaps no longer welcome, perhaps rescued from an untenable situation by his brother. It was not easy to find a new school for a boy as old as Ben. Ward was corresponding with his friend Acklom Harrison, who had been injured along with Benjamin Hallowell Sr. in the fracas over the *Liberty*. Harrison had found it desirable to leave Boston and assume a position in the somewhat less exciting British Customs service. He suggested that Ward consider a school at Warrington. Whether it was at Warrington or elsewhere, sometime in late January 1776 Ben was delivered into the hands of a new master.

In the same letter Acklom Harrison makes a very curious reference:

> *What I have to communicate to you on the subject of your brother Ben would be more satisfactory to us both to have one hour's conversation together than the exchange of twenty Letters. I really wish to*

see you very much, for I have a Commission to execute from your Mother relating to your Brother, which has not been in my power yet to do, and lays upon my Conscience.

Before Harrison left Boston Mary Hallowell must have asked him to perform some unknown action that concerned Benjamin, of such delicacy that Harrison needed to consult Ward. The incident reinforces the impression that there was something out of the ordinary in the mother's relationship with her younger son.

By the time of the First Continental Congress at Philadelphia in September 1774 many American leaders were resolved on independence even at the cost of rebellion, and although this was not openly acknowledged they began to plan accordingly. Meanwhile the British government remained one step behind events, unable to find a balance between its conflicting aims of asserting the right to govern and avoiding decisive action that might further inflame the situation.

By spring of 1775 Boston was a city under siege, crowded with troops and loyal colonials seeking refuge in this last bastion of British rule in Massachusetts. On April 18 Governor Gage took aggressive measures by sending troops to capture suspected stores of arms in the city's suburbs. They encountered colonial militia at Lexington and Concord, in the first armed skirmishes of the revolution. The British troops dispersed the formed bodies of the militia with relative ease, but during their return march they suffered severe losses under constant sniping by the colonial marksmen.

On June 12 Gage imposed martial law. The American response was swift. On the night of June 16 they occupied and entrenched Bunker Hill, from which artillery could dominate the city and harbour. Throughout the next day British infantry and marines launched a series of frontal attacks. After heavy casualties on both sides they at length drove the Americans from their positions.

Again the Hallowell family had a direct involvement, this time through Captain Thomas Bishop. From the deck of the *Lively* he was the first British officer to spot the new American entrenchments. He at once opened fire but soon received orders to desist, so great was the confusion and indecision among the British commanders. He was later told to re-engage in support of the land assaults, but at extreme range his 9-pounders had little effect. In the eyes of the patriot party the Hallowells were already entirely committed to the Loyalist position, but if any additional evidence had been needed this incident would have provided it.

The British often undermined their interests by appointing unsuitable senior officers to important posts in North America. Some harboured an ill-concealed disdain for colonials. Others were incompetent or indecisive, perhaps understandably so in light of the vacillations of government policy. Still others were simply unpleasant characters who provoked resentment among both supporters and enemies of the Crown. Prominent among these last was Rear Admiral Samuel Graves, who took over as naval Commander-in-Chief in 1774. Accompanying him were his four relations, Samuel, John, Thomas, and David Graves, all of whom he caused to be appointed lieutenants in his flagship *Preston*, positioning them for promotion to command of their own ships as vacancies arose.

Admiral Graves and Commissioner Benjamin Hallowell engaged in a personal squabble that would have been farcical had it not involved two of the principal Crown officials in the midst of a fateful political crisis. There had been previous friction between the two over the unloading of a merchant vessel in Boston Harbour, and Benjamin Hallowell is supposed to have criticized Graves to his face for his conduct of the naval side of the Bunker Hill battle. Moreover, Graves had ordered the court-martial of Thomas Bishop of the *Lively* over a question of salvage from the wreck of a Spanish vessel. The complainant in the case was the Admiral's nephew Thomas, whom Graves had promoted to command of the armed schooner *Diana*. The court found the charge proven in part, but considered it an error of judgment rather than an act of indiscipline, and let Bishop off with a reprimand.

The culminating quarrel began over hay, which Graves needed for his stable of horses. He wished to obtain it from Gallup's Island at Nantasket, on which Hallowell had purchased the haying rights. Hallowell refused to sell, and Graves then prohibited all haying on the islands. A polite letter offering Graves half the crop went unanswered, as did several increasingly less polite reminders. For Hallowell the issue was no longer the hay but the perception that Graves was not treating him as a gentleman ought to be treated; his status was at stake.

In August 1775 the two encountered each other on the street. Hallowell called Graves a scoundrel, fisticuffs erupted, Graves drew his sword, and Hallowell took it from him and broke it over his knee. There were numerous witnesses: the affair became a *cause célèbre* in the besieged city and was reported in both Boston and London newspapers.

Benjamin Hallowell Sr. had displayed great physical courage, extreme obstinacy and disregard for authority when a principle was at stake. His younger son's career would illustrate that he had inherited these traits, perhaps to excess.

After the debacle of Bunker Hill, General Gage was superseded by General Howe. He had been advised to occupy the Dorchester Heights overlooking Boston from the south, but had failed to do so. On 10 May 1775, a force from Connecticut and Vermont had surprised the unsuspecting British garrison of Fort Ticonderoga, which fell without a shot being fired. To his consternation, on 5 March 1776, Howe discovered that General Washington had forestalled him and that the captured guns of Ticonderoga now dominated the city. The Hallowells' beloved Roxbury retreat was taken over as a hospital by the rebels and they commenced heavy bombardment of the city.

Two choices remained: for the British to mount an attack to recapture the Heights or to concede that Boston was indefensible and evacuate. Even if successful an attack would have risked the slaughter of another Bunker Hill.

Howe chose evacuation, and with that decision ended the Hallowells' hopes of holding on in Boston until the rebellion was squashed. With thirteen thousand soldiers to be evacuated shipping was scarce, but Howe offered to embark any Loyalists who wished to accompany the departing British.

Now the Hallowells had less than two weeks to prepare to leave the city that had been the family home for generations. There was no question of embarking any possessions beyond their immediate personal effects.

The Roxbury retreat where the Hallowell family sometimes sought refuge from disturbances in Boston

Benjamin Hallowell had to make what arrangements he could for the family property. He entrusted its care to Moses Gill, the husband of Mary Hallowell's sister Rebecca and a strong supporter of the patriot cause.

Hallowell's mother, his wife and daughter, aunt Rebecca Bishop (wife of the captain of the *Lively*) and the family of Robert Hallowell were crammed with many others into the hold of the *Hellespont*, a transport that had not been designed to carry passengers. In the absence of berths they slept on the bare deck — servants, farmers, merchants, and officials crowded together without regard to rank or wealth, their situation desperate, their future unknown.

Loaded with its human freight, *Hellespont* moved from Boston harbour to Nantasket, where it remained at anchor for three weeks while other ships were filled and the convoy completed. After riding out a gale the convoy made a six-day passage to Nova Scotia, under an escort that included Captain Bishop's *Lively*. It arrived in Halifax on April 2, the passengers having been confined on board in appalling conditions for twenty-seven days. Mary Hallowell was confined to her bed immediately, due not so much to seasickness as to the trauma of three nights of bombardment before the refugees embarked.

Halifax at this time was a struggling pioneer settlement of only 4,000 inhabitants, one-tenth the population of Boston, which was over a century old when Halifax was founded. To the evacuees it seemed a poor place indeed. The inhabitants were mainly occupied in supporting the naval and military facilities that were the city's *raison d'être*. Since most of these forces had been transferred to Boston the place was far from prosperous. The hinterland of Nova Scotia was virtually empty, and the infant town obtained most of its supplies from overseas.

Housing was mostly substandard, and the town was not prepared to handle the influx of returning troops and civilian evacuees from Boston. Rents and other prices rose alarmingly, and many of the refugees felt that the local inhabitants were gouging them in their time of distress. It cost Benjamin Hallowell more than £200 to house and feed his family for less than four months, far more than he would later pay in the great metropolis of London where the cost of living was generally regarded as exorbitant.

The refugees' morale was not improved by the climate, which is at its miserable worst in March and April. Those who could lost no time in arranging their passage out.

As for Commissioner Hallowell, his sense of duty would not permit him to leave his post until the American Board of Customs was actually ordered to England or driven from the continent. He offered his services to both the naval and military authorities, who were busy preparing an expedition to capture New York. In a May 12 letter from Halifax to his son Ward he remained optimistic that the rebellion would be subdued, although he recognized that after the evacuation of Boston 'the King has not a foot of land in America but this place, Newfoundland and we hope Quebec.'

By that date people in Halifax must have been aware that on the last day of 1775 British regulars and French Canadian militia had repelled an American attack on Quebec. But the invaders continued the siege, and everything depended on the arrival of a relieving force from

England as soon as the St. Lawrence became free of ice. Unknown to Hallowell that event had occurred six days before he wrote.

The authorities declined Benjamin's offer to serve in America, perhaps because he was anathema to the Patriots, with whom it was still hoped to negotiate a compromise. He and his wife sailed from Halifax in the transport *Aston Hall* on July 15. By October 1776 the exiles were established in their own residence in London. Scarcely had they arrived when they learned that, with disastrous timing, young Benjamin had just been expelled after a fight with a schoolfellow named Rogers.

Events in America may have played a part. Benjamin Hallowell's affray with Admiral Graves was sensational enough to be reported in the *London Chronicle* of November 1775. Ben's father was described as 'a native of Boston, the son of a Carpenter, bred to the sea, much liked in the town.' The report provided Ben's new schoolfellows with at least two reasons for taunting him. Firstly, he was revealed as a native of a colony in rebellion, whose father had had the impudence to strike a British admiral — useless for Ben to protest that his father was the most loyal of the loyal. Secondly, it inaccurately described Ben's grandfather, the prosperous ship-builder and merchant, as a 'Carpenter.' In class-conscious Britain, a carpenter's grandson would have been a great oddity at a public school, and a boy so identified could expect no mercy from his fellows.

Ward reacted decisively. He made arrangements for the unfortunate Rogers to go home, quite probably paying his way. He also put Benjamin on the coach for London carrying a letter of explanation. As yet there had been no reunion between the two sons already in England and the newly arrived parents. After years of separation Benjamin's first act had to be to present the account of his disgrace.

The father's reaction is summed up in his immediate reply to Ward.

Kentishtown ye 26 October 1776

My Dear Ward

Your brother got home last evening about 9 o'clock, by whom I received your letter, and am most exceedingly sorry that his behaviour complained of is so strongly confirmed; if the boy has understanding he keeps it to himself, neither your mother or myself can discover the least of the Character by which he has been recommended to us. I have taken the hint about his treatment; it is now four o'clock afternoon, tho he appears like a stupid lad he has not had the best guide for what he is not blamable. We express our concern for his wellfare and endeavour to impress on his mind the importance a good behaviour must be to himself; that he has nothing to recommend or introduce him into life but a fair reputation, the part that you have taken in advice to the poor unfortunate Rogers and in sending of him home I dare say is exceeding proper. I wait impatiently for his master's letter which I shall desire the youth to read until then I shall be quiet indeed I do not intend to be in any way violent.

Ben's feelings may well be imagined, although apparently not by his parents. He has not seen his father for six years or his mother for eight. His dearest wish is to be reunited with them in circumstances that would make them proud to embrace him once again within the family. Unexpectedly, they arrive in England under appalling circumstances, refugees from their native land, their lives fundamentally transformed by the politics of revolution. Far from making a good first impression, Ben manages to turn the longed-for reunion into a traumatic experience and to place an additional burden on his exiled parents. Little wonder he is struck dumb in his mortification and disappointment.

2

THE WOODEN WALLS
1777–1778

To Our Ships   To Our Men

Naval toasts of the day for Mondays and Tuesdays

Hallowell's parents hoped that their exile would be only temporary, but the reality was that they were three thousand miles from Boston, in straitened financial circumstances, and burdened with a son who had just been expelled from school. The question of his career had unexpectedly become urgent. They chose the classic last resort for younger sons: service in the military. Given his father's connections, only the navy need be considered. The entire course of Hallowell's life had just been determined. All other possibilities had been foreclosed by a revolution in a far-off land he no longer remembered.

At sixteen, Hallowell was already too old for the standard route of entry. Expert opinion was that a boy destined for the navy should be put into a mathematical school at the age of twelve, and should join his first ship between the ages of thirteen and fifteen. In most cases, a captain had to agree to enroll the lad as a servant as a favour to a relative, friend, or patron. The future Admiral Nelson, for example, first sailed at thirteen in a ship commanded by a maternal uncle.

Such boys were actually unpaid apprentices, roughly equivalent to the modern-day cadet. (In later years they were called first-class volunteers, and that term will be used hereafter.) If a boy learned his trade and showed an aptitude for the sea, the captain could rate him midshipman, usually at the age of sixteen or seventeen. On passing an examination and reaching the age of twenty, a midshipman became eligible for a lieutenant's commission. To qualify he had to have been on a ship's books for at least six years, of which at least two had to have been as midshipman. This provision was frequently evaded by the simple expedient of entering a boy's name in the ship's books well before he actually joined, although since 1749 that practice had been illegal and punishable by dismissal from the service.

It would have been easy for the Hallowells to enter their son at the standard age. Benjamin Hallowell was well acquainted with many commanding officers who would have considered his son favourably.

But now the senior Hallowell would have to employ all the influence at his command to short-circuit the system. The young man must bypass the volunteer stage and be accepted by some captain directly as a midshipman, as befitted a sixteen-year-old. The rule demanding six years service before commissioning would still have to be satisfied, so that by regulations Ben would be twenty-two before qualifying for lieutenant, two or three years older than those following the usual stream. In the competition for promotion it would be difficult to overcome such a handicap, a permanent penalty for the belated choice of career.

Less than three months after their ill-starred reunion Hallowell was enrolled in his third boarding school, that of a Mr. Alexander. The fees were nearly double those at Mr. Morrice's establishment. The boy's age and checkered academic career may have forced his father to pay a premium to induce Mr. Alexander to take him at all. There is a charge of twelve shillings 'for a large book for Mathematics,' another for six shillings and sixpence for Thompson's 'The Seasons,' a popular work of English literature. Latin, Greek, and French do not appear. His previous breadth of study, appropriate to a well-rounded gentleman, had narrowed to a naval focus, concentrating on the essentials of effective communication and on the mathematics indispensable for the study of navigation.

Ben must have done a great deal of written composition; in a period of three months his father was billed for 700 quills! Dancing and drawing lessons were continued, the former a social necessity, and the latter with a very practical military application in the days before photography. Finally, there is a most interesting charge of six shillings 'for cash for Sergeant,' almost certainly for teaching the aspiring officer the basics of swordplay in preparation for battles to come.

After less than four months Hallowell was withdrawn and embarked on a whirlwind of activity — shopping for suitable clothing, packing his kit, and completing a round of farewell visits. Every spare moment was no doubt spent with his father, learning the basics of seamanship and naval lore that his colleagues-to-be had already absorbed through actual experience. On 11 May 1777, he joined his first ship, HMS *Sandwich*.

Hallowell would be rated midshipman, a title and position grounded in naval history. Until the late Middle Ages there was no real distinction between warships and merchant vessels. When danger threatened, merchant vessels were hired or requisitioned with their crews, and soldiers were drafted aboard to do the actual fighting. The ship's master simply handled the vessel as directed by the soldier's commanding officer, who remained quite ignorant of the seamanship involved.

As cannons were adapted for use at sea it became important to carry the maximum number of guns, sacrificing most of the space hitherto used for cargo. The new purpose-built warship lead to a permanent fighting navy maintained at public expense in both peace and war.

Despite this revolution, old distinctions persisted between the mariner who sailed the ship and the gentleman who fought her. 'There were seamen and there were gentlemen in the navy...., but the seamen were not gentlemen, and the gentlemen were not seamen'. Since gentlemen were borne and not made, it seemed inconceivable that a seaman could be turned into a gentleman. The solution was to turn gentlemen into seamen, by sending suitable young men to sea to acquire essential technical knowledge.

The title of midshipman had originally belonged to a petty officer in charge of the midships area of the upper deck. The aspiring young gentlemen were to be payed at the same rate, and with the passage of time they assumed the title as well. Their status was that of petty officers, and as such they were punished, demoted or dismissed the ship at the absolute discretion of the captain. On the job training was emphasized, but at the same time they were expected to assume important leadership roles, in command of ship's boats and parties of men, and in charge of a section of guns in battle. This system had proved itself over the years in a noticeable improvement in naval professionalism, and young Hallowell was now to be absorbed into it.

With the resilience of youth, young Hallowell put his familial stress behind him. Excited anticipation of new adventures was tempered with a healthy recognition of his own insignificant place in the great system of the navy and of his responsibility to his family and to himself to meet the new challenges.

Outwardly, the *Sandwich* was an impressive vessel, a three-decked ship of the line mounting ninety guns, the largest ship then lying in the Spithead anchorage off Portsmouth. Hallowell's entry was made official by the recording of his name and rating in the ship's muster roll. His place of birth was supposed to be entered, but that space is blank, not only in the *Sandwich's* roll but in the rolls of other vessels in which he was to serve. Like all newly joined personnel he was assigned a number on the ship's books against which all further entries would be recorded, including his presence at pay musters, and any ship's clothes or 'slops' and tobacco issued to him.

His eventual departure from the ship could be noted in one of only three ways. If he was posted to another ship or left the navy his name would be marked 'D,' signifying his 'discharge.' If he became a deserter he would be marked 'R' for 'run' and subject to severe punishment if recaptured. Finally, if he were to die of illness or in battle, by accident, or by drowning, the notation would be 'DD,' or 'discharged, dead.'

With the paperwork completed, the midshipman of the watch would conduct him to his future home. The way was down ladder after ladder, traversing the upper deck, the main gun deck and the lower gun deck, with their silent rows of 12-, 24-, and 32-pounder guns. The two gun decks were also home to the six hundred men of the ship's company. Finally, they would reach the orlop deck, below the waterline and immediately above the reeking hold.

The orlop never saw the light of day or felt a breath of air, and under its low deckhead men moved in a permanent stoop by the fitful light of oil lanterns. At its after extremity was a cramped compartment, the cockpit, where the midshipmen slept, ate, studied, and took their leisure. Lockers serving as seats ran down both sides of a long table, alongside which the inmates slung their hammocks or cots. In battle, the cockpit became the ship's operating room: the grim joke was that the stains on the table were not gravy, but blood.

Apart from the midshipmen, the denizens of this nether region included the surgeon's mates, the captain's clerk, and the master's mates, all rated as petty officers, and undergoing what would now be known as on-the-job training in their chosen careers. In essence, the cockpit was a way station through which all must pass en route to the privileges of higher rank.

Their unsupervised mess constituted an informal democracy in which each new member acquired the ability to get along with others while at the same time standing up to bullying from his older and larger colleagues. Big for his age and more than willing to defend himself, Hallowell would have had little trouble establishing himself among his messmates. Hard drinking was not just acceptable but virtually compulsory.

Not all midshipmen succeeded in passing the exam for lieutenant, but there was no limitation on how often they could try. A mid who repeatedly failed could remain aboard at his captain's discretion, watching succeeding batches of his juniors do the requisite penance, pass their exams, and leave him behind. There were instances of men who were still midshipmen at the age of fifty, contemptuous of anyone below the rank of admiral, with no hope of promotion but condemned to sailor on, since they knew no other life.

A sailing line of battle ship and its complement of sailors and marines formed probably the most complex social-technical system in existence before the Industrial Revolution. For an aspiring midshipman his first seagoing ship was a critical step in achieving the mastery of this system upon which his career and even his life would depend. (See the Appendix for an overview of the ships, men, and tactics of the late age of sail.)

The second-rate *Sandwich* was far from an ideal ship in which to learn. As the Portsmouth guard ship she seldom if ever went to sea but instead swung for months on end at her Spithead anchorage. A guard ship was a floating barracks into which new entries were enrolled and subsequently distributed to make up the crews of the operational ships. Apart from endless disciplinary problems (in a period of six weeks twenty-one deserters were marked 'Run') there was little to break the monotony or contribute to the development of the officers under training. Moreover, *Sandwich* was in poor shape, her captain complaining to the Admiralty that the ship was 'in general so weak and works so much that when it blows neither officers nor men sleep dry in her. It was necessary to move guns from aft to forward to ease her in the last blow, when she made 14 inches of water per hour.'

Eighteenth-century wooden ships were never entirely watertight. When underway every vessel found it necessary to pump bilges at least once a day, and much more often in heavy weather, after battle damage, or if the hull had begun to rot. But having to pump almost constantly when at anchor was by no means usual.

The revolutionary colonies lost no time in attacking British trade, the principle source of her maritime strength. Nor were these attacks confined to the North American side of the Atlantic. The famous John Paul Jones, having plundered the defenseless Nova Scotian fishing communities of Canso and Arichat, arrived in France to equip a commerce raiding squadron.

In this autumn of 1777 France and Britain were still officially at peace, but there was no doubt where French sympathies lay. There could hardly have been a greater contrast than that between the French regime and the democratic ideals espoused by the revolutionaries, but the French monarchy appeared blind to the effect the American example might have on its own far more seriously oppressed people. Too cautious to commit themselves until it was certain that the revolt had staying power, they nevertheless gave the Americans every assistance short of war, including support to American commerce raiders in European waters.

Jones sailed from Brest on his first successful mission exactly a week before Hallowell joined the *Sandwich*. Indistinguishable in appearance from ordinary merchant ships, but more heavily armed and with a much larger crew, the raiders could lie in wait for their prey even in sight of British shores and easily overpower an unfortunate merchant vessel. A prize crew would be placed on board to sail the vessel to a French port, where she and her cargo would be sold and the profits distributed among the crew. Meanwhile, the mother ship searched for new victims.

The British had developed a standard response to the privateer threat. First, the navy would establish a close blockade of enemy ports to prevent the raiders from getting to sea in the first place. But this was not possible in 1777, since the bases were those of an ostensibly neutral country. Besides, the navy had been caught unprepared, and there were simply not enough ships to make a blockade effective. In fact, blockade was never to be successfully established in this war, a strategic failure of the first order. Second, a convoy system would be implemented, requiring all trade to sail in organized groups under naval escort. But even when in convoy merchant vessels were often picked off before the escort could intervene.

Finally, small and medium-sized naval vessels were sent on independent anti-raider patrol. These cruisers had some success; when young Hallowell joined the *Sandwich* she was holding seventeen American prisoners. At least half had French names, concrete evidence of that country's support of the new republic. (The prisoners were only given two-thirds the authorized food ration. This sounds harsh, but it was an internationally recognized practice considered fair because the prisoners were not required to do any work.)

Even a newly joined midshipman could be useful, and Hallowell soon volunteered to be 'lent into cruisers.' He probably saw little or no action, but for a midshipman just beginning his career the experience was invaluable. With its off-lying rocks, shoals, and fierce currents, the stormy Channel presented a constant challenge to the navigator. A cutter would have a small crew commanded by a lieutenant with one or two midshipmen or master's mates to assist him. Even a seventeen-year-old newly joined midshipman would quickly be expected to take charge of a watch on deck by day and night. In meeting the challenge the young man acquired a familiarity with basic seamanship and a confidence in his own ability to accept responsibility.

On 1 January 1778, Captain Samuel Hood became Commissioner of the Portsmouth Dockyard. Ten years earlier he had commanded the small British North American squadron based at Halifax. Hood had first dispatched naval reinforcements to the assistance of the customs authorities in Boston and had later transferred his own headquarters to that difficult town. There he certainly became friendly with Benjamin and Robert Hallowell, who as customs officials were at the centre of the disturbances. Very possibly Hood had noticed the six-year-old Ben Hallowell just before his departure.

Hood had likely met the elder Benjamin Hallowell much earlier, when the latter was in command of the *King George* and Hood of the *Lively*. In any case, in 1778 Commissioner Hood would have been filled with sympathy for his exiled friends and well disposed to advancing the naval career of the younger son. As a mere captain, apparently destined for retirement and in a not very prestigious post, his influence would have been relatively small, but in the navy of the time any influence was valuable. No one in 1778 could have foreseen that Hood was about to begin a remarkable series of wartime successes that would bring him to the pinnacle of the service and to ennoblement as Lord Hood.

The British strategic concept for 1777 was to isolate the more militant New England colonies by means of a pincer movement. General 'Gentleman Johnny' Burgoyne was to advance southward from Montreal via Lake Champlain, capture Ticonderoga, and move down the Hudson valley, where he was to be met by the other pincer driving north from New York. Burgoyne took Ticonderoga, but instead of advancing to meet him most of the British troops were diverted to the capture of Philadelphia, a showy success that had no strategic effect. Without support, short of supplies, and unable to live off the country, Burgoyne was forced to surrender at Saratoga on 17 October 1777.

This was a decisive event. Now the rebellion was not going to be suppressed before winter brought campaigning to an end. The French hesitated no longer. In February 1778 they signed a treaty of alliance with the Americans, and the official declaration of war followed in the middle of

March. By July Admiral d'Estaing's fleet had arrived in Chesapeake Bay carrying regular French troops under the Marquis de Lafayette. A new episode had opened in the ancient French-English struggle for maritime supremacy.

India would again be a theatre of war, and the Admiralty hastened to reinforce its small squadron in Far Eastern waters. The first ship available was the 64-gun third-rate *Asia* under Captain George Vandeput. With the support of Commissioner Hood, Benjamin Hallowell Sr. persuaded Captain Vandeput to accept his son.

Vandeput was probably receptive. His ship had been in New England waters at the time of the evacuation of Boston. If Vandeput had not actually met Benjamin Hallowell Sr. he would certainly have known of him and of the total disaster that had befallen the Hallowells and other Loyalist families. Also, the *Asia* would have had more difficulty than most ships in reaching its authorized strength of sixteen midshipmen. Service in the Far East was highly unpopular, because there were few opportunities for prize money and because of the prevalence of tropical diseases in the days before immunization.

On 22 April 1778, a 'D' was marked against Hallowell's name in the books of the *Sandwich*, and the next day he was entered in the *Asia* muster roll. His father barely had time to convey a draft for ten guineas to Captain Vandeput to be doled out as necessary to supplement the meagre stipend of a midshipman. Within days *Asia* sailed on its six-thousand-mile journey to the other side of the world.

The route led south through the Atlantic Ocean, around the Cape of Good Hope, and finally north and east across the Indian Ocean to Bombay. The story of this journey highlights the navy's problems in controlling the sea on which Great Britain depended for the trade-generated economic strength that enabled her to wage war. Merchant ships had to be gathered into convoys and provided with a naval escort to discourage enemy warships and privateers. When Captain Vandeput sailed, he had in his charge a convoy of four vessels of the East India Company: the *Colebrooke, Royal Henry, Calcutta,* and *Royal Admiral*.

The group was forced to proceed at the speed of the slowest ship. For the merchant masters, time was money, and the most aggressive would be itching to find an excuse to leave the convoy and run the risk of proceeding on their own. In the *Asia's* convoy, the slowpoke was the *Colebrooke*.

The first leg of the voyage was down Channel, beating against the prevailing westerly winds, sometimes helped and sometimes hindered by the swiftly running tidal currents. Giving the dangerous Cape Finisterre a wide berth, the convoy tacked to the southward, running across the mouth of the Bay of Biscay, where swift privateers lurked in every haven. This was the most dangerous leg of the voyage, and here, at least, the merchantmen were happy to remain as close as possible to their escort.

With luck, if the westerlies were favourable, a ship on the starboard tack could make good time in these waters for hours and days together. Part way down the coast of Portugal, again with luck, the convoy would enter the prevailing northeasterlies and continue its southward run with the wind to port.

For this particular trip, the winds were usually adverse or absent altogether, and it was not until May 26 that the lookouts descried the six-thousand-foot peak of Pico Rive on the Portuguese island of Madeira. The convoy had taken thirty days for the roughly twelve-hundred-mile voyage, for an average speed made good of less than two knots or two nautical miles per hour. Fresh provisions had long since been exhausted and water was running short. Men cursed the *Colebrooke* and longed for a break in the tedium of the voyage.

The convoy spent five days at anchor in Funchal, a beautiful colonial town surrounded by rich green hills contrasting with the azure waves of the harbour. Madeira was one of the first way stations established by the Portuguese as they groped along the African coast seeking a sea route to Asia. Portugal was England's oldest ally, and although the Portuguese were not now at war they afforded all possible assistance to the visitors. Captain Vandeput made his courtesy call on the Governor and the ships' pursers hurried ashore to arrange the purchase of fresh provisions and water. Load after load was carried out to the anchored ships in lighters and hoisted into the holds by tackles rigged on the yards. Because of the risk of desertion, only the most reliable men were granted shore leave, but boats from the city hovered around the ship selling delicacies to the sailors through the gun ports.

Hallowell would have been in charge of one of the *Asia's* boats plying to and fro between ship and shore. While making sure that none of his boat's crew seized the chance to slip away, he would have had more opportunity than most to savour the unfamiliar sights, sounds, and smells of a subtropical foreign port. It is possible also that Captain Vandeput, satisfied with the behaviour of his midshipmen, permitted them leave to stroll through the town, perhaps to exchange glances with the heavily chaperoned Portuguese girls and certainly to sample the much-prized wine of the island, grown from vines first introduced by Prince Henry the Navigator. When mixed with a small amount of brandy Madeira wines kept well during long sea voyages, and doubtless the young men clubbed together to purchase a few casks for later consumption. Here young Hallowell began his lifelong love affair with good wine.

The convoy weighed anchor early on May 31. Rookies such as Hallowell would have hoped that the worst of the voyage was over. But the more seasoned sailors spoke grimly of the doldrums, a two-hundred-mile belt of calms north of the equator in the gap between the extreme limits of the northeast and southeast trade winds. Within this band the convoy might feel no wind for days and nights on end. Eyes would be peeled to spot the ripples raised by even the most insignificant breeze and the watch would make feverish efforts to trim the sails to win even a few yards toward their goal. All too often the wind would die as swiftly as it arrived, and once again the sails would droop on the motionless ships.

These maddening calms were often punctuated by sudden squalls which might set a ship on her beam ends if the watch was slow to react. In one such squall the *Asia* suffered her first death of the voyage, when one of the volunteers, a mere boy, fell overboard and was drowned.

Taking advantage of the southeast trades, ships bound for the Cape sailed on the port tack to the south-southwest, executing the first leg of the great circle course to the Cape. The preferred track almost reached South America before ships entered the prevailing westerlies that would carry them on the final leg to Cape Town. It was in pioneering this route to the Far East that the early Portuguese explorers had first stumbled unexpectedly upon the Brazilian coast.

Averaging less than four knots the convoy took just under a month to sail the first eighteen hundred miles of the southward run from Madeira. By this time the masters of the fastest ships were bursting with impatience at being held back by the *Colebrooke*. On June 29 the convoy was in latitude 4° north. For once, the wind was favourable and steady, but a new delay arose. Some of Captain Vandeput's charts depicted a dangerous shoal at approximately latitude 4° north and longitude 19° west.

In fact, the so-called French Shoal does not exist. The erroneous reports have been attributed to surface disturbances caused by volcanic activity on the ocean floor, now known to be on the collision boundary between the South American and African tectonic plates. The truth being unknown to Captain Vandeput, he prudently ordered the convoy to heave to for the night, reluctantly giving up several hours of much-needed progress to avoid the risk of running upon the shoal in the darkness.

When dawn broke the *Calcutta* was no longer to be seen. As Vandeput reported dryly, her captain later claimed it was all 'a mistake of the Officer of the Watch, who imagined he perceived that we had made sail.' Everybody of course knew the *Calcutta* had deliberately parted company. A week later the *Royal Henry* followed suit and disappeared over the southern horizon.

Not long after, the convoy crossed the equator, and the tedium of the voyage was relieved by a nautical ritual that was already ancient and that survives to our own time — the ceremony of crossing the line. Members of the crew making their first crossing of the equator must be initiated into King Neptune's realm. For the duration of the ritual ordinary discipline was suspended and the tadpoles, whatever their rank, were completely at the mercy of the King and his court.

Dressed in the most elaborate costumes, the shellbacks who had already crossed the line played the roles of the King and his Queen, Davy Jones, the Royal Surgeon, the Royal Barber, and other characters. The Queen was always one of the largest and ugliest of the shellbacks, gowned and bonneted and padded to voluptuous proportions, her appearance spoiled only by a luxuriant beard. From time to time she would bestow an embrace and a wet kiss on one of her subjects, the more senior officers being especially favoured in this regard.

Davy Jones and the Royal Police would present the tadpoles one by one to their majesties, who subjected them to a series of probing questions to which their answers were always wrong. The sentence was invariable: a large dose of foul-tasting 'medicine' administered by the Royal Surgeon, lathering with an equally foul cream in preparation for a shave with a dull blade by the Royal Barber, and finally total immersion and ducking in a tub of filthy water set up on deck. It was a wise

Very similar scenes occur to this day as naval vessels preserve the ancient ceremony of crossing the line.

new shellback who obtained a certificate from his captain to avoid a repetition of the ordeal on some future voyage.

Having picked up the southeast trade winds, the convoy began to make slightly better progress, averaging just fewer than four knots. On 17 July the masthead lookouts sighted Martin Vas, six hundred miles off the Brazilian coast, in latitude 20° south. Over three hundred feet high, this group of barren rocks could be seen at a distance of twenty-five miles even from the deck. Sure of their position, and having entered the zone of the prevailing westerlies, the *Asia* and her remaining charges altered course to the southeast for the final twenty-two hundred nautical miles of the journey. At some point another East India Company vessel, the *Gatton*, caught up with them and accompanied them for the remainder of the voyage.

Unfortunately, the winds again tapered to light breezes, speed fell to the familiar two and a half knots, and it was not until five in the morning

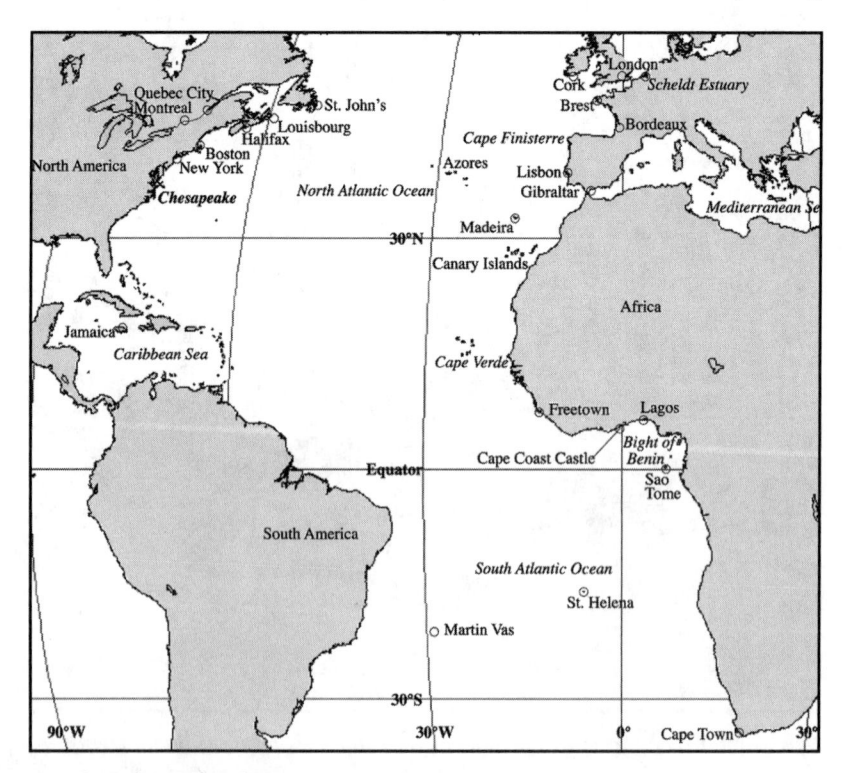

North and South Atlantic Oceans

of 24 August that the high land of the Cape of Good Hope was sighted to the northeast. They were seven months and twelve days out of Spithead. (By contrast, with no convoy to escort, the *Asia* would spend only three months between Cape Town and Spithead on the return journey.) Since Madeira, eighty-five days earlier, no one from the *Asia* had set foot on shore or received any news of the outside world.

One more delay was to befall the convoy. In what many may have seen as just retribution, disaster struck the *Colebrooke*. As Captain Vandeput later reported, 'Hauling in to False Bay at halfpast eleven the *Colebrooke* unfortunately struck upon a rock not known before, at which time she must have been five miles from the shore. When she struck the *Gatton* was so near to her that it was with difficulty that she could veer clear of her, and had 27 fathoms of water, and the *Royal Admiral* who was nearer to the land by three-fourths of a mile than the *Colebrooke* had no less at any time than 20 fathoms.'

The *Colebrooke* had found an uncharted pinnacle at the entrance to a harbour that European ships had been using for almost three hundred years. Such was the state of oceanographic mapping. She soon slid off the rock, but as the sea poured through the gaping hole in her bows, her captain quickly recognized that she was doomed and resolved to run her ashore to save the lives of the crew and as much as possible of the cargo.

She reached the land with minutes to spare, but so steep was the foreshore and so heavy the surf that several men were drowned in leaving the vessel, despite the assistance of the *Asia's* boats, one under the command of Midshipman Hallowell. Conditions were so dangerous that only a small amount of the cargo could be taken off before the stricken ship was abandoned to the battering of the South Atlantic rollers. Sobered by this reminder of the risks of their profession, the rest of the convoy entered Simon's Bay, today a major base of the South African Navy.

On modern charts the isolated pinnacle on which the *Colebrooke* came to grief is shown as Whittle's Rock. It is indeed nearly five miles from shore and reaches within two fathoms of the surface at low water. In bad weather the seas break over it, but on the day of the disaster this visual warning was unavailable. Today it is well marked with a light and bell buoy, and leading marks ashore also help the mariner to avoid the danger.

The men of the *Asia* had been suffering from scurvy for weeks. It was not then accepted that scurvy resulted from a deficiency of vitamin C due to a lack of fresh fruit and vegetables. After the first few days at sea, the diet consisted mainly of salt beef and pork, beer (it kept better than fresh water), dried peas (made into soup), oatmeal porridge, biscuit (often weevily) and very hard cheese.

After about five months of such a deficient diet small lesions begin to appear on the body, accompanied by weakness and pain in the joints. Eating becomes painful and difficult due to a loosening of the teeth and severe hemorrhaging of the gums. So afflicted, men soon became unfit for duty, and ultimately the majority died.

As early as 1753 a naval surgeon named James Lind had experimented with different diets and had shown that the consumption of oranges and lemons rapidly affected a complete cure. Tragically, his work did not receive the official attention it deserved. The East India Company may have known the secret earlier, but it was not until 1794, after the voyages of Captain James Cook, that the Royal Navy would begin to issue a compulsory daily ration of lemon or lime juice to every man, a custom that gave rise to the nickname 'Limey' for British sailors.

In 1778 this remedy was still in the future, but many captains had independently recognized that scurvy had something to do with the sailors' diet. Captain Vandeput had embarked a store of 'sour crout.' Preserved cabbage would indeed have been of help in preventing scurvy, but his supply was soon exhausted. On reaching the Cape, he had to report that 'about this time [mid-July, in the vicinity of Martin Vas] the people began to fall down very fast with the scurvy, and those that had recovered from the fevers they had had in the lower latitudes, not gaining strength so as to be able to do duty, our sick list increased to a great number.' In fact, on arrival at the Cape, ninety-eight seamen and thirteen marines were unfit for duty, more than a quarter of the four hundred men on the ship's books. None had died yet.

The Cape of Good Hope had been in Dutch hands since 1632. In this year of 1778 the Dutch and British were not at war, so the *Asia* and her convoy could avail themselves of the port facilities and land their scurvy patients to the Dutch hospital. The *Asia* would be too undermanned to sail until the hospitalized men recovered, even though Captain Vandeput had pressed a number of men from the unfortunate *Colebrooke*.

With their own crews in good health, and already well behind schedule, the masters of *Calcutta* and *Gatton* balked at waiting for their escort, and requested permission to proceed without one. Captain Vandeput was well aware that if the East India Company were to suffer financial losses because of his decision the directors would most certainly complain to the Admiralty and his conduct of the voyage would come under severe scrutiny. He approved the request, but covered himself by making it very clear that in choosing to sail without escort the two captains did so at their own risk.

It was not until 12 October that the *Asia* finally got under way with what was left of the convoy, plus the *Stafford*, which had arrived carrying General Sir Eyre Coote en route to take command of the troops in India. At least six precious weeks had been squandered for health reasons. The object lesson would not be wasted on young Hallowell.

The convoy first steered up the east coast of Africa, passing between the continent and the huge island of Madagascar, before emerging into the Indian Ocean proper and picking up the southwest monsoon winds for the final leg to Bombay. There was a risk of encountering warships or privateers operating from the French base on Île de France, (now Mauritius), but the ocean remained empty except for themselves and the occasional Arab dhow trading between Zanzibar and the Persian Gulf.

In order to lead an officer had first to learn to follow, and the midshipman's position was uniquely designed to make that possible. Under the guidance of trusted petty officers Hallowell spent many days acquiring the skills of an able seaman: steering, splicing, and handling sails and lines. He learned to heave the lead and read the soundings by feel alone, the line being marked at each fathom by a different material — a strip of calico or a piece of leather with a hole in it, and so on. Mistakes might earn the perpetrator a severe dressing-down or a few hours at the masthead to ponder his shortcomings, but provided he did his best and learned from his errors, no lasting harm would be done.

It was equally important to achieve a high level of competence in navigation. As a midshipman, Hallowell would take his own observations and work out the ship's daily position every day the weather permitted. The master checked his work, and poor results would earn him extra practice. Neither the astronomic theory nor the calculations involved were simple, and whatever else he may have felt about his school days he must have blessed the mathematical instruction he had endured in the establishments of Mr. Morrice and Mr. Alexander. (The Appendix contains a more detailed discussion of the principles of seamanship and navigation in the age of sail.)

Hallowell was fortunate in that one of his mentors in the *Asia*, Lieutenant Wilfred Collingwood, was already recognized as an officer of great promise and an ideal role model for the young midshipman. Wilfred and his older brother Cuthbert, also a naval officer, came from a locally respected but far from rich family. Wilfred had always looked much older than his real age, but his energy and intelligence rapidly undeceived anyone who underestimated him on first acquaintance. Despite the lack of family influence both brothers were to win rapid advancement. Based on the early connection between Hallowell and his younger brother, Cuthbert Collingwood was later to become one of Hallowell's greatest friends.

The *Asia* finally reached Bombay on 12 February 1779, 121 days out of Cape Town with no news of the outside world. During the voyage one of Hallowell's fellow midshipmen, died, 'Discharged Dead' in the muster book. In such cases the dead man's clothing and possessions were auctioned off, and the proceeds sent to the next of kin. In a gesture of sympathy Hallowell was among those who purchased some of his dead colleague's belongings.

The voyage just described was by no means untypical. As a learning experience for an aspiring midshipman it lacked only an encounter with the enemy. He had entered foreign ports, experienced gales and calms, the trials of convoy escort, drowning, shipwreck, and scurvy. Discussed at length with senior officers during the long night watches, and with his colleagues in the cockpit, the events and lessons of the journey would be there for recall when he in his turn should assume the responsibilities of command.

News of the outbreak of the new war between Britain and France had reached India in July 1778. By August the British-Indian troops were laying siege to the principle French seaport of Pondicherry on the east coast of the peninsula, supported by a squadron of four ships under Commodore Sir Edward Vernon. A French squadron soon appeared to relieve the place, but after an inconclusive action returned to the Île de France, and Pondicherry capitulated in mid-October.

When the *Asia* arrived, Vernon's ships were wintering at Bombay. At any time the return of a French fleet with reinforcements could have completely changed the situation. Command of the sea was essential, and the *Asia* was a valuable addition to Vernon's small force. However, the ship's nearest approach to action occurred two weeks after it reached Bombay, when it embarked guns and ammunition to assist the army in the siege of Mahe, a French post some four hundred fifty kilometres to the south. With no hope of relief the place soon surrendered.

Thereafter, the squadron functioned as a deterrent, making relatively short patrols separated by long periods at anchor in strategic ports. While in India the *Asia* spent 350 days in harbour and only 84 at sea. For Hallowell and the other midshipmen meaningful training and experience virtually ceased.

Initially, the midshipmen must have been enthralled by the wonders of India, a civilization vastly older and vastly different from their own, so different indeed that anything more than superficial interaction with its people was impossible. Once the novelty had worn off, the ennui and discomfort of endless days in harbour was overwhelming, especially during the monsoon season from March to September. To counteract the heat and humidity springs were bent to the anchor cables so as to swing the hull across the wind, with gun ports open and canvas wind scoops rigged on the upper deck to funnel fresh air to the sweltering gun decks. The midshipmen's mess in the cockpit was barely habitable. Not surprisingly, at least ten per cent of the ship's company was on the sick list throughout the *Asia's* time in India. The routine was modified so that no work was done in the full heat of the day, a necessary change, but one that added to the stupefying boredom.

With the prospect of action remote and no chance at all of prize money, even the consoling thought that the ship was performing a worthwhile function evaporated. Deserters would have been numerous except that their complexions made them so conspicuous that recapture was inevitable. Even so, three men were desperate enough to 'Run,' including two who did so from the hospital in Madras.

Perhaps most depressing of all was the feeling of remoteness from the real world. In these days of rapid communication it is difficult to imagine the isolation of Indian service two centuries ago. Niall Ferguson has pointed out that a journey measured in hours in a modern jetliner would have required the same number of weeks by sea in the eighteenth century. At best a letter took at least six months to arrive from England and the reply another six months to get back.

Hallowell's father wrote him often, but received only one reply, written from Trincomalee nearly two years after the *Asia's* departure. Nothing from Madeira, nothing from the Cape, and nothing from Bombay or Madras, when most young men would have been bursting to tell their families about their new life and experiences. Given the distances and uncertainties some letters may have gone astray. It seems far more likely that Hallowell refrained from writing, a conscious or unconscious protest against the way he had been packed off to England as a boy, all but ignored during his school days, and placed under an undeserved cloud after his expulsion. At the same time, his anxiety regarding the fate of his uprooted family must have been intense.

Letters from his father did nothing to ease his resentment or reassure him about the future. None have survived, but the following excerpt from one to Captain Vandeput clearly shows the general tone. 'I have wrote my son several letters, laying the greatest stress on his own good behaviour, that nothing could be expected from me, having lost my whole fortune in the American rebellion, that I had nothing for my support but the salary I have from my office, which at my decease, if not before, would then be lost to my family.'

Hallowell was obliged to contribute his share of the funds with which the mess supplemented the monotonous ship's diet and supplied themselves with wine and spirits. Like most of his colleagues he was purchasing pipe tobacco from the ship's stores. It was possible to pay his way only because his father continued to accept any bills that Captain Vandeput endorsed as being essential. Hallowell may have resented the pressure his father applied, but in providing stern advice and essential financial support his father was showing his love in the only way available to him.

In the spring of 1779 seven more ships were sent to India under Rear Admiral Sir Edward Hughes, who superseded Commodore Vernon. Vernon's disappointment was mitigated by news of his own promotion to rear admiral, and he was ordered home. He had been flying his commodore's broad pennant in the *Ripon*, but it was the *Asia* that was selected to carry him back to England, no doubt to the intense joy of all on board and the disgust of the *Ripons*. The lucky ship departed Madras on 7 April 1780, just under two years after leaving Spithead.

Admiral Vernon was an able officer but never matched the achievements of his famous father, Admiral Edward Vernon, a hero of the wars of the early part of the eighteenth century. The admiral was borne as a passenger only, not flying his flag and not empowered to direct the movements of the ship. Nevertheless, the situation would not have been easy for Captain Vandeput, his every action observed by a senior officer living at close quarters in the same accommodation. In one way at least Vernon did assert his rank. Contrary to regulations he ordered that some French prisoners captured at Madras should receive full rations rather than the two-thirds proportion authorized for prisoners.

The ship's log carefully records that the increase was granted solely as a result of Admiral Vernon's personal intervention. Otherwise, the purser's provision accounts would not have passed the Navy Board's stringent review at the end of the commission. Until the Navy Board was satisfied, the purser was personally liable for any shortfalls and the captain also remained under a cloud.

Having called at Madagascar, the *Asia* reached the Cape of Good Hope on 26 August 1780. News at last. Like France, Spain had lost much by the Treaty of Versailles, and in the summer of 1779 she joined the Franco-American alliance. In previous struggles with their maritime rivals the British had always had allies in Europe, thereby forcing their enemies to divide their resources between the continental and the overseas theatres of conflict. In this war no such allies were available. While trying to suppress the rebellion, the British found themselves contending single-handed with the French and Spanish.

The Dutch would join the alliance in December 1780. Next to Britain, France, Spain, and Holland were the strongest naval powers in the world. Together, they threatened to wrest control of the sea from the island nation, strangling its overseas commerce and inevitably causing its economic and military collapse.

For the moment at least the Royal Navy was holding its own. A combined French and Spanish naval expedition to the English Channel in the summer of 1779 had been a failure. The allies then laid siege to Gibraltar, the key to British control of the Mediterranean. With the fortress on the point of surrender, in January 1780 Admiral George Rodney fought his way through with a relieving fleet. Rodney then sailed for the West Indies where he successfully engaged the French fleet in the Battle of Martinique in April 1780, a few days after the *Asia* left Madras for home. The welcome tidings would have greeted the *Asia* on the ship's arrival at the Cape.

All this was positive, but the news from North America was not. The overstretched navy had been unable to prevent a French squadron from basing itself at Rhode Island and landing four thousand troops in support of the New England rebels. These trained and disciplined regular troops were a valuable addition to the American army that General George Washington was gradually bringing into existence. The British had been successful in several minor engagements, but their achievements were largely nullified by geography and by faulty control and strategy. Each victory enticed them to occupy additional territories that their resources were inadequate to hold in the long run, a strategy orchestrated from London by the incompetent administration of Lord North and Lord George Germaine. Rather than being concentrated for decisive action, strength was dissipated in expeditions with transitory objectives and without mutual support.

As Benjamin Hallowell Sr. wrote bitterly in early 1781:

> As to the war in America I wish I could speak more favourably of the management of the public affairs there, a whole summer gone and winter commenced, and nothing done that looks like bringing the war to an end. The Jerseys taken and abandoned, Rhode Island taken, afterwards evacuated, Philadelphia the same, Virginia after collecting vast numbers of Loyalists to the King's forces a second time abandoned, and the poor people who had gone over, and shown their attachment to their country, left to the mercy of the rebels, has done the royal cause the greatest injury.

The plight of the abandoned Loyalists was magnified by their anomalous position in the context of the Revolution. The British treated captured American troops as prisoners of war, entitled to the protections traditionally extended to a conquered enemy rather than a rebel force. The Americans treated their captives from the regular British forces in the same way, but saw the Loyalists as traitors to the Patriot cause, not as recognized combatants. They were often harshly treated when they fell into the hands of the rebels and not infrequently retaliated when in a position to do so.

By the winter of 1781–2 the British controlled only the areas of Savannah and Charleston and the vicinity of New York City. One significant mobile army remained in the field, that of General Cornwallis, operating in the Carolinas and southern Virginia. The slim hopes remaining to the British now rested entirely on Cornwallis gaining a decisive victory. As Benjamin Hallowell Sr. wrote: 'our hopes have been so often disappointed that I do not build much on appearances however all is in the womb of time and we must await the event.'

For most of the *Asia's* officers, as for the British public, the war situation appeared to be relatively favourable, stalemate in America balanced by success in Europe and the Indies. Midshipman Hallowell could not share this perspective. To him the American side of the war was all-important, since its outcome would determine the future of his family and himself.

Concerns on that score were reinforced by more immediate personal and professional worries. He must have worried about his problematic relationship with his parents, from whom he had parted more or less in disgrace and with whom he pointedly failed to remain in touch.

Then there was the all-important question of his professional advancement. As his father had made abundantly clear, Hallowell's future depended entirely on making a success of his career. Two hurdles had to be surmounted in the very near future. In the first place, he had to be accepted aboard by another captain as soon as possible after Vandeput's *Asia* paid off. Even more critical was passing the examination for lieutenant, a prerequisite to being commissioned and beginning to earn a barely adequate income of his own.

Midshipmen were normally examined by a board of captains at the Admiralty, but local boards could test those on foreign stations. The candidate had to produce certificates of good conduct totalling at least four years. Having joined his first ship in May 1777, Hallowell would not reach the four-year point until May 1781, eliminating the option of a Far East board. He would still be some months short of the four years when the *Asia* reached home. If he was without a ship his time would cease to accumulate and he would need more qualifying sea service.

Already the consequences of his late start in the navy were becoming apparent. Faced with multiple stresses he needed to call upon all his strength of character to perform his duties and maintain an outwardly cheerful demeanour before his shipmates

The *Asia* left Cape Town in mid-October 1780. In contrast to the outbound passage she fairly flew along under the southeast trades, traversing the first 2000 miles to St. Helena in just 17 days. Fifty square miles in area, St Helena is a tiny speck on the map of the south Atlantic, 950 miles from the coast of Africa, 1700 from Brazil, and, of future significance, nearly 4000 from France. In the days of sail the island's position on the great circle route made it a valuable port of call for homeward-bound ships. It would be thirty-five years before its isolation made it the exile home of the ex-Emperor Napoleon Bonaparte. On 17 May 1779, as the *Asia* swung at anchor in Bombay, the eight-year-old future conqueror had entered the French military academy at Brienne.

A week at St. Helena sufficed to renew the *Asia's* stocks of fresh water and provisions. The equator was crossed once again, this time without ceremony since the crew was all shellbacks. The doldrums were negotiated, Madeira was bypassed, and in the first week of January 1781 the *Asia* entered the Irish inlet of Crookhaven in County Cork. For better or for worse, Midshipman Hallowell's uncertainty would soon be resolved.

3

THE WORLD TURNED UPSIDE DOWN
1781–1783

Your Excellency will have observed that whatever efforts are made by the land armies, the Navy must have the casting vote in the present contest.

George Washington to the Comte de Grasse,
October 1781

Early in the American Revolution Admiral Richard Howe had acquired an excellent reputation, and seemed destined for the command in the West Indies. However, the British government tried to pin the blame for the failures of the American land campaign on his brother General William Howe, and in family loyalty the admiral refused to serve the current regime. Thus, Admiral Sir George Rodney was now to command in the vital theatre. His second in command was to be Captain Samuel Hood, who had appeared destined to finish out his career in the unglamorous role of Commissioner of the Portsmouth Dockyard. Hood and Rodney had previously served together but were not on good terms. In September 1780 Hood was promoted rear admiral and sailed with reinforcements to join Rodney in the West Indies.

Nothing could have been more favourable for Hallowell than to have this suddenly powerful family friend in a position to exercise real influence. He could be sure that his father would be working hard to make the most of this unexpected stroke of good fortune. With a renewed feeling of optimism he served out his last few weeks in the *Asia*, which made a quick passage to the Downs, the offshore anchorage for the port of London.

It was essential for Hallowell to actually come under Hood's command, which meant getting to the West Indies as soon as possible. This his father accomplished by convincing Captain George Christian to take him aboard HMS *Fortunée*, then outfitting at Spithead. No doubt Admiral Hood's name was mentioned to good effect. Even better, there was no break in service, Hallowell being entered on the books of the *Fortunée* on 27 April 1781, one day after he was marked 'D' from the *Asia*.

Admiral Lord Hood

He did not actually join his new ship until 13 May. He had to make his way from the Thames to Portsmouth and found time to spend a few days with his family in London. His father had continued to draw his salary as Commissioner of the American Board of Customs, so the exiles lived relatively comfortably in the expensive metropolis. Perhaps young Benjamin's welcome was that of the prodigal son. More likely the atmosphere was strained thanks to the circumstances under which he had departed and his almost total failure to write. Instead of the confused adolescent who had sailed in the *Asia*, his parents beheld a strapping young man who was in many ways a stranger, hardened and matured by the sea, fully committed to his naval future, and ambitious for promotion.

For Hallowell perhaps the biggest change was in his sister Mary, a mere girl when he left but now a young woman of eighteen. Elder brother Ward had hardly begun to revive his business activities, distracted as he was by the need to bring his disastrous marriage to an end. Unable to return to Boston in the current state of affairs, he had to beg the assistance of his uncle Thomas Boylston in realizing debts owed to him by Boston merchants. They corresponded through the American ambassador at Paris, Benjamin Franklin: at a personal level it was still possible to maintain trans-Atlantic contacts in a roundabout fashion. Ward was commissioned lieutenant in the East Norfolk militia, constructing fortifications and watching the coast in case of a French invasion.

Conversation would have revolved around the disappointments of the campaign in America, and the potentially disastrous consequences for the Hallowells if the Revolution were to succeed, as appeared increasingly probable. As he prepared to leave for the theatre of operations the young man may have felt an unrealistic personal responsibility to win the war for his family.

The friendship between Hood and Benjamin Hallowell Sr. would undoubtedly stand the younger Benjamin in good stead. But his father had an even more important acquaintance, Hood's superior Rodney. Now sixty-seven years old, Rodney had distinguished himself during the Seven Years War in the destruction of a French landing flotilla assembled for the invasion of England and by the capture of Martinique, St. Lucia, and Grenada. After the peace he became Governor of Greenwich Hospital and later commander-in-chief in Jamaica.

A gambler, reckless with money, he had spent heavily to win a seat in Parliament and had been forced to flee to France between the wars in order to evade his creditors. Earlier in this war he had already defeated a Spanish fleet off Cape St. Vincent. Despite his personal shortcomings he was well known for his care of his men, and he was clearly the best choice for command in the most critical theatre at this juncture in the war.

The senior Hallowell had already asked Captain Vandeput of the *Asia* to write Rodney in his son's favour. He had once had a conversation with Rodney on the subject of America, probably when both were in Halifax during the Seven Years War. On the strength of that brief acquaintance and their mutual patron Lord George Germaine, he wrote to the admiral in May 1781. He explained his losses as a Loyalist and commended his son to Rodney's consideration, requesting 'that you will give him such countenance and promotion in the Navy under your command as you may think he merits. Having lost all my property by the rebellion in America I must depend upon my friends to give a kind helping hand to my best endeavors in making some provision for my children.'

The *Fortunée* was a frigate of forty guns, originally French, captured just two years earlier. The design and construction of European warships differed very little from one nation to another, so there were few impediments to making use of captured enemy vessels. Usually it was necessary to replace the guns with those of one's own calibre, and the masts and spars might have to be changed for ease of maintenance, but hulls were basically interchangeable. It was common practice to retain the original name under the new flag, a morale booster for one's own crews and a humiliating reminder of defeat for the enemy.

The *Fortunée* was carrying numerous military and naval passengers to join the forces in the West Indies. All the midshipman positions being filled, Hallowell was enrolled as an able seaman, a common expedient and no disgrace. In terms of pay, there was little difference, and despite his nominal rating he berthed in the cockpit with the mids and master's mates, rather than on the mess deck, and stood his watches with the officers on the quarterdeck. Nelson himself had once served as an able seaman under similar circumstances.

The *Fortunée* left Spithead on 5 July and made a rapid twelve-day passage to Antigua. Hallowell immediately joined Admiral Hood in HMS *Barfleur*, still as a nominal able seaman, but positioned for better things in his patron's flagship. Within a few days the fleet was on its way north, partly to avoid the West Indies hurricane season, as was the usual practice, but also in response to strategic movements of the French fleet.

Hallowell had arrived at a critical juncture in the Revolutionary War. After a series of aimless advances and withdrawals, General Cornwallis had allowed himself to be penned into the Yorktown Peninsula in

Chesapeake Bay. Here the one remaining mobile British army was besieged, now running short of supplies, and dependent on receiving reinforcements from the sea or from the commander-in-chief, General Clinton, in New York. The Americans had cut communications between the two. Unaware of the gravity of his subordinate's predicament, Clinton was unable to make up his mind how to act. Not so the Americans and French under Washington and Rochambeau, who had been facing Clinton, but were now hastening to the critical point with more than 10,000 fresh troops.

Moreover, unlike the British, the allies were effectively co-ordinating their efforts by land and sea. On 5 August Admiral de Grasse sailed from Haiti for the Chesapeake with the twenty-eight battleships of the French West Indies fleet and 3,000 additional troops, and the French squadron of eight ships of the line based in Rhode Island was also en route to the same place.

The Jamaica and America stations were separate from Rodney's command in the Leeward Islands, but in practice Rodney's rank and prestige allowed him to act as a virtual commander-in-chief. Initially, he misread the situation. He believed that de Grasse would only take a portion of his fleet to the north, and that it could be dealt with by the squadron under Hood, joined with the ships already in America. In the meantime, sufficient British ships would remain in the Caribbean to protect the trade. By the time Rodney developed a better appreciation he was on his way back to England, suffering from ill health, and his new conception came too late.

Hood was left in command of the Leeward Islands, but he was junior to the admirals commanding in Jamaica and America. Aware of Cornwallis' predicament, he sailed from Antigua on 10 August, having collected all the ships that Rodney had not detached on convoy duties. Despite sailing five days later than de Grasse, Hood arrived at Cape Henry at the mouth of Chesapeake Bay ahead of the French admiral. Not finding his opponent there he sailed on to New York, anchoring outside the harbour bar on 28 August.

Hood had fourteen ships of the line. Already at New York were seven others under Rear Admiral Thomas Graves, cousin of the disgraced

Samuel Graves of the siege of Boston. One year younger than Hood, Graves was one year senior to him in rank, and therefore took command of the combined force. One of his ships, the *Bedford*, was commanded by Captain Thomas Graves, who when serving under his uncle in Boston had challenged Hallowell's father to a duel as recounted in Chapter 1. Although the younger Hallowell and this Thomas Graves both had long naval careers and must have known about each other, there is no indication that they ever met.

For a few days after Hood's arrival contrary winds prevented Graves's ships from crossing the harbour bar, but on 31 August they were able to do so and the whole force sailed for the Chesapeake. On the same day Able Seaman Hallowell was rowed across from the *Barfleur* with his kit to become acting fifth lieutenant of HMS *Alcide*, 74, 'per Order from Admiral Hood,' as the move was recorded in the *Alcide's* muster book. (Amplifying information on ships' armament and rates is included in the Fighting section of the Appendix.)

One day earlier de Grasse had arrived at the Virginia Capes. The French troops were landed and four ships remained off Yorktown to co-operate with the land forces. The remaining twenty-four of the line proceeded to anchor inside Cape Henry, at the mouth of Chesapeake Bay, well placed to prevent any relief of Cornwallis from the sea.

At dawn on 5 September Cape Henry was visible four or five leagues to the west of the British fleet, then heading west on the starboard tack, the wind at north-northeast. At 9:30 Graves's scouting frigate sighted the anchored French, and at 11:00 the admiral steered for the bay and gave the order to clear for action. In all the ships men raced to their quarters to the rattle of the marine drums and the ship became a hive of purposeful activity: temporary wooden screens were removed; galley fires extinguished; boarding nettings rigged; decks wetted and spread with sand to provide better footing; small arms, cutlasses, and boarding pikes placed in readiness; buckets of water positioned to douse fire; and the cockpit turned into a surgery. Within minutes the ports were opened and the loaded guns run out, the crews stripped to the waist, and gun captains holding their slow matches ready to fire. In the sudden silence first lieutenants reported to captains that the ships were at quarters and the waiting began.

Hallowell had been through this many times for practice, but the reality was different. As a junior lieutenant he was in charge of the guns on one side of the lower deck, with a more senior lieutenant commanding the other side as well as the gun deck as a whole. Once he had reported his broadside ready there was nothing to do until the firing should begin. The occasional glance through the open ports revealed the shadow of Cape Charles far to the north, the surface of the sea, and the ripples as the ship glided slowly toward the invisible enemy. Between decks a man of his height had to adopt a perpetual stoop, a growing torture as the waiting dragged on. Perhaps the discomfort helped him to avoid thinking about the coming baptism of fire: how would it feel, how would one behave? His father had written that death would be preferable to disgrace in battle, adding, 'Your courage I have never had the most distant idea of suspecting, a failure in that cannot happen'.

From time to time news filtered to the men on the gun decks who could see nothing for themselves. Because of the northerly wind the French ships were with difficulty emerging one by one from behind Cape Henry. By 1:45 in the afternoon de Grasse cleared the Cape in his flagship, the 104-gun *Ville de Paris*, but his van remained in some disorder and his rear had not yet sailed clear. Instead of taking advantage of his opponent's difficulty, Graves continued to steer to the westward with his ships in line ahead. Meanwhile de Grasse succeeded in forming his own line on the larboard tack, on an easterly course. Having allowed his opponent to get organized, Graves first reversed his course to parallel the French, and then altered inwards in succession to intercept.

In consequence, at about four o'clock the leading British approached the French in line ahead, at an acute angle, unable to engage with all their guns, but suffering severely under the concentrated fire of the enemy van. In the meantime, because of the angle of attack, the ships under Hood in the British rear could only fire at long range, and in fact some of them never engaged at all. By sunset both fleets were sailing to the southward, still in sight of one another, but the battle was over.

The *Alcide* was one of the ships able to engage the enemy, albeit at long range. For the first time Hallowell heard the thunder of an enemy's guns, the shriek of the arriving broadside, and the crash as a shot struck home. For the first time he experienced the heat, smoke, and noise of the gun deck as hundreds of men toiled over their weapons.

If a man was killed his body was immediately thrown overboard without ceremony; the wounded were carried to the cockpit for the surgeon's attention, administered without anaesthetic. In the *Alcide* two men were killed and eighteen wounded.

In the heat of action and with his ship suffering damage and casualties, Hallowell discovered that he was too busy to worry about himself. Fear he must have felt, but he had kept his head and done his duty, and now knew that his father's detested 'failure of courage' would not happen.

For several days the fleets remained in sight of one another, gradually moving to the south. Joined by the eight ships from Rhode Island, de Grasse had thirty-six ships against Graves's eighteen, the British *Terrible* having been so badly damaged she had to be abandoned and burnt. With other ships in poor shape Graves had no inclination to renew the battle, and de Grasse did not do so. Hood suggested that the fleet enter the Chesapeake, but probably wisely Graves refused, fearing that superior numbers would bottle him up without achieving anything. Graves returned to New York to effect repairs, and on September 10 de Grasse re-entered Chesapeake Bay, sealing Cornwallis's fate.

During the Seven Years War, after a battle off Minorca, Admiral Byng and several of his captains, including Graves, had been court-martialled for failing to do their utmost to engage the enemy. Graves had escaped with a censure, but Byng was convicted and shot. Graves's error at the Chesapeake was almost exactly the same as Byng's at Minorca and led to much the same tactical results and infinitely greater consequences.

'Yesterday the British fleet had a rich and most delightful harvest of glory presented to it, but omitted to gather it.' So began the letter Hood dispatched to the Admiralty immediately after the battle, expressing his view that Graves had not only missed a great opportunity to attack, but also that he had not pressed the action when he did finally engage. The issue was a complicated one involving the need to achieve a decisive concentration of force without violating the sacred principle of maintaining the line of battle. The tactical issues were to recur through much of Hallowell's professional life.

(Whole books have been written on the subject; the Appendix contains a brief analysis.)

According to Hood, as the French fleet emerged vessel by vessel from behind Cape Henry, Graves should have concentrated his whole force against a portion of the enemy's, and thus won the decisive victory which alone could have saved Cornwallis. Instead, a slave to the principle of the line, he allowed de Grasse to form his fleet for the inevitable indecisive engagement of the type that had been fought so often before. Graves did not lose the battle, but he did prove incapable of grasping the final slim chance for Britain to win the war in America. In Washington's words, the naval vote had been cast in favour of American independence.

Hood also felt that, having missed his great opportunity for concentration, Graves then went on to mishandle the standard line encounter he had chosen instead. The British line approached the French at an acute angle, with the signal for the line of battle flying in the flagship. Graves made the signal to engage when his leading ships came within range of the French, but did not haul down the signal for the line. Thus, the leading British ships were heavily involved, but those further in rear, and therefore further from the French, were firing at long range or in some cases unable to reach the enemy at all. In the centre of the line Graves's own flagship the *London* was not in the thick of the fight.

Naturally, Hood's disgust would filter down, and for days the battle would be the sole topic of conversation in the wardrooms of the fleet. Anyone who has served at sea can imagine the heated discussions that swirled around the wardrooms of the anchored fleet as it licked its wounds and undertook repairs off New York. Over a glass, or perhaps several glasses, of wine even a junior lieutenant such as Hallowell could venture an opinion. We can be sure that he loyally supported the ideas of his patron Hood. Stimulating as they were, such professional discussions could not conceal the collective sense of failure or the anxiety all felt over the fate of Cornwallis.

On 19 October Graves sailed again. When five days later he reached the Chesapeake all was over. Cornwallis had surrendered the day before, outnumbered two to one with no prospect of relief. As the disarmed British troops marched out their own bands played a popular tune of the day, 'The World Turned Upside Down.'

Of the former Thirteen Colonies the British now held only Charleston, Savannah, and New York. In his heart Hallowell must have known that for him and his family the world had indeed turned upside down forever.

With the North American winter approaching and the hurricane season ended, the fleet sailed on for the West Indies, whither de Grasse had already returned. Hood gave Hallowell another sign of his patronage by appointing him fifth lieutenant of the *Alfred*, which unlike the *Alcide* was in Hood's squadron rather than Admiral Drake's. Adjustment would be easy, for both ships were third-rates of seventy-four guns, 32-pounders on the gun deck, 18-pounders on the upper deck, and 9-pounders on the quarterdeck and forecastle.

Although the Admiralty records are silent on the matter, Hallowell must have passed his examination for lieutenant before a board convened in Hood's squadron, allowing him to become a commissioned sea officer, the junior lieutenant in his ship.

Devastated by the disasters in America, the senior Hallowell nevertheless continued to support his son's progress in every possible way. He followed up Hood's on-the-spot commissioning of his son to make sure it was confirmed by the Admiralty. Visiting Rodney during his convalescence in England, he obtained the Admiral's promise to make the young man a lieutenant as soon as he returned to the West Indies. Of course, Hood had already done that, but Rodney's favour meant that the next step to commander was not out of the question if the war lasted long enough.

Hallowell also wrote in turn to the captains of every ship in which his son served — *Fortunée, Barfleur, Alcide,* and *Alfred* — not pleading directly for special treatment, but asking them to recommend his son if the latter's conduct deserved it. Uncle Robert Hallowell was also pressed into service to write to acquaintances like Rodney on his nephew's behalf. Highly inappropriate from our perspective, such lobbying was part of the accepted way of conducting public affairs in that place and time. Fortunately for young Hallowell his father was very good at it, and continued to enjoy the respect and sympathy of people of influence.

As a customs official Benjamin Hallowell Sr. would have met Samuel Hood, commanding the North American station; and George Vandeput, captain of the *Asia*, part of the Boston squadron. Lieutenant Cuthbert Collingwood of the flagship *Preston* would have known all about the violent quarrel between Admiral Graves and Hallowell. Benjamin Hallowell Sr.'s earlier command of the *King George* would also pay unanticipated dividends: at various times in and around Halifax, Louisbourg, and St. John's, the *King George* was in company with the frigate *Dolphin*, captain John Jervis; and with the *Dublin*, 74, under Captain George Rodney.

All these officers would later play a role in the career of the younger Hallowell. Four of Britain's most distinguished admirals — Rodney, Hood, Jervis, and Collingwood — were to retain positive memories of the father when they were much later in a position to help the son.

But getting the opportunity through interest was just a first step. In letter after letter Benjamin Hallowell impressed his son with the need to justify his good fortune by his own performance. 'Do credit to your new appointment behave so as to recommend yourself to your superiors ... behave so as to deserve the countenance of your superiors ... you are now an officer who must stand or fall by his own merit or demerit....' The earnest injunctions, however well meant and perhaps necessary, must soon have lost their impact through sheer repetition. His father also strongly advised the newly-minted officer to remain as long as long as possible under the command of Rodney and Hood, even urging him to exchange with another officer if the ship he was in was ordered home.

Lack of money weighed heavily on the elder Hallowell. As long as the fate of the Revolution remained in doubt he continued to receive his salary as commissioner, but it was always in arrears and collected with difficulty. (His brother Robert had to personally attend the

Treasury offices every day for months in order to collect his own stipend.) If the colonies were lost he would be without employment and his family penniless.

He informs his son with pleasure that Uncle Samuel Vaughan had given his nephew a present of £20, but expresses his annoyance at receiving one of his son's bills from Madras, a debt incurred more than a year before, after having been assured that no more charges would be forthcoming from the *Asia*. Moreover, now that Hallowell is a lieutenant his father expects him to live on his pay and quotes with approval a remark of Admiral Montague to his own newly commissioned son: 'He that cannot live on his pay ought to be damned.'

The newly-commissioned lieutenant on the American station was just as bad a correspondent as the midshipman in the Far East. After the action of the Chesapeake there came no letter to describe the experience or even simply to say that he was unharmed. From the official dispatches his family was aware of the twenty casualties in the *Alcide* and suffered unnecessary anxiety until they learned from another source that their son was not among them. Nor did he write before the fleet left New York for the West Indies. Pathetically the father pleaded, 'Whenever there is an action and you are in it I shall always be fearful if I don't hear from you. Pray write by every opportunity.'

It is hard to know what to make of young Hallowell's silence. His emotional ties to his family were being steadily eroded, thanks to his almost total separation from them since the age of seven. Moreover, for a naval officer, the substitute family of the wardroom was always at hand. Working and living together at close quarters, depending on each other in battle, relaxing or carousing together ashore or around the mess table, the intensity of the shared experience created ties not unlike those of a real family, albeit a transitory one.

Hood's squadron, including the *Alfred*, reached Martinique from New York on 26 November 1781, and then proceeded to Barbados. Here Hood complained bitterly about conditions in the naval hospital. Most of the men sent there simply deserted if they could crawl, and those who remained had their clothes stolen and usually perished from inadequate care. Indeed, desertion and sickness caused far more

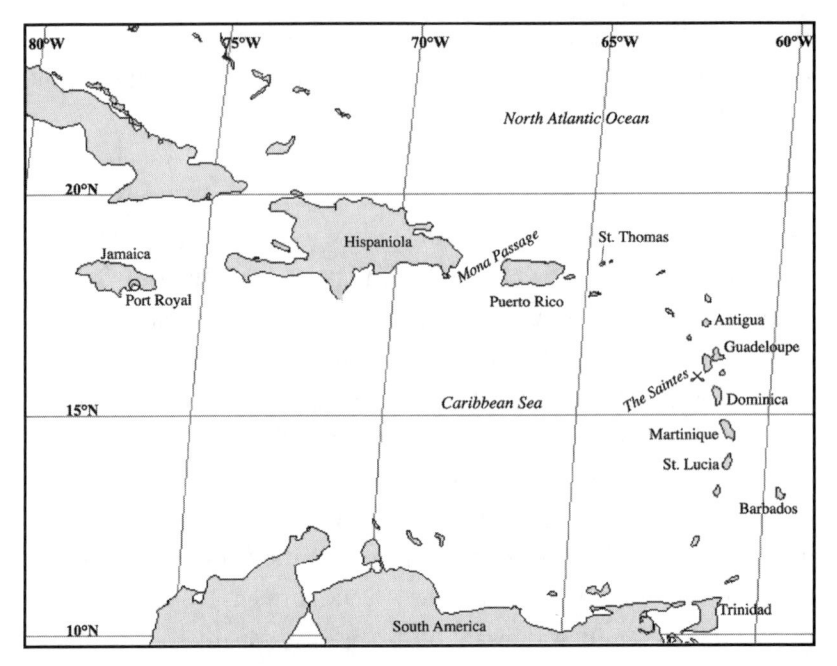

The Carribean Sea

casualties in the British forces than the French ever did. Hood also railed at a contractor who was gouging the seamen by setting exorbitant prices for shoes and clothing. (Twenty years later Hallowell was to become embroiled in controversy on the same theme; perhaps he remembered his patron's reactions at Barbados.)

Early in 1782 de Grasse's ships landed a French army on the island of St. Kitts. The little capital of Basseterre fell on 13 January but a British garrison continued to hold out on the fortified Brimstone Hill above the town. Hood hastened to their relief, collecting troops from Antigua en route. He anticipated that he would find de Grasse at anchor off Basseterre and intended to surprise him by attacking him in that position.

Unfortunately, the fleet was delayed by a collision between the frigate *Nymph* and the *Alfred* that sent the *Alfred's* fore-topmast crashing to the deck and severely damaged her bowsprit. Hood ordered both officers of the watch to be court-martialled — Hallowell was not one of them — but because of the delay Hood could not put his original plan into effect. Undaunted, he tempted de Grasse out of harbour, and then by a series of brilliant manoeuvres slipped around him and anchored his fleet in the very spot the French had vacated!

The next morning de Grasse attacked. The head of the line of anchored English ships was too near the shore to be turned, and the ships themselves were moored so close together that there was no room to pass between them. The leading French ship approached almost head on, unable to use its own guns but exposed to the concentrated fire of every British ship. 'Whole pieces of plank were seen flying from her side,' and she was soon forced to draw off. Succeeding ships suffered the same fate. The French pressed their attack bravely, but by afternoon the action had ceased with Hood still firmly ensconced in the bay.

The troops were landed and at first drove off the French forces. But they returned in increased strength and penned the British in along the shore. Captain John Inglefield of the *Centaur*, 74, managed to reach General Frazer commanding the fort on Brimstone Hill, but it proved impossible to relieve him. The troops were re-embarked, and on January 13 Brimstone Hill surrendered.

Hood's squadron was now apparently trapped in Basseterre harbour, with the coast of St. Kitts entirely in French hands and de Grasse hemming him in from seaward. The wily Hood ordered his ships to display false lights from rafts and then to cut their anchor cables at a predetermined time and slip out in the darkness. The ruse succeeded, and by dawn the British were well away.

Hood had proven himself a master of manoeuvre and surprise as well as a tactical thinker of the highest order. For aspiring officers like Hallowell, Hood became a professional role model and a source of invaluable lessons not only in tactics, but also in his concern for his men.

Returning from England with reinforcements, Rodney resumed command. Although still in ill health, he was determined to bring de Grasse to battle in the hopes of scoring a decisive victory as a counterbalance to the failures in America.

de Grasse was a superb commander and tactician, and the French navy had fully recovered from the defeats of the Seven Years War and so far had proven itself at least a match for the British. But circumstances were gradually shifting in the Royal Navy's favour. Some of the more experienced French captains and crews had returned home, and the British would for the first time enjoy a numerical superiority in the critical theatre. Moreover, they were gradually introducing technical changes in construction and gunnery that would make their vessels superior on a ship-to-ship basis.

The British were starting to sheathe their ships' hulls in copper. Especially in tropical waters, wooden sailing vessels were slowed by accumulated seaweed and barnacles, and their hulls were bored by teredos, also called shipworms. Copper sheathing greatly slowed the accumulation of weed and barnacles and defeated the teredos. In consequence, British vessels tended to sail faster than French ones that had been in the water for similar periods and British ships needed to be careened less often.

Hitherto, guns had been fired by applying a slow match to the powder-filled touchhole through which the spark was communicated to the charge. The innovation was to introduce a flintlock firing mechanism as used in the muskets of the time, except that the gunlocks were tripped with a lanyard rather than a trigger. The spark from the flint was carried to the charge through powder-filled goose quills placed in the touchholes. Ignition was quicker and the time delay before firing more predictable. Gun captains could improve accuracy by synchronizing the jerk of the lanyard with the roll of the ship.

A further innovation was in large part due to Captain Charles Douglas, Rodney's First Captain of the Fleet (chief of staff in modern terminology). By having the framing at each side of the gun ports altered, he made it possible to train the guns through a considerably greater arc than had previously been possible. When opposing ships were moving relative to each other, the target vessel came into the gun's enhanced firing arc earlier and left it later, enabling a ship to get off more broadsides than its opponent could.

Naval and military reinforcements had reached the French stronghold of Martinique. de Grasse had thirty-six ships of the line and ample troops to carry out the French strategy of capturing the island of Jamaica, worth more to the British than all the Leeward Islands put together. Loss of Jamaica was regarded in that day and age as being just as serious as the loss of the Thirteen Colonies.

On 8 April the French troop convoy sailed north from Port Royal, remaining close inshore and screened to seaward by the fleet of de Grasse. On the same day the British sailed from St. Lucia in pursuit. In light winds over a hundred warships manoeuvred to attack or defend the slow-sailing convoy.

On the morning of 9 April Hood, with the British van squadron, made contact with the French and in a sharp engagement several British ships were damaged. The *Alfred* was in the thick of the fight, but opened fire at too great a range and had only ten charges of powder left at the end of the action. One French shot carried off Captain Bayne's leg about mid-thigh, and before a tourniquet could be applied he died. Throughout the next two days the main British force slowly overtook the French, de Grasse having lingered to protect the *Zele*, dismasted in a collision and under tow by a frigate.

Dawn of 12 April found the two fleets still in the twenty-five-mile channel between Dominica and Guadeloupe. At the northern end of the channel is the group of islands known as Les Saintes, which was to give its name to the forthcoming battle. The French fleet was to the north of the British and the wind light easterly. Having decided to cover the crippled *Zele*, de Grasse formed his line on a southerly course and steered to gain the weather gauge by crossing ahead of Rodney's line, which was then approaching from the south. Quite prepared to fight from leeward, the British admiral allowed de Grasse to complete his manoeuvre. Having crossed ahead, de Grasse turned his ships a few points to starboard in succession. The head of the British line similarly altered to its larboard as it approached within range, and the stage seemed set for a standard line-to-line engagement on opposite courses and within musket shot of each other. The first broadside was fired at about 7:45 in the morning.

Rodney had six more ships than de Grasse, but he had ordered an interval of only a hundred yards between them, setting a station-keeping challenge that could only be met by the best of captains. His line was thus only two-thirds the length of the French formation, which was somewhat irregular as well as having larger gaps between ships. The passing situation maximized the benefits of the recent improvements in British gunnery and highlighted the deterioration in professionalism of the French personnel.

As usual the terrific British fire was directed at the hulls rather than at the rigging of the enemy ships. The French suffered heavily, and for the first time in this war there were reports of their gun crews running from their posts in anticipation of a British broadside. At about 8:30 de Grasse tried to order his ships to wear onto the opposite tack, but the smoke of battle had become so thick that his signals could not be read.

So far nothing disastrous had occurred, although the French were getting the worst of the fight. But fate presented Rodney with an unexpected opportunity. Crippled by gout, he was directing the battle from an armchair on the quarterdeck of the *Formidable*. Shortly after 9:00 the wind suddenly veered from easterly to southerly, forcing the French ships to steer more to starboard. This tended to widen the already-existing gaps in their line, and through one of these Rodney ordered his 100-gun flagship, which raked the French ships to either side from end to end as she passed between them. The *Glorieux* to starboard was dismasted and the *Diadème* to port so damaged that she paid off in irons, forcing the ships astern of her to stop.

Five British ships of the centre squadron followed the *Formidable*, and the *Bedford* led the ten ships of Hood's rear division through a second gap in the French line, the centre of which was now in complete confusion. For a time the wind failed altogether, a phenomenon then believed to be the result of prolonged gunfire in a confined area. Wreathed in smoke and unable to manoeuvre, the two sides continued to cannonade away at any enemy within range while attempting to repair their own damage.

Shortly after noon a breeze sprang up. As the smoke cleared it was seen that the French fleet had been separated into three parts. Rodney now hauled down the signal for the line, and the individual ships of his centre squadron and Hood's in the rear ran down to engage the isolated vessels in the French centre. Some of the ships of the French rear and van attempted to rejoin their comrades, largely unsuccessfully since they were well to leeward of de Grasse's flagship *Ville de Paris* and the ships with her. At one point no fewer than eight British ships were engaging the 104-gun *Ville de Paris*, which put up a tremendous resistance. By the end of the action she had fired off all her made-up cartridges and was loading with loose powder from barrels hoisted on deck.

To avoid futile slaughter de Grasse at length surrendered the ship; he was one of only three unwounded men left on deck. Four other French ships also surrendered, and as dark fell Admiral Vaudreuil led the badly damaged remainder out of the fray. The *Ville de Paris* alone had suffered more casualties than had the entire British fleet. Boarding the surrendered ship, a British officer, 'over his shoes in blood,' conveyed Rodney's invitation to de Grasse to join him in the *Formidable*.

Rodney had won the greatest naval victory in living memory. At last Britain had a triumph to set against the now inevitable loss of America and an assurance that its possessions in the West Indies would not be forfeited to the French. Hood, always inclined to be critical of his superiors, thought that the badly damaged French should have been pursued immediately, but with six ships taken and his illustrious foe a prisoner, the sick old admiral was justifiably content with what had been achieved. In this case, in Washington's analogy, the naval vote had been cast in favour of the British.

The wind shift had been a critical factor, but it need not have been decisive. It needed an admiral of Rodney's calibre to perceive the possibility of breaking the enemy line and then to follow up by releasing his ships from the constraints of his own line of battle. It was later claimed that Captain Douglas had actually been first to suggest the manoeuvre. Regardless, it was Rodney who gave the order, and in seizing the moment he had achieved the elusive goal of concentrating his forces at the critical point. Once that situation had been brought about, superior British gunnery proved decisive.

As after the Chesapeake, the events and tactics of Les Saintes would be endlessly discussed. It was now seen that a decisive concentration of force could be attained even within the constraints of the line of battle. Graves might have done this at the Chesapeake had he attacked before de Grasse could form his fleet; Rodney had done so at Les

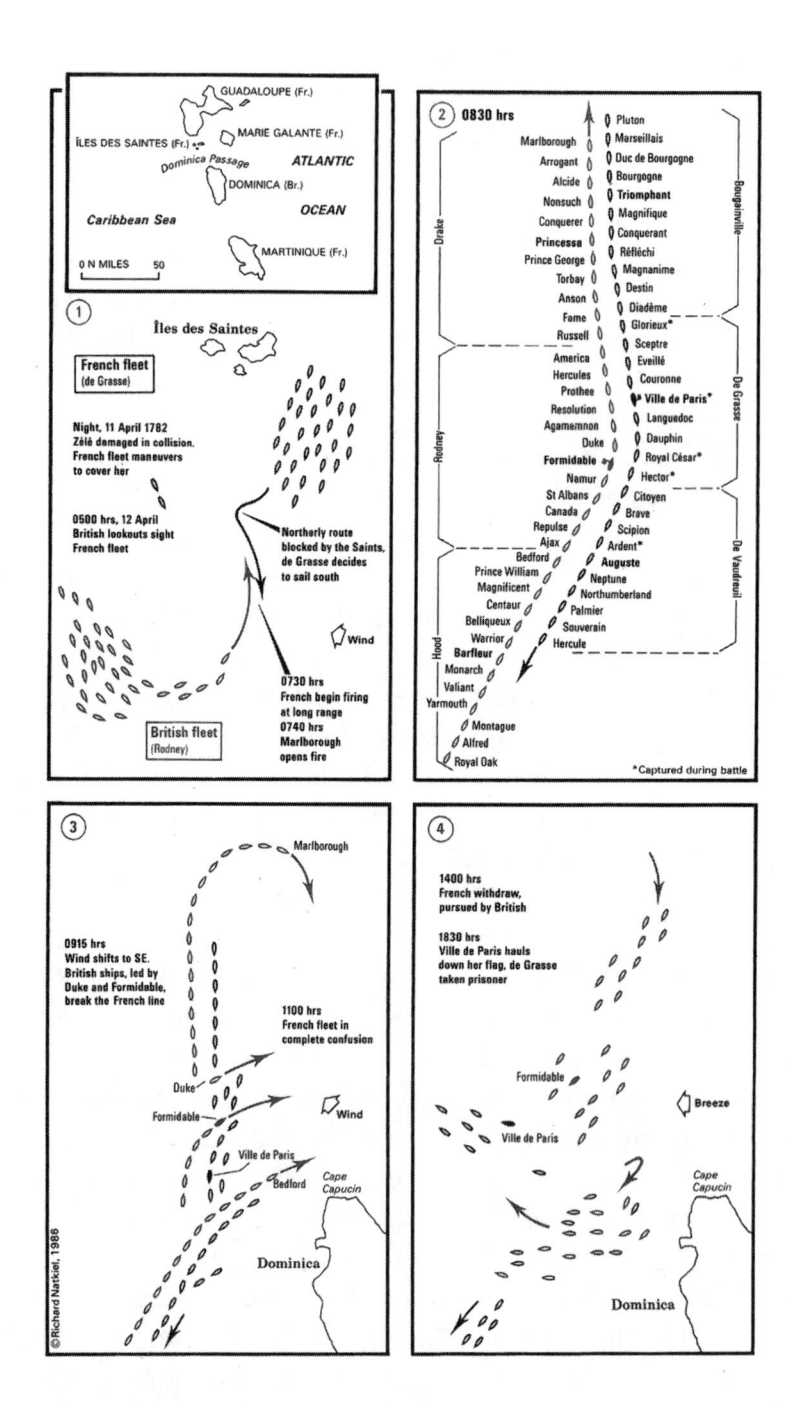

Plan, Battle of Les Saintes, 12 Apr. 1782.

Saintes because a change in wind direction allowed him to break the enemy's line. What was needed was a commander prepared to seize any opportunity presented to him by his opponent's difficulties, the weather, or any other favourable circumstance.

Hallowell had joined the *Alfred* as its fifth lieutenant. By early January 1782 he had became fourth, and in early April, second. With the death of Captain Bayne in the engagement of April 9, the first lieutenant, Lind, had taken command during Les Saintes on 12 April, and Hallowell had in consequence become first lieutenant.

The first lieutenant was responsible for organizing the crew by drawing up Watch and Quarter and Station bills. The Watch Bill assigned every man to either the larboard or starboard watch for normal sailing, the two watches relieving each other in rotation around the clock. The Quarter Bill expressed the fighting organization. When the drum beat to quarters, each man knew his post. For the majority of the ship's company this would be at the guns, one man for each five hundred pounds weight of the piece, plus the gun captain for a total of eight to ten men.

By the evening of the final battle the *Alfred* had lost twelve men, including Captain Bayne, and forty wounded. These were more casualties than any other British 74, and much worse than the *Alcide* had suffered at the Chesapeake, reflecting the much harder fighting at Les Saintes. Hallowell had sustained a contusion but chose not to report himself injured.

As acting first lieutenant, it was Hallowell's job to make the ship once again fit for action, as well as to reorganize the diminished crew in a new Watch and Quarter Bill. Having been at quarters for nearly twelve hours, the exhausted men now had to be put to work repairing hull and rigging and restoring the ship's combat readiness while the sea around them swarmed with sharks feasting on the bodies of the dead. He had scarcely achieved his goal before the ship was once again committed to action.

Rodney did not choose to take the whole fleet in immediate pursuit, but he intended to proceed to Jamaica in case the French continued with their invasion plans. The impatient Hood was ordered to sail first with his van squadron, including the *Alfred*. A week later and four hundred miles to the northwest they chanced upon a small French detachment in the Mona Passage between Hispaniola and Puerto Rico. Outnumbered and outsailed thanks to the copper sheathing of the British ships, the French surrendered, and the *Jason*, 64; *Caton*, 64; *Amiable*, 32; and *Ceres*, 16, fell into the squadron's hands.

When merchant vessels were captured the ships and cargoes were sold, the proceeds were distributed as prize money among the crew of the capturing ship in accordance with a formula promulgated by the Admiralty. The reward for capturing enemy warships not sold was known as head money, calculated at the rate of £5 for each man alive aboard the enemy ship at the beginning of the action. Head money was distributed more equally than prize money but was seldom as lucrative. The captures in the Mona Passage would have netted Hallowell a few pounds, no doubt welcome but probably not actually paid out for many months.

On the same day as the captures, Hood appointed Robert Barbor, captain of the *Fame*, to command the *Alfred*. Lind and Hallowell both moved down a notch to their former rungs on the lieutenant ladder. The scene in the Mona Passage must have been one of great activity, with the British and ex-French ships hove to and boats plying to and fro in the bright sunshine with prisoners, prize crews, and, in the case of the *Alfred*, a new captain. No fewer than twenty-four men rated 'servants' accompanied Barbor.

With its prizes Hood's squadron rejoined Rodney and the rest of the fleet in late April. Barbor's son, also a Robert, had been a volunteer on the *Fame*. The new captain took the opportunity to bring him into the *Alfred* and rate him midshipman, an act of favouritism so typical of the time that it would have passed quite unnoticed; indeed, for him not to have done so would have been considered remarkable. Once again there was much coming and going of personnel, prisoners, and prize crews, and on 26 April the *Alfred* took aboard 155 captured Frenchmen.

At this juncture Hallowell must have felt his chances of quick advancement to be very good. Although only twenty-one he had fought bravely in four actions and assumed growing responsibilities, fully justifying the faith Rodney and Hood had placed in him. He might even have been in line to become commander of one of the

French prizes after Les Saintes had he not been too busy as acting first lieutenant of the *Alfred*. Above all, he must have cursed the consequences of his late entry into the navy, brought into sharp focus by the example of a young man of very similar background.

Just two years older than Hallowell, Isaac Coffin had also been born in Boston, where his father Nathaniel had been a subordinate of Benjamin Hallowell Sr. Unlike the younger Benjamin, he had entered the navy at the typical age of fifteen through the patronage of Admiral Montague, then Commander-in-Chief in America. Like Hallowell he became a protégé of Admiral Hood. As flag lieutenant to Admiral Arbuthnot at the Battle of the Chesapeake, he was already marked out for advancement and was soon a commander. By June of 1782 he had been made captain of the *Shrewsbury*, 74. A mere two years difference in service meant that he caught the wave of promotion that was to elude Hallowell for more than ten years.

Hallowell's prospects were about to change for the worse. The *Alfred* was one of the ships detached to reinforce the Jamaica station, meaning that Hallowell could no longer count on the direct interest and support of Rodney and Hood. Sir Peter Parker, the admiral commanding in Jamaica, had his own protégés, who would take precedence over a newcomer, however meritorious his service and however prestigious his now remote patrons. Moreover, Rodney was superseded in August 1782 and returned home to be elevated to the peerage and receive the acclaim of his countrymen.

Hood had caused some of the crew of the departing *Alfred* to be transferred to ships that were to remain under his command, and the *Alfred* was now very short of men. The French prisoners were therefore included in the Watch Bill for the passage. By virtue of keeping watches the French received full rations instead of the two-thirds they would have got as prisoners, and they no doubt preferred to spend time on deck rather than being confined below.

That enemy sailors could be so employed despite the language barrier well illustrates the similarity of sailing technology among the navies of the time. It also illustrates the feelings of mutual respect between French and English seamen, who when not actually trying to kill each other were quite able to co-exist and work together to counter the common enemy, the sea. For the prisoners the biggest hardship probably was being forced to consume beer or rum rather than the wine to which they were accustomed. Nevertheless, the crew of the *Alfred* had to be constantly on guard against any attempt by the prisoners to rise up and take the vessel.

In mid-May the *Alfred* arrived in Jamaica, the largest of the British 'sugar islands,' and of immense importance to the nation's economy. Prior to the arrival of Columbus in 1494, Jamaica had been inhabited by Arawaks; but under Spanish rule ill-treatment, new diseases, and migration had destroyed the indigenous population. The climate proving unsuitable for European labour, the Spanish had imported African slaves in large numbers.

In 1655 the British captured the island and it became a haven for privateers and pirates until the early eighteenth century, when the cultivation of sugar cane was initiated. The demand for sugar seemed insatiable, bringing fabulous prosperity to the plantation owners and to the traders and merchants who marketed the crop in Europe.

When the Spanish gave up the island they freed their black slaves, who developed an independent warrior society that in course of time began preying on the British settlements. Hallowell heard many tales of a people known as Maroons who maintained a fierce independence in the interior highlands. The name probably derives from the Spanish *cimmaron*, meaning wild. The Maroons' numbers were continually augmented by escaped slaves.

The British army undertook several campaigns against them with limited success. Some of the Maroons finally made peace on the basis of being given sovereignty over their local territory and agreeing to assist in the recovery of escaped slaves. Other groups continued to maintain their relative independence. Twenty years later and on the other side of the Atlantic one such group would re-enter Hallowell's life.

The Jamaican climate began to take its toll, and the number of men sick on board or in hospital steadily mounted. After a short illness Captain Barbor died, having enjoyed less than two months in his new command. He was marked 'DD' in the ship's book on June 12, and the very same day the twenty-four volunteers with whom he had arrived were discharged from the ship, marked 'D' with the laconic amplification 'master dead.' Mostly adolescent officer apprentices, they were aboard only because of the captain's personal wish, and with his demise they no longer belonged.

The new captain was Peter Dumaresq, and like Barbor he arrived with his own generous retinue, consisting of twenty-three volunteers, his clerk, five midshipmen, a schoolmaster, and the coxswain and thirteen-man crew of his barge.

A captain resembled a comet, trailing his dependents and favourites like a tail as he moved from one appointment to another. Nepotism it may have been, but to an extent it also made for efficiency, because the little teams tended to stay together in support of the central figure as he moved up the ladder. In his turn Hallowell was to use the system to advantage like everyone else.

The *Alfred* spent less than two months at Port Royal in Jamaica. Soon after sailing the sick list dropped significantly and had virtually disappeared when the ship anchored at New York on 5 September 1782. It was just over a year since Hallowell had arrived there and been commissioned in his first ship, and a year to the day since the fateful action of the Chesapeake.

General Cornwallis's surrender had ended the British attempt to defeat the Revolution, and it was now simply a question of holding New York, Savannah, and Charleston as havens for despairing Loyalists who had fought for the losing side. On May 1 an order had been issued to cease hostilities at these ports. A few days later General Clinton had been relieved by Sir Guy Carleton, who had successfully defended Quebec against the rebel invasions. His task was to make the final arrangements to end the war.

New York was crowded with families so committed to the Loyalist cause that there was no chance of their being accepted in the triumphant new republic. Admiral Robert Digby, commanding on the station, was already organizing their evacuation by sea to a new life in the remaining loyal colony of Nova Scotia. So well did he perform this task that his name was given to the county and town at the mouth of

Annapolis Basin where many of the Loyalists found a new home.

Hallowell went ashore as the houseguest of Edward Winslow, an old friend of his father's and at this time an officer in the Loyalist forces. Immersion in the atmosphere of the doomed city must have been a melancholy experience for the young exile, recalling as it did his parents' account of their own evacuation from a besieged Boston six years earlier. Then the prospects for a return to America had been good; now they were non-existent.

Captain Dumaresq pressed eighteen men before sailing for Jamaica, and three men actually volunteered to join the *Alfred*, perhaps fearful Loyalists anxious to get out of New York and not enthusiastic about starting over in Nova Scotia.

The *Alfred* reached Port Royal, Jamaica, on 5 February 1783, to learn that the long-anticipated peace had been concluded at Versailles a month earlier. Whatever hopes Hallowell still had for quick advancement evaporated. Even worse, a drastic demobilization of the fleet was sure to follow. When the *Alfred* paid off he would be left without active employment and facing the stark reality of an indefinite existence on half pay. Even peacetime service in the unhealthy West Indies would have been preferable.

There was a brief respite while the ship awaited instructions, but all too soon she was ordered home, leaving Port Royal on 25 April. Two months later, the *Alfred* was at Plymouth, the exceptionally slow passage easily tolerated by officers who stood to lose their jobs when it was over. These feelings would not be shared by the men of the lower deck, who could count on being reabsorbed into the merchant service from which they had mostly been pressed.

On 5 July the *Alfred* arrived at the Chatham dockyard. Hallowell could have left at once, but he squeezed out every day of full wages until the *Alfred* at last paid off on 26 July.

4

ON THE BEACH
1783–1790

To a bloody war or a sickly season.

Naval toast of the day for Thursday

The temporary but tightly knit family of the *Alfred's* wardroom had dissolved, never to be reunited, and the young man was welcomed again into his natural family. Seven years before, the reunion with his exiled parents had been blighted by young Ben's expulsion from school. Now a commissioned officer tested in battle and a mature professional, the young man had again become a family problem. At least this time he could not be blamed. Had the war lasted a little longer, he could have taken the all-important step up to his own command. But history had decreed otherwise, and like thousands of others he had become that figure of pity, the lieutenant on half pay.

In the interests of economy the strength of the navy was greatly reduced in peacetime. Apart from a few on active service, the ships were tied up in the royal dockyards, almost completely unmanned. At the threat of war the noncommissioned portion of the crews would be brought up to strength from the pool of merchant seamen and if necessary by impressment. In the case of officers there was a permanent reserve, consisting of those who remained available for service in consideration of a sort of retainer known as half pay. This was a regular stipend of approximately fifty percent of full salary, payable on condition that the recipient swear quarterly before a justice of the peace that he had not accepted any other employment under the Crown (i.e., government employment).

For officers with private incomes half-pay status would not be a major hardship, but poor lieutenants like Hallowell, who relied entirely on their pay, suffered severely. Saving was out of the question, and only a small minority of junior officers was lucky enough to have accumulated a nest egg from prize money.

A lieutenant's half pay at this period amounted to slightly more than £50 per year at a time when a skilled worker might earn something like £40. But the two individuals would have regarded these comparable sums very differently due to class expectations. Not aspiring to the niceties of middle-class existence, the skilled worker would be well above his perception of the poverty line. The lieutenant, on the other hand, would find himself financially on the brink of the social chasm separating the middle class and the lower orders. It was not just his standard of living but also his very position in polite society that was at risk.

It was said of half-pay officers that 'though they hardly live they never die,' where 'hardly living' meant the inability to enjoy much of what counted as essential within their milieu. Not the least of the consequences was that the impecunious half-pay officer was virtually disbarred from seeking a marriage partner within his own class.

Of course Hallowell was taken in by his parents and supported to the best of their ability, with his own meagre stipend thrown in to supplement his father's income. At first the situation would not have been too serious, because the elder Hallowell continued to draw his full salary. But in November 1783 the government revoked the patent of the American Board of Customs. On an annual pension of only £250, the former commissioner too was now on half pay, but with no prospect of future employment.

By exercising strict economy, such as giving up a carriage and horses, the Hallowells maintained the essential aspects of middle-class life, including two live-in domestic servants. Their household in Stafford Row, Buckingham Gate, consisted of the parents, the shore-bound lieutenant, his sister Mary, and young Nicky, Ward's son by his now dissolved marriage. Benjamin Sr. also rented a house in Cavendish Square for his widowed mother Rebecca and his cousin Martha Hallowell, the old lady's long-time companion.

John Adams, later the second president of the United States, had been appointed his country's first ambassador to the Court of St. James. The Adamses, Boylstons, and Hallowells had been friends in Boston, despite their political differences, and Mrs. Hallowell and Mrs. Adams were cousins. At this time Mrs. Adams was temporarily alone in

Benjamin Hallowell's father, very much the busy man of affairs.

London awaiting the arrival of her husband, and the Hallowells offered her lodgings until her husband took up his post. She declined, but did accept their invitation to 'an unceremonious family dinner,' and found them living in some style, but not as splendidly as they had in Boston.

Ward resided in rooms at Barnard's Inn and had entered into a promising business partnership with his uncle Thomas Boylston. Thomas was friendly with John Adams and Thomas Jefferson and took an active part in re-establishing the trade between Britain and the former colonies. Young Benjamin might have joined them, but despite his penury there is no indication that this career change was even considered.

The senior Hallowell's Boston property had been confiscated, but in her own name Mary Hallowell continued to own the house at Roxbury, as well as a share in other family real estate. Her sister Rebecca had married Moses Gill, who acted as agent for the property and very occasionally remitted a small but welcome share of the rents to London. With revolutionary feelings still running high there was no immediate prospect of any of the family returning to Boston to make more advantageous use of Mary's inheritance. Grandfather Benjamin Hallowell had died in 1773, but his estate had not been settled. His land on the Kennebec was potentially valuable, but of no current benefit.

Any improvement in the family's financial situation had to be looked for elsewhere. Two possibilities were at hand. The British government had established the Loyalist Claims Commission to investigate claims of loss from the rebellion and to recommend compensation where justified. Benjamin Hallowell Sr. and Ward Boylston both submitted claims, but there would be a considerable delay before any restitution could be expected.

The second possibility was to make something out of the twenty thousand acres in Nova Scotia granted to the senior Hallowell in 1765, but still totally undeveloped in 1783. To avoid speculation the provincial government imposed conditions on all such grants. The most important was that the grantee must 'settle on every 200 acres one Protestant settler within ten years from date here of.' If this condition was not met and the land was required for settlement, the grant was subject to escheatment, that is, takeover by the government.

Most of those who migrated from New England preferred to settle the already cleared lands of the deported Acadians. Hallowell had gone to some expense and entered into contracts with several families, but none had settled on his grant by the time the ten-year condition expired in October 1775. By that time revolutionary and later wartime circumstances precluded further attempts at settlement.

With the success of the American Revolution the picture had changed dramatically. Now thousands of disbanded military personnel and fleeing Loyalists were seeking new farms in Nova Scotia and Canada. Escheatment had become a real possibility. In July of 1783 Hallowell Sr. wrote to Governor Parr of Nova Scotia, pointing out that he had lost all his possessions in Massachusetts, and explaining that, 'having been absent from America on public business in England two years and a half, together with the threatened rebellion which broke out in 1774, it was not in my power to fulfill the conditions of the grant.' On these grounds he pleaded with the governor for further time.

Hallowell's first response from Nova Scotia came from the lieutenant-governor, Colonel Fanning, also a Loyalist. Writing in December 1783, he commented very favourably on a recent tour of the Annapolis Valley and on the prospects for development in the province. He enclosed a report from surveyor Charles Morris to the effect that Hallowell's grant was very suitable for farming, fishing, and forestry. He recommended that Hallowell survey the tract in lots of 200 acres and give away every other lot in order to stimulate settlement and increase the value of the remainder.

Hallowell had not received this letter when early in 1784 he wrote somewhat testily to Fanning reminding him of the problem of escheatment and his promise of assistance. This is the first example of the difficulty of managing his grant at long range. He frequently expressed his intention to go to Nova Scotia, but some circumstance had always turned up to prevent it. Business had therefore to be carried on by means of a trans-Atlantic exchange of letters, which sometimes went astray and often crossed in passage. At best, months would elapse before any question could receive a reply or any decision was put into effect. To make matters worse, Hallowell was frequently unable to attend to business for weeks at a time due to ill health.

John Wentworth was much better placed to be of assistance. In colonial days the Wentworths had been a politically powerful family in New Hampshire. Born in 1737, Wentworth was a graduate of Harvard, a participant in his father's business affairs, and a friend of the Marquis of Rockingham, a leading British political figure to whom he was distantly related. Wentworth played a prominent part in the campaign to repeal the Stamp Act, but remained completely loyal to the mother country. At the time of the Revolution he was governor of New Hampshire, but in 1775 he had been forced by mob action to flee to Boston and was subsequently evacuated with the Hallowells and other Loyalists.

On the fall of the Lord North government, Rockingham formed a ministry and appointed his protégé governor of Nova Scotia, as well as Surveyor General of the King's Woods. Rockingham soon died, and the next ministry revoked both his appointments and appointed Parr as governor. Still another change of ministry brought Wentworth's friend the Duke of Portland to power. It was too late to stop Parr's appointment, but Portland was able to reinstate Wentworth as Surveyor General of the King's Woods.

It was Wentworth's job to inspect the province's forests and set the most suitable trees aside for the Royal Navy, always in need of timber and especially of the tall, straight, knot-free trunks required for the towering masts of the line of battle ships. Until he was well into his sixties he ranged the virgin forests in all seasons by canoe, on foot, or on snowshoes and probably came to know the province as well as anyone alive, including the aboriginal inhabitants.

It was not until the end of April 1784 that Wentworth was able to give the elder Hallowell some news. It must have been received with mixed feelings. Ten thousand acres or half the total grant had to be given up for settlement; that area was to include an allowance for a town. Hallowell would retain ten thousand acres plus a share of the lots within the town limits. This plan came as a shock, but as Wentworth wrote, 'The ten thousand acres remaining to you will then be a valuable and inexpensive property — in any other mode it would be useless and in continued hazard of being lost.' Wentworth promised to have his surveyors protect Hallowell's timber, 'with which the Acadians residing on the adjacent harbour have hitherto made free.'

Perhaps to cushion the loss of ten thousand acres, Wentworth went on to paint a glowing picture of Nova Scotia's potential to supplant New England as a supplier of commodities to the sugar islands:

> *If properly managed it would immediately afford a good relief to the West Indies of lumber, and in time supply them amply, and with corn, fish, provisions, cattle and horses — indeed with every article that the United States supplied except rice, tobacco grows here perfectly well, and as to fish and lumber it exceeds any country I ever saw. The latter can be exported much cheaper than from New England.*

At this period the Hallowell family situation reached its nadir. Unable to maintain a household in central London, where, according to one refugee, '£600 per annum is but a drop in the ocean,' they were forced to move to Edgware Road, then a semirural area. The ex-Commissioner's meagre pension had to be collected in person from the Treasury and was frequently in arrears, and his claim before the Loyalist Claims Commission was unsettled. The remaining New England property was out of reach, half the Nova Scotia grant had been given up, and there was little demand for the remainder. Daughter Mary had no dowry, and son was unemployed. According to Thomas Boylston:

> *The circumstance of the Hallowell family is very melancholy. She is broken with cares and disappointments; their dependency on government has very much embarrassed them: he has but a few months I fear to live, being far advanced in a wasting declining state; and the salary he now gets from government is thro more trouble than a man not in necessity would think worth pursuing — and which when he dies, dies with him, and leaves his children in a very pitiful situation.*

The unemployed Lieutenant Hallowell must have felt acutely guilty at burdening his family with his presence at such a time. Quite likely he took any available opportunity to escape the depressing atmosphere of Edgware Road by visiting his Uncle Robert and his now-widowed aunts Anne Gould and Rebecca Bishop in Bristol. They were no better off than his parents — indeed they were worse off — but the cost of living outside the capital was significantly lower. In Bristol Hallowell would again have come in contact with his cousin Anne Gould, now thirteen, and it may have been at this time that their lifelong attachment began.

With others on half pay he would spend hours in the waiting room at the Admiralty, hoping for an opportunity to remind officialdom of his existence and to plead for a ship. His father was also hard at work through Rodney and Hood. It no doubt helped that Hood had become the Member of Parliament for Westminster, Parliament being the most powerful source of influence. On 1 May 1784, Hallowell at last received a commission as lieutenant in HMS *Falcon* on the Leeward Islands station. According to his uncle, 'he was half dead when he left London,' but he would have considered himself fortunate to have employment after barely a year on half pay.

The *Falcon* was already in the West Indies. Perhaps tiring of that unhealthy station, her original lieutenant may have asked to be relieved, causing the vacancy that Hallowell was very glad to fill. He joined his new ship at Antigua on 29 July. Immediately below his name in the ship's muster book is that of Nicholas Boylston, listed as Lieutenant Hallowell's servant. This was Ward's young son Nicky, now a volunteer, hopefully on the first step of a naval career. Each sea officer was allowed to bring aboard one such protégé. In taking his nephew Hallowell had relieved some of the pressure on his distressed family and placed his brother Ward under a considerable obligation. At this time Nicky must have just turned thirteen, quite old enough to enter into this new world.

The *Falcon* was the smallest vessel in which Hallowell had yet served, her armament consisting of ten 4-pounder guns and ten swivels. She was rated as a brig-sloop, with two masts, and all her guns were mounted on the upper deck. At this time she was commanded by Commander V. C. Berkeley, which meant that she was referred to as a sloop; if Berkeley had only been a lieutenant the same ship would have been called a brig. Her complement was just seventy men, with no marines, and, apart from the captain, Hallowell was the only commissioned officer and thus first lieutenant. She carried no purser, her accounts being kept by the naval storekeepers at Antigua and Barbados. A comedown after a 74, the *Falcon* nevertheless provided an excellent opportunity for Hallowell to assume hands-on administrative and operational responsibilities that would prepare him for larger vessels.

His new posting brought him into contact with two old acquaintances and with three men who would play significant roles in his future. The admiral in command was Sir Richard Hughes, whose arrival in India in 1780 had been the occasion for the *Asia* to leave that unpopular station. On a more intimate level, Hallowell's mentor in the *Asia*, Wilfred Collingwood, was here as commander of the sloop *Rattler*. Through Wilfred, Hallowell met his older brother Captain Cuthbert Collingwood of the fifth-rate *Mediator*, Hughes's flagship. It was the start of a close relationship that would end only with Collingwood's death twenty-five years later. In command of the frigate *Pegasus* was His Royal Highness Prince William, Duke of Clarence, second son of King George III and the future King William IV. The social gap between Hallowell and the prince was too great for any true friendship to develop, but in the distant future a favourable remembrance by royalty would contribute to both the final reward and the final disappointment of Hallowell's life.

For the first time Hallowell came into regular contact with the young man who was to become the Royal Navy's greatest hero. In all probability they had already met when Hallowell was in the *Alfred* at New York in the autumn of 1782 and Horatio Nelson arrived there in command of the frigate *Albemarle*. The twenty-four-year-old Nelson had already been identified as an officer of great promise.

Prince William was then a midshipman in Hood's flagship *Barfleur* and happened to be on watch when Nelson arrived to pay his respects. Many years later he wrote,

> *Captain Nelson of the Albemarle came in his barge alongside, who*

appeared to be the merest boy of a captain I ever beheld [he] produced an appearance which particularly attracted my notice; for I had never seen anything like it before, nor could I imagine who he was, nor what he came about. My doubts were however, removed when Lord Hood introduced me to him. There was something irresistibly pleasing in his address and conversation; and an enthusiasm when speaking on professional subjects that showed he was no common being.

In the small naval circle of the Leeward Islands, Nelson and Hallowell inevitably became known to each other both socially and professionally, beginning a relationship that would play a major role in Hallowell's life.

The primary duty of the Leeward Islands squadron should have been to enforce the Navigation Acts, requiring that all cargoes originating in Britain and her colonies should be carried in British or colonial vessels. Now that the thirteen former American colonies were independent, they no longer enjoyed the right to participate in the trade of the British empire. Wentworth and others believed this prohibition would provide a major impetus to the economy of Nova Scotia. In helping to enforce the rules young Hallowell could feel that he was contributing in a small way to the value of his father's Nova Scotia grant.

In the West Indies local interests wanted American trade to continue as though the Revolution had never happened. Nelson in the 28-gun frigate *Boreas* was given responsibility for the northern part of the station with Wilfred Collingwood's *Rattler* and Prince William's *Pegasus* under his command. Hughes remained mainly in the southern area, based on Barbados. He led the comfortable and highly social life of a commanding admiral on a peacetime station and was loath to court the enmity of influential merchants and officials by interfering with their interests.

In contrast to his chief, Captain Nelson was determined to enforce the law. By the time he left the station he had arrested numerous American ships, antagonized the planters and merchants, quarrelled with government officials and his own admiral, complained to the Secretary of State and the King over the heads of his superiors, and was being sued for damages for assault and imprisonment.

Hallowell would especially admire Nelson's conduct because it closely resembled his father's unpopular enforcement of customs regulations in pre-revolutionary Boston. Not being captain of his own ship, he had little scope for emulation, all the more because the *Falcon* spent most of its time in inactivity. From the time Hallowell joined until she sailed for home the ship spent 535 days in harbour and only 183 days, a mere one-fourth of her commission, at sea.

Much of the inactive time was spent at the island of Antigua. At 108 square miles Antigua is the largest of the Leeward Islands and was strategically well placed to guard the northernmost British territories from the French at Martinique. English Harbour on its south shore, almost landlocked and sheltered by hills, made Antigua one of the few places in the West Indies where ships could lie in reasonable safety even during the hurricane season. By the 1780s a dockyard had been constructed and English Harbour had become the refit and replenishment centre for the whole station. Warm in winter and hot in summer, the island receives comparatively little rain, and its climate is moderated by the nearly constant northeast trade winds. In the late eighteenth century sugar cane, cultivated in large plantations with African slave labour, was virtually its only product.

As in the other sugar islands, the white plantation owners, merchants, and colonial officialdom formed a small but all-powerful governing class with whom the naval officers on the station enjoyed extensive social relations, Nelson being somewhat of an exception since in many places he was ostracized by the elite. For many a naval officer the daughter of a wealthy planter would be a desirable match, while for the lady the social status of the officer and the prospect of escaping the confines of island society were great inducements. Nelson was to marry just such a sugar heiress, and Hallowell's captain, Berkeley, was at one time courting an unidentified 'Miss E.'

Prince William lived ashore in a specially-built residence. With no need to marry wealth, he mixed with the fair sex in less wholesome ways and managed to contract venereal disease in his 'pursuit of the Dames de Couleurs.'

Hallowell would no doubt have been invited to the planters' estates on occasion, but accepting their hospitality on a regular basis would have incurred reciprocal obligations that he could not afford. As a mere lieutenant with no private means it would have been useless for him to pay court to any of the island belles.

Running the ship in harbour while his captain socialized would have kept him fairly busy, but we can imagine him tramping the roads through the cane fields and climbing the hills around English Harbour as an outlet for his energy and a means of passing the time. Probably he spent a great deal of time with nephew Nicky, encouraging and instructing him in nautical matters.

The *Falcon* was ordered home in May 1785. Two years earlier, on his return from America in the *Alfred*, Hallowell had faced the prospect of an indeterminate period on half pay and a reunion whose joy would be tempered with the knowledge that he had once again become a burden on his distressed family. Quite unrealistically he might have blamed himself for not single-handedly quelling the rebellion while in the *Alfred*. Now, as he returned in the *Falcon*, there loomed again the awful prospect of half pay. Equally unrealistically he might now blame himself for not being another Nelson in thwarting the illegal trade of the hated rebels.

The *Falcon* paid off in the River Thames, conveniently near his parents' home, in July 1785. He found few changes. Both parents remained in poor health. His father had appeared before the Loyalist Claims Commission a few months earlier, but his claim had not yet been adjudicated. Now twenty-two, sister Mary remained without a dowry, essentially unmarriageable.

The partnership of brother Ward and uncle Thomas Boylston was beginning to prosper in the operation of a sugar refinery in London and the import of whale oil from the United States.

Benefits from the Nova Scotia lands seemed as far in the future as ever, and the task of managing them at long range just as frustrating. On Fanning's advice the senior Hallowell had appointed a Mr. Lodge, actually on the ground in the area of the grant, as his agent. At the same time both Fanning and Wentworth remained actively engaged.

To anticipate the tangled story by a few years, an impossible situation was to arise in which Fanning and Lodge each had the impression that he was Hallowell's sole agent. Fanning was granting lots of 200 acres each, while Lodge had his own plan involving parcels of only 150 acres that he was allotting to entirely different settlers!

Hallowell dismissed Lodge, politely requested Fanning to stop helping, and appointed Messrs. Cutler, Stuart and Wyatt of Guysborough as his agents. (Thomas Cutler was a graduate of Yale University and had held a senior logistics position at British army headquarters in New York.) There is no escaping the conclusion that age, worry, and illness were taking their toll on the ex-commissioner, formerly so businesslike and competent but now becoming incapable of managing his affairs. Nevertheless, by 1792 the 200-acre lots were gradually being sold off for about £10 each, payable in installments over three years.

A coastal tract was surveyed and a town plot laid out. Thomas Boylston had promised to provide financial assistance in establishing a church and school on condition that the place was named after him. Hallowell duly applied to the authorities, and was gratified in August of 1784 to hear from Lieutenant Governor Fanning: 'I desire my compliments to Mr. Boylston, and that you will inform him that I have stood God-father to the town now settled on your land, and that I have called its name Boylston. Which neither time nor chance can kill, or take away.'

Boylston never reached the dignity of a town, but the village, perhaps the most beautifully situated in the area, still exists. The original plan is clearly evident in the layout of the streets and houses. With the original forest cover and its south and west facing aspect, the Hallowell parcel must indeed have been very attractive to prospective settlers. In 1788 agent Lodge laid out another town site at Clam Harbour, to be named Hallowell, but it never became established.

Apart from the sheer poverty of Hallowell's half-pay periods, the most soul-destroying aspect was that there was no way of predicting their end. In 1785 Europe was tranquil and the prospect of war and mobilization of the fleet correspondingly remote. Nevertheless, Hallowell would haunt the Admiralty pleading for a ship, while his father pursued the same objective through his network of connections. As on his first period of half pay, the young man made the round of visits of his relatives, a pleasant enough occupation, but carrying with it the inescapable sense of being a sponger and thus wounding to his pride.

In the course of his visits to Bristol, Hallowell again came in contact with his cousin Anne Gould, and their earlier friendship seems to have ripened into love. Perhaps it was with her rather than his family that he had corresponded while in America and the West Indies; that was certainly to be the case in later years. The only direct testimony comes from the memoirs of Robert Hallowell Gardiner, the son of Robert Hallowell and thus another of the younger Benjamin's first cousins. According to him:

> [Anne] had been educated with great care by her mother and to a good person added a fine understanding and excellent principles. In her youth she and her cousin, now Admiral Hallowell, had been strongly and mutually attached, but marriage was out of the question, he being only a poor lieutenant, and she dependent upon her mother, who, having only a life annuity could make no provision for her.

The mother was already searching for a rich match for her daughter, and the feelings of the two young people were irrelevant beside the issue of property. Crushed by the disappointment, Hallowell's energies and aspirations were focused even more on his career.

The Hallowells passed the summer of 1787 at Aldsworth in Sussex, conveniently near the Hood estate and never far from Hood's notice. A letter of Thomas Boylston in August 1787 illuminates the family situation:

> Mrs. Hallowell is in better health than she has been for some time, and he is also mended in his health. They are both gone to a country town about 50 miles from London, near the saltwater, to reside for the summer season; they think the sea air will recruit their spirits, mend and establish their health. Polly their daughter, as they call Mary, is gone with them. She's grown a stately fine figure, gay and agreeably plump, good shaped and a complete woman, wanting

nothing to finish her wishes but what is common to her age, the one thing needful. Their son Ben also accompanies them; he is out of employ and waits for a war, being a lieutenant in the navy. God grant he may be long disappointed and give us peace in our day.

Peace was preserved, but Hallowell's purgatory was on the point of ending. Once again the patronage of Lord Hood proved invaluable. On October 1 of the same year Hallowell wrote to his Uncle Thomas:

Lord Hood has (unsolicited) applied to the lords of the Admiralty to have me appointed one of his Lieutenants, and I am in consequence of his application to be commissioned tomorrow for the Barfleur, the ship on board which his Lordship is to hoist his Flag, placing me immediately in the line of preferment.

We may well question the reference to 'unsolicited,' but however it happened, the young man had taken an important step. It was usual for the most promising or favoured lieutenants to be sponsored to a flagship, where they could be closely observed and be available for promotion when a vacancy arose in the admiral's squadron. Normally the first lieutenant of the moment would get the first such appointment, with the remaining lieutenants moving up one step, and the process would be repeated as often as new opportunities arose — hence the 'line of preferment.'

Service in a flagship was expensive. Hallowell's letter to his uncle turns into an unabashed request for money. He has been unable to save anything from his half pay, and

I am really destitute of the means myself, I shall immediately upon my embarkation be called upon for thirty or forty pounds for the Mess, exclusive of the unavoidable expenses I must be at to furnish myself with every kind of apparel. When you consider the necessity of my situation and the inability of my parents to assist me I hope you will excuse my presumption and either give or lend me such aid as you may think proper.

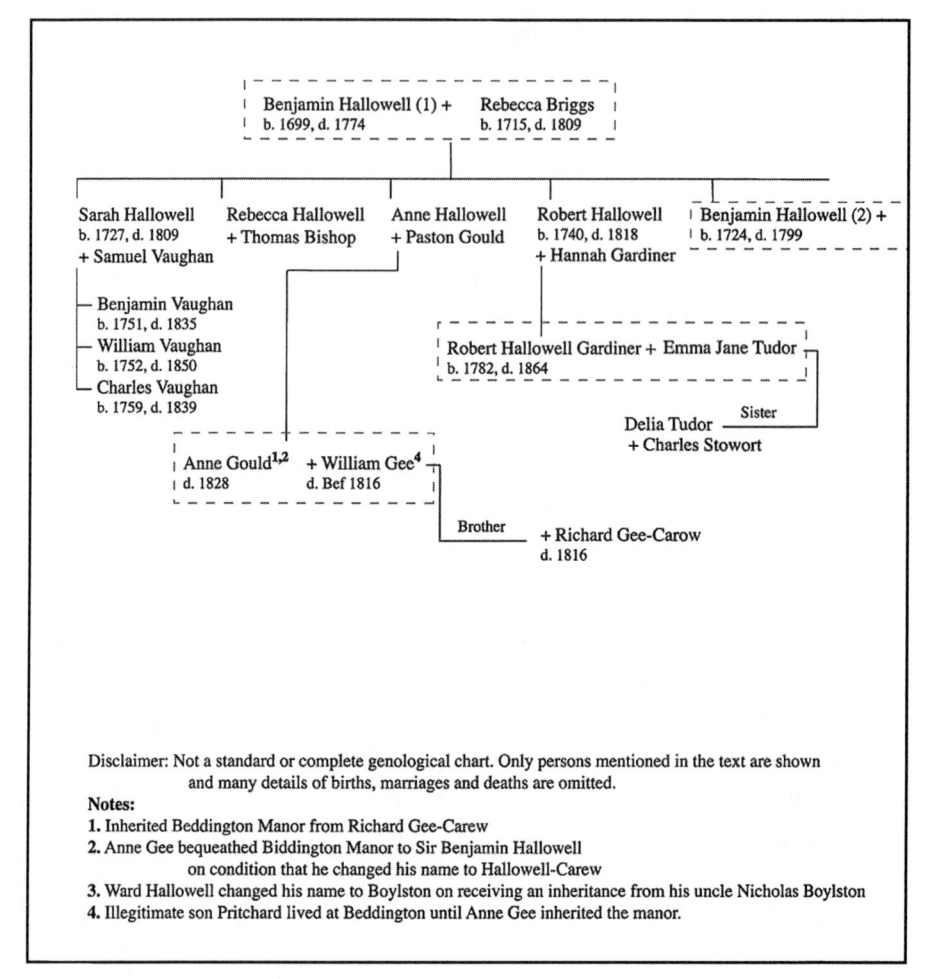

```
                    ┌─────────────────────────────┐
                    │ Benjamin Hallowell (1) +    │
                    │ Rebecca Briggs              │
                    │ b. 1699, d. 1774            │
                    │ b. 1715, d. 1809            │
                    └─────────────────────────────┘
```

Sarah Hallowell	Rebecca Hallowell	Anne Hallowell	Robert Hallowell	Benjamin Hallowell (2) +
b. 1727, d. 1809	+ Thomas Bishop	+ Paston Gould	b. 1740, d. 1818	b. 1724, d. 1799
+ Samuel Vaughan			+ Hannah Gardiner	

— Benjamin Vaughan
  b. 1751, d. 1835
— William Vaughan
  b. 1752, d. 1850
— Charles Vaughan
  b. 1759, d. 1839

Robert Hallowell Gardiner + Emma Jane Tudor
b. 1782, d. 1864

Delia Tudor —— Sister
+ Charles Stowort

Anne Gould[1,2]   + William Gee[4]
d. 1828   d. Bef 1816

Brother   + Richard Gee-Carow
             d. 1816

Disclaimer: Not a standard or complete genological chart. Only persons mentioned in the text are shown and many details of births, marriages and deaths are omitted.

Notes:
1. Inherited Beddington Manor from Richard Gee-Carew
2. Anne Gee bequeathed Biddington Manor to Sir Benjamin Hallowell
   on condition that he changed his name to Hallowell-Carew
3. Ward Hallowell changed his name to Boylston on receiving an inheritance from his uncle Nicholas Boylston
4. Illegitimate son Pritchard lived at Beddington until Anne Gee inherited the manor.

This may well have been the only letter from his nephew that Thomas Boylston ever received. Boylston was notoriously parsimonious, and at this time he and Ward Boylston were quarrelling over their business affairs. He declined to assist, and it was left to Samuel Vaughan and Ward to provide the minimum funding for Hallowell to take his place in the *Barfleur*.

Shortly after he joined, Hallowell witnessed the beginning of what became one of the most famous episodes in maritime history. A small vessel hired by the Admiralty left Spithead on an unusual mission. HMS *Bounty* was bound to the South Pacific to collect breadfruit plants. It was hoped this dietary staple of the natives of Tahiti could be trans-

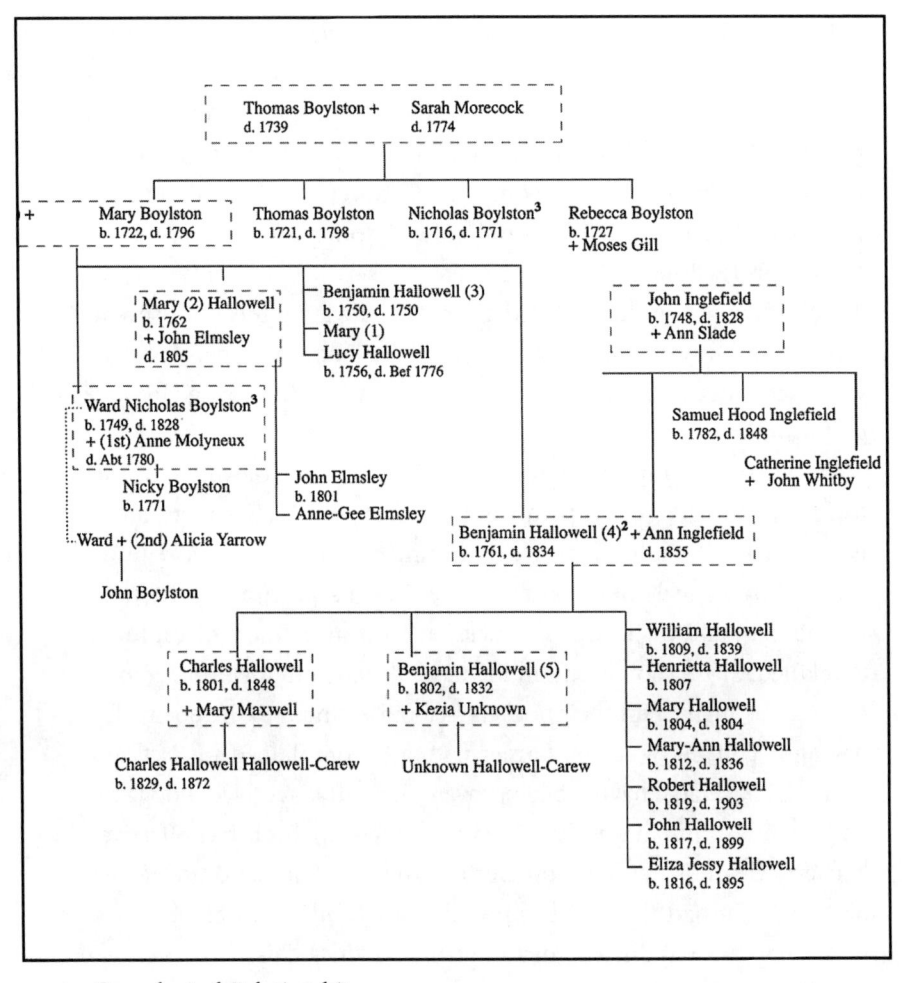

```
                    Thomas Boylston + Sarah Morecock
                         d. 1739         d. 1774

   + ── Mary Boylston ── Thomas Boylston ── Nicholas Boylston³ ── Rebecca Boylston
        b. 1722, d. 1796   b. 1721, d. 1798   b. 1716, d. 1771    b. 1727
                                                                  + Moses Gill

        Mary (2) Hallowell    Benjamin Hallowell (3)           John Inglefield
        b. 1762               b. 1750, d. 1750                 b. 1748, d. 1828
        + John Elmsley        Mary (1)                         + Ann Slade
        d. 1805               Lucy Hallowell
                              b. 1756, d. Bef 1776
        Ward Nicholas Boylston³                                Samuel Hood Inglefield
        b. 1749, d. 1828                                       b. 1782, d. 1848
        + (1st) Anne Molyneux
        d. Abt 1780                                            Catherine Inglefield
                              John Elmsley                     + John Whitby
        Nicky Boylston        b. 1801
        b. 1771               Anne-Gee Elmsley
                                                 Benjamin Hallowell (4)² + Ann Inglefield
        Ward + (2nd) Alicia Yarrow                b. 1761, d. 1834         d. 1855

        John Boylston
                                                                    William Hallowell
                                                                    b. 1809, d. 1839
             Charles Hallowell      Benjamin Hallowell (5)          Henrietta Hallowell
             b. 1801, d. 1848       b. 1802, d. 1832                b. 1807
             + Mary Maxwell         + Kezia Unknown                 Mary Hallowell
                                                                    b. 1804, d. 1804
        Charles Hallowell Hallowell-Carew   Unknown Hallowell-Carew Mary-Ann Hallowell
        b. 1829, d. 1872                                            b. 1812, d. 1836
                                                                    Robert Hallowell
                                                                    b. 1819, d. 1903
                                                                    John Hallowell
                                                                    b. 1817, d. 1899
                                                                    Eliza Jessy Hallowell
                                                                    b. 1816, d. 1895
```

Genealogical Relationships

planted to the West Indies as a local food supply for the plantation slaves. *Bounty's* captain was an officer who had been commissioned in the same year as Hallowell, Lieutenant William Bligh.

At this time a quarrel between France and the Netherlands had seemed likely to trigger a war in which Britain would be involved. Indeed, that possibility was the main reason the King had forced his ministers to give Hood the command in the Channel, for he was not popular within his own service. However, the dispute blew over, and life in the flagship settled down to a dreary peacetime routine.

Richard Gardner, a midshipman in the *Barfleur* at the time, later wrote the story of his naval career. He gives a thumbnail sketch of every officer with whom he served, characterizing Hallowell as 'a brave and skilful officer.' The word 'brave' appears in many of the sketches, but Hallowell is the only one Gardner calls 'skilful,' a rather remarkable distinction in a catalogue of some of the navy's best-known professionals.

According to Gardner, 'We led a very lazy life at Spithead for several months and it was expected we should strike upon our beef bones, as we never shifted our berth. We had nothing to do but row guard and go for fresh beef.'

He describes a number of midshipmen's escapades, of which the following is typical: A midshipman and a boat's crew had been sent on an errand ashore. While passing a farmyard on their return they were attacked by a gaggle of ducks. Like true British seamen the party took up the fight and dispersed the ducks, apart from a few they captured and killed. Spying some fruit in the farmer's orchard, the midshipman ordered his men to fill their pockets as a punishment to the enemy for having begun the war. The farmer naturally complained to *Barfleur's* captain. The charge having been proven, the sailors received a flogging and the midshipman was dismissed from the ship, his career effectively over. 'The midshipman thought this extremely hard, and on leaving observed that had the case been tried before a jury he was sure they would have brought in a verdict of justifiable duckicide.'

Such incidents would become known throughout the fleet, to be chewed over endlessly in an atmosphere where events of real significance were rare. For Hallowell, even ennui at Spithead was preferable to half pay, but, short of war or an unexpected outbreak of disease, his advancement would be long delayed. In the years 1788 and 1789 no officers were promoted to the rank of captain and there seemed no end in sight to the drought.

But in late 1789 war suddenly became imminent thanks to an incident half a world away. Spain laid claim to the entire west coast of North America. Spanish captains such as Juan de Fuca had indeed explored the coast, but its effective occupation was limited to southern

California. British vessels had been trading with the aboriginals further north for some time without molestation. Suddenly reasserting their sovereignty, the Spanish arrested four trading vessels in Nootka Sound on the west coast of what is now Vancouver Island. The British demanded their release.

When Spain did not back down Britain made ostentatious preparations for war, mobilizing additional ships, recalling captains and admirals, and preparing troops for overseas service. With no hope of assistance from France, Spain finally agreed to the Nootka Sound Convention of October 1790. Captain George Vancouver, a contemporary of Hallowell's, was sent with two ships to chart the coast, opening the Pacific Northwest to British trade and settlement.

As tension rose, Hood had shifted his flag to the *Victory*, taking the officers of the *Barfleur* with him. By now Hallowell had risen to second lieutenant, just two steps away from preferment; his father said he would already have been first lieutenant had not parliamentary interest placed someone ahead of him against Hood's wishes. Now there was to be no war, and promotion again receded into the indefinite future. Hallowell was twenty-nine and still a lieutenant. In bloodier times he might like Nelson, Coffin, and many others have been a captain while still in his early twenties.

But the most demoralizing period of his life was at an end. On 6 December 1790, Hallowell was at last commissioned master and commander.

5

PROMOTION
1790–1792

*Go on board and take upon you the charge
and command of Captain.*

New commanding officer's commission

Benjamin Hallowell's first command was a very desirable one. The *Scorpion* was only five years old, a sloop of the Echo class, the first class to have been especially designed to mount carronades. She carried sixteen 6-pounders on her upper deck, and eight 24-pounder carronades on her quarterdeck and forecastle.

Named after the Caron Iron Works in Scotland, the carronade was just coming into service at the end of the Revolutionary War. Much shorter and lighter than a standard gun of the same calibre, it was easier to reload and fire. Its lightness and shortness of barrel meant that its range was limited, but at close quarters it was a terrifying weapon. The earliest carronades had simply been fitted to existing ships where space permitted and were not counted when characterizing a ship's armament. Even when designed into new construction this convention persisted. Thus, the *Scorpion* was a sixteen-gun sloop, despite her total of twenty-four guns, and a third-rate 74 remained a 74 no matter how many carronades were added.

The *Scorpion* was square rigged with two masts, with a complement of one hundred twenty-five men including twelve marines. The wardroom consisted of one commissioned officer as first lieutenant, a master, a surgeon, a purser, and a marine second lieutenant. She was big enough to present a challenge to an officer in his first command but small enough for him to manage, and Hallowell could not have been happier. At a cost of £20 his proud father presented him with a new full-dress uniform, emphasizing his new status.

The only shadow was the station to which his ship was assigned. It was the west coast of Africa, which had a worse reputation for discomfort and disease than even the West or East Indies. For that very reason the *Victory's* first lieutenant may have declined the opportunity, but Hallowell as next in line was only too happy to accept, whatever the risks.

Some months of preparation were to pass before the *Scorpion* could depart. A ship's company had to be found, a protracted process in peacetime when pressing was not authorized. Stores and guns had to be embarked; masts stepped in place, sails bent, and miles of running and standing rigging set up. With few officers to help him, there would be long days of work for Hallowell, overseeing every detail, the safety of his first ship and her men his personal responsibility.

Nevertheless, there was time to share in the activities and interests of his family, which continued to revolve around the Nova Scotia grant. In 1792 Benjamin Hallowell Sr. could rejoice at the appointment of his old friend John Wentworth as lieutenant governor of Nova Scotia. His support would be all-important for the development of the Boylston lands. Ward had given up on Nova Scotia and was liquidating his investments there. He had terminated his partnership with his uncle, Thomas Boylston, but his sugar refinery on the London docks was very profitable and he was carrying on a busy trade with Boston. He was well on his way to becoming rich. By comparison, brother Benjamin was still more or less penniless, but at least as long as he remained captain of the *Scorpion* he was not a burden on his parents.

Fifteen years had passed since the family's exile, and now for the first time they could enjoy a sense of security and stability. Indeed, Benjamin and Mary Hallowell were living a life comparable to what they had enjoyed in Boston. His pension of £250 per year was being paid with more certainty and punctuality. His £7882 claim before the Loyalist Claims Commission had finally yielded £6010, allowing the family to abandon the supposed rural charms of Edgware Road and return to the more fashionable location in Stafford Row, Buckingham Gate. In 1791 the house was insured for £355, with an annual property tax of just less than £9, including two shillings for each of its twenty-four windows, and five shillings for each of the two resident female servants.

The Hallowells embarked on an orgy of gardening and decorating, and the household accounts begin to reflect the purchase of small luxuries, such as leather gloves and purse and a silk gown for daughter Mary, now very much in the matrimonial market. Moreover, in April 1792 Robert Hallowell had returned to Boston to expedite the settlement of their father's estate, still outstanding nearly twenty years after his death.

Like most other first-generation Loyalists, the elder Hallowells would never feel truly at home in Britain. But thanks to the Vaughans and to Benjamin's earlier residence in England, they had non-Loyalist friends and relations to help them avoid the isolation and boredom experienced by so many of the exiles.

There was one cloud on the horizon: the health of the elder Mary Hallowell. In November of 1791 the accounts show an expenditure of more than £3 for 'stomachick mixture,' pills, febrifuga drafts, and, ominously, opium wine. In the following April Benjamin advised his brother Robert in Boston, 'the complaint in [his wife's] breast continues very obstinate, not yielding to the application that has been tried.' Benjamin has heard of a 'medical gentleman' in New York or Long Island who is famous for a medicine which never fails of curing cancer, and if Robert is able to 'procure some for my best friend we should both be as happy as this World can make us.'

Commander Hallowell was now twenty-nine, an age when many men feel a need to settle down and establish a family, especially perhaps a man who had been separated from his own family as a child. Consciously or unconsciously he was also on the rebound. His attachment to his cousin Anne Gould had been thwarted because of his status as an impecunious lieutenant with gloomy prospects. But the two could cherish the hope that something might occur to overcome Mrs. Gould's objections. And now something had: he was a commander, employed even in peacetime when positions were scarce, signs that he was marked for advancement.

But it was all too late. By the summer of 1791 he knew that in obedience to her mother's wishes Anne was irrevocably engaged to another and richer man, and that whatever his feelings he must now look elsewhere for a wife.

Among the Hallowells' Loyalist friends was the Coffin family. As cashier for the customs Nathaniel Coffin had been one of Benjamin Hallowell's subordinates in Boston and he was father to Isaac Coffin who had enjoyed such rapid promotion during the American Revolution. The Coffins resided at Aldsworth House near Emsworth in Sussex, only a few miles from Portsmouth. The senior Hallowells were frequent guests, rejoicing in the rural visits as an escape from London and an opportunity to renew their health in the quiet countryside. Daughter Mary accompanied them, as did their younger son whenever he was not at sea. Ward necessarily remained in London under the pressure of business, but corresponded with his father almost daily.

The Coffins had two daughters. It appears that Hallowell Sr. hoped that frequent contact between his son Benjamin and the elder girl would lead in due course to marriage. Perhaps he threw them together to take Benjamin's mind off the loss of Anne Gould. To an extent his plan, if such it was, succeeded. Eventually the younger Hallowell had convinced himself that he was in love, but the lady was reluctant to commit herself.

Her younger sister, Catherine, had made an astonishingly good match at an astonishingly young age. A few miles from Aldsworth lies the estate of Stansted Park, the Saxon 'Stone Place,' a manor since ancient times. Successively in the possession of the Earls of Arundel, Lumley, and Halifax, it had been purchased in 1781 by a Mr. Barwell, who had acquired great wealth in the service of the East India Company. In 1785 the marriage was reported thus:

> *Mr. Barwell the great East Indian of Stansted to Miss Coffin, a very pretty little Girl, not 16, of American extraction. Till a fortnight*

> before this Event he kept a very Beautiful Mistress close to this Park, by whom he has several children, and till very lately He declared most strongly against Matrimony. He seems a good-natured man, but the Mogul prevails strongly in his way of Life and Conversation. Mrs. Barwell is in possession of a most Noble Park and immense Riches.

Like other nabobs who had made their fortunes in India, Barwell flaunted his wealth in a way foreign to the established landed gentry. He gave magnificent balls and allowed his friends, including Hallowell, to shoot over his extensive grounds, amounting to more than five thousand acres.

In the summer of 1790 the object of Hallowell's affections was spending much of her time with her fortunate sister at Stansted House, and it was there that he pursued his courtship whenever he was able to leave his ship. From the mansion, *Scorpion* could be seen tugging at her anchor in Portsmouth harbour, an ever-present reminder that his suit must succeed now or never.

His friends were advising him against the match. The reputation of the Coffins may have been tainted by whispers that they had in effect sold their scarcely nubile daughter to a known rake, and Captain Isaac Coffin had recently been dismissed from his ship for falsifying the muster book. Barwell had just insulted a parliamentary committee investigating affairs in India, but was soon to be elected a member himself, his campaign no doubt lubricated by his unlimited financial resources. In normal circumstances a family connection with a Member of Parliament would have been a major plus for a naval officer's career, but Hallowell's friends would argue that Barwell's *nouveau riche* behaviour and lurid sexual past would have just the opposite effect.

A decision had to be made and on September 3 Hallowell made it. The next day he explained everything in a very strange letter to Ward. In the characteristically flowery style of the day he begins:

> Wholesome advice and a little reflection on my part have made a wonderful improvement in the unfortunate heart of your poor brother and has not only made me abjure the plan of happiness I had fool-

> ishly proposed to myself but has been productive of no small stock of indifference to the object I so lately idolized. Such is the mutability of the mind of fickle man — and I believe it is best it should be so — for if my mind had not been relieved by the assistance of my friends from its late load, I am certain I should have foundered. — it is all over. I have been a cursed fool, but will never be in love again.

So far, the rather conventional lament of a man who has made a difficult decision and emerged from a doomed love affair wiser but with a broken heart. Pitiable, perhaps, but the effect is quickly spoiled by what follows:

> I have received my orders and believe I shall go to sea tomorrow week. We are certainly to touch at Madeira, and I would be glad to know if you would wish me to execute your former commission for a pipe of wine, and on whom I am to draw for the amount. My father wishes to take one third of the pipe with you and Mr. Chandley if you have no objection. I will be much obliged to you if you will enclose some tooth powder, as I felt the want of it much last voyage and I can use none but yours.

Already the affair is fading into the background, making way for really important things like wine and tooth powder. The letter ends:

> I was at Stansted yesterday, the Lady is excessively angry with me, I believe her pride is astonishingly hurt to think she has not had the pleasure of dismissing me but that I have withdrawn myself. You may be assured Ward that it ~~is~~ was an attachment that never shall be renewed, and I think myself a lucky fellow in making my escape from the jaws of matrimony.

The word 'is' has been firmly struck out and replaced by 'was' in the original.

Perhaps the obvious interpretation is the right one. Having decided to bring the uncertainty to an end Hallowell acts decisively by breaking off the affair himself, and only a day later he is already well on the way to putting it behind him and even turning the result into a lucky escape. On the other hand, the 'I will never be in love again,' suggests that he has received a permanent emotional wound. Or perhaps that phrase is tongue in cheek and throughout the letter he is simply laughing at himself for having been so foolish, inviting Ward to join in the joke at his expense.

Hallowell now focused completely on his approaching deployment. The Company of Merchants Trading to West Africa, hereafter the West Africa Company, maintained a number of fortified trading posts along the Gold and Slave Coasts of the Gulf of Guinea from Fort Appolonia to Accra. The British government provided a subsidy for maintenance and a small number of soldiers. The company's influence did not extend much beyond the fort walls. The hinterland was populated by states at various levels of development, frequently at war with one another.

Conflicts among the African states were the main source of the West Africa Company's chief commodity, human beings. The British slave trade began in 1662 and was not prohibited until 1807. During this period more than three million men, women, and children were transported in British ships to the plantations of America and the Caribbean. This number does not include the extensive slave commerce of Spain, Portugal, France, Denmark, the United States, and other countries.

Shackled together in long lines or coffles, their native captors or Arab middlemen brought the slaves down to the coast to be exchanged for cheap manufactured articles and muskets. Much of the shoreline consists of mangrove swamps, and the slaves had to be carried in boats to the anchored vessels that had carried the trade goods from England. Men, women and children were crammed naked into the holds in a rough proportion of three to every one ton's burden of the ship. To increase the carrying capacity, tiers of temporary decking were fitted so close together that there was only room to lie down.

Once out of sight of land the demoralized captives were let out on deck in small groups once a day and the holds might be sluiced out with the ship's pumps. Those who refused to eat were whipped. Shortly after the slaves had recovered from their seasickness, they often began to die of disease, and if the passage was a lengthy one more than a quarter might perish. The survivors were sold at auction, and the ships that brought them were loaded with sugar, rum, or tobacco for the return voyage to Britain. Each leg of this triangular trade produced its own profit, making the fortunes of the merchants and cities of Liverpool and Bristol.

The Royal Navy's patrols consisted of two or three vessels under an officer holding the temporary rank of commodore and commanding his own ship in addition to being the 'admiral' of his tiny squadron. In his first command it was critical that Hallowell should have a good working relationship with his commodore. As a lieutenant, John Inglefield had been serving in the *Romney* in Boston at the time of the senior Benjamin Hallowell's ill-fated seizure of the *Liberty* and would be favourably disposed toward the Loyalist's son from the beginning.

In command of the *Centaur* in Hood's squadron, Inglefield had fought at the Chesapeake and Les Saintes. At the latter battle the *Centaur* had captured the French *César*, but a member of the boarding party searching for wine had upset a candle near the magazine, and the resulting explosion killed four hundred of the French and fifty-eight men of the *Centaur*.

Inglefield's ill luck continued. After the battle he was dispatched to England with a convoy including some of the captured French ships. In mid-Atlantic a hurricane sank several of the vessels, among them the *Ville de Paris*. While hove to riding out the storm, the *Centaur* was taken aback in a sudden shift of wind and laid over on her beam ends. Her masts went by the board and as she righted herself with a lurch many of her guns broke adrift and began to crash from side to side with the ship's roll.

Inglefield and eleven others escaped in an open boat just before their ship foundered. With a bag of bread, some small pieces of meat, some liquor, and two quarts of water and a blanket as a sail, they set course for the Azores Islands, more than seven hundred miles to the southeast.

To keep up their spirits Inglefield led the survivors in singing and storytelling. On the sixteenth day, having consumed the last of their provisions and with hope almost gone, they sighted the island of Faial. Farcically, the Portuguese officials at first refused to let the famished survivors come ashore for fear they were the bearers of an epidemic! At the mandatory court martial Inglefield was acquitted, but admiration for his epic journey was tempered by doubts on the manner in which he had abandoned his sinking ship and his men.

He was now flying his commodore's pennant in the 50-gun fourth-rate *Medusa*. His eight-year-old son was also on the books. He must have been conceived immediately after his father's epic voyage, and had been christened Samuel Hood Inglefield in a rather obvious compliment to the admiral.

Inglefield had already made two patrols on the Africa station. Like Hallowell, he had no money and no influence and was happy to serve on a station that more fortunate officers avoided. He thoroughly understood the environment and set an excellent example in the matter of health and hygiene, boasting to the Admiralty that his ships had suffered only one death from disease during the latest cruise. Before sailing he had obtained permission to conduct a trial of 'White's air machine.' Just what this was and how it worked are unknown, and the device does not seem to have entered common use, but his request gives evidence of real concern for his men and openness to new ideas.

The *Medusa* and the *Scorpion* sailed in the autumn of 1791. Ever thoughtful, his father made Hallowell a present of two charts of the African coast issued by William Fadden, geographer to the King, costing a full guinea. Apparently the Admiralty was too niggardly to provide the latest information to its captains.

The outward journey was made via Madeira, already familiar to Hallowell from his first voyage in the *Asia*. Here he purchased the pipe of the island's famous wine to fulfil his promise to Ward. The ships also touched at Tenerife, the largest of the Canary Islands, dominated by the twelve-thousand-foot peak of el Teide, snow-covered at this time of year even though the island is nearly within the tropics. In the late fifteenth century the Spaniards had wrested control from the aboriginal Guanches, and thereafter the Canaries served as a vital way station on their route to America. As usual when visiting foreign ports, the ships' officers carefully observed the facilities and defenses of the main city of Santa Cruz; in just a few years Hallowell would put this intelligence to good use.

The squadron's first African stop was in Sierra Leone, several hundred miles to the north of the Slave Coast. In dramatic contrast to the purpose of the slave-trading Africa Company, the mission of Sierra Leone was to provide a home for freed slaves. A local chief named King Tom had ceded a small coastal enclave to Captain Boulden Thompson of the Royal Navy, or so the latter believed, and under the auspices of British abolitionists about four hundred freed slaves were settled there in 1788.

In King Tom's eyes the supposed cession was by no means permanent and his continued interference led to friction between the settlers and the surrounding tribesmen. Moreover the land proved unsuitable for many crops and susceptible to flooding during the rainy season. Within a few years the remaining settlers had fled to slave traders' establishments for protection. The experiment was on the point of failure when it was saved by a change of governance and an infusion of new blood.

In 1791 Parliament chartered the Sierra Leone Company to develop the settlement and engage in trade with the hinterland in all commodities except slaves. The pressing need for new immigrants to Sierra Leone was met from an unlikely source.

Among the Loyalists who fled at the end of the American Revolution were many thousands of blacks, both slave and free. About 3,000 of these went to Nova Scotia, where they should have participated in the general allocation of lots to the refugees. Most received less than the equal share they had been promised, partly because of administrative problems and partly through incompetence and prejudice on the part of the authorities. Similarly, they frequently received less than their entitlement of the free provisions distributed in the early years while the exiles were establishing their farms. Thus they suffered even more than the white Loyalists during the lean years of 'Nova Scarcity' in the late 1780s and early 1790s.

By 1791 many were quite ready to abandon the province, a circumstance that fitted nicely with the Sierra Leone Company's need for settlers. On 15 January 1792, about 1,100 sailed from Halifax in fifteen ships bound for the continent of their ancestors. While at Freetown, Hallowell would have learned of their imminent arrival and would have been struck by the coincidence of their exodus from the very province in which his father was facing such frustration.

From Sierra Leone Inglefield's ships made their way southward and eastward along the coast, stopping to inspect each of the West Africa Company's forts. A typical report of such an inspection, at Accra, showed that the fort was manned by the chief and the factor of the company; an interpreter; and a sergeant, a gunner, and eight mulatto soldiers. Also within the walls were fourteen male slaves — including qualified carpenters, bricklayers, and blacksmiths, together with their apprentices — and eighteen females. Whether or not they were aware of it, the life of the skilled fort-slaves was paradise compared with the fate of their fellows who were transported to the New World. Even those too old to work were supported until they died. Accra mounted twenty-seven cannon and was in good repair, unlike others, such as Commenda and Whydah, whose walls were disintegrating and whose guns were unusable because their wooden carriages were rotting in the oppressive humidity.

The whole region is less than ten degrees north of the equator, and the climate is hot and extremely humid, especially during the rainy season from about May to November. Malaria and other tropical diseases flourished. The death rate among soldiers serving in Sierra Leone was thirty times higher than in Britain or Canada. The Royal Navy had learned to make its inspections in winter and early spring, when temperature and humidity were just bearable, although this meant contending with a prevailing northerly wind known as the harmattan. Laden with dust from the Sahara Desert, the harmattan often reduced visibility to almost zero and covered the decks with fine sand.

Having completed their inspections, the ships hastened to return to England before the equatorial summer made conditions unbearable. Leaving Accra on 3 March 1792, Inglefield detached Hallowell in the

Slaves brought from the interior were confined in such coastal forts while awaiting transport to the Americas.

Scorpion to finalize the inspection circuit at Whydah and then to rejoin the *Medusa* at the island of São Tomé, a Portuguese possession situated almost on the equator at the southeastern entrance to the Gulf of Guinea. Here the purser of the *Medusa* caught fever and died, according to Inglefield because he had been so rash as to walk in the equatorial mid-day sun.

When unexpected vacancies occurred there was always a general reshuffle to fill the gap. The purser of Hallowell's *Scorpion* filled the dead man's shoes, while the captain's clerk from *Medusa* advanced to be purser of *Scorpion*, in each case with a welcome increase in pay. Such promotions were only provisional, but almost always the decision of the officer on the spot would be confirmed.

The home trip began with the departure from the notorious Bight of Benin at the north of the Gulf of Guinea. This might take weeks in the face of winds and strong currents setting in an easterly direction. It is said that the crews of ships who had succeeded in making their escape would taunt those entering with the doleful warning:

> *Beware and take care*
> *Of the Bight of Benin,*
> *There's one comes out*
> *For forty goes in.*

Having won clear of the Bight, the first leg of the voyage from São Tomé was not north to Europe but west to the Antilles, to take advantage of the southeast trade winds and the equatorial countercurrent to carry the ship through the doldrums. With some good fortune the thirteen-hundred-mile voyage could be made in as little as ten days. After an interval at Barbados or Antigua for rest and repair, returning vessels would complete the final leg to the English Channel, propelled by the Gulf Stream and the prevailing westerlies. In fact, on each patrol the ships of the navy's Africa squadron sailed precisely the same three-legged route as the slave vessels bearing their successive cargoes of trinkets, human beings, and tropical products.

On this voyage the tiny squadron was detained at Antigua by the commander of the Leeward Islands station. Hallowell's finances were still so precarious that this unexpected sojourn forced him to cash a cheque on his brother Ward to pay for new tropical clothing. His explanation is straightforward and unapologetic:

> *The unexpected orders I had to remain in this Country has embarrassed me much and put me to many difficulties, principally in the article of cloaths which are very extravagant here; I have therefore drawn on you for the sum of £25, being the only resource I had — to say I have borrowed it of you for any fix'd period would be deceiving you, but that I will repay it whenever I possibly can (and with gratitude) is my full intention.*

In a postscript he adds, 'I am here refitting now, and have scarce time to pay attention to any thing but the Ship as the Adm'l is expected here any day.'

The Admiral's unusual interest in the transient Africa squadron stemmed from the situation in France. In supporting the American revolutionaries the French monarchy had sown the seeds of its own destruction. Ideas of political freedom already current in European thought gained new impetus from the American example. The contrast between such ideas and the absolutist ethos of the Bourbons was glaring. Moreover, the enormous expenses of the war had devastated France's finances without any compensating gains in territory or influence. By 1789 the monarchy was bankrupt, and King Louis XVI was forced to summon the ancient representative body known as the Estates General for the first time in centuries. On July 14 the populace stormed the Bastille prison and released the prisoners. The Paris mob would continue to play a decisive role as events unfolded.

Most of the delegates to the Estates General looked forward to establishing a constitutional monarchy along British lines, but the energetic Jacobin minority wished to go much further. In the enthusiasm of the moment the nobles and clergy of the first two estates vied with each other in giving up their privileges. The middle-class third estate assumed the lead in stripping away the King's prerogatives one by one; he continued to reign in name only while being kept a virtual prisoner. The sight of royal absolutism under threat in the most powerful state in Europe struck fear into the equally absolute rulers of Austria and Prussia. The former also had a personal interest: his sister was France's Queen Marie Antoinette. Austria and Prussia formed an alliance, and in their fear and loathing proceeded to threaten the Estates General with military action if its mistreatment of the King continued.

On 20 April 1792, a defiant Estates General declared war on Austria and Prussia, making it certain that the two allies would soon invade France in aid of their fellow monarch. This news would have reached the admiral commanding in the Leeward Islands about the time Inglefield's squadron arrived there. Britain might very easily be drawn into any continental war, might indeed already be at war for all the admiral knew. Hence his decision to hold on to the *Medusa* and the *Scorpion* and to restore their combat readiness as a matter of urgency.

However, there were a few more months of peace. Inglefield's little squadron was allowed to leave, borne homeward by the westerlies and the current of the Gulf Stream. On the way, he passed again through the waters in which the *Centaur* had been overwhelmed, and Inglefield's officers and son were no doubt regaled with the cautionary but stirring tale of the survivors.

The squadron reached Blackstakes in the Thames on 25 September 1792. Five days earlier the enthusiastic French volunteers had beaten the invading Prussians and Austrians at the village of Valmy and were driving them from the soil of France.

For the third time in his career Hallowell had arrived from the West Indies with half pay on the horizon. But this time the threat of imminent war promised that the purgatory would be brief. In France the radicals had instituted the period of wholesale executions known as the Reign of Terror. Early in 1793 Louis XVI went to the guillotine, followed soon after by Marie Antoinette and a host of nobles, clergy, and moderate revolutionaries who dared to disagree with Robespierre, Danton, and the other extremists. On 1 February France declared war on Britain and Holland, and its armies marched to invade the latter country, carrying with them the terrible doctrine of revolution.

Three weeks later Hallowell assumed command of the aptly christened *Camel*. The ship was familiar, since Cuthbert Collingwood had commanded her in the Caribbean under her former name *Mediator*, when Hallowell was there in the *Falcon*. The new name had been assigned when she was designated an armed store ship, and her lower deck guns removed to provide room for cargo. She still mounted her upper deck armament, but her humble role was to carry supplies to the fleet, if necessary through enemy-controlled waters.

Hallowell was now thirty-two and still only a commander, his career frustratingly slowed by ten years of peace. He could be forgiven for welcoming the prospect of active service, even in the unglamorous *Camel*. As a store ship she was really only a lieutenant's command, but getting to the Mediterranean in any capacity was absolutely necessary in the days of interest, because his patron Lord Hood had been appointed to command in that vital theatre of war.

Once again Hallowell became immersed in the manifold details of getting a newly commissioned ship ready for deployment. This time there was an enemy to be faced in addition to the normal dangers of the sea. As though this were not enough he had to ask for his purser to be replaced, because his accounts for the previous commission had not been cleared. The whole fleet was being mobilized, resources were strained to the limit, and when it came to the allocation of workmen and *matériel*, the penurious captain of a humble store ship suffered from low priority with the dockyard officers. The *Camel* was not yet ready when Hood sailed from Spithead on 22 May with eight ships of the line, flying his flag in the *Victory*.

After touching at Gibraltar, in mid-July Hood established a blockade of Toulon, the base of the French Mediterranean fleet of twenty-two ships of the line. An imposing fleet on paper, but in fact almost valueless, discipline having all but vanished under the influence of revolutionary principles. It was there in early August that the *Camel* joined the fleet.

By this time the excesses of the Terror had provoked a counter-revolution in many parts of France, including Marseilles. But the city was retaken by the national revolutionary troops, and large numbers of its inhabitants were massacred. The same fate seemed to await Toulon, which was also in a state of insurrection and moreover running short of supplies because of Hood's blockade. In their terror the people of Toulon asked Hood to take possession of the city and hold it in the name of the son of the guillotined Louis XVI.

There was no time for the admiral to consult with the British government. On his own responsibility he accepted, and on August 27 landed a force of 2,000 sailors and marines to join the Toulonese who were already in arms. Shortly afterwards Spanish, Neapolitan and Sardinian ships and troops arrived, bringing Hood's total force to about 12,000 men. Unfortunately, the allied troops proved to be mostly of low quality, and the Spanish admiral Langara and Hood were was soon at odds.

Leading the landed seamen was Captain George Keith Elphinstone, who took command of Fort la Malgue at the entrance to the harbour. He was not without military experience, having served ashore at Charleston during the American Revolution. It was necessary to replace him as commanding officer of the *Robust*, 74. At last Hallowell was in the right place at the right time, and on 30 August 1793, Hood signed his commission to take over from Elphinstone. Hallowell's first act on boarding his new ship was to formally establish his authority by reading out his commission to the assembled ship's company, most of whom could not have read it for themselves. In the solemn words of such documents he was ordered:

> *Forthwith to go on board and take upon you the Charge and Command of Captain in her accordingly, strictly Charging and Commanding all the Officers and Company of the said Ship to behave themselves jointly and severally in their respective Employments, with all due Respect and Obedience unto you their said Captain, and you likewise to observe and execute the General Printed Instructions and such Orders and Directions as you shall time to time receive from Me, or any other your Superior Officers, for His Majesty's Service, hereof nor you nor any of you may fail as you will answer the Contrary at your Peril; and for so doing this shall be your Warrant.*

Hallowell had been 'made post,' the pivotal step in an officer's career. His future was in a sense pre-determined, his seniority on the list of captains set once and for all by the date of his appointment. There was no jumping the queue, no matter how outstanding his performance. He would gradually rise on the list as those above him died, were killed, or were promoted to admiral. Even when on half pay this upward progression would continue until length of service brought him to the top, when he would automatically become a Rear Admiral, as a reward for remaining alive.

The Jacobin government had sent an army of 17,000 men to retake Toulon. Under indecisive commanders the besiegers settled down to blockade the city on the landward side, but British control of the sea ensured that the defenders could not be starved out, and as long as the city resisted, the revolution would be in jeopardy. The stalemate might have continued indefinitely but for one man — Napoleon Bonaparte.

On leaving the preparatory military school at Brienne at fourteen Napoleon had wished to pursue a career in the navy. From his final report of 1784 we learn of him: 'Conduct most satisfactory, has always been distinguished for his application in mathematics. He is fairly well acquainted with history and geography. He is weak in all accomplishments — drawing, dancing, music and the like. This boy would make an excellent sailor.' How the history of the world might have been changed had that come to pass! But various difficulties made it impossible, and the young man was instead admitted to the École Royale Militaire in Paris. In September 1785 he was commissioned a second lieutenant in the artillery. In pre-revolutionary France this arm and the engineers were the only branches in which intelligence and ability outweighed the accident of aristocratic birth.

By 1793 Napoleon was still only a captain and had seen no action. He had, however, dabbled in the chaotic politics of revolutionary Paris and had made powerful friends among the ruling Jacobins. Assigned to the army besieging Toulon, he intrigued against his commanding general and succeeded in having him replaced by General DuGommier, both more energetic and more inclined to take advice from newly promoted Major Bonaparte.

Napoleon had identified the critical importance of Fort l'Aiguillette, whose guns dominated both the inner and outer harbours. As long as this stronghold remained in British hands Hood's fleet was safe, but if it fell to the French the ships would have to sail or be battered to pieces and Toulon must fall. Fort l'Aiguillette was protected from the landward side by Fort Mulgrave, the key to the whole allied position.

Napoleon concentrated the French artillery against the critical point. By mid-December he could report that the guns of Fort Mulgrave had been silenced and that an assault was practicable. The defenders resisted desperately in hand-to-hand fighting, but at length gave way when Napoleon, now a colonel, himself led a last charge in which he suffered a severe pike wound in the thigh. Almost immediately he was promoted to brigadier general at the age of only twenty-four. Bonaparte was on his way.

On 18 December, the day after the attack, Hood took the inevitable decision that Toulon must be evacuated at once. From a military standpoint it was necessary to achieve two aims: to embark the troops and to destroy the captured French ships. There was also a moral obligation to embark as many as possible of the citizens of Toulon who faced a horrible vengeance at the hands of the victorious Jacobins.

Despite a panic among the Neapolitan soldiers, the vast majority of the troops were carried to the ships, along with 15,000 inhabitants, amid scenes of indescribable confusion and despair. The spectacle of the terror-stricken civilians crowding into the boats must have vividly reminded Hallowell of his family's tales of the evacuation of Boston seventeen years before, but this was incomparably worse. Despite heroic efforts many fugitives had to be left behind, and in the succeeding days several thousand of them were guillotined or shot.

Hallowell had charge of the embarkation of the troops and civilians from Fort la Malgue, directing the rearguard action under the covering fire of the fleet. He was one of the captains especially mentioned in the final dispatch of the army commander, General Dundas: 'to their indefatigable attention and good dispositions we are indebted for the happy success of so important an operation.' The decks of the *Robust* were thronged with refugees, and when she got underway there was hardly room enough to work the ship.

The navy had performed miracles in saving thousands of military and civilian lives, but the attempted neutralization of the French fleet was less successful. The task had been entrusted to Capt. Sir Sidney Smith and Admiral Langara, who planned poorly and failed to co-operate with each other. The British and Spanish carried off only four ships. The remainder were set afire but for the most part escaped with little damage, and almost all were ready for sea by the following summer.

Hallowell had just experienced his first action on land; there were to be many more. Incongruous as it appears, not only marines but also seamen often fought ashore, a feat made possible by the great similarity of military and naval weapons. At close range both sailors and soldiers relied on the musket, the bayonet, and the sword or cutlass, while at longer ranges both used cannon of similar calibres and capabilities. Of course, seamen could not face masses of drilled professional soldiers in the open field, but in static situations or in surprise attacks they proved time and again that they were just as formidable ashore as in their traditional element. Like the United States Navy today, the Royal Navy was a self-contained striking force, capable of applying its power not only at sea but also on any shore where men could be landed. Mobility gave a fleet the advantage of surprise as to both time and place, tying up enemy men and resources by keeping an entire hostile coastline in a state of perpetual alert.

With the evacuation of Toulon, Captain George Elphinstone returned to the *Robust*. It may have been at this juncture that the two men developed a mutual dislike that would reverberate throughout Hallowell's career. Elphinstone had correctly perceived that Hallowell was one of Hood's protégés, and perhaps out of jealousy wrote to several friends expressing his displeasure at being superseded by a newly made captain. Even if their first contact had been in less contentious circumstances the two men were separated by a huge gap. Elphinstone was son of a Scottish Lord and a Member of Parliament. He was already near the top of the captains list and had been hugely successful in winning prize money. Elphinstone had little in common with a newly promoted captain fifteen years his junior, the penniless son of a Loyalist refugee.

Later events conspired to deepen the antipathy. Elphinstone was a Whig, and a friend of the Prince of Wales, while Hallowell's father was an active Tory, and, as we shall see, Hallowell himself may later have offended the Prince. Elphinstone would soon leave the Mediterranean to take command of a successful expedition to capture Cape Town, for which he was rewarded with a peerage as Lord Keith. But before his departure he was to deal Hallowell's career a potentially fatal blow.

Hood's confidence in Hallowell had been justified by his conduct during the evacuation. Once again Hood appointed him to a temporary command, this time of the *Courageux*. Captain Waldegrave of that ship had been sent home with Hood's report of the evacuation, and Hallowell was to act in his absence. The *Courageux* was a third-rate of 74 guns. She had been captured from the French in 1761 and like most French ships was considered better built than her British counterparts.

(As usual, the original enemy name had been retained for morale purposes, but it is hard to imagine that the typical sailor pronounced it in any other way but 'courageous.') On 24 December 1793, Hallowell read himself on board with his new commission, all the Christmas present he could desire.

Hood had again exerted his patronage. No doubt he was glad to give pleasure to his old friend Benjamin Hallowell, but if the younger Hallowell had ever let Hood down his patron's influence would have immediately been withdrawn, friend or no friend. A fellow Admiral said of Hood:

> I never saw an officer of more intrepid courage or warmer zeal; no difficulties stood in his way. Without the least disposition to severity, there was something about him which made his inferior officers stand in awe of him. He was so watchful upon his post himself that those who acted with him were afraid to slumber.' Impossible to disappoint such a leader, and many such as Hallowell who were fortunate enough to serve under him based their future conduct on his example.

The loss of Toulon brought a change to British strategy. Early in 1794 Hood contented himself with blockading the evacuated port. This was tactically difficult because observation posts on the high coastline enabled the French to observe the British at a great distance. But the British had to venture close to the harbour if they wished to ascertain the presence or state of readiness of the enemy ships. The British scouting ships frequently came under fire as they turned away at the last moment.

The French fleet was not yet a threat, but might become so at any time. Occasionally, the shape of the giant three-decker *L'Orient* could be made out in the outer harbour. At any time a northerly wind would be fair for the French to exit while at the same time driving the blockading vessels southward, allowing the enemy to reach the open sea.

A blockading fleet needed a forward operational base where supplies could be obtained, crews rested, and the never-ending wear and tear on masts, yards, and sails made good. Gibraltar was too far from Toulon and lacked facilities for hull repairs to large vessels. A Spanish port might have served, but the attitude of Spain was uncertain and she might at any time withdraw from the war. The Kingdom of the Two Sicilies, better known as Naples, was another of Britain's allies with Mediterranean ports. Its Queen Caroline was the sister of the guillotined Marie Antoinette, and she had vowed to obtain vengeance for her sister's death. Her husband King Ferdinand meekly accepted her policy. It seemed certain that Naples at least would remain faithful to the alliance. The fleet could use the Neapolitan port of Livorno (called Leghorn by the British) for provisions and minor repairs.

The British fleet also needed a secure anchorage closer to Toulon. The Bay of San Fiorenzo on the north coast of the island of Corsica offered a refuge in bad weather within easy reach of the enemy base. The patriot Paoli continued to lead an active independence movement against French occupation. Expecting to be supported by the inhabitants, the British determined to take the island and especially the two northern ports of Bastia and Calvi. Hood would command the fleet in landing and supporting the troops under Lieutenant General Charles Stuart.

A preparatory attack at Mortella was repelled by a tower of a new design with a heavy gun on its upper story and walls too thick to be damaged by the ships' armament. Manned only by a sergeant and fifteen men the tower inflicted two hundred casualties on the *Fortitude*, 64, and was only captured when the attackers hoisted artillery to the hills above it. When Corsica was later evacuated, it took three hundred barrels of gunpowder to level the stronghold to the ground. So impressed were the British that they later copied the design in many of their fortifications around the world; the name became corrupted to 'Martello Tower.'

After this setback the army commander was reluctant to proceed with the attack on Bastia. Fearing that the enemy would be reinforced, on April 4 Hood landed two-hundred and fifty seamen and 1,200 marines under Captain Nelson and laid siege to the city on his own initiative.

A week later Hallowell's command of *Courageux* came to an end with Captain Waldegrave's return from England. However, Waldegrave was very near the top of the captains list, and it was understood that on his promotion to rear admiral Hallowell would return to the *Courageux*, on a permanent basis.

For the moment he was again without a ship. He immediately volunteered to take part in the attack on Bastia and was appointed to command the boats operating an inshore blockade. He also led a dramatic rescue of the *Proselyte*, a captured frigate converted to a floating gun platform. The *Proselyte* was set afire by red-hot shot, and Commander Serocold and crew would have perished had Hallowell not braved the flames and gunfire to save them.

Bastia capitulated on 19 May. Over 4,000 French troops starved out by the close naval blockade surrendered to the much smaller naval landing force. Hood's dispatch after the victory contained the statement, 'I feel myself much indebted for the vigilance and attention of Captain Hallowell who became a Volunteer whenever he could be useful by guarding the harbour's mouth of Bastia with gunboats and launches well armed the whole of every night.' This letter was published in the *London Gazette*; Hallowell's parents would read it with pride and also with relief that their son had again emerged unscathed.

The second British objective was Calvi, which promised to be a

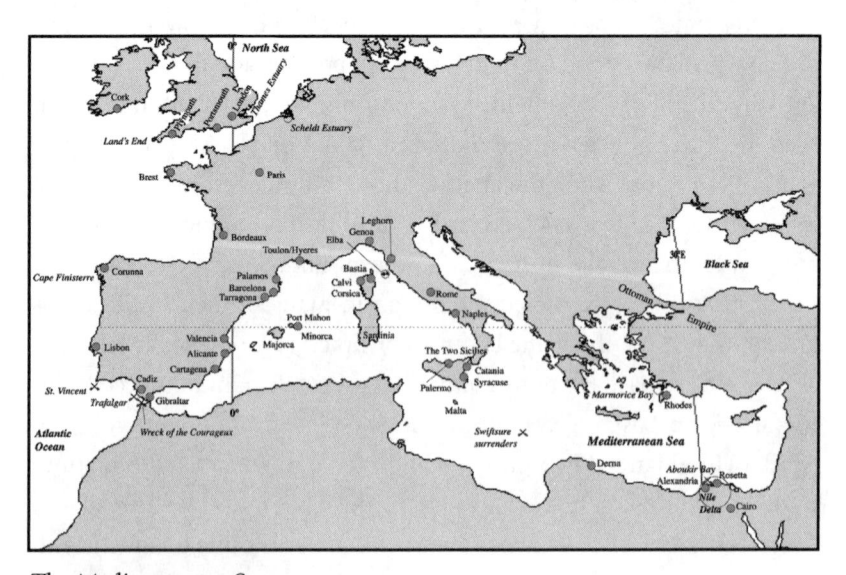

The Mediterranean Sea

much harder nut to crack. The citadel was situated on a promontory connected with the strongly walled city by a defended causeway. On the other three sides sheer cliffs fell to the rocky shore. Thus fortified, and with ample supplies, the garrison could only be defeated through intensive bombardment with heavy artillery. The only nearby beach suitable for landing such guns was commanded by the batteries of the citadel.

In a night reconnaissance by boat, Captain Nelson identified a very difficult alternative landing spot in a tiny inlet called Porto Agro. The entrance was strewn with rocks, and when the wind blew onshore the surf made landing impossible. Beyond the narrow beach, hills rose steeply to the broken terrain stretching the three and a half miles to Calvi. Before the bombardment of the fortress could even begin it would be necessary to haul the two-and-one-half-ton cannon and all their ammunition and stores over this trackless waste and erect the platforms and parapets of the batteries. The prospect was daunting, but there was no other way.

Nelson was given two hundred and fifty seamen to perform the task, with Hallowell and the rescued Serocold as his deputies, 'very able, willing and zealous officers,' as Hood referred to them. The enormous weapons were manhandled forward by brute force and by skilful use of systems of blocks and tackles with which seamen were well acquainted. All depended on the morale of the men and the leadership of their officers. After witnessing a similar operation an army officer wrote:

> *You may fancy you know the spirit of these fellows but to see them in action exceeds any idea that can be formed of them. A hundred or two of them with ropes and pulleys will do more than all your dray horses in London. Let but their tackle hold and they will draw you a cannon or mortar on its proper carriage up to any height, though the weight be never so great. It is droll enough to see them tugging along with a good 24-pounder at their heels; on they go, huzzaing and hullooing, sometimes up hill and sometimes down hill; now sticking fast in the brakes, presently foundering in the mud and mire; swearing, blasting, damning,*

sinking and as careless of everything but the matter committed to their charge as if death or danger had nothing to do with them.

Eighteenth-century sieges proceeded with an air of inevitability toward a usually predictable conclusion. An assaulting battery would begin an artillery duel with its guns concentrating fire on one section of the fortress. As the attacking guns gained the upper hand, the approach trenches would be pushed forward and new batteries brought into action at ever-decreasing ranges. At this stage the besieged often attempted a surprise sortie to occupy and demolish he attacker's entrenchments and disrupt his plans. Eventually, the defending fire would be completely suppressed and the attacking guns would concentrate on demolishing a section of the walls.

Once a breach had been opened it was customary to give the defenders an opportunity to surrender with the honours of war. If they refused, an infantry charge with artillery support would be expected to carry the attackers through the breach, and the defenders would be overcome in hand-to-hand fighting within the walls. In this event there would be heavy casualties on both sides, and the defenders would be given little opportunity to surrender until the battle fury of the attackers had died away.

The first British battery came into action two weeks after the landing. Seamen manned the pieces, with Nelson and Hallowell taking twelve-hour turns in charge of the position. General Stuart himself slept every night in the most advanced battery. The French replied energetically, and there was a constant trickle of casualties among the gunners as the enemy shells burst in front of and within the parapet. Guns too were often disabled as they were hit by especially well-aimed or lucky shots. Serocold, so recently saved from the *Proselyte*, was killed by grape shot early in the siege. Short of officers, Hood told Nelson, 'If you and that brave fellow Hallowell feel equal to the strains that may arise will not send you another officer.'

Nelson himself was struck in the face by a handful of stones thrown up by a bursting shell. It was feared at the time, and indeed transpired, that he would lose the sight of one eye, but he continued to take his

Hallowell participated alongside Horatio in the siege of this French stronghold in Corsica, during which Nelson lost the sight of one eye.

twelve-hour turns in the batteries. The sailors were fighting something very like a battle at sea, a gunnery slogging match where leadership, drill, and sheer endurance would determine victory or defeat. As Nelson reported, 'Hallowell and I are always on the batteries with them, and our jacks don't mind it. Hallowell, who is a very good, worthy man, and myself feel equal to the duty here.' In his diary he noted 'the indefatigable zeal, activity and ability of Captain Hallowell, and the great readiness he ever shows to give me assistance in the laborious duties entrusted to us.'

The climate was as much an enemy as the French. The Corsicans referred to the days of high summer as the Lion Sun; on one day alone sixteen British seamen suffered heat stroke. Malaria was endemic, and dysentery and typhus began to spread in the unsanitary conditions of the trenches. At first, the seamen appeared to suffer less than the soldiers, a fact Nelson attributed to their hard exercise serving the guns and to the excellent quality of the Corsican wine! A few days later, however, he had to report seventy sick among the gun's crews in addition to thirty who had been sent back on board their ships.

Hallowell too eventually succumbed. As late as July 25 he was 'as active and good as ever' according to Nelson, but two weeks later the latter wrote to Hood: 'Captain Hallowell, I am sorry to say, is quite unwell and much reduced. If Dr. Harness is on board I wish he would have a look at him; I think, poor fellow, he would like it.' Harness was the well-respected Physician of the Fleet and one of the navy's pioneers in the use of citrus fruits to combat scurvy. At his direction, Hallowell was invalided on board just as the siege reached its climax.

By 19 July the British guns had been pushed forward to within six hundred fifty yards of the centre of the citadel, and under a white flag General Stuart invited the garrison to surrender. The answer of the French commander was to quote the motto of the town: *Civitas Calvi semper fidelis (City of Calvi, ever faithful)*. A week later thirty heavy guns had been brought within five hundred and sixty yards, and the final bombardment began. Ever faithful or not, at eleven in the morning on 1 August the doughty Frenchman was forced to surrender, with much of the wall beaten down, the citadel either in ruins or in flames, and almost half the defenders too ill to resist.

During the siege Hood had temporarily withdrawn his line of battle ships to pursue Admiral Martin's French fleet, which the Directory in Paris had ordered to sail and fight a battle. With inexperienced and ill-disciplined crews and badly outnumbered, Martin wisely disobeyed his orders by taking his ships to anchor in Hyères Bay east of Toulon. Hood planned to sail into the bay and anchor his own ships one on either side of each Frenchman, thus achieving an overwhelming concentration of force. The weather prevented an immediate attack and Hood was forced to return to Calvi to assist in the siege. However, concentration of force as a tactic was once more in the air, and Hood's concept was later to be revived with decisive results.

As a result of this foray, ill feelings arose between Hood and General Stuart, who felt he had been left unsupported at a critical time. They also quarrelled over the disposition of the French prisoners, and many considered that Stuart's final report down-played the navy's contribution. Always hungry for glory, Nelson especially was incensed that his own role had not received the praise he thought was due.

No doubt Hallowell shared this feeling to some degree, but he had

PROMOTION

no time or energy to spare for such fancies. Family circumstances made it essential for him to make a success of his career, and in this regard there was both good news and bad news after Calvi. As usual, all captured military and naval *matériel* became lawful prize. The proceeds were shared out among those who had participated in the siege, according to the usual complicated rules, even more complicated in this case because both the army and the navy were involved. Since at the time Hallowell was not in command of a ship he was not strictly entitled to a share, but a special commission decided an exception would be made for him and a few others in his situation. (The heirs of the dead Serocold received his portion.) The amount would not be particularly significant, but there had also been a small distribution after Toulon, and for the first time Hallowell's financial situation was not immediately critical.

Satisfaction at this windfall was eclipsed by a setback that might have ended Hallowell's career. While ill and in quarantine Hallowell could comfort himself with the prospect of resuming command of the *Courageux*, for which he had actually been commissioned on Waldegrave's departure. To his mortification the prize was snatched from him through the agency of Captain George Elphinstone. Resentful when Hallowell temporarily replaced him in the *Robust*, he now reported to Admiral Hotham that the crew of the *Courageux*'s barge had told him that the men would mutiny if Hallowell returned to command them. Without further investigation, Hotham rescinded Hallowell's commission to the *Courageux*.

6

COURAGEUX
1793–1797

Such a ship, so commanded.

Admiral Sir John Jervis

Hallowell had been sure that he had been liked and respected during his few months in command of the *Courageux*. How could he have been so mistaken, and how would his brother officers regard him after this slur on his professionalism? His consolation prize — command of the *Lowestoffe* — added insult to injury, the ship being a fifth-rate of only 32-guns, after he had commanded two 74s with apparent success. The decrease in pay on going to the smaller vessel – from thirteen to eight shillings per day – would be significant, as well as a constant reminder of his disgrace. Hood would not have taken such drastic action on the uncorroborated word of another captain, but in his absence the opportunity to do Hallowell an injury had presented itself and was seized.

Hallowell somehow mastered his emotions and resolved to make the best of his new situation. The *Lowestoffe* was attached to the fleet blockading Toulon. The duty of a frigate in these circumstances was to cruise as close inshore as possible, so as to provide the larger ships cruising further out with early warning of a French sortie. Sometimes the work brought the ship within range of the shore batteries with the constant risk that an unexpected shift in the wind would trap an unwary vessel on an unfriendly lee shore. The strain on the captain was enormous and unremitting. The trauma of the lost *Courageux* was submerged, but not forgotten.

When the wind was unfavourable for a French sortie, the fleet could withdraw to the San Fiorenzo anchorage on Corsica for reprovisioning and rest, and there would be many social contacts. Hallowell sought every opportunity to find out just what was behind the injustice he had suffered. No one professed to be aware of any animosity toward him on the part of the ship's company. This was welcome information, but not conclusive, and insufficient to make a claim for redress.

On the last day of January 1795 the mystery was resolved. Hallowell happened to be waiting with his friend Nelson at the landing place in San Fiorenzo Bay when the barge of the *Courageux* came alongside. Led by the coxswain, the barge crew approached their former captain and expressed hope that he would soon resume his position. Astonished, Hallowell demanded to know how they could make such a wish after declaring to Captain Elphinstone that Hallowell's return would spark a mutiny. It was the turn of the barge crew to be astonished: not only had they never made such a comment but they were sure that not one man would object to his return; they had never had a captain they so much wished for again.

Hallowell's emotions can be imagined, but he retained the presence of mind to ask the barge's crew to repeat their statements with his friend Horatio as a witness. The next day he wrote a letter to Admiral Hotham, respectful in tone but impossible to ignore. After recounting the circumstances he went on 'to most earnestly request that Captain Elphinstone may be desired to name the men who told him of their determination to mutiny on my going on board, and that the company of the *Courageux* may be desired to express if they have the smallest objection to my commanding them....' If Elphinstone's statement was proven erroneous, 'I flatter myself that you will allow my commission to take effect, and that I may instantly take possession of my proper ship.'

This placed Hotham in a dilemma that he resolved by referring the whole mess to the Admiralty, while persuading Hallowell to remain quietly in the *Lowestoffe* until an answer was received. Hotham was a very likeable man, but he was no Hood in his powers of decision, either administratively or operationally. As he informed the Admiralty, 'My only intention in the steps I have taken being to keep things in a state of tranquility.'

The incident sheds an unusual light on the sociology of the Royal Navy at the close of the eighteenth century. The accepted picture is of an inflexible hierarchy with an unbridgeable gulf between tyrannical officers who commanded and robot-like men who unquestioningly obeyed. In reality, just as today, there was constant informal interaction between wardroom and lower deck, and there were many ways in which the true feelings of the men could be made known to wise officers who were prepared to listen.

Even more revealing is the tacit acknowledgement that a ship's company had a legitimate interest in the issue of who was to command them. Both the spurious original message about the opinions of the crew of the *Courageux* and the second much more reliable message were acted upon. (It is also true that some considered Hotham to be a poor disciplinarian, and that the incident could hardly have occurred under his very different successor Jervis.)

The chance meeting on the quay also points up the special status of the coxswain of the ten-oared barge in which a ship's captain made his official trips. The coxswain prided himself on training a crack crew that would reflect the efficiency of the ship itself. Unofficially, the coxswain might perform an even more important function. By virtue of his job, he came into personal contact with his captain more often than any other member of the lower deck. A wise commanding officer cultivated a relationship of mutual trust with his coxswain, a relationship in which differences of rank might be temporarily relaxed. Thus, he could benefit from a perspective that might differ from the reports reaching him through the chain of command. In Commonwealth navies, the position of coxswain still exists with very different formal responsibilities, but still enjoying a special relationship with the commanding officer.

Some time must elapse before the Admiralty reply was received, and in the meantime the *Lowestoffe* remained with the fleet. The routine was broken in mid-March of 1795 when a French squadron appeared off Genoa and was intercepted by a squadron under Nelson. A confused encounter ensued in very light winds that left many ships more or less out of control for long periods. In the 32-gun *Lowestoffe* Hallowell found himself in just such a position, unable to manoeuvre and stern on to the *Duquesne*, 74, which opened fire on him with her port battery. Unable to reply, Hallowell ordered his men to take shelter below, meanwhile continuing to pace the quarterdeck with only the officer of the watch and the helmsman. Fortunately, the range was long and the French gunnery inaccurate, but the *Lowestoffe*'s stern was badly knocked about before the *Duquesne*'s attention shifted to a more attractive target.

It needed a good deal of personal courage to function under enemy fire when fighting back as Hallowell had already done at the Virginia Capes, Les Saintes, Toulon, and Calvi, but that brand of courage was common enough. To deliberately expose oneself as a target, unable to return fire, and with nothing to occupy one's mind except the wait for the next broadside carries the idea of courage to a rarer level. The accompanying decision not to expose others unnecessarily shows a genuine concern for the safety and well-being of subordinates, which if not rare was by no means universal; in fact there were no casualties.

Inevitably, the story became generally known, and the incident went far to restore Hallowell's reputation, not least on the lower decks of the fleet. A week later the *Lowestoffe* shared in the rescue of the crew of the *Inflexible*, which had run aground trying to enter Livorno for repairs. For Hallowell another positive step on the road to rehabilitation.

At length the Admiralty reply to Hotham arrived, and on 19 June 1795, Hallowell reassumed command of the *Courageux*. In that very month a new uniform policy for the first time required captains to wear epaulettes with their dress uniforms, in his case just one, on his right shoulder. When he had spent three years in his new rank (September 1796), he would be entitled to put up the second epaulette on his left shoulder, marking him as a senior captain, equivalent to an army colonel.

In his previous tenures in relief of Elphinstone and Waldegrave,

Hallowell had always been aware that he was a temporary fill-in. The *Lowestoffe* also could be seen as a waiting appointment. In contrast, this time he could feel secure, captain of a 74 and certain of a positive reception from the ship's company. Barring disaster from the weather or in battle or from a trial by court martial, as long as the war continued he could count on commanding the *Courageux* or a ship like her. If the war lasted long enough, his inexorable progress up the captains list as his seniors were killed or promoted might even make him an admiral.

He had, however, lost the on-the-spot support of his patron. When Hood left in the summer of 1794, he had been expected to return to the Mediterranean as soon as his health permitted. But in England he became involved in a policy dispute over the strength of his fleet, which he considered inadequate for its mission. The new First Lord of the Admiralty, the second Earl Spencer, resisted Hood's demands, and the resulting antagonism caused Hood to relinquish his command, allegedly for health reasons.

Hood was never to be employed at sea again, but instead became a member of the Board of Admiralty. He certainly became aware of Hallowell's problem in the *Courageux* through reading Hotham's letter, and no doubt also through his friend Benjamin Hallowell Sr. In a final act of support, it is very probable that he used his still enormous influence to ensure that his protégé was reinstated.

The officer appointed to take over from the complacent Hotham was sixty-year-old Admiral Sir John Jervis. There could hardly have been a greater contrast. At the age of twelve Jervis had run away from home to join the navy. As a young commander, his ship *Porcupine* had guided the fleet carrying General James Wolfe's army up the St. Lawrence to the attack on Quebec. He was present on the Plains of Abraham on the day of the decisive battle and is said to have carried the dying Wolfe's last message to his fiancée. Between wars he had gathered intelligence of numerous continental harbours on his own initiative. He had been made a Knight of the Bath for a successful single-ship action in which he outmanoeuvred and captured the French *Pegasus*, 74, with no casualties among his own ship's company.

Jervis was what would now be called a workaholic; he completed a day's work by the time others rose in the morning. Although capable of humour, his commanding presence and habitually stern demeanour conveyed an irresistible impression of a demanding leader. Intelligent and a student of his profession, he was a strict disciplinarian and demanded from his subordinates as much as he demanded from himself. The trait he most valued was the ability to accept great responsibility, and he believed only a few possessed this capacity. These rare officers would enjoy his unstinting support and assistance.

Hallowell was to find a new patron in this distinguished officer, thanks to contacts his father had made while in command of the *King George*. Officers whom Benjamin Hallowell Sr. had known in those pre-revolutionary days had now risen to positions of influence and power. Just before Jervis's departure to supreme command in the Mediterranean, the senior Hallowell wrote him, stressing his son's good reputation in the fleet, of which Jervis was already well aware, and hoping that 'he will be no less deserving of your approbation.' Nothing so crude as to ask directly for special treatment for his son. Well he knew that Jervis was not to be swayed from his duty by old friendships and that if the Admiral's approbation were won, it would be through the younger Hallowell's own professionalism and in no other way.

From time to time letters arrived keeping Hallowell more or less up to date on family matters. The news was not pleasant. Early in 1793 his mother underwent a second operation in which two tumours were removed from her breast. She was under the knife for twenty-five minutes — an unimaginable ordeal in the days before anaesthetics. The family still placed great hope in the fabled cancer root, unavailable in England but to be obtained in America, they hoped, by Robert Hallowell or Moses Gill. In the meantime they were applying a poultice of flaxseed and oatmeal mixed with porter and goose grease, 'recommended by an old woman said to have cured many people.' Mary was also taking hemlock internally, but as her husband wrote, 'has not much benefited. Dear soul, she is struggling hard to get the better of this dreadful malady, the pain of which is hardly to be borne.'

Benjamin Hallowell hired a nurse to provide a week of immediate postoperative care at the enormous cost of £2 5s. Although the woman was illiterate, her skills must have been in great demand for her to command twice the wages of a naval lieutenant. When the worst was over, daughter Mary Hallowell assumed the role of nurse. Writing to his brother Robert in Boston, Benjamin Hallowell was lavish in her praise and full of pride in his son's progress in the navy:

> *Your valuable niece is beyond all comparison in her attention to her mother, who says she does not know how to put a sufficient value on her worth. The poor girl has borne the fatigues most wonderfully well. Ward and myself are in pretty good health and the captain was well the 20th July, commanding the Courageux in the Mediterranean, and I have the pleasure to say that no man in the navy is more highly spoken of than your nephew, who when the war is over will command a ship on the Halifax station. He will have one of the first vacancies that are made in America.*

Hallowell was never to serve in Canada. Nevertheless, it is interesting that Halifax rather than anywhere else in the far-flung empire was his peacetime station of choice. Exiled as a child from the United States and in some ways a stranger to England, perhaps in the Nova Scotia lands he felt the nearest approach to permanency that he could imagine or aspire to.

By now the Boylston grant was doing well. Not for the last time, war had brought prosperity to Nova Scotia and land values were rising steadily. Governor Wentworth's letters to Benjamin Hallowell Sr. are full of pride in the colony's progress and optimism for its future. 'There is more cash in Halifax than was ever known.' The 1795 harvest had been very productive and the first frost of the year had not occurred until October 27. Wentworth claimed to be growing oranges and myrtle outdoors in summer, an achievement that would be difficult to replicate today.

The big news for the grant at Boylston was that Wentworth had found a new route for the road from Guysborough to Halifax via Musquodoboit and Preston that would shorten the distance by 35 miles.

Wentworth sent his letters away in the ships that had begun to make regular voyages from Nova Scotia laden with spars for the Royal Navy.

But now there was a new problem. The Duke of Cumberland's Regiment had been disbanded in Nova Scotia, and by mistake a 5,000-acre section of Benjamin Hallowell's grant had been surveyed and parcelled out to the thousand-odd soldier-settlers and their dependants. By the time the error was detected it was too late to stop the process. Hallowell immediately appealed to the Duke of Portland for redress, Wentworth argued in his support, and Benjamin Hallowell was soon compensated.

The new parcel was near the shore of Antigonish Harbour on the Northumberland Strait in a part of Sydney County that was eventually to become part of Antigonish County. This area also would benefit from Governor Wentworth's new road, which would reduce its distance from Halifax by sixty miles. According to Wentworth the replacement land was preferable in every way to the lost portion of the Boylston tract.

At this time, summer 1795, the Austro-Prussian invasion of France had definitely been repelled. With this threat removed, a political reaction in Paris sent the rabid Jacobins of the Committee of Public Safety themselves to the guillotine. They were replaced by a five-man Directory drawn from the bourgeoisie. The revolution seemed to have spent itself and a more moderate outlook on the part of the French government might lead to productive negotiations.

The unbounded ambition of Napoleon Bonaparte would soon dispel that hope. After the capture of Toulon, Napoleon had returned to Paris, where he continued to intrigue for advancement. His chance came when he succeeded in suppressing a Royalist rising against the Directory. His reward was to be given command of the French Army of Italy, as much to remove him from the political scene as in recognition of his military talent. Just before leaving Paris he married Josephine Beauharnais, the former mistress of the Director Barras.

The stalemated conflict now flared up anew. Napoleon invaded Italy on 9 April 1796. He infused his troops with a new élan, and under his brilliant generalship they outmarched, outmanoeuvred, and outfought his Piedmontese and Austrian opponents. Within a month the former had withdrawn from the coalition and Napoleon was in Milan, where he and his troops proceeded to loot the city.

While maintaining the blockade of Toulon, Jervis's ships under Admiral Lord Keith had also operated along the northern Italian coast in support of the Austrians, without being able to affect the final result. The key base of Livorno surrendered to the French; the undeveloped Corsican ports and anchorages could not replace the loss and Gibraltar was too far from the scene of action. With Spain about to join the French, the British strategic position in the Mediterranean had suddenly become untenable.

During 1796 the fleet blockaded Toulon for 150 days, constantly on the watch for a French sortie. With scouting frigates inshore the ships of the line waited in a standoff position dictated by the winds and expected weather at any given time. The strain on masts, rigging, and men was unending, but the combination of stress and boredom as months passed without a French deployment placed an even greater strain on morale. Jervis's answer to this was to drill the fleet at every opportunity. By day or night ships would be ordered to make and reduce sail, to tack and wear together or in succession, to form on lines of bearing, to deploy from cruising formation to line of battle and vice versa — to practise and repractise every manoeuvre they might be called upon to make in a general action.

Even keeping rigid station with one or two cables' distance between ships demanded unceasing vigilance and swift reaction. Each captain would quickly learn exactly how much canvas he must set to match his ship's speed to that of the flagship as the latter made or reduced sail. When wearing or tacking, he would learn to time his own helm-over according to the rate at which his next ahead or astern was already changing course. Poor judgment, momentary inattention, or a slack response from the men working the sheets would earn an immediate rebuke from the admiral even if no collision resulted.

The *Courageux* frequently operated close inshore with a select squadron under Captain Thomas Troubridge. As Jervis reported, in a period of five months only one ship managed to elude their vigilance and escape from Toulon: 'The copper of the *St. George, Captain* and *Courageux*, is off in many places, very low down, in other respects they are sound ships, and their commanders men after my own heart, with whom I should be very sorry to part.' And in a later report, 'how highly I think of the three captains who blockaded the port of Toulon last summer, Troubridge, Hood, and Hallowell, who will achieve very important services to their King and Country when I sleep with my fathers.'

From time to time it could be confirmed that the French fleet was in no condition to go to sea, and even the inshore squadron could temporarily withdraw to San Fiorenzo on Corsica, about a hundred and thirty nautical miles from Toulon. Here there would be some relaxation from the unremitting strain of blockade service, an opportunity for much-needed rest and recreation, in today's terminology.

In this summer of 1796 the fleet was providing a refuge to the wealthy Wynne family, father, mother, and teenaged sisters Betsey and Eugenia. Despite the war, they had been touring Europe in leisurely and luxurious fashion, but unluckily found themselves in Livorno as Napoleon's whirlwind campaign carried him through northern Italy. They were rescued by the navy just before the city fell, and there being nowhere else to go they spent several months aboard different ships in the San Fiorenzo anchorage. Both sisters kept diaries, later published in a collection, that provide a unique outsider's perspective on daily life in the fleet.

Captains were not members of the officers' mess and normally ate in solitary splendour in their own cabins. But by custom they were often invited to dine in their ships' wardrooms on Sundays at the usual hour of four o'clock and the Wynnes frequently joined the company. On occasion they also dined with the gallant Admiral Jervis in his flagship, along with those captains who happened to be in harbour.

Betsey Wynne fell in love with the dashing young Captain Fremantle, but as he lacked a fortune, her parents would not permit them to marry. Hallowell had the same problem, but Fremantle was soon to earn enough prize money to make him an eligible suitor.

After one such dinner Betsey wrote: 'On our return to our ship we stopped near the Courageous [sic] to hear some very pretty musick. Capt. Hallow [sic] who commands that 74 (taken from the French the war before last) has a very good band. They played the charming tunes and the flutes and bugle horns made a most delightful affect. Happy listening to the charming tunes and admiring the beauty of the sky and sea.' That night there was a dance in the *Britannia* attended 'by all the gentlemen who had dined, plus Captain Hallow and Captain Sotheby of the *Bombay Castle* came.'

No doubt Hallowell put his schoolboy dancing lessons to good use on such occasions, but it is clear that he made very little impression on Betsey Wynne, despite the excellence of his band. He was of course nearly twenty years older than she. She even gets his name wrong, although it is just possible that 'Hallow' was a nickname by which he was generally known at that time; if so, it never appears again. At Calvi, Nelson had called him 'a worthy, good man' and 'a brave fellow'; to Jervis he was 'a man after my own heart.' But something of a social failure, at least in the eyes of a teenaged civilian.

Perhaps Hallowell's normal nature was not in evidence. He had good reasons to be subdued. On 22 November 1795, Mary Hallowell's long battle with cancer had ended with her death, seen by her husband and daughter as a merciful release. As her husband wrote to his friend Wentworth: 'the best of women that ever was borne, my partner in life for half a century, 49 years and five months, the last five of which she has been laboring under the severest malady, and for more than eight months in the most excruciating pain, that beggars all description.'

The younger Benjamin and his mother had never been close. She had had very little to do with his upbringing, and since he had left Boston he had spent less than two years in her household. Ward had always been by far her favourite child and she had made no attempt to conceal her preference. The mysterious errand of Acklom Harrison confirms that theirs was not a typical mother-son relationship. Nevertheless, her younger son would be distressed by her death, if only out of sympathy for his father, sister, and brother.

Prospering though he was in his London sugar business, Ward had been steadily laying the groundwork for a return to Boston. He owned an American-registered ship that traded with both France and England, and through his uncle, Thomas Boylston, he was in correspondence with the American ambassador in France. Covering all bases, he was also providing the British Admiralty with intelligence from French naval ports as observed by the master of his ship. Concurrently, he was petitioning to have the Massachusetts General Court waive the prohibition against the children of banished Loyalists inheriting property in the state. Moses Gill, husband of Hallowell's sister Rebecca, had been elected lieutenant governor and promised to use his influence with Governor Adams. He expressed cautious optimism, since the newly elected General Court would likely be 'of more liberal sentiments than has been since the Revolution.' Ten years after the event, resentments were beginning to fade.

Moses Gill might well succeed in restoring the property rights of Benjamin Hallowell Sr.'s children, but as one of the most notorious of the banished Loyalists Hallowell himself had no prospect of resuming his previous life in Boston. Mary's ill health had prevented the family from starting over in the frontier conditions of Nova Scotia. Thus, the tacit assumption had always been that the family would live permanently in England, except perhaps for Ward.

The death of Mary Hallowell set in train a series of totally unforeseen events almost as disruptive as the original exile from Massachusetts. Released from the duty of caring for her dying mother, the younger Mary Hallowell was at length free to marry at the age of thirty-two, very late for the times. Moreover, the success of the Boylston grant and the new and supposedly even better parcel at Antigonish made her a woman of substance, at least potentially, and thus an eligible bride for someone from the same social stratum as the Hallowells. Indeed, the new and shorter road in Nova Scotia was a major factor. As her father wrote to Governor Wentworth, 'The new road ... enables my children to hold up their heads, and as property is the greatest motivator in the matter of matrimony in this country, I banter my daughter that she may soon receive an offer worthy of her acceptance.'

Quite probably Mary had met her future husband before the death of her mother, and some understanding may have been reached. In any event, on 23 July 1796, she was married to John Elmsley, an aspiring lawyer.

In the previous month her father had taken an active part in the year's parliamentary elections. Despite his advancing years the consummate lobbyist assumed a prominent role as campaign manager for Vice Admiral Sir Alan Gardner, the Tory candidate in the constituency of Westminster. The race was keenly contested, Westminster being one of the few ridings where most male citizens were eligible to vote. For the same reason the results were often seen as a barometer of the real state of British public opinion. Voting was open rather than by secret ballot, and bribery and intimidation were common although illegal. Alcohol must have played a major role in the chaotic contest, since Hallowell appears to have done most of his managing from public houses, including The Goat and The Bag of Nails, both in Pimlico; The Red Lion in Chelsea; and The Marquis of Granby, Knightsbridge.

Sir Alan was successfully returned. Benjamin Hallowell's main objective in managing the campaign had probably been to assist his younger son by gaining direct access to parliamentary interest, critical to advancement in the navy. However, the new Member of Parliament does not appear to have rendered any special support before his death in 1809. But campaigning for Sir Alan may also have enabled Hallowell Sr. to help his new son-in-law. Within six months of the election, the Duke of Portland chose John Elmsley to be the second chief justice of the infant colony of Upper Canada. He was required to take up his post immediately.

Of course Mary would accompany her husband. It was probably she who first suggested that her father join them. The more they thought about it the more attractive the idea appeared. Although the elder Hallowell had just displayed his vigour in a tough campaign his health was not good; despite his many friends, the prospect of entering old age with none of his family around him was not appealing. Why not accompany his daughter, to live in some degree of comfort with a high official of the colony, undeveloped frontier though it was? Albeit far from his Boston roots, he would at least be back in a part of North America that was still British. As Loyalists both he and his daughter would be entitled to substantial grants of land in Upper Canada, the new home of thousands like himself displaced by the Revolution.

The capital of Upper Canada had been established at Newark, now Niagara-on-the-Lake, and it was there that the chief justice and other officials would reside. The family's heavy luggage was sent to Newark via Montreal, the shortest route. It would be some time after his arrival before John Elmsley could set up a household for his wife and father-in-law. The family would therefore travel first to Boston. John would at once make his way to Canada, while the others were to spend the winter in their native city before joining him. Also in the party was Thomas Radish, who was to become the first Anglican cleric in Upper Canada.

On 2 August 1796, just days after the wedding, they were aboard a ship anchored at Ramsgate, awaiting a fair wind for the passage through the Downs. Benjamin reported proudly that the servants were seasick even at anchor but he was not. The short voyage from the Thames already appeared to have helped his chronic cough. The sea dog was glad to be afloat once again, but the nautical life may have palled by the time the ship reached Boston in late October, after an eleven-week voyage.

When the younger Hallowell left Britain in 1793 there had been no sense of a final parting. Now his mother was dead, his father and sister en route to the Upper Canadian frontier, and his brother actively preparing to return to Boston. It was quite possible that he would never see any of them again. Unmarried, rootless, and in a sense a second time abandoned by his family, the navy took on new importance as the one firm anchor in his life. Quite literally, everything he possessed or aspired to be was embodied in the *Courageux*.

Shortly after the fall of Livorno, Naples withdrew from the allied coalition, despite the objections of the Queen. Spain switched sides and joined the French. Eluding a British squadron under Admiral Man, Admiral Langara succeeded in reaching Toulon to unite the fleets of France and Spain in a force that was greatly superior to that of Jervis. Deprived of bases and with no remaining allies in the Mediterranean, Jervis sailed for Lisbon, which was to be his new station, and en route brought the fleet to anchor in Rosiers Bay, Gibraltar, on 1 December 1796.

Calder, the Captain of the Fleet, had drawn up a detailed anchor plan, calling for the ships to be moored two cables apart on two concentric arcs. On the way to Gibraltar the captains had been called on board the *Victory* and provided with copies, and the master of *Victory*, who was well acquainted with the anchorage, explained its dangers and obstructions. The *Courageux* was the northernmost ship in the outer arc, about a thousand yards from the harbour mole, with the gigantic rock of Gibraltar looming to the southeast and the Spanish shore at Algeciras a few miles to the west.

On 10 December a portion of Langara's fleet was seen passing through the Straits of Gibraltar toward the Atlantic. A gale from the east prevented Jervis from sailing in pursuit. The storm increased in violence and during the night *Courageux*'s anchors failed to hold and she dragged a considerable distance before the wind. Hallowell dropped a third anchor just before the cable to one of the others parted, and the ship was successfully brought to after some anxious hours. However, when dawn broke Hallowell was concerned to observe that the *Courageux* had drifted within range of the shore batteries at Algeciras. They did not immediately open fire, but he at once commenced to unmoor preparatory to returning to his original anchor berth.

In the middle of this complicated evolution he was summoned to sit as a member of a court martial convened in the *Britannia*, flagship of the second-in-command of the fleet. There was nothing for it but to have himself rowed to the *Britannia* in his barge and personally beg permission from the president of the court, Vice Admiral Charles Thompson, to be excused and return to his ship. By an odd coincidence, Thompson had been captain of the *Alcide* in which Hallowell had fought at the Battle of the Chesapeake fifteen years earlier. Permission was refused, and in some trepidation Hallowell took his seat, having requested the captain of the *Victory* to direct Hallowell's ship to carry on with the planned evolution.

Apprised that his captain would not be returning, Burrows, the first lieutenant, continued getting the *Courageux* underway, taking advantage

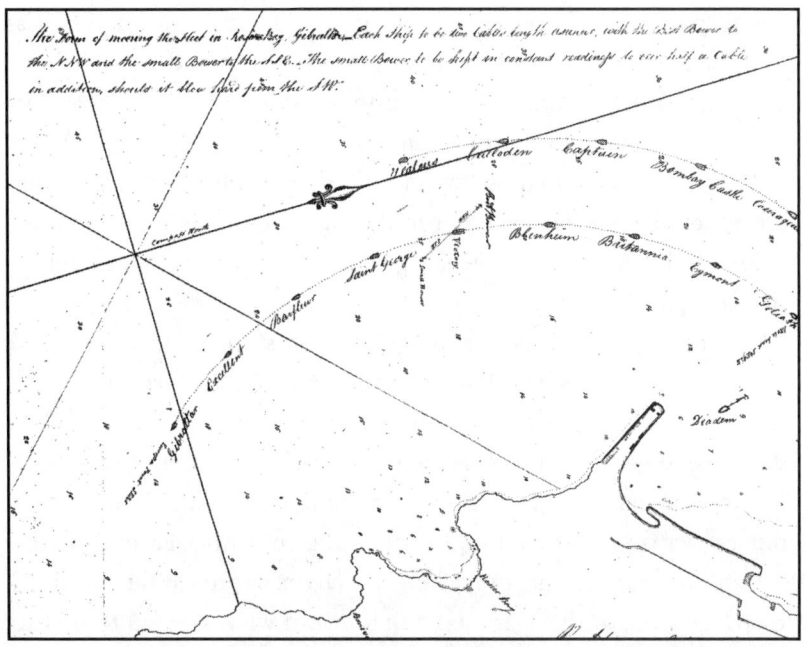

Jervis's Gibraltar anchorage plan, demanding consummate seamanship from his captains; the gale drove the Courageux *from her position on the extreme right.*

of temporarily favourable tides to unmoor the two remaining anchors. This was about eleven in the morning. Before she reached her former anchorage the gale became so intense that bringing to in the midst of the fleet would have been dangerous.

In preparation for another attempt the master, Mr. John Morton, recommended to Burrows that the best of the remaining cables be spliced to the best anchor. Burrows directed Mr. Morton to remain on deck and retired to his cabin, claiming that he was ill. He declined Morton's suggestion that in view of his illness he temporarily relinquish command, which would allow the master to manoeuvre the ship legally in the role of pilot.

About three o'clock the ship re-entered the bay for a second try. At this point the master was advised that the cables had not been overhauled and that nothing had been done to clear away the stores, casks, and other *matériel* that had been in the process of being loaded or unloaded at the anchorage. Morton suggested to Burrows that they display a signal indicating that there were problems with the anchors, thinking that when Hallowell was informed he would at once return on board. His advice was not taken.

He thereupon advised Burrows to give up the idea of re-anchoring, recommending instead that he run through the strait before the wind under storm staysails only, keeping well clear of the land, and return when the gale had abated.

But Burrows was aware that a few Spanish ships had just transited the Strait, and that he might encounter them if he allowed the ship to be driven too far westward. Unable to bear the whole responsibility, he discussed the matter with Lieutenants Prior, Chapman, and Ainslie. At length he made the decision to beat back and forth on north-south courses across the fifteen-mile strait between the European and African shores, wearing or tacking away on approaching the land, accepting a known navigational risk to avoid what seemed to him to be a greater potential risk from the enemy. Mr. Morton reiterated his advice, then declined to take further responsibility for the safety of the ship; but assured Burrows that he would carry out his orders to the best of his ability.

Later in the evening, with the ship standing toward the African shore on the port tack, the weather became very squally and visibility was much reduced. No bearings had been taken since about five o'clock, when Cabritta Point near Algeciras bore NW by N about three or four miles. Having been on deck all day, Mr. Morton went to the captain's cabin to study the charts and make an estimate of the ship's position, leaving Lieutenant Prior on watch with strict instructions to wear the ship directly land was sighted ahead.

With normal care all should have been well, but the strain and responsibility seems to have been too much for Burrows. All hands had been required since dawn, and at this juncture he ordered dinner and the daily issue of wine, leaving only a skeleton watch on deck. At the same time the fifth lieutenant, Ainslie, took charge of the watch. Ainslie was newly joined and very inexperienced. Hallowell had not yet allowed him to keep his own watch even for an instant. Why Burrows did so is a mystery; perhaps he simply didn't know that Prior had turned over the watch to the fifth lieutenant. Two lieutenants were on detached duty with the ship's boats, but Chapman and Prior were still on board, apart from Burrows and the master. There was no need for the least capable officer to take charge in this demanding situation.

With darkness descending and rain falling in sheets the lookout suddenly made out the shape of the land almost directly ahead and hailed the officer of the watch. Even then disaster might have been averted had Ainslie at once put the helm to windward and eased the mainsheet to wear the ship out of danger. Apparently paralyzed, he took no action.

The master returned to the quarterdeck at this juncture and to his horror found Ainslie on watch and saw land on both bows and right ahead. He instantly ordered the helm put over in a last attempt to wear clear of the danger. The *Courageux* began to turn, but too late. With the wind almost right astern she ran bows on into the steep cliff at the foot of Ape's Hill on the coast of Morocco.

The bowsprit and fore-topmast toppled on impact, and almost at once the ship began to break apart as it pounded against the rocks. At first she held together and the master calmed the crew, advised them to stick by the ship, and endeavoured to work her off the shore by trimming the mizzen and mainsails. But the carpenter soon reported that the water was up to the orlop deck. With the ship obviously sinking Mr. Morton had the mizzen and mainmasts cut away to provide a sort of bridge to the shore. The crew abandoned ship as it disintegrated under them. The master, along with Captain Wise of the marines and three other men, jumped to a small rock four or five yards from shore. Two were quickly washed away in the raging surf and Captain Wise died during the night. The next morning the master and the remaining man succeeded in reaching shore, where they found 121 others alive but terribly bruised and battered by the rocks. One master's mate and one midshipman had survived, but Lieutenants Burrows, Prior, Chapman, and Ainslie all drowned.

The longboat with four men in it had been towed astern throughout the day, and one more sailor managed to leap into it from the quarterdeck before the ship disintegrated. Cutting the towline, the five were swept away from the wreck into the strait.

During the storm several other ships had dragged and touched ground; the *Gibraltar* was driven right over Pearl Rock by a tremendous sea, and came off with a chunk of rock that remained wedged in the ship's bottom until the vessel was drydocked in England weeks later.

Hallowell spent a sleepless night in the *Britannia*, beside himself with concern for his ship and his men. At dawn on December 11, with the *Courageux* not in sight, he left in his barge in a vain search for his ship. News soon arrived that the frigate *Andromache* had sighted some wreckage apparently from the *Courageux*, and hope began to fade. The worst was confirmed when the frigate *Niger* picked up the five men in the longboat. By their account it seemed certain that everyone else aboard had been lost.

Jervis reported to the Admiralty:

> *There is too much cause to apprehend she is wrecked, and every soul on board at the time, perished. Captain Hallowell, than whom a gallanter officer or more honourable man does not exist, is on board the* Victory *with two boats crews, a list of whose names is also enclosed. At any time the loss of such a ship to his Majesty, so manned and commanded, would have been very great, but in the present circumstances of my force, compared with that of the enemy in these seas, it is beyond all calculation.*

On 16 December Jervis departed for Lisbon with his ten remaining ships, Hallowell sailing with him in the *Victory*. Three days later a cutter overtook them off Cape Saint Vincent with a letter from Mr. Matra, the British consul at Tangier. To their great surprise and joy they learned that 123 men, including the master, had in fact escaped from the doomed *Courageux*. According to Matra, many of them had been terribly injured by the jagged boulders. Fortunately, just at this time relations between the British and the Barbary corsairs were relatively good, and the survivors were eventually repatriated.

Hallowell, two boats crews, and a number of men on detached

service had not been aboard at the time of the disaster. In the end, of the total complement of 610 men, 439 were drowned. As a fighting unit the *Courageux* had ceased to exist, along with her 'famous band of musick.'

On New Year's Day 1797, Hallowell wrote to Ward to advise him of the calamity:

> *By this unfortunate disaster I am not only deprived of the command of one of the finest ships in the navy, where I had the most flattering prospect of obtaining some reputation in the present war, but have also lost everything I possessed. I am at present on board the Victory, awaiting the arrival of the Master and some of the crew in order to take my trial at a court martial.*

Hallowell's stoic tone conceals the impact of his loss. Apart from the uniform he stood up in he was in fact virtually penniless, all his hard-won gains set at nought. Without a ship there was no chance of recovery from the blow. The only positive factor was that he still retained the approval of the commander-in-chief. 'Sir John Jervis has done me the honour of promising to appoint me to the first ship that may be vacant ... and expressed a desire to have me continue under his command.' Unfortunately there seemed little likelihood of a vacancy in the foreseeable future.

In this letter Hallowell confides some particulars that did not emerge at the court martial. On seeing the land Ainslie had actually left the deck and reported the danger to the first lieutenant in the wardroom. Lieutenant Burrows rushed to the quarterdeck but panicked, and nothing was done until the master appeared from the captain's cabin and ordered the helm over. No doubt these unflattering details were suppressed in testimony.

Great events were about to unfold, in which Hallowell would play his part, but it is convenient to anticipate by a few days and finish the story of the *Courageux*. On 17 February Hallowell, the master, and the surviving members of the crew were tried by court martial, an obligatory procedure whenever a ship was lost. The court was made up of two vice admirals, a rear admiral, and ten of Hallowell's fellow captains, including Wilfred Collingwood's brother Cuthbert. The president was the same Admiral Thompson who had refused to excuse Hallowell from the Gibraltar court martial.

Defending himself, Hallowell clearly showed that he was right in ordering the ship to get under way in his absence and that he had made every effort to rejoin her, but had been prevented from doing so. There was an awkward moment when he put a direct question to the president designed to show that he had in fact asked to be excused, but Admiral Thompson explained his refusal by saying that the *Courageux* was already under sail and could be expected to re-anchor in her original position on the next tack.

The master read out his account of events, called witnesses from the survivors to corroborate his evidence, and answered questions from members of the court. It was abundantly clear that he had kept his head throughout the ordeal and had shown a high degree of professionalism. Mr. Morton refrained from adverse comments regarding Burrows, the deceased first lieutenant, but the facts left little doubt that his leadership and judgment had been at best inadequate. He had retained command in a formal sense but had abdicated it in practice.

The evidence having been heard, the accused withdrew, leaving the members of the court to reach a decision, which could not have taken long. By custom, at the commencement of a trial the sword of the accused would be taken from him. As he re-entered the court to hear the verdict he would see the weapon on a table in front of him, point toward him if guilty, hilt first if not guilty. In this case, there can have been little suspense. Hilt first it was, and the court's decision read:

> *The Captain being on duty ... at the time the ship went to sea there can be no charge against him, he is therefore honourably acquitted; it also appears that if the Master's advice had been taken, in all probability the ship would not have been lost, the Court do therefore acquit him, the other surviving officers and the ships company, and they are hereby acquitted accordingly.*

There can be no doubt that if Hallowell had been on board, the ship would have succeeded in re-anchoring; or she would have stood down the gut as the master recommended; or, if Hallowell had elected to beat back and forth across the strait as Burrows did, the ship's company would have been kept to their duty and for certain Lieutenant Ainslie would not have been left in charge.

Admiral Jervis esteemed Burrows very highly: 'He has been brought up under me, and was a very capable man.' Allowance must be made for the likelihood that he was ill on the fatal day, but even so it is hard to account for the fact that neither he nor the other commissioned officers provided any real support to Mr. Morton. In Hallowell's absence they totally failed to rise to the occasion. Perhaps the wardroom was made up of mediocre officers whom Hallowell had inherited and had to make the best of. Ainslie for instance was the son of a general, and there is more than a hint that he had been promoted beyond his level of competence. Interestingly, the only sea officer to appear to advantage in the disaster was Morton, who had previously been master in the *Lowestoffe* and whom Hallowell had brought with him to the *Courageux*.

Blockade duties had demanded Hallowell's unremitting attention, and he had probably taken direct charge of all but the most routine manoeuvres. Jervis expected commanding officers to be on deck for every alteration of course, day and night. Under Jervis there would be no tolerance for mistakes, even the natural errors of officers learning their trade. It would have been difficult for any captain to train his officers by challenging them with increasing responsibilities. In the presence of the captain, all would be well; in his absence his subordinates might easily find themselves out of their professional depth in a novel situation.

We must now return to the fleet at Lisbon in the days before the 17 February court martial.

On 6 February Admiral Parker joined with a reinforcement of five line of battle ships, bringing Jervis's total strength to fifteen. He was aware that Admiral Cordova had twenty nine, including six of 112-guns, plus his flagship, the enormous *Santissima Trinidad*, with 130. Moreover, it was generally agreed that the Spanish constructors built vessels that were much superior to those produced by British shipbuilders.

Despite the discrepancy in paper strength, Jervis was determined to bring Cordova to battle if the opportunity offered. His fleet no longer had a Mediterranean base, Napoleon was carrying everything before him in Italy, and the continental allies were wavering. If the Spanish fleet were allowed to join with the French they would achieve an overwhelming superiority that might decide the war. Jervis was also aware that mutinies were brewing in the British fleets in home waters. At this critical time in world affairs he saw clearly that Britain had a pressing need for a victory, and that his force was the only one by land or sea that was able to provide one.

Without underestimating his opponents, Jervis knew that a large proportion of their crews consisted of conscripted landsmen, untrained and inexperienced. Moreover, their fleet had had little time to work together at sea and practice their gunnery, while his was at peak efficiency after the long years of blockade. Finally, he had a plan, which was to nullify the overall Spanish superiority by concentrating his entire force against a portion of the enemy's. At dinner in the great cabin of his flagship on the eve of the battle, with Nelson and Hallowell among those present, he proposed the punning toast 'To Victory.'

On the night of 11 February Jervis's scouting frigates reported hearing the signal guns from Cordova's fleet. Certain that they were making for Cadiz, Jervis took up an intercepting position off Cape St. Vincent. He was rewarded when on the morning of 14 February the leading Spaniards were spotted to the southward, sailing free before a westerly breeze. As their topsails emerged one by one over the horizon, Jervis received a stream of reports: 'There are fifteen sail of the line, Sir John'; 'There are eighteen sail of the line'; 'There are twenty-two sail of the line, Sir John.' Tired of this, the admiral ordered that there be no more reports, and stated quietly that he would fight no matter how many Spaniards there proved to be.

At this remark Hallowell took the extraordinary liberty of clapping his Admiral on the back and exclaiming, 'That's right, Sir John, and we'll give them a damned good licking too.' The bystanders were aghast at this breach of discipline, but Jervis was unperturbed: apparently coming from the combative Hallowell the outburst was forgivable.

With the enemy fully visible it was seen that they were in two groups, the seventeen-ship main body to windward of the British and eleven others to leeward. In failing to keep close order they had presented Jervis with the opportunity he sought. He formed his line on the starboard tack and steered southward for the gap. Having interposed between the two groups, he intended to tack in succession as he reached the rear of the windward group, and engage it on a parallel course on the port tack. He accepted the risk that his own ships would be subject to the fire of both Spanish groups as he thrust between them.

Forty line of battle ships and over thirty thousand men were now committed to a life-and-death struggle in this small patch of ocean. With mainsails clewed up the fleets approached the point of intersection

"We'll give them a damn good licking." Just before the Battle of Cape St. Vincent. On the quarterdeck of the Victory, *from left to right Captain Calder, Hallowell, Sir John Jervis.*

agonizingly slowly, admirals and captains anxiously tracking the scarcely changing bearings, which nevertheless showed that Jervis would in fact break through the gap before the Spanish could close it. The Spanish main body now altered more to the north, so that the two fleets were closing on nearly reciprocal courses. The first shots were fired at 11:30 as the *Culloden*, leading the British line, engaged the leading ship of the leeward enemy group, which sheered away to starboard. Soon afterwards the action became general as the fleets passed each other on opposite tacks.

Step one of Jervis's plans had succeeded, but perhaps absorbed with the threat from the leeward enemy group, he delayed the second step, the order for his fleet to tack in succession. Instead of turning immediately his leading ships were still on their interception course while the Spanish main body drew steadily away in the opposite direction. By the time the British had reversed course the Spanish would be well ahead, the opportunity for close action might easily be lost, and the battle so brilliantly begun might end in the usual indecisive standoff.

Nelson was flying his commodore's pennant in the *Captain*, the third ship from the rear of the British line. From this vantage point he perceived what was likely to happen if nothing was done, and without orders from Jervis ordered the *Captain* to wear and head directly for the head of the Spanish line. After first laying the *Captain* alongside the *Santissima Trinidada*, he proceeded to engage the *San Josef*, thus throwing the Spanish centre into confusion and allowing the leading British ships to complete their turns and overtake the enemy. Cuthbert Collingwood in the *Excellent* at the rear of the British line immediately followed Nelson's example, and Jervis also ordered the *Culloden* to wear and cut off the rearmost ships.

A furious melee ensued. *Victory* was trading broadsides with the *Salvador del Mundi*, 112. There were no more tactical decisions to be made. Jervis was pacing the quarterdeck with Hallowell and other senior officers when a cannon ball took off the head of a nearby marine. The admiral's uniform was spattered with brains and blood. Apparently unmoved, the admiral asked someone to fetch him an orange and refreshed himself with it until the *Salvador del*

Mundi surrendered. The *San Isidore* also struck her colours. Meanwhile, the severely damaged *Captain* grappled with the *San Nicolas*, 80, which had become entangled with *San Josef*, 112. Nelson himself led a boarding party to capture the *San Nicolas*, and from there onto the deck of the *San Josef*, which also surrendered. With courtly grace the Spanish officers of both ships gave up their swords to Nelson; he handed them one by one to a sailor called Fearney who very coolly bundled them together under his arm.

Cordova's fleet had fought stubbornly: the *Excellent* had expended 170 barrels of powder; the *Captain*, 146; and the *Blenheim*, 180. None of the splendid Spanish ships was sunk, but once close action was joined superior British gunnery had tilted the scales. The *Excellent* had attained the extraordinary rate of fire of two broadsides in seventy-five seconds, and some ships claimed to have delivered five or six broadsides to their opponent's one. Against such firepower the numerical superiority of the Spanish counted for little, no matter how bravely they fought.

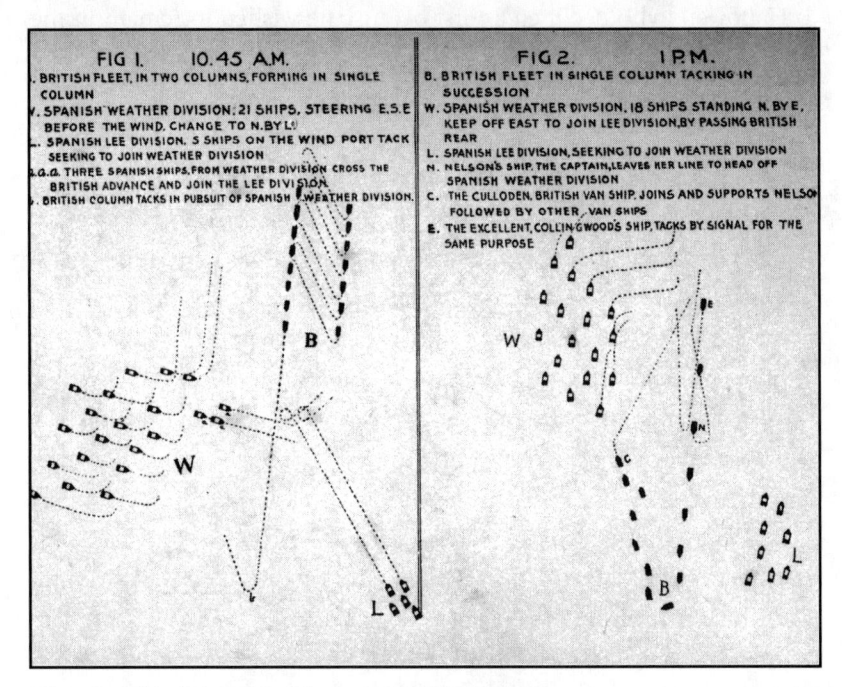

Plan, Battle of Cape St. Vincent, 14 Feb. 1797.

The British casualties totalled three hundred killed and wounded; the Spanish, 1,000, plus more than 3,000 captured. Late in the day Cordova succeeded in reuniting his fleet and was reinforced by two more ships of the line. He made an attempt to recapture the four ships that had surrendered, but Jervis formed a protective line and Cordova drew off to the safety of Cadiz.

Church bells rang out when news of the victory reached Britain. Jervis was elevated to the peerage as Earl of St. Vincent, testimony to the national relief at this enormous piece of good news. But the real hero of the hour was Nelson. He had made the victory possible by his well-judged and timely disregard of orders. His use of one Spanish ship as a bridge to board and take another enraptured the popular imagination.

It was three days after this battle that Hallowell emerged with honour from the *Courageux* court martial. Jervis's dispatches announcing the victory had already been sent home in the care of the Captain of the Fleet, Calder. Hallowell probably acted in his place for a brief period. However, as a mark of favour, Jervis entrusted the duplicate dispatches to Hallowell, who declined at first because he wished to remain in the operational area in case Jervis continued to need him. In the end, he was persuaded, and departed in the lugger *Hope*. Jervis wrote:

> *I am so penetrated with the zeal and disinterestedness of Captain Hallowell, who refused to go to England in the Lively, and now declines carrying duplicates of the despatches in the Hope, because he thinks he may be of use to me, in case of our again keeping in with the Spanish fleet, that I beg you will represent it to the Lords Commissioners of the Admiralty, who, I am sure, will do justice to his extraordinary merit upon this occasion as on all other occasions since he has been under my command.*

Leaving nothing to chance, Jervis also wrote directly to the First Lord, Earl Spencer, asking for his personal support of Hallowell. Coming from the victor of the most decisive engagement of the war, these recommendations guaranteed that Hallowell would not be without a ship for long. Privately, Jervis may also have offered to lend the penniless

John Jervis, Earl of St. Vincent

Hallowell sufficient funds to outfit him for a new command.

His fellow captains gave him their own testimonial. He had been without a ship and was therefore not entitled to prize money from the victory. Nevertheless, the captains present at St. Vincent voted unanimously to include him when their one-quarter share was portioned out 'as a mark of the very high respect we entertain for the character of Captain Benjamin Hallowell, late commander of His Majesty's Ship the Courageux.'

7

THE NILE
1797–1798

Almighty God has blessed his majesty's arms.

*Nelson's victory dispatch,
3 August 1798*

The *Hope* landed Hallowell at Plymouth. He was expected to present his dispatches in London without delay, and with the Admiralty paying he could afford the luxury of coach travel, jolting along the turnpike through Exeter, Dorchester, and Salisbury, stopping only to change horses at the eighteen relay stations. By 10 March he had delivered his documents and submitted an expense claim for £27 covering coach, tolls, drivers, and refreshments. Thanks to Jervis's strong recommendation, within a week of his arrival he was given command of the frigate *Lively* and ordered to sail from Portsmouth by month's end.

There was just time for a brief reunion with Ward, who brought Ben up to date on the rest of the family. They had reached Boston early the previous October. John Elmsley and Thomas Raddish soon departed, hoping to complete the journey to the Niagara region before winter. On the Hudson River the boat they were in filled with water and John lost much of his baggage, including an irreplaceable set of books.

The capital of the new colony at Newark was redolent of the wilderness, a far cry from Boston, let alone London. The clergyman Raddish lost no time in returning to England, but Elmsley immersed himself in his duties and in preparing for the arrival of his wife and father-in-law.

Father and daughter at first stayed with Lieutenant Governor Gill and his wife, Mary's aunt Rebecca, at their Princeton, Massachusetts, estate. Gill had done very well out of the Revolution. By contrast the former commissioner was one of the twenty-nine Loyalists who had been banished by law and could never again become permanent residents. But Gill's assessment that the public mood had changed proved correct. Hallowell's former friends cordially received the old man.

He followed the presidential election, in which Jefferson and Adams were the contenders, and kept Lord Hood informed on American politics. But he spent most of his time settling his very complicated financial affairs, a task his brother Robert had failed to complete. Assets in the former colonies included 'no inconsiderable amount of property belonging to my children, some thousands of dollars in right of their mother, and considerable property of my father's that was my portion, that has not been sold by the state, which the General Assembly has allowed them to possess, they paying a reasonable compensation.' The lands acquired in Maine as part of the Kennebec Proprietorship formed the major part of the assets. Some money had been realized, but it was clear that the family's expectations had to be significantly reduced.

Many years later Robert Hallowell Gardiner was still tidying up the estate and would complain bitterly that his father Robert and uncle Benjamin had spent too much time reminiscing and not enough on business. Perhaps they could be forgiven. Benjamin's departure for Upper Canada was imminent, and they must have known that there would be no more reunions.

Early in 1797 confusing reports of the wreck of the *Courageux* began arriving in Boston. Concern became something very like despair with the arrival of a report from the southern states with the specific information that only Mr. Morton and 125 others had struggled ashore. Not until late March did Benjamin Hallowell receive the letter left at Gibraltar by his son on 16 December bearing the news that Captain Hallowell had not been aboard when the disaster occurred. The thankful father wrote to Admiral Jervis congratulating him on his victory at

Cape St. Vincent and thanking him for his kindness to his son after the loss of the *Courageux*.

John Elmsley strongly advised his wife and father-in-law not to travel to Newark by the route that had proved so disastrous for him the previous autumn. Governor Wentworth pleaded with his old friend to go by sea to Halifax and thence to Montreal and even offered a provincial vessel to carry the family to Halifax. In the end they took the overland route through Vermont to Montreal and thence to Newark. They were there by the end of July 1797; John Elmsley reported to Ward that his father was pleasantly surprised by the country, seemed years younger, and was perfectly happy.

The border town of Newark being judged too vulnerable to American attack, the capital of Upper Canada was moved to York, the future Toronto, in the summer of 1797. John Elmsley necessarily followed, his family arrived in the new capital in 1798, and Benjamin Hallowell and his daughter petitioned for the land grants to which they were entitled as Loyalists. Each received 1200 acres, subdivided into 200-acre lots situated in Concessions III to VII in the township of Pickering, just east of York. At the time the land was of course completely undeveloped and for the most part remained so until the early decades of the nineteenth century.

In June 1797 the Executive Council approved a 'Plan for the Enlargement of York,' expanding the town to the westward. The family received three one-acre lots, all located in the northwest corner of Wellington and Simcoe Streets, where the Roy Thompson Hall now stands. The Elmsleys constructed a two-storey brick and log house, one of the most impressive in the little capital; in later years it was used as Government House. Mary's father lived with them, paying a very generous £100 a year toward expenses.

Alexander Grant was a member of the Executive Council of Upper Canada and the senior official in charge of government vessels in the province. Concurrently, he traded on the upper lakes in his own vessels and had become a wealthy man. He was not in the Royal Navy but nevertheless went by the courtesy title of 'commodore.' A shared interest in matters nautical led to a firm friendship between him and Benjamin

Hallowell. Grant was totally unpolished and very stout with a red pockmarked face. On being introduced to Prince Edward Augustus he inquired, 'How do you do, Master Prince, and how do your Papa do?'

One of the earliest Loyalist settlements was west of Kingston on the peninsula of Quinte. Surveys began in 1783, and by 1797 an increasing population made it necessary to split off a new jurisdiction from the original townships of Marysburgh and Sophiasburgh. The Executive Council had the responsibility of choosing a name. Under the influence of Chief Justice Elmsley and Alexander Grant it chose 'Hallowell' as a compliment to the old man. The township also gave its name to a small village that grew up on the Bay of Quinte and later merged with the town of Picton, the county seat of Prince Edward County.

Back in England the younger Hallowell was busy at Portsmouth, preparing the *Lively* for sea. This was not the *Lively* of Bunker Hill and the evacuation of Boston. After Captain Bishop had left her, that ship had been captured by the French in 1778 and later recaptured and sold. Hallowell's new *Lively* mounted thirty-two guns rather than twenty, and was only three years old. On the recommendation of Jervis (now Earl of St. Vincent), the Admiralty had given Hallowell this fast frigate rather than a ship of the line because she would be a superior vehicle for winning prize money, the quickest way to recover his losses from the wreck of the *Courageux*.

The *Lively* had returned from Jervis's fleet badly in need of repair, and both her standing and running rigging needed to be replaced. Hallowell was obliged to inform the Admiralty that she would not be ready to sail by the end of March as ordered, but that he hoped to do so in the first week of April, carrying dispatches and private letters for the fleet.

His instructions required him to escort to Lisbon any merchant vessels awaiting convoy. To collect his charges he posted notices in the Customs House requiring the masters of all vessels awaiting escort to report to him for orders. He also sent a cutter ahead to Falmouth to order any Lisbon-bound ships to stand in readiness to join the convoy as it passed down the Channel. In the World Wars of the twentieth century convoys were organized by specialized staffs in the major ports — it is interesting that in Hallowell's time the senior officer of the escort was expected to organize his convoy personally. On one of Hallowell's letters to the Admiralty reporting his arrangements an unknown member of the Board has scrawled 'Good,' in recognition of his efficiency and initiative.

He sailed on 8 April 1797. Only a week later mutiny was to break out in the fleet at Spithead. It did not come as a complete surprise to the Admiralty, and Hallowell may have been aware of the discontent. Fresh from the Mediterranean, the crew of the *Lively* had not had prolonged contact with the Spithead seamen, and discipline in Hallowell's ship was not affected. A few months later it would be a different story.

A full gale was raging as the convoy approached Falmouth. Hallowell realized that he could not stand in to collect any waiting ships. He could carry on without them or await better conditions. Today a captain can obtain almost instant advice and direction, but Hallowell had to make up his own mind. He wasted no time in deciding to press on and bypass the Falmouth contingent. Jervis would have applauded his readiness to assume responsibility, that rarest of qualities. The *Lively* and her convoy reached Lisbon on April 16 after an uneventful and exceptionally fast nine-day passage.

Portugal was one of Britain's few remaining allies, and Lisbon was crucial as the fleet's main operational base for maintaining the blockade of Cadiz. If the Spanish fleet could escape from Cadiz it might join the French at either Toulon or Brest, producing an overwhelming force able to control the sea in whatever area it chose to operate.

Shortly after his arrival Hallowell was ordered to patrol off the Canary Islands to intercept Spanish vessels returning from America with their valuable cargoes and also to negotiate an exchange of prisoners. The *Minerve*, 38, Captain Cockburn, was placed under his command. Originally French, *Minerve* had been captured by the *Lowestoffe*, by coincidence just a few days after Hallowell left that ship. Typically bad luck, as Hallowell must have reflected.

A few months earlier two other frigates had cut out a prize worth £30,000 from Santa Cruz, the port of Tenerife. Hallowell's mission was operationally justifiable, but in sending the two captains Nelson acted as much from friendship as from strategic considerations. 'I long to see poor Cockburn and Hallowell enrich themselves.' This would not be the last time Nelson tried to help his friend by putting profit in his way.

On May 28 the two ships were off Santa Cruz. Hallowell met with the port authorities under a flag of truce to carry out his negotiations — taking the opportunity to reconnoitre the port. One very desirable prize was present, a galleon from Manila no doubt crammed with the spices of the East. Unfortunately she was moored too far into the harbour to be captured, but a warship flying French colours was nearer the harbour mouth, and Hallowell resolved to cut her out.

When the truce expired, the ships' boats were manned with seamen and marines under Thomas Hardy, the first lieutenant of the *Minerve*. In mid-afternoon, the siesta hour, they started for the harbour, the men rowing like mad to board their quarry under heavy musket fire. Taken by surprise, the French were unable to bring their guns into action and were quickly overpowered. The boarders cut the anchor cable and loosed the sails for the escape. Unluckily, the wind was light, and the ships' boats had to tow the prize for nearly an hour under continuous if inaccurate fire from the now alerted fortifications. The French captain Xavier Pommier and many of his men were ashore at the time, and could only watch impotently as their ship disappeared over the horizon.

Surprise and careful preparation had paid off. Amazingly, the boats had suffered only sixteen casualties, all wounded. The prize turned out to be the fourteen-gun brig *Mutine*, a beautiful little vessel whose sailing qualities made her a valuable addition to the fleet as scout and messenger. Hardy, who was one of the wounded, became her commander in the first step on the path that would make him captain of Nelson's flagship at Trafalgar.

An individual share of head money from the little *Mutine* was nothing compared with Nelson's hopes for enrichment of the two captains. However, more might be in store if Hallowell continued in command of his fast frigate. But in a climate of threatened mutiny St. Vincent's policy at this time was to post reliable captains to badly disciplined line of battle ships, regardless of seniority. Hallowell was junior to some of the other frigate captains on the station, but St. Vincent offered him command of the third-rate *Swiftsure,* and his sense of duty impelled him to accept. Taking command of his new ship off Madeira on 26 October 1797, he was ordered at once to the Cadiz blockade.

Thus, he missed Nelson's rash and unsuccessful night attack on Tenerife two months later, in the course of which the admiral lost his right arm. By stimulating the defenders to greater alertness and more accurate gunnery, Hallowell's recent exploit may inadvertently have contributed to Nelson's only real failure. Xavier Pommier, the unlucky captain of the *Mutine*, redeemed himself by playing a major role in the Spanish defence.

At Lisbon Hallowell played a part in a black chapter in the history of the Royal Navy. One week after the *Lively* left Portsmouth mutiny had broken out in the Channel fleet. The sailor's grievances centred on discipline, pay, food, and lack of freedom. Discipline was necessarily harsh, although tempered to some extent by rules that did not exist in the merchant service. Wages had not been increased for over a hundred and fifty years and by now were far below what a merchant seaman could earn. To allow for spoilage, pursers only had to issue seven-eighths of the ration they had purchased, and many took unfair advantage of this allowable gap between outlay for food and food provided. Finally, men could not change voluntarily from one naval ship to another and were seldom granted shore leave even when in home port.

Nevertheless, naval service was in some ways preferable to merchant service. Despite the cheese-paring of the pursers, navy food was usually better than in merchantmen. Men always received their admittedly inadequate pay rather than being cheated out of it by unscrupulous merchant captains, as often happened, and the prospect of prize money was a big inducement. Men could and did desert from merchant vessels to the navy as well as the other way around. As Nelson said, 'They would desert from heaven to hell simply for the change.'

At first the disturbances were more in the nature of a strike than a mutiny. Sailors used no violence against ships' officers and made it clear that they were ready to return to duty if the French put to sea. The authorities reacted quickly. On 23 April the King's pardon was read to the fleet and the men were promised that their grievances would be addressed. The mutiny seemed to be over, but it reignited on May 7 when it appeared to the sailors that the promises were not being fulfilled. This time unpopular officers were singled out and some of them were forcibly put ashore. Four days later the highly respected Admiral Lord Howe visited each ship with a 'Seaman's Bill' that met the sailors' wishes, about half the landed officers were allowed to return, and the fleet sailed on May 16 with no problems.

Four days earlier a much more serious mutiny had begun at the Nore, the fleet base on the Thames estuary down river from London. In a political dimension that had not been present at Spithead, the ringleaders raised democratic issues associated with the ideas of the French Revolution. London's apparent defencelessness caused near panic in financial circles, and interest rates on government bonds more than doubled. The authorities refused to negotiate beyond the concessions of the Seaman's Bill, cut off supplies to the anchored ships, and lined the shores with guns and troops. The former mutineers at Spithead addressed a remonstrance to their counterparts at the Nore, urging them to return to duty. One by one over the next few weeks the ships hauled down the red flag of rebellion and surrendered unconditionally. The ringleaders were tried for mutiny and on conviction were hung or transported to Australia.

The mutinies in home waters were over, but the contagion threatened to spread to the Earl of St. Vincent's command at Lisbon. To exacerbate matters, rebellion was brewing in Ireland and discontent was rife among the numerous Irish in his ships.

The Earl acted on the premise that only iron discipline would avert an outbreak. When the *Marlborough* arrived from England after a mutiny en route the ringleader was court-martialled and sentenced to be hanged at the yardarm by his own ship's company. The captain reported to St. Vincent that the crew refused to carry out the hanging, to be told that if he couldn't enforce obedience the admiral would send someone to take command who could. With armed boats from every ship in the fleet surrounding the *Marlborough*, the man was duly hanged. In another case Admiral Thompson protested when a mutineer was ordered to be hanged on a Sunday. St. Vincent went ahead with the punishment as an example to the men and had Thompson ordered home as an example to the officers.

Always a strict disciplinarian, St. Vincent became harsh and dictatorial under the strain of suppressing the mutiny: 'a torrent of impetuous reproof in unguarded language would rush from his lips.' He was later challenged to a duel by one of his subordinates, Admiral Orde, but declined to fight over his public as opposed to his private conduct. The example he set in this instance would be remembered by Hallowell when years later he faced the same dilemma.

Serving under Hallowell was a boy named John Lee. He had been entered in the books of the *Cambridge* at the age of seven and had actually gone to sea at ten in the *Barfleur*, where his father was first lieutenant. He had been present at the capture of Bastia, and before he was twelve had taken part in the Battle of Cape St. Vincent. When his father was given command of Hallowell's old ship the *Camel*, he was unable to take his son with him and persuaded Hallowell to accept him in the *Swiftsure*. In later life Lee published his memoirs, a first-hand source of information on the stirring events of his boyhood.

We are indebted to him for the account of near mutiny in the *Swiftsure*. Water was in short supply and was being strictly rationed. Patrick Crick, an Irish marine, had been allowed two drinks from the cask on the quarterdeck in a short period of time, but was forbidden to take a third by the midshipman of the watch. Crick became insolent and threatening, and a sympathetic crowd was gathering when the marine was put in irons and taken to the flagship for trial by court martial. He was convicted and sentenced to be hanged, as usual in his own ship.

The *Swiftsure* was anchored in the middle of the fleet. Two boats from every ship, each manned by suspected malcontents, were gathered around her to witness the punishment. Crick had been confined in the clerk's office, and when the time came could not stand without assistance. (Lee does not say so, but out of mercy the condemned man may have been unofficially allowed a quantity of rum.) Crick was half carried to the larboard cathead where the boatswain placed a white hood over his head and adjusted the noose around his neck. His arms and legs were tied.

As was the custom he held a handkerchief, and could choose the moment of his death by dropping it as a signal for his shipmates to run away with the rope and hoist him to the yardarm. He could not do it, so the signal was given by the firing of a gun. At this, says Lee, 'He was quickly run up to the yard arm where he hung for half an hour before being lowered down and consigned to the deep.' Examples such as this, repeated in any ship where symptoms of mutiny were detected, 'had a wonderful effect on the fleet.'

Today one recoils at this account, but Lee describes the incident without emotion and as something quite within the bounds of normalcy. It was a harsher age, and the country was in a desperate single-handed struggle against a France that seemed invincible on land. Without her fleet Britain was doomed. St. Vincent's unflinching rigour preserved the discipline of that fleet at a critical juncture. There is no way of knowing whether less ruthless measures would have been as effective in that place at that time.

Meanwhile the blockade of Cadiz continued. Stationed just out of range of the shore batteries an inner screen of guard boats provided early warning. They were backed up by a flying squadron of the fastest line of battle ships, under Nelson's command, of which the *Swiftsure* was one. This squadron normally anchored off the port, but one ship was always underway, ready to support the guard boats against a sortie by the numerous and efficient Spanish rowing galleys. Depending on the enemy's state of readiness the main fleet either manoeuvred well offshore or remained at Lisbon. The British permitted the local fishermen to carry on as usual, bought some of their catch, and allowed them to land the rest. In return they obtained amazingly accurate intelligence of the Spanish fleet.

French and Spanish privateers swarmed in the Bay of Biscay and along the coast of Portugal. They were difficult to distinguish from innocent merchant vessels even at close range, and some actually operated in the very mouth of the Tagus. One countermeasure was to disguise a British ship as a merchantman and entice a privateer into approaching what was revealed at the last moment as a hornet's nest. The *Aurora* was so successful with this tactic that each of her able seamen was reputed to have won £600 in prize money, all too often laid out in silver buckles, silk handkerchiefs, and even gold buttons on their jackets.

On one occasion the *Bellerophon* was trapped in calm and carried by the tide within range of the shore batteries. They opened fire and enemy galleys hastened to the attack. Unmanoeuvrable as she was, their heavy bow guns could rake her from astern with complete impunity. Hallowell in the *Swiftsure* came to her assistance only to be becalmed in his turn, supposedly because the gunfire caused what little wind there was to die away entirely. Fortunately, it soon sprang up again and with the help of the *Culloden* and the *Theseus* the two ships escaped after suffering heavy casualties.

A similar scenario was played out not long afterwards. The *Swiftsure* and other ships were escorting a convoy to Gibraltar when the wind failed and the *Hannibal* was becalmed under the guns of Algeciras. Again Hallowell hastened to assist, and again the *Swiftsure* was becalmed as a swarm of active and daring galleys gathered around their

Seemingly endless blockade eventually won the war at sea; here a squadron including Swiftsure *manoeuvres off Cadiz.*

prey. Hallowell lowered his boats to tow the ship's head around to bring her guns to bear, but the nimble Spaniards maintained their vantage point off his stern. Four more British ships soon found themselves in the same uncomfortable position, with as many as seventy galleys tormenting them and causing heavy casualties. A potential disaster was only averted when a freshening breeze carried the threatened ships out of danger.

Even in the midst of war there were lighter moments. Hallowell permitted his men to consume wine over and above the daily allowance providing the privilege was not abused, as it never was in the *Swiftsure*. Midshipman Lee was sent ashore in Gibraltar to purchase two hundred and fifty gallons of Malaga to replenish the stock. He felt it was his duty to sample every cask, and could hardly make it up the ship's side when he returned. Hallowell happened to be on the quarterdeck and chided Lee for setting a bad example to the boat's crew, but Lee swore that he wasn't drunk. Hallowell challenged him to walk a seam in the deck. The mid accepted, but found that he could not stay within seven seams and had to be assisted to his bunk by the grinning quartermaster.

A few days later Hallowell gave a ball on board the *Swiftsure*, inviting his fellow captains and the officials of the Gibraltar garrison with their families. As in the lost *Courageux*, he had encouraged the crew to form a voluntary band. Colourful signal flags decorated the upperworks, there was dancing on the quarterdeck, and solid and liquid refreshments were available in the captain's cabin. Of course, the story of Midshipman Lee's ill-fated expedition went the rounds, to the vast amusement of the guests.

Among these was Captain John Inglefield, Hallowell's commodore on the coast of Africa five years before and now Commissioner of the Gibraltar Navy Yard. He was accompanied by wife and his three daughters Ann, Lucretia, and Catherine. Ann, the eldest, was twenty-two, the other two in their late teens. All three were very much in the market for a husband. In Ann Inglefield, Hallowell had met his future wife, whether or not either of them realized it at the time. Probably nothing can be made of the fact that his future wife bore the same Christian name as his unattainable first love.

The *Swiftsure* soon returned to blockade duties, but not for long. The Austrians had been forced to make peace in October 1797. Strong French forces were massing on the Channel coast in ostentatious preparation for an invasion of Britain, the only power as yet unconquered. Commanded by Napoleon, a second expeditionary force was gathering at Toulon, its destination unknown. The French and Spanish together possessed ninety ships of the line against the British sixty-five, and the aftermath of mutiny still pervaded the fleet. In this desperate situation the government decided on a daring strategic initiative. Earl Spencer directed St. Vincent to send a detachment into the Mediterranean, with the dual objectives of encouraging Austria and the other continental powers to renew the struggle and of countering the threat from Toulon, whatever its destination.

That destination was Egypt. In September 1797 the British had captured the Cape of Good Hope, consolidating their sea route to the east while rendering French sea communications around the Cape much more difficult and dangerous. A foothold in Egypt would open the possibility of establishing an overland connection as a substitute. In any case, France had long been interested in Egypt as a potential replacement for the colonial losses of the Seven Years War.

The country was a province of the Ottoman Empire, theoretically ruled by a pasha appointed by the sultan, Selim III. In practice Egypt was governed by the Mamelukes, a military society replenished by recruits from the Caucasus, who were nominally slaves of the sultan. They were rightly regarded as the best fighting men in the Middle East. Their beys governed the various provinces, collected the taxes from the wretched peasantry, and remitted a token tribute to Constantinople.

France's Directorate decided to conquer Egypt and gave the command to Napoleon Bonaparte, partly because of his ability and partly to get the ambitious general well away from Paris. Napoleon was sincerely interested in Islamic religion and culture, and his strategic vision went much further than the mere occupation of Egypt. He planned to overthrow the Mamelukes and place the administration in the hands of native Egyptian religious officials. Using the country as a base he would create a Muslim army with a core of French veterans and repeat the march of Alexander the Great through Arabia and Iran to wrest the riches of India from the British. A daunting challenge to be sure, but Bonaparte if anyone might have succeeded.

He was given an army of nearly 37,000 soldiers collected at Toulon and Marseilles and at several Italian ports. The force was embarked in three hundred transports and escorted by thirteen ships of the line and fourteen frigates, plus numerous smaller vessels, the whole armada under Admiral Brueys. It was the largest expedition to cross the Mediterranean since the Crusades.

In sending a counterforce Spencer left it to St. Vincent to decide whether to go himself or to appoint Nelson in command. The second option was chosen. Nelson left Gibraltar on 8 May 1797, in the *Vanguard*, accompanied only by two 74s and four frigates. But reinforcements were on the way. Nine ships were sent from England to the Cadiz blockade, and as they joined, St. Vincent detached Troubridge to catch up to Nelson with ten of his best ships including the *Swiftsure*. The relief took place in darkness; the arriving ships were painted the same as those departing to conceal what was happening from the Spanish.

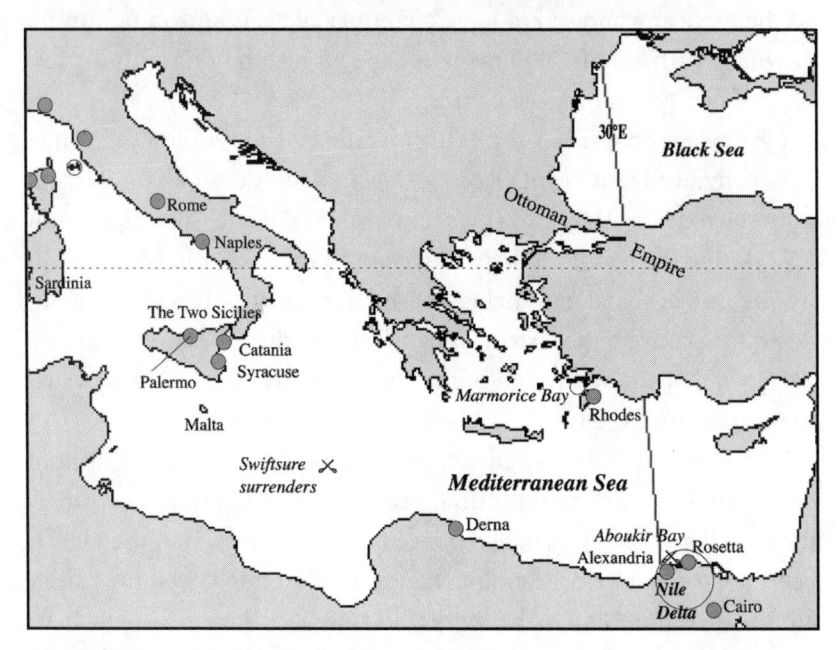

Map of Eastern Mediterranean

Troubridge joined Nelson off Sardinia on 7 June, only to learn that Napoleon had sailed from Toulon on 19 May, had collected his contingents from the other ports, and was now loose on the high seas. Numerous strategic possibilities were open to the French, including Ireland and the West Indies as well as anywhere in the Mediterranean. Egypt was not considered to be one of the more likely objectives.

The British fleet steered to the south and was off Elba on 12 June, sighting numerous waterspouts in the midst of a severe electrical storm. Nelson's frigates became separated and would not rejoin until the campaign was over. Deprived of his scouts, the admiral had to rely on intelligence obtained from merchant vessels or from ports as he sailed past. Obtaining no news at Naples, the fleet passed swiftly through the dangerous Strait of Messina, the Scylla and Charybdis of myth. The inhabitants came out in boats to watch the spectacle and the buildings on the Sicilian shore were draped in flags and banners; the bulk of Mount Etna dominated the scene.

The French arrived off Malta on 10 June and easily conquered the island from the military order of the Knights of Malta. Napoleon looted their treasury and seized large quantities of arms and ammunition. Leaving a garrison of 3,000 men, he sailed for Alexandria with the rest of his force, proceeding via Corfu.

On the twenty-second the British learned of the capture of Malta, and, convinced that Egypt was indeed Napoleon's destination, Nelson also steered for Alexandria. No contact was made, although from 22–24 June the two fleets were very close to each other in poor visibility, the British signal guns being clearly heard by the French. Not hampered by a convoy, the faster-sailing British reached Alexandria on July 28; since they found no sign of the enemy, they immediately departed to reconnoitre Cyprus.

Two days later the French arrived; it is said that observers ashore could see the British topsails disappearing over the eastern horizon as those of the French gradually emerged from the west. Had the French been intercepted before landing, the expedition might well have been annihilated and Napoleon's career and perhaps himself might have been drowned in the waters of the Mediterranean.

The French army landed near Alexandria on the night of July 1 and captured the city the next day. With characteristic energy Napoleon immediately led his troops toward Cairo where the Mamelukes prepared to meet him. They wore steel helmets under their turbans and mesh armour that could deflect bullets under their quilted jackets, and were capable of cutting a man in two with their swords. The Battle of the Pyramids was fought on 21 July 1798. For over an hour the Mamelukes repeatedly charged the French squares, but the disciplined firepower of the infantry ultimately prevailed over the individual skill and courage of the attacking horsemen. Perhaps 10,000 of the Mamelukes were killed. French losses were trifling in comparison, and Napoleon established his headquarters in Cairo three days later.

Meanwhile the British fleet continued its search. Frustration and tension grew by the day, as it appeared increasingly likely that they had been completely outwitted. Finding nothing at Cyprus, they sailed to Syracuse in Sicily to replenish their provisions. Hallowell and some of his officers relieved the tension by playing the part of tourists in the ancient city. They crawled on their hands and knees through the catacombs, led by an old friar with a light. Young Lee claimed to have counted 5,000 mummified bodies, each clad in the costume of its day. By way of contrast they then visited a subterranean garden with high rock walls, where pomegranates, olives, and oranges grew in profusion. As they returned to their anchored ship, the submerged ruins of the ancient city could be clearly seen at the bottom of the bay.

The fleet left Syracuse on 24 July. Off Greece it was learned that the French had been seen sailing for Egypt a month before, and course was again shaped in that direction. As the fleet sailed west the *Swiftsure* recovered a floating object that turned out be a lifebuoy from the French frigate *l'Artémise*. By its appearance it had not been in the water very long. Hallowell ordered the signal 'Intelligence to Communicate' to be hoisted and was ordered to close the flagship. As his boat approached the *Vanguard*, Nelson leaned over the side and asked, 'Hallowell, what have you got?' The reply was, 'They are not far off; here is the lifebuoy of one of their frigates.' This discovery encouraged the admiral to push on to Egypt for a second time in renewed confidence that he would at last discover his quarry.

Maddening though it was, the fruitless search had provided time for Nelson and his captains to become acquainted. Individually or in groups most of the captains were summoned to the flagship, where the admiral gradually forged the famous 'Band of Brothers.'

The group studied a recent example of success achieved through concentration of force. On 1 June 1794, Admiral Howe had intercepted a grain convoy en route to France, escorted by a fleet under Admiral Villeneuve. The supplies were absolutely critical to the revolutionary government. Attacking the escort, Howe ordered his ships to break the enemy line. Not all captains understood or obeyed, but the result was a significant if only partial defeat of the escort. However, the convoy escaped.

The encounter illustrates a profound difference in the way the two navies conceptualized the war at sea. The French had evolved the doctrine of the 'mission.' Its modern counterpart is the principle of war referred to as 'selection and maintenance of the aim.' Villeneuve's mission or aim on June 1 was the safe arrival of his convoy, and in this he succeeded. Failing, he would no doubt have lost his head.

The pragmatic British would scarcely have admitted to having anything as abstract as a doctrine, but invariably their intention was to come to grips with the enemy fleet. In the short term this might lead to missed opportunities. If Howe had somehow manoeuvred to destroy the convoy rather than Villeneuve's fleet a starving Paris mob might have turned against the revolutionaries. But in the long run the relentless British pressure on the enemy's fighting power would secure for them the decisive advantage of control of the sea, their aim from the beginning.

Nelson had a final conference with all his captains on the morning of July 31. He had inculcated them with his tactical principles and inspired them with his enthusiasm, and under his leadership personal animosities and professional jealousies were put aside. It would be as a supremely confident and cohesive team that the fleet would finally go into action.

After landing the troops the French fleet had no useful role, but

Napoleon wished it to remain available until he was well established inland. The harbour of Alexandria was deemed too dangerous because its entrance was shallow and easily blockaded. Accordingly, unaware of the fast-approaching danger, Brueys anchored his fleet in the Bay of Aboukir to the east of Alexandria. Ironically, Napoleon did finally dispatch orders to sail for Corfu, but they were intercepted by Arabs and never reached Brueys.

Anticipation was high at dawn on 1 August as the British fleet approached the Egyptian coast. While the remaining ships stood on to the east, Nelson ordered the *Swiftsure* and the *Alexander* to close Alexandria and reconnoitre. Again hopes were dashed. Apart from a few small vessels there were no warships in the harbour, although it was crowded with merchant shipping. The bad news was signalled to the admiral. Meanwhile the *Swiftsure* bore down on a French brig and a galley near the harbour entrance. Just as she was about to run on a subsequently discovered uncharted rock, the flagship hoisted the recall signal, a providential escape from disaster.

Again the fleet had missed its quarry, and in the British ships lunch was a gloomy affair; Nelson would not eat a morsel. So much, it seemed, for the lifebuoy of *l'Artémise*.

By two-thirty all was transformed. Aboukir Bay is hidden to ships approaching from the west by the peninsula of Aboukir, with a ruined castle at its end, and by the Island of Bequires a few hundred yards to the east. As the bay opened up beyond the island, the two leading British ships simultaneously signalled 'Enemy in Sight.' The entire French fleet was soon visible, lying at single anchor in a formidable slightly curved line nearly two miles long, with the ship's heads pointing into the westerly wind and the ships about two hundred yards apart. Inshore of the line of battle were four frigates and some gunboats and brigs. Brueys dispatched one of these to draw the leading British ships into shoal water, but the ruse did not succeed.

At quarter past three Nelson made the signal to prepare for action and shortly afterwards ordered his fleet to prepare to anchor by the stern. At four o'clock the crews went to dinner as usual. At this time the *Swiftsure* and the *Alexander* were about twelve miles astern of the main body.

Many of the French seamen had gone ashore to obtain fresh water. They were hastily recalled, but not all returned. Some men were also transferred from the frigates to make up numbers in the most undermanned ships of the line. Brueys briefly considered getting his ships underway, but he recognized that this would likely lead to confusion and make it impossible to form his line of battle in time, and therefore decided to await the British attack at anchor. It was late in the day. Brueys believed that Nelson would not choose to fight in the dark, so that the French would have overnight to complete their preparations.

Brueys was wrong. The British fleet formed a line of battle on a southerly course, steering to pass clear of Bequires and its off-lying shoals. They had no charts, but Nelson had a sketch of the bay Hallowell had captured from a French prize. Under topsails the fleet gradually closed the French line at a speed of only six knots. There ensued the usual agonizing interval between the decisions for action and actually coming within range, so typical of battles in the age of sail. Some men joked, others waited silently. An officer jotted down this conversation at one of the guns:

Jack: There are thirteen sail of the line and a whacking lot of frigates and small craft. I think we'll hammer the rust off ten of them, if not the whole boiling.

Tom: We took but four on the first of June, and I got seven pounds of prize money. Now if we knock up a dozen of these fellows (and why shouldn't we?) damn my eyes, messmates, we will have a breadbag full of money to receive.

Jack: Aye, I'm glad we have twigged them at last — I want some new rigging for Sundays and mustering days.

Tom: So do I. I hope we'll touch enough for that, and a dammed good cruise among the girls besides.

Forty-year-old John Nichol was considered too old for active labour at the guns. To his disgust he was assigned to assist the gunner making up powder charges in the main magazine of the *Goliath*. He and others actually looked forward to battle:

> A serious cast was to be perceived on every face, but not a shade of doubt or fear. We rejoiced in a general action; not that we loved fighting; but we all wished to be free to return to our homes, and follow our own pursuits. We knew there was no other way of obtaining this than by defeating the enemy. 'The hotter the war, the sooner the peace' was a saying with us.

If these remarks are in any way representative, they portray a fatalistic but supremely confident body of men, if not eager for battle at least resigned to it. Prize money and the hope for peace were powerful motivators. Scarcely a year before, many of these same men had been on the brink of mutiny.

As Nelson was a rear admiral of the Blue Squadron, his ships should have flown blue ensigns. However, they were ordered to hoist white ensigns, probably because that colour would be easier to distinguish in the upcoming night action. Once past the Island of Bequires, the fleet altered in succession to the west-southwest on the starboard tack, steering a gradually converging course for the head of the French line. Nelson hoisted the signal of a red pennant over a blue flag, signifying 'Engage the enemy more closely,' prompting cheers from the British ships. At about six o'clock, as the range closed, the French ships opened fire one by one and the British began to reply just as the sun set.

Brueys may have believed that Nelson would anchor his ships in a line parallel to and seaward of his own, so that a standard one-on-one engagement would ensue between roughly equal numbers. His ships would only need to man the guns on their starboard sides, more than making up for any shortages in his ships' complements. The *Swiftsure* and the *Alexander* were still out of sight, so Brueys could see eleven British line of battle ships against the thirteen in his own fleet. The British also had the 50-gun *Leander*, but she was too weak to take a place in the line. The numbers altered further in Brueys's favour when the *Culloden*, 74, ran aground on the seaward edge of the shoal off Bequires. There she remained throughout the battle despite the frantic efforts of Captain Troubridge and his crew to get her off.

Brueys also may have counted on an interval during which his opponents were swinging to their anchors, well within range, yet unable for the time being to bring many of their own guns to bear. But Nelson had ordered his ships to prepare to anchor by the stern. During the approach the anchors would still be visible in the bows, but when let go the ships would be brought to by cables run through their stern ports and would come to rest with stern rather than head to the wind, ready to engage. Springs attached to the cables enabled a ship's heading to be altered to bring the broadside to bear in any desired direction.

Nelson was not going to fight a standard battle. He was mobile and the French were not, so he had the opportunity to concentrate his whole force on a portion of the enemy's. No further orders were necessary for captains he had imbued with his philosophy. Many of them would also be aware of Hood's intended action against Martin in 1794, when he had planned to place his ships on both sides of each anchored Frenchman.

The leading ships wore around the head of the French line, one after the other raking the *Guerrier*, which was soon a dismasted wreck. Each then proceeded inshore of the French on an opposite heading, before letting go and paying out cable until it arrived in its chosen position. Later ships performed the same manoeuvre but on the outer side of the enemy line, so that the eight or nine leading French ships faced all eleven British. Many of the French were fired on from both sides with their inshore batteries in many cases not even cleared for action.

Sunset was at 6:31 p.m. By the time the *Swiftsure* and the *Alexander* rounded the Island of Bequires it was completely dark. To starboard Hallowell could make out the lights displayed by his friend Troubridge in the grounded *Culloden*, serving the useful if frustrating purpose of marking the limit of safe water. As Hallowell passed clear on the starboard tack, with the ship heeling slightly to port, a shot from a French shore battery smashed through the hull below the waterline. The carpenter and his mates tried desperately to plug the hole, but soon there were four feet of water in the hold, and exhausted men had to labour constantly at the pumps to keep the *Swiftsure* afloat and in the fight.

Hallowell was well aware that he and Captain Ball in the *Alexander* represented a crucial reinforcement that could decide the struggle in favour of the British. In choosing his anchorage position he had nothing to guide him but the flashes of the guns, spread on an arc of over a mile across his bows. Somewhere in the melee was his future brother-in-law, Samuel Hood Inglefield, a lieutenant in the *Theseus*.

The British night signal was four lights at the mizzen peak, but in many ships they had been shot away, and the rest were indistinguishable against the gun flashes. The line of almost continuous illumination was highly confusing, because the British ships that had passed inshore of the French were actually firing in Hallowell's general direction, just as the French were, while those British vessels outside the French line were firing away from him.

Soon, however, he recognized what had happened, and from the pattern of flashes identified the French flagship *L'Orient*, 120, the only three-decker on either side. He determined to anchor in the gap between this powerful vessel and her next ahead, which, although he did not know it, was the eighty-gun *Franklin*. From this position he could employ one broadside with doubled crews or by using his spring bring both broadside to bear, engaging both *L'Orient* and the *Franklin*. He gave strict orders that not a shot was to be fired until the ship had her anchor and the sails had been clewed up. Silently, except for the groaning of the pumps and the depth reports from the leadsman in the fore chains, the *Swiftsure* glided toward her intended position.

Unknown to Hallowell, the *Bellerophon*, 74, had missed her intended anchorage opposite the *Franklin* and had not brought to until she was immediately abreast of *L'Orient*, only fifteen yards from her giant opponent whose upper deck was twelve feet higher than her own. Not surprisingly, she had got much the worst of the ensuing one-on-one duel. Severely damaged, with her captain and two hundred others killed or wounded, she cut her cable and ran for safety. Without warning she suddenly emerged from the smoke and darkness ahead of the *Swiftsure*.

Some overeager gun captain might well have fired upon the menacing

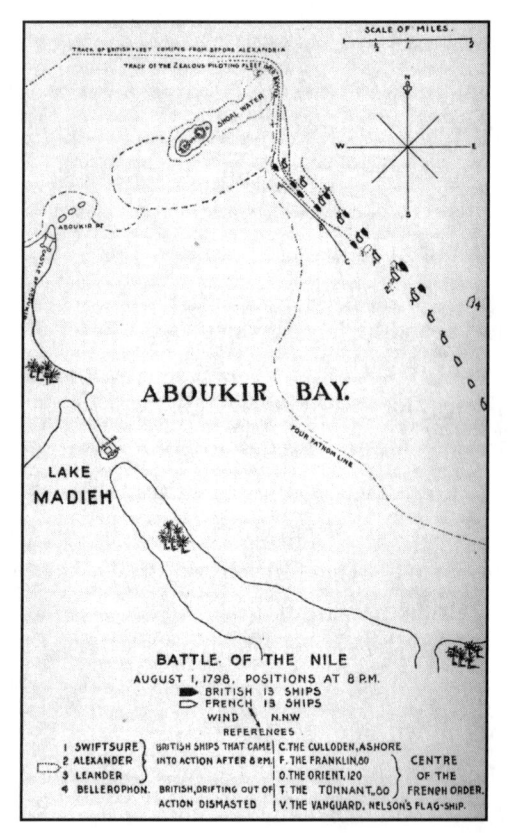

Plan, Battle of the Nile, 1 Aug. 1798

shape suddenly glimpsed through his gun port, triggering a broadside that could have finished the *Bellerophon*. Not a gun was fired by Hallowell's well-disciplined crew. At the last moment Hallowell noted that the fallen sails of the mystery ship were loose rather than furled as the French would have been. To his hail the ship replied 'Bellerophon going out of action disabled' and the shattered vessel limped away unmolested.

Both *L'Orient* and the *Franklin* were already firing on his ship when at 8:03 the *Swiftsure* anchored by the stern in the exact position Hallowell had chosen: opposite the strongest part of the French line, less than two hundred yards fine on the starboard bow of *L'Orient* and on the starboard quarter of the *Franklin*. The sails were clewed up, at 8:05 the anxiously awaited order to engage was given, and the *Swiftsure*'s double-shotted broadside roared out. From the *Swiftsure*'s position some of its guns could engage the *Franklin*, but most were brought to bear on the French flagship, which could only train a small number of its guns far enough forward to menace *Swiftsure*.

Following the *Swiftsure*, the *Alexander* passed between *L'Orient* and her next astern, the *Tonnant*, and anchored inside the French line opposite the gap between them, from which position she engaged them both. All the British ships were now in action. Even the 50-gun *Leander* had contrived to anchor athwart the gap between the *Peuple Souverain* and the *Franklin*, a position which allowed her to rake both vessels while avoiding exposure to their much heavier broadsides that otherwise would have quickly sunk her.

On this night young Midshipman Lee served as Hallowell's messenger and aide de camp. His memoirs include an account of the battle as seen from the *Swiftsure's* quarterdeck, from which Hallowell was directing the fight. As Lee remembered it, the flashes of the hundreds of guns 'were so vivid at times as to enable each party to distinguish clearly not only the colours of the respective contestants, but the disastrous results of battle upon them.' In need of refreshment, Hallowell asked Lee to fetch a few bottles of ginger ale for himself and his companions. While consuming his beverage on the starboard gangway, Hallowell remarked approvingly on how well *L'Orient* was shooting. He and Lee had just turned away when the truth of his observation was confirmed: a heavy shot shattered the bulwark at the very spot where the two had been standing.

The battle was approaching its climactic moment. By about nine that evening word spread through the British fleet that Admiral Nelson in the *Vanguard* had been wounded and carried below; the seven forward guns of his flagship were to have all their crews killed or wounded three times before the fight ended. Nelson's opponent, Admiral Brueys in *L'Orient*, had lost both legs, but with tourniquets applied continued to direct the battle from an armchair until he was cut in two by a shot from the *Swiftsure*.

About this time it was observed that a fire had broken out in the mizzen chains of *L'Orient*. Hallowell sent Lee to order the lieutenants and Captain Allen of the marines to direct the fire of every gun and musket that would bear upon the seat of the fire. At the same time he ordered ropes, spars, and gratings to be flung into the water for rescue purposes.

The French watched in consternation as the flames leapt up the rigging and worked their way down toward the ship's magazine. Lieutenant Berthelot was in charge of the 42-pounder battery on the lower gun deck. His men had been fighting with great bravery and tenacity, but now the middle deck above their heads caught fire and threatened to cave in upon them under the weight of its guns. To avoid certain death, the French sailors began to make their escape through the gun ports.

Realizing that nothing could be done, Berthelot himself stripped naked, dived through a gun port, and swam in the direction of the *Swiftsure*. Partway there he realized he had nothing to confirm his status as an officer and gentleman. Accordingly, he returned to the blazing ship and retrieved his hat, once more entered the water, and swam to the *Swiftsure*. Hauled aboard, he was escorted to the quarterdeck, still stark naked except for his precious headgear. In his schoolboy French, the astonished Hallowell asked, 'Who the devil are you?'

But there was little time for conversation. *L'Orient* was obviously doomed, and any ship near her when the inevitable explosion came might suffer the same fate. The heat was such that the pitch was running out of the *Swiftsure*'s deck seams. Hallowell was urged to move further off, but he reasoned that being within half a pistol shot (under a hundred yards) and slightly upwind he would be inside the radius of greatest danger. He directed marines to be posted with strict orders to shoot anyone who tried to cut the anchor cable. Hatches and gun ports were closed, each man was provided with a scrap of sail and bucket of water to extinguish fires, and everyone but he and a few others took shelter below. Firing decreased or ceased altogether as the attention of all the combatants focused on the doomed flagship.

At 9:37 'an awful and terrific glare of light blinding the very sight showed *Orient* blowing up with an astounding crash.... It was like an earthquake, the air rushing along the deck and below with inconceivable violence and creating a tremendous motion in the ship which existed for some minutes.' Bodies and debris were flung high in the air

Swiftsure illuminated as L'Orient *explodes at the Battle of the Nile*

before falling back like rain onto the sea and nearby ships. As Hallowell had foreseen, most of the fragments flew right over the *Swiftsure* and she suffered astonishingly little damage. He himself received only a 'slight graze.'

It is recorded that for many minutes after the awful end of *L'Orient* the guns fell nearly silent, as friend and foe paused in awe at what they had witnessed. When the firing resumed it was much less intense. The *Swiftsure* engaged the *Franklin* until she hailed that she surrendered. Since all *Swiftsure*'s boats had been smashed to pieces, Hallowell had to ask the captain of the *Defence* to take possession. Most French ships, including the *Tonnant* next astern of *L'Orient*, either surrendered or cut their cables and allowed themselves to run ashore, as did *l'Artémise*, she of the telltale lifebuoy.

As dawn broke, fighting spread toward the rear of the French line, where Admiral Villeneuve and the ships with him had been spectators throughout the battle. Being downwind of the engagement, he claimed successfully that he could not have joined in and he survived to lead another fleet to an even greater defeat seven years later. He weighed anchor and made his escape in the *Guillaume Tell*, along with the *Genereux* and two frigates, the British being too badly damaged to pursue.

Chaplain Willyams led the crew of the *Swiftsure* in offering thanks to God as the French prisoners looked on amused.

Of the eleven French ships of the line actually engaged, *L'Orient* was completely destroyed, seven were captured, and three were beached and burnt by their crews. No British ships had been destroyed or taken, but almost all had lost at least one mast and only the *Zealous* was combat ready the next day.

Over 5,000 French sailors were killed or missing, nearly 1,000 of them in *L'Orient*, which had only about seventy survivors. More than 3,000 French were captured. On the British side only two hundred and eighteen were killed and six hundred and seventy-seven wounded. Such were the fruits of concentration of force and superior gunnery.

To finance the expedition *L'Orient* had carried £600,000 in gold and treasure looted from the Swiss and Italians, plus three tons of gold and silver plate, twelve life-sized silver statues of the apostles, and the decorated gates from Malta's Valletta cathedral. All went to the bottom, where they remain.

At one stroke the British had regained control of the Mediterranean, ended Napoleon's dreams of the conquest of the east, and locked the French troops and their much-feared general out of Europe. The fact that the fate of Egypt had been decided by two European powers marked a milestone in the long decline of the Ottoman Empire. The victory led directly to the Second Coalition of Austria, Russia, and Naples against France, and to a series of allied victories on land. Some French historians believed that the Nile was such a crushing defeat that the French no longer had any possibility of achieving sea supremacy. In this view, Trafalgar was merely an epilogue. At the Chesapeake, Hallowell had already fought in one battle that changed history; arguably, this was his second.

The Nile was the second battle for which the Royal Navy awarded medals, a gold badge embossed with the letter 'N,' worn in the third

A commemorative collage of Nelson and his 'Band of Brothers'

buttonhole on the left side of the coat.

The French captured Nelson's first report, and for months the British government and people remained ignorant of events subsequent to Napoleon's landing in Egypt. The duplicate report finally reached London on October 2. It was another seven weeks before Halifax greeted the news with salutes and illuminations, and only on 31 January 1799, did the *Upper Canada Gazette* proclaim the glad tidings to the inhabitants of 'little muddy York.'

For old Benjamin Hallowell it was just in time. On the day news of the victory was published William Jarvis reported, 'Benjamin Hallowell fell from his horse yesterday. Much bruised but thinks lightly of it. I fear the old gentleman is not to last long.' There was time to receive congratulations from Governor Wentworth and to share with his daughter and his friends his pride in his son's exploits, but on 30 March the *Gazette* noted, 'DIED. Thursday last Benjamin Hallowell, Esq., in the 75th year of his age. The funeral will be on Tuesday next and will proceed from the house of the Chief Justice to the Garrison burying ground, at one o'clock precisely. The attendance of his friends is requested.'

In the early twentieth century, navy and army veterans in Toronto erected a memorial to those who had fallen in the War of 1812. It was placed in an enclosure in Victoria Park at the corner of Wellington and Bathurst Streets, the site of the original garrison burying ground. The enclosure also contains several much older headstones whose weathered inscriptions can no longer be read. It is impossible now to tell which one marks the grave of the last Commissioner of the American Board of Customs.

8

SURRENDER
1798–1801

Preserve us from the violence of the enemy.

From the Naval Prayer

Over the next several days the British made good their battle damage. As well as restoring the combat readiness of his own ship, Hallowell somehow found time to assist Admiral Nelson in his manifold responsibilities for the fleet as a whole. With Troubridge he approached the Castle of Aboukir under a white flag to negotiate the landing of the French prisoners. This was duly arranged, the French promising that the seamen would not serve again under arms. As soon as Napoleon learned of the transaction he broke the promise and augmented his army by forming the sailors into what he called the Nautic Legion.

On 8 August Hallowell took possession of Aboukir Island, demolished the battery, and brought twelve brass field guns and two thirteen-inch brass mortars on board the *Swiftsure*. The battery's iron guns were thrown into the sea, and the platforms and battlements destroyed.

Water was always a problem, so Hallowell set some Cornish miners of his crew to work digging wells on the island. They broke through into a cavern full of human bones with Greek writing on the walls, evidence of the antiquity of the spot, perhaps the site of the ancient city of Canopus.

By 10 August the *Swiftsure* was nearly combat ready. At dawn a French warship stood into the bay and the British ships lured her on by hoisting French colours. Too late she became suspicious and lay to. Hallowell gave chase and captured the *Fortune,* a corvette under the command of Citoyen Marchand. Uninformed of the fate of the French fleet, he broke down when told of the end of *L'Orient,* in which two of his brothers had been serving. The *Fortune* was not large, but she would yield a welcome addition to Hallowell's prize money from the battle, which came to something over £3,000 for each captain.

Three weeks after the battle, Nelson sailed for Sicily, leaving Troubridge with three ships, including the *Swiftsure,* to blockade Alexandria. The boredom of blockade service was often relieved by minor incidents of no importance except to those directly involved, but casting an interesting light on the realities of war in the Mediterranean.

A French cutter was sighted trying to elude the blockade and enter Alexandria. The *Swiftsure* gave chase and forced the cutter to beach itself short of the harbour. The cutter's crew wished to surrender but their passenger, General Cormin, insisted on landing and trying to reach Alexandria on foot. Suddenly the cutter's crew showed signs of great alarm, and Hallowell's crew saw a party of Arabs emerge from the dunes. Hallowell at once sent a boat to the rescue, and the midshipman in charge swam ashore with a line to enable the French to escape. The crew was more than willing to go, but the general and his aide refused to surrender to the British. The Arabs immediately shot them down and plundered their possessions.

The blockaded French suffered from a severe shortage of provisions. From time to time the mainly Danish and Swedish transports Napoleon had hired attempted to escape, but up to seventy of them were intercepted. Invariably the vessels were burned and their crews landed so that the number of useless mouths in Alexandria should not be reduced. The British lacked the manpower to detach prize crews, and could only watch in disgust as many hundreds of pounds of prize money went up in smoke.

On occasion French officers came on board the *Swiftsure* under a flag of truce to discuss the exchange of prisoners. They were astonished to find the ship in perfect order despite the recent battle. They were always dined on the best of the remaining provisions, including the fowl otherwise reserved for the sick berth. Their judgment was not improved by the copious quantities of wine they were pressed to consume. They left with the false impression that the blockading ships were well provisioned and could keep their station indefinitely, their shaky descent into their boats a source of much amusement to the watching sailors.

The Egyptian Club, as the captains present at the battle had styled themselves, had commissioned a jewelled and decorated sword as a gift to the man who had led them to victory. As it happened, a substantial portion of *L'Orient*'s mainmast with its iron fittings had either been caught in the *Swiftsure*'s rigging or recovered from the water. From it Hallowell ordered his ship's carpenter to fashion an additional, more personal, memento for his friend and commander. A desk, chair, or other article of furniture was possible but too commonplace. Hallowell's choice was anything but — it was a coffin, made to measure for Nelson's slight frame.

While the coffin was being built, young Midshipman Lee frequently

Arabs on Board the Swiftsure. *Watercolour by* Swiftsure's *Chaplain.*

climbed into it for a lark. On one such occasion Hallowell surreptitiously sent for the carpenter, and standing near the coffin, ordered him to screw the lid down, saying that the admiral's memento was to be not only the coffin but also the youngest person to have served in the battle. Lee emerged like a shot and never repeated his prank. The story spread through the ship like wildfire, to be chuckled over for days, a welcome break in the routine of blockade.

When the French took Alexandria they had captured a Turkish admiral. They now allowed him to sail from the port in a small vessel. Suspicious at the French generosity, Hallowell interrogated the admiral on board the *Swiftsure*. Not satisfied with the answers he boarded the Turkish ship and found a Frenchman named Beauchamp, dressed like a Turk, and some Arabs smoking their pipes in the captain's cabin. Troubridge ordered Hallowell to take Beauchamp to the Turkish island of Rhodes for investigation.

The *Swiftsure* had long been on short rations, reduced as Lee says to a noon meal of rice and pork and a dinner of pork and rice, supplemented by a small piece of Turkish black bread. Hallowell had maintained morale by ordering the miserable rations to be shared equally by the officers and crew, but the opportunity to replenish his provisions was very welcome. On 28 September the *Swiftsure* set sail.

One week later the *Swiftsure* was anchored off the town of Rhodes at the extreme eastern end of the island of which it was the capital. Hallowell called upon the ex-slave Hassan Bey, whom the sultan had promoted to the position of governor. Passing through a crowd of Mameluke guards, he was led to a seat where he bargained for provisions over cups of strong Turkish coffee. He was able to obtain fourteen bullocks and very welcome onions, lemons, and pumpkins. He also arranged to replenish the ship's stock of wine — an item of at least equal concern to the crew — with a local product. It arrived in goatskin bags, hairy side in, 'of good quality but not the best flavour.' The crew passed five very pleasant days embarking water and provisions in beautiful weather.

Hallowell formally turned Beauchamp over to the bey. The Frenchman produced a large sum of money that he claimed to be his own. Believing him, Hallowell had the coins counted out before the bey and wrote a letter to the British consul in Istanbul, verifying the tally as a precaution against robbery by the Turks.

It later transpired that Beauchamp was an agent of Napoleon. With the connivance of the Turkish admiral he was under orders to proceed to Constantinople and convince the new sultan to switch sides. The money had been given to him by his master to support his mission. Honest himself, Hallowell was reluctant to suspect a European gentleman of dishonesty, being at the same time perhaps too ready to suspect it of a Turk.

The harbour of Rhodes is open to winds from the east and southeast. Hallowell had ascertained that if gales were expected, ships weighed anchor and sailed for the sheltered Gulf of Marmorice on the Turkish mainland. Early in the morning of 12 October it began to blow very hard, and at one thirty in the morning the *Swiftsure* fired a gun as a signal for a pilot, who came on board about an hour later. By the time the ship had cleared the harbour a tremendous electrical storm was raging, the worst display of lightning the most veteran seamen had ever seen. The gales increased to hurricane force and even with the sails close-reefed both the main and mizzen topsails split and were torn to rags. The Gulf of Marmorice could not be reached, so the ship sought shelter in the Gulf of Simia.

The *Swiftsure* was able to enter a narrow inlet that seemed to offer shelter. The channel gradually widened, and Hallowell attempted to anchor. In the furious gusts of wind the anchor failed to hold and the ship dragged at a fearsome rate. So poor was the visibility and so desperate the situation that Hallowell was forced to con the ship from the forecastle, with the master standing by the quarterdeck wheel and personally directing the helmsmen.

Hallowell suddenly made out the shape of land perilously close and right ahead of the ship. There was no time to pass orders. Those on the quarterdeck were dumfounded to see their captain race aft, seize the wheel from the helmsman's hands and reverse the port turn the master had ordered. The bows steadied and began to move to starboard with agonizing slowness. The crew held its collective breath as the jib boom swung over a small island and the port side actually brushed the rocky shore. 'One minute more and Swiftsure and her gallant crew would have been forever lost to Britain had not the energy and decision of Captain Hallowell saved them.'

Disaster had been averted for the moment, but there was no time to relax. The demoralized pilot was on his knees praying, but otherwise took no further part in the proceedings. The rock-bottomed inlet had turned out to be a trap, and Hallowell decided to take his chances in the open sea. The wind continued to blow in furious gusts with a terrifying noise that drowned out even the claps of thunder, but so high were the overhanging cliffs that the water was almost smooth. This made it somewhat easier to make out the numerous rocks and shoals that beset the passage, and at length the open sea was reached. Providentially, the gale abated, and the *Swiftsure* set her course to return to Rhodes.

This may have been the first occasion on which a British warship had visited the island. Hallowell submitted a full description of the harbour describing the navigational dangers, sailing directions for anchoring in safe water, instructions for obtaining provisions and water, and the state of the fortifications. Two hundred years later warships visiting foreign ports are still noting such details to update the Port Information Book covering virtually every major harbour in the world.

In October the British were joined by a mixed squadron of Turkish and Russian ships. Thus reinforced, it was possible to consider an offensive operation. A few Turkish gunboats were placed under Hallowell's command to attack the Castle of Aboukir. He embarked five British seamen in each one, and in the *Swiftsure*'s gig led the little flotilla to within point-blank range of the fortifications. As he wrote to Hood, 'I kept my boat ahead of them to lead them on, sometimes coaxing, sometimes dancing and swearing at them for poltroons, but to very little effect.' Despite his leadership the Turkish sailors fell flat on deck or ran below each time a shot was fired from the castle, and their infrequent shots in reply were wildly inaccurate. The attackers were forced to withdraw.

Both the Turks and the Russians were wretchedly led. Hallowell found some of their senior officers smoking their pipes behind a breakwater at the height of the fight and had to force them to go to the scene

Assault landing at Aboukir, Hallowell in the stern of the leading boat. Watercolour by an eye-witness.

of action. He now added fifteen Russian sailors to the five British in each gunboat and renewed the attack. The Turkish sailors refused to row, so the boats of the *Swiftsure* had to tow the gunboats into position. One of the Turkish captains cut his tow and steered to Aboukir Island where he took refuge. Not surprisingly the second assault achieved no more than the first.

The next day Hallowell tried an assault landing on the beach to the eastward of the castle, using the *Swiftsure*'s boats and the Turkish gun vessels, their crews again augmented by British seamen. The French were strongly posted behind the sand dunes and opened a murderous fire as the boats neared the shore. In the gig the marine sitting between the captain and Lee was killed by a musket ball, but Hallowell pressed on. The gunboats refused to follow and open fighting broke out between the British and Turkish sailors. Hallowell had to break off his attack and personally quell the disturbance, but not before one Turk had been killed by a seaman with a handspike and the Turkish commanding officer wounded with the same weapon. Hallowell reported, 'Had I not gone on board initially I believe every Turk would have been slaughtered.'

Inter-allied problems reached a climax when the crew of one of the Turkish frigates mutinied. Bringing the *Swiftsure* within close range, Hallowell threatened he would sink the malcontents' ship if they did not return to duty. His previous firmness convinced the mutineers that he meant what he said, and they were soon brought to order. But it was obvious that the Turks in general were so lacking in training and discipline and were so badly led that any idea of offensive action was out of the question. Hood felt that Hallowell 'managed the Turks very nicely,' but Hallowell had lost all respect for his allies. Under better leadership on other occasions the Turks fought well. Hallowell had seen them at their undisciplined worst.

Occasionally, the *Swiftsure* bombarded the shore batteries. Following one such action a party of French officers came off under a flag of truce to protest that the British had employed an infernal weapon in the form of an inflammable projectile, contrary to the accepted usages of war. Well knowing the answer in advance, Hallowell summoned his gunner and in the presence of the French officers asked him to explain the matter. Mr. Parr answered forthrightly that the unusual projectiles had been taken from the magazine of the captured *Spartiate* and that he, Parr, was simply experimenting with them. Hallowell with difficulty managed to keep a straight face as the discomfited Frenchmen left the ship.

The next day two of the shells were taken to Aboukir Island and detonated. One duly exploded but the other merely burnt furiously and could not be extinguished even under water. Perhaps they were based on some form of the ancient Greek fire. Hallowell believed that the conflagration in *L'Orient* might have been started by one of these projectiles fired inaccurately from the *Tonnant* anchored close astern of the flagship. Parr had the projectiles that remained thrown overboard.

It was not until February 1799 that the *Swiftsure* and the *Zealous* were relieved on the Egyptian station and sailed to join Nelson at Palermo. It was storm season in the Mediterranean, a time when if possible ships remained in a sheltered anchorage. The unlucky *Swiftsure* once again encountered a terrific storm with winds of hurricane force. One of the quarter galleries was stove in and wooden covers had to be secured over the windows of the wardroom to prevent them from being shattered. The oldest seamen said they had never seen such waves — when in the troughs the crests seemed higher than the masthead. Men laboured at the pumps continuously to keep pace with the leakage through the strained hull. Lying to under a single storm staysail the *Swiftsure* made three or four knots of leeway and rolled her main yard and foreyards under at every lurch. The creaking of the beams and guns was truly frightening. Had a gun come adrift and begun careening from one side to the other it would probably have smashed the ship to pieces. Thanks to superb seamanship she survived.

A few days later the *Swiftsure* sighted Sicily, with Mount Etna and its plume of smoke dominating the scene. Her destination was the port of Palermo, temporary capital of the Kingdom of Naples. Approaching from seaward, the scene was magnificent, the green of the surrounding orchards contrasting with the dazzling whiteness of the stone from which all the buildings of the city were constructed. As the *Swiftsure* came to anchor in this entrancing setting, the tribulations of blockade and hurricanes faded from men's memories, and for the first time in months there was a release from seemingly unending stress.

That very evening Hallowell was invited to a magnificent ball at the royal court. The hostess was Lady Hamilton, wife of the British ambassador Sir William Hamilton. A week later Hallowell repaid her hospitality by hosting a ball on board the *Swiftsure*, even more elaborate than the one he had given in Gibraltar. The quarterdeck was hung with the flags of all the countries allied with Great Britain, those of Naples and Britain being intertwined with great taste. The guests included Lord and Lady Hamilton, Nelson, Neapolitan nobility and Hallowell's fellow naval officers. There was dancing on the quarterdeck, cards on the poop, and unlimited refreshments everywhere. It was broad daylight by the time the last of the guests departed. Staging such an entertainment was a huge personal expense; Hallowell had not yet received his share of the Nile prize money, but it was known that it would be significant.

Rumours had reached the blockading ships, but these were Hallowell's first opportunities to assess for himself the relationship between his friend Nelson and the wife of the ambassador. Lady Emma

Hamilton had begun her career as a vivacious girl of humble background caught up in the escapades of the wilder spirits of fashionable London. She had borne an illegitimate and unacknowledged child before becoming the mistress of Charles Greville, second son of the Earl of Warwick. Greville more or less passed her on to his uncle, Sir William Hamilton, who was so captivated that in 1791 he regulated their arrangement by marrying her. He was sixty-three and she twenty-four. She was extraordinarily beautiful and was frequently painted by the fashionable portraitist Romney.

In Britain their social status would have been problematic, but at the Neapolitan court they were fully accepted and Emma did nothing to excite scandal. Sir William was an aesthete interested as much in the antiquities and customs of Italy as in his ambassadorial duties. Lady Hamilton more than compensated for his detachment by throwing herself into public affairs and becoming the trusted confidante of the Queen. As sister of the guillotined Marie Antoinette, the Queen was an inveterate opponent of revolutionary France — and she exercised enormous influence over her husband.

Nelson had met Lady Hamilton briefly in 1793, but their relationship really began when the *Vanguard* was towed into Naples Bay in late September 1798, fresh from the victory of the Nile. Lady Hamilton accompanied her husband on board to welcome him and threw her arms around him in an excess of hero worship. A week later she hosted a huge party to celebrate his fortieth birthday and at every opportunity continued to feed his vanity by incessant flattery. Fluent in French and Italian, she became Nelson's go-between to the Neapolitan court and royal family. It was not long before gossip suggested that the working relationship was becoming something more. If so, Sir William showed no objection.

Always eager to be at the enemy, Nelson joined with Queen Maria Carolina and Lady Hamilton in persuading King Ferdinand to declare war on the French. Although not yet ready to go to war herself, Austria appeared supportive and sent General Mack to lead the Neapolitan forces. Rashly relying on immediate assistance, King Ferdinand was persuaded, and in November 1798 'the most beautiful army in Europe' advanced to Rome. Here it encountered the French. The Austrians failed to assist and the Neapolitans were driven back in a disgraceful rout. By January 1799 the French had taken the city of Naples and established the bourgeois Parthenopean Republic espousing the ideals of the French Revolution. In disarray the royal family and the Hamiltons fled in Nelson's flagship to the alternative capital of Palermo, safe as long as the British fleet could prevent a landing on the island of Sicily.

At the Nile, Nelson had refused to be treated out of turn for the blow to his head, nor did he take the rest appropriate to a possible concussion. Thereafter he was frequently subject to splitting headaches. He was depressed that Troubridge had been left out of the rewards for the Nile victory because the grounded *Culloden* had taken no direct part. Perhaps most of all he felt slighted that he had been made only a lord, whereas Jervis had been made an earl after what was arguably a less decisive triumph. He was more than usually susceptible to the adulation of a beautiful woman.

Nelson was severely criticized by his enemies in the service, of whom Keith was one, and even many of his friends were disappointed and warned him against the potential scandal. Hallowell was not among the critics, but he did not immediately present the coffin made from the mast of *L'Orient*. Perhaps a few finishing touches were needed. Perhaps there was no suitable opportunity during the ten-day period during which Hallowell and Nelson were both in Palermo, filled as it was by the hectic round of entertainments and gambling that occupied the Neapolitan court. Most likely Hallowell found a Nelson he hardly recognized, the result of the most recent wound, overwork, late nights, and entanglement with Lady Hamilton. He might have feared that his extraordinary memento would be perceived as a veiled warning against the brewing scandal and would be resented for that reason.

At the end of March the *Swiftsure* was dispatched to join Troubridge in the reconquest of the mainland portion of the Kingdom of Naples. Most of the French had withdrawn to counter the threat of the Second Coalition between Austria and Russia, and a Neapolitan army under Cardinal Ruffo was advancing on Naples city. The Cardinal was assisted by the ordinary people who were devoted to King Ferdinand and far from sympathetic to the puppet Parthenopean Republic. On 2 April the city was recaptured, apart from two forts held by the republicans, and the citadel of St. Elmo which was garrisoned by the French rearguard.

Again Hallowell served on shore. In order for a siege battery to come into action against St. Elmo it was necessary to cut down a tree that obstructed the line of sight. It was well within range of enemy fire and the Neapolitan gunners refused to perform the task. Hallowell and Troubridge went forward to distract the enemy, who duly fired a shot that luckily struck the ground just between the two officers. Meanwhile the tree was levelled.

The French Admiral Bruix had escaped from Brest. Admiral Lord Keith, commanding the blockade of Cadiz, sighted but did not molest the French fleet as it passed and successfully joined the Spanish in Cartagena. There were now forty-three allied ships in the Mediterranean against thirty-five British, the latter divided into several widely separated squadrons. Believing the combined fleet to be destined for Sicily, Nelson gave orders for his squadron of nine third-rates, including the *Swiftsure*, to concentrate at sea in mid-May.

Hallowell sensed that there would never be a more auspicious occasion to present his memento; indeed, with the vastly superior allied force at large it seemed that the coffin might well be needed shortly. Moreover, away from the temptations and intrigues of Naples, Nelson was much more his former self and less likely to take offence at what was, to say the least, a most unusual gift. Accordingly, on 22 May Hallowell made his presentation along with an explanatory note:

Sir;

I have taken the liberty of presenting you with a coffin made from the mainmast of 'L'Orient,' that when you have finished your military career in this world you may be buried in one of your trophies. But that that period may be far distant is the earnest wish of your sincere friend,

Benjamin Hallowell

The secret had been well kept. Nelson was astonished but after the initial surprise declared himself to be delighted. The crew of the *Vanguard* was aghast when they realized that the gift was a coffin. 'We shall have hot work of it indeed, you see the Admiral intends to fight until he is killed, and there he is to be buried,' said one of his old shipmates. The gift was placed upright on the after bulkhead of his cabin behind the chair where he sat at dinner. When he transferred his flag to the *Foudroyant*, the coffin went with him and was displayed on the quarterdeck. Seeing some of the officers scrutinizing it, Nelson remarked, 'You may look at it gentlemen, but depend on it none of you shall have it.'

There has been considerable speculation on the message Hallowell may have been trying to convey by his unusual choice of gift. One recent author has characterized it as 'mawkish,' that is, 'sentimental in a feeble or sickly way.' To associate such terms with the hard-headed and independent Hallowell is ludicrous. Equally unlikely is the theory that it expressed disapproval of Nelson's liaison with Emma Hamilton. Hallowell must have conceived the idea shortly after the battle, when the romance had not even begun. Nelson would hardly have treasured the memento if he saw it as a criticism of his private life, nor would he have employed Hallowell as a personal messenger to Emma, as he afterwards did.

The most likely explanation is the simplest — Hallowell had been with Nelson at Calvi when he lost his eye, he had fought at Santa Cruz just before Nelson lost his arm there, and had been at the Nile when the admiral was carried below with a dangerous-looking wound. With this background he was better placed than most to remind his friend and commander of his humanity and his mortality, and he did so in a way that commanded attention, with 'an offering so strange and yet so suited to the occasion.'

At the end of the month Nelson expressed to St. Vincent his continued high opinion of the two captains he had had no opportunity to observe while they were blockading Alexandria: 'Hood and Hallowell are as active and good as ever, not that I mean to say any are otherwise, but these are men of resource.' Apparently the gift had done nothing to alter Nelson's opinion of its highly capable if slightly eccentric donor.

Having failed to intercept Bruix as he passed Cadiz, Keith sailed to reinforce St. Vincent in the Mediterranean. Soon afterwards St. Vincent was forced to give up his command due to ill health and on 6 June Keith became commander-in-chief. St. Vincent commented on this appointment to Earl Spencer in ambiguous terms. According to this very demanding admiral, the Scots were naturally deficient in their ability to assume responsibility: 'You will never find an officer of that nation figure in supreme command; they are only fit for drudgery. Lord Keith is by far the best I have met with by land or sea.'

One week after taking command Keith ordered Nelson to join him with all or part of his squadron to help defend Minorca. Nelson refused because in his probably impaired judgment Naples was more important than Minorca. The issue was not really whether one of the two possible objectives was more important than the other, but whether without reinforcements Keith's outnumbered force would have been defeated by Bruix if the fleets had met.

Nelson later sent four ships under Duckworth, but was nevertheless reprimanded by the Admiralty for what amounted to outright disobedience of orders. Bruix had achieved what might have been a decisive superiority, but did nothing with it. Long before Duckworth reached Minorca the French repassed Gibraltar westward en route to Brest, and Keith followed, leaving Nelson temporarily in command in the Mediterranean.

There followed a series of amphibious mopping up exercises as Nelson used his squadron to help free southern Italy. Again Hallowell fought on land, this time alongside Troubridge, leading a thousand seamen and marines in successful siege operations against the city of Capua, where Troubridge praised him for staying night and day in the field to erect the siege batteries. After the place fell, Troubridge returned to Naples and Hallowell went on to Civitavecchia, the port of Rome.

In discussions with representatives of the French garrison in Rome he displayed great perception and a talent for dissimulation:

> *This day a flag of truce came off from Civita Vecchia with General Dubardieu bearing the enclosed letter from General Belair. As the whole was but French humbug I fed them well and sent them ashore with my answer. I rather suspect their object was to sound me with regard to any attack that was to be made on them. I gave them to understand, but in indirect terms, that they would soon be besieged. I believe they are sensible that they cannot hold out long, and I am confirmed in this idea by their overstrained civility to me, and the many fulsome complements they paid to the English nation. But to everything they said I turned a deaf ear.*

It is interesting to contrast this meeting with Hallowell's encounter with the agent Beauchamp. He perceived Beauchamp as an innocent gentleman at risk of being cheated, and somewhat naively assisted him. Perhaps he had learned a lesson. However, at Civitavecchia he was dealing with a recognized enemy, against whom it was legitimate to employ deception and psychological pressure. The negotiations would almost certainly have been conducted in French, the international language of diplomacy. If so, Hallowell's early schooling must have given him excellent command of that language.

The forces of the Second Coalition went from success to success, undermining the popularity and credibility of the Directorate. In Egypt Napoleon Bonaparte recognized that his political opportunity had come. Abandoning his army, he evaded the blockade on 18 August 1799, with a small squadron of frigates. His passage was slow, but on 9 October he landed at Frejus near Toulon and hastened to Paris. Within a month he had staged a coup against the discredited Directory and made himself First Consul of France. The other two consuls were nonentities, and the revised constitution eliminated most of the few remaining vestiges of revolutionary democracy.

Rather than capitulate to the despised Neapolitan army, General Belair chose to surrender Rome to the Royal Navy on 22 September 1799. Just before Rome fell, the *Swiftsure* was ordered to join Admiral Duckworth off Minorca, and Captain Louis took the surrender in Hallowell's stead. It was not every day that a French army surrendered

Nelson at Naples 1799, under physical and emotional stress, wearing the Sultan's jewelled ornament.

the papal capital to the Royal Navy. It must have rankled that after having done most of the work Hallowell was deprived of the unique if largely meaningless distinction of being Rome's captor.

But there was welcome compensation. At the Nile the heat from the doomed *L'Orient* had melted the tar from the *Swiftsure*'s deck seams, and ever since then water had leaked into the mess decks whenever it rained or heavy seas came aboard. The ship had been through two hurricanes, and Hallowell had reported on more than one occasion that it had become impossible for men to sleep dry under such conditions.

Bruix's fleet had left the Mediterranean and the campaign on the Italian coast was successfully concluded. Hallowell now felt justified in requesting that his ship be detached to have her decks recaulked and the wear and tear of the last year and a half made good. En route to Gibraltar he fell in with two small French merchant vessels and captured both. They were not particularly valuable, but as the only captain present he retained the whole of the captains' one-quarter share of the prize money.

On arrival at Gibraltar his first duty was to meet with Commissioner Inglefield to initiate the repairs to his ship. Inglefield had been commissioner at Gibraltar since November 1794. The two had served together in the West African squadron, and by coincidence both had also served at different times in the *Lively* and the *Robust*. Business concluded, his old friend would certainly invite him to the official residence for his first meal ashore in many months. Since the *Swiftsure* was swarming with workmen, Hallowell may well have accepted an invitation to live with his old commander for the duration of the repairs.

If Inglefield had an ulterior motive for his hospitality, his stratagem succeeded. Hallowell had met young Ann Inglefield two years before when she was twenty-two. At twenty-four she was still unmarried, and perhaps not particularly marriageable, since Inglefield was by no means wealthy. Her later portrait is not particularly flattering, but we have no idea of her attractiveness as a young woman. Absolutely nothing is on record concerning her character or personality, but she later raised a large family almost single-handedly.

Distribution of the Nile prize money had begun after the obligatory one-year delay, and Hallowell's share would be nearly £2200, more than four years' pay. He was at last in a position to convince an anxious father that he could support a wife. When he had parted from Miss Coffin eight years before Hallowell had vowed never to fall in love again. Whether he did so now we cannot know, but with seeming inevitability Benjamin Hallowell and Ann Inglefield were married at the Garrison Church at Gibraltar on 17 February 1800.

After a honeymoon of less than a month, the *Swiftsure* returned to Admiral Duckworth's squadron blockading Cadiz. In early April the force captured two Spanish frigates and nine richly laden merchant vessels. Notwithstanding the rewards of the Nile, the prize money would have been particularly welcome for the newly married Hallowell — but the *Swiftsure* was not with the rest of the squadron when the captures occurred and he did not share.

In late 1799 Admiral Keith returned to the Mediterranean as commander-in-chief, superseding Nelson. By this time Nelson and Lady Hamilton were lovers and their no-longer-concealed relationship was the scandal of Europe. Ill and distracted, Nelson had virtually abdicated his duties and wished nothing more than to return to England with Emma. A disgusted Keith made every effort to accommodate his wishes.

The British army had played little part in the war up to now, and what it had done was far from glorious. A major detachment had just been evacuated from Holland after failing to take Amsterdam, and a landing at Ferrol in Spain had been equally unsuccessful.

A large expeditionary force was assigned to the Mediterranean theatre under General Abercromby, and the government was pressing Keith and Abercromby to so something with it. Their first intention was to assault Cadiz, but they could not agree on a plan and the idea was abandoned with some mutual acrimony.

It was decided to land in Egypt and defeat the French army Napoleon had deserted. Success would give the British an important bargaining counter in the peace negotiations that were expected to begin in the near future. French strength in Egypt was estimated at 13,000 men when it was actually 32,000. The British force amounted to 16,000, but some help was hoped for from the Turks.

Hallowell was one of the few officers who knew anything about Egypt, and Keith asked him for his recommendations as to where the landing force was to concentrate before making its assault. Sir Sidney Smith had recommended Malta, but Keith also accepted Hallowell's advice to concentrate at Marmorice, the Turkish harbour that the *Swiftsure* had failed to find in the terrible storm off Rhodes. Hallowell also provided advice on the navigation along the Egyptian coast and the best source of water for the fleet and troops after the landing.

On 1 January 1801, Hallowell's fortieth birthday, the fleet of seven warships and over one hundred and fifty transports anchored at Marmorice. Here the men were rested and exercised in the techniques of assault landings. The bad weather that seemed to follow the *Swiftsure* manifested itself in a terrific storm of hail and wind that lasted for two days. A torrent of water swept away the soldiers' tents and the *Swiftsure* was struck by lightning, fortunately with no loss of life.

For the only time in his career, a ship under Hallowell's command carried a flag officer, Admiral Sir Richard Bickerton, second in command to Keith. Whenever possible admirals hoisted their flags in three-decked first- or second-rate ships, where they had their own separate suite at the after end of the upper deck. A two-decked third-rate such as the *Swiftsure* did not offer this luxury, and admiral and captain necessarily lived together in the latter's cabin. If the two men were not congenial or if the admiral interfered in the working of the ship, strong antipathies could arise, but Hallowell and Bickerton seem to have got along well and they remained lifelong friends. Bickerton's flag lieutenant was Hallowell's new brother-in-law, Samuel Hood Inglefield, already with eight years of sea service under his belt.

Hallowell's local knowledge made him the obvious choice to lead the fleet into Aboukir Bay. On anchoring, the cable of Keith's flagship the *Foudroyant* actually snagged the wreck of *L'Orient*. The fleet waited out bad weather until March 8, and then made the amphibious attack vividly described by veteran seaman John Nichol:

> Belonged to one of the boats. Captain Cochrane was beach-master and had the ordering of the troops in the landing. We began to leave the ships about twelve o'clock, and reached the shore about sunrise in the morning. We rowed very slow with our oars muffled. It was a pleasant night; the water was very still; and all was silent as death. No one spoke; but each cast an anxious look to the shore then at each other, impatient to land. Each boat carried about 100 men and did not draw nine inches of water. The French cavalry were ready to receive us but we soon drove them back, and landed eight thousand men the first morning. We had good sport at landing the troops, as the Frenchmen made a stout resistance. We brought back the wounded to the ships.

The army captured the Castle of Aboukir and marched on Alexandria. Having failed to prevent the landing, General Menou decided to attack the British on the isthmus between Lake Mariotis and the sea. 21 March saw a desperate battle, the likes of which even the French veterans of the Army of Italy had never seen. The result was a decisive defeat for the French, but the respected General Abercromby was severely wounded and died a week later on board the *Foudroyant*. The victory opened the way to Alexandria, but had an even more profound and lasting psychological significance. As the Marquis of Buckingham wrote to Grenville, 'We appear to have broken that magical invincibility *sur terre* of the great nation.'

For the only time in his career Hallowell was present at an amphibious operation without being in the forefront of the fighting ashore. Admiral Keith managed the complicated business of the landing and ongoing support to the army, functioning as his 'own controller, contract and purchase agent, director of transports and director of works.' Whatever his operational capabilities, he had no rival in the navy for administrative ability and sheer hard work.

Under Keith, Admiral Bickerton in the *Swiftsure* was responsible for watching the army's back against an attempt by the French navy to disrupt the operation or reinforce the French General Menou. Their Mediterranean squadron was commanded by the skilful Admiral Ganteaume. He had been Admiral Brueys' chief of staff at the Nile, but had escaped in a launch before the flagship exploded. He was under Napoleon's strict orders to aid the army in Egypt at any cost. Ganteaume had made more than one unsuccessful attempt to obey his orders, so continued vigilance was essential. Nevertheless, Hallowell found the time to embroil himself with Admiral Lord Keith in a quarrel that would adversely affect the rest of his career.

For long there had been bad blood between the two, arising in the first place from Hallowell's temporary relief of Captain George Elphinstone (who became Lord Keith) of the *Robust* during the siege of Toulon. Perhaps motivated by resentment, the latter's fabricated report of possible mutiny had triggered Hallowell's removal from command of the *Courageux* in 1794, a wrong that was only righted thanks to information Hallowell received in a chance encounter. Under any circumstances Hallowell would have found service under

Keith distasteful in the extreme.

Unfortunately, at this juncture, Hallowell's personal feelings about Keith meshed perfectly with opinion among his colleagues. Keith used to say that his father had given him £5 when he joined the navy and told him to make his fortune. This he had more than accomplished and some of his fellow officers murmured that he was a little too much concerned with the acquisition of prize money. Some believed that Keith retained prize money received for distribution to the fleet and used it in order to profit from foreign exchange dealings, that he interfered too much in minor matters, and even that his word was not to be trusted. Hallowell's friend Nelson was no admirer of Keith, and had apparently got away with flatly disobeying one of his orders. Some officers felt that Keith's failure to bring Brueys to action in the summer of 1799 showed that he was simply not up to the job of commander-in-chief.

On 1 April 1801, Lord Nelson won a hard-fought battle against the Danish fleet at Copenhagen. (This was the occasion of the famous and probably true story of Nelson putting his telescope to his blind eye and announcing that he really did not see his superior officer's signal to break off the action.) His victory put an end to the League of Armed Neutrality, rendering the French much more susceptible to the idea of a negotiated peace. Keith's discontented subordinates were almost certainly aware of this development by early May, and the contrast between the remembered teamwork of Nelson's Band of Brothers and the atmosphere in Keith's squadron would have been painful.

On 4 May all captains were summoned to a routine court martial held on board Bickerton's flagship the *Swiftsure*. After the trial they took advantage of this rare opportunity to compare notes. There was general dissatisfaction with Keith's alleged failure to procure fresh provisions for the sick and wounded, although such provisions were supposed to be readily available on shore.

The three senior captains — Cochrane, Louis, and Martin — signed a letter on behalf of all of them strongly urging Keith to do something about stocking fresh provisions. Keith replied that he was doing his best and severely admonished the captains for their highly improper interference. The captains replied the same day that they were only doing their duty by bringing the matter to the admiral's attention — in effect rejecting Keith's criticism. This time the letter was signed by all eleven captains, including Hallowell. Still on the same day Keith replied, reiterating his opinion of the captains' interference and advising them that he was forwarding all the correspondence to the Admiralty, which in due course issued a mild castigation of the captains.

In remonstrating collectively with their superior officer, the captains had come perilously close to an act of mutiny. On 9 May, the day of their first letter, Hallowell sent Keith one of his own which was to lead to an extraordinary paper war between the two of them. It eventually involved the Admiralty and the Navy Board, very nearly deprived Hallowell of a peacetime command that he could not have afforded to lose, and was still reverberating nearly fifteen years later.

The issue was mundane enough, the price of shoes. Keith's secretary, Mr. Brown, had been entrusted with a large sum of money and the authority to purchase clothing and other necessities, known then (as now) as slops, for resale to the crews of the fleet. Keith allowed him 'a liberal commission' to prevent 'the unnecessary multiplication and consequent complication of accounts.' Although the *Swiftsure* already had an ample stock of shoes, she was ordered to take on board part of a large consignment purchased at Palermo by Brown's agent Meek. A general fleet directive then fixed the resale price at a level ten per cent higher than Hallowell understood the *Northumberland* to have paid for the same type of shoe at the same place at the same time.

The inference was that the difference was being pocketed by Brown with or without Keith's knowledge. Hallowell always showed great concern for his men and went out of his way to treat them fairly, and no doubt this was his main motivation in the action he took. But there was certainly more to it than that. One can picture the scene: the captains gathered in Hallowell's cabin discussing their remonstrance over the provisions for the sick, in the context of a general antipathy toward Keith, Hallowell casually mentioning the high price of the shoes and Captain Martin of the *Northumberland* making an off-hand statement that his own purser had paid much less for the same shoes at the same place and at the same time as Brown's agent. No doubt libations were being consumed. In the enthusiasm of the moment Hallowell immediately put pen to paper and his letter was probably carried to Keith in the same boat as the captains' collective remonstrance, an unfortunate juxtaposition.

Keith's reaction on reading the two missives can be imagined. His response to the captains we have already seen. He waited until next day before replying to Hallowell and then wrote that he had already examined the vouchers 'and was perfectly satisfied that the transaction was honourable and correct,' and that he had kept the Navy Board fully informed.

Nursing his personal grievance, and swept up in the general dissatisfaction, Hallowell now committed a huge error of judgment. On 11 May, one day after receiving Keith's reply, he went over his commander's head and sent copies of both letters to the Navy Board, with the request that the board investigate further. Typically, he also informed Keith in writing of what he was doing.

Before he wrote, Hallowell had taken the precaution of checking with Captain Martin that his facts were correct. Martin confirmed his story as to quality, price, and origin of the shoes, but was no longer completely certain that the *Northumberland*'s purchase was made at exactly the same time as Brown's. Nevertheless, Hallowell remained convinced that any time difference was certainly too brief for any meaningful changes to have occurred in either the price of shoes or the exchange rate. Much later he was to learn that at least nine months had actually elapsed between the two purchases, and that in the interval the price of Sicilian shoes had risen and that the exchange rate had moved against the pound.

Meanwhile a more serious subject of contention had developed between Hallowell and Keith. The *Swiftsure* had last had a long maintenance period in February 1800, at the time of Hallowell's marriage. Fifteen months of hard service later, the shipwrights of the navy yards at Gibraltar and Minorca were reporting that she was in a dangerous state and in need of repairs that could only be carried out in a dockyard, of which there were none in the Mediterranean. Hallowell wished to remain, but it was imperative that the ship return to England as soon as possible. Admiral Bickerton requested Keith to allow him to shift his flag to a more seaworthy vessel and to exchange captains in order to retain

Hallowell as commander of his flagship. A few days after receiving the joint letter and Hallowell's complaint about the shoes, Keith authorized Bickerton to shift his flag, but refused to allow Hallowell to change ships.

In the meantime Ganteaume had sailed from Toulon in yet another attempt to carry out the orders of Napoleon. His zeal was stimulated by the presence on board his flagship of the First Consul's youngest brother Jerome Bonaparte. Some ships were so badly manned that they had to be sent home, but Ganteaume continued with four line of battle ships and one frigate and some smaller vessels and transports. Keith learned of his sortie on 19 May, and Ganteaume reached the North African coast on 25 May. One of his corvettes succeeded in getting into Alexandria, but a few of his transports were captured. The rest of his force lingered near Derna on the Libyan coast in hopes of landing reinforcements, but were deterred by the unfriendly attitude of the local Arabs. Unaware of Ganteaume's exact position, Keith believed the danger had passed and detached four of his line of battle ships to Malta under Admiral Sir John Borlase Warren.

On 26 May Hallowell addressed a strong yet respectful letter to Keith on the issue of the *Swiftsure*'s combat readiness, of course making no mention of the shoes. He first drew Keith's attention to the fact that the prevailing winds were shifting to the west and northwest, foul for a passage from Alexandria to Gibraltar. He went on to remind the admiral of the adverse reports from the chief shipwrights at Gibraltar and Minorca testifying to his ship's unseaworthiness, which in their opinion had actually rendered her so weak that they would have to treat her very carefully even to repair her. Then came a detailed description of her many defects, which meant that:

> In our last gale, notwithstanding the hand pump was constantly going, we were obliged to pump her out thrice, sometimes four times in a watch with the chain pumps. While your Lordship was in expectation of an Enemy Squadron here you never heard complaints from me; but as the defects are daily increasing I have been induced to make this representation to you.... I am of opinion that every exertion and care will be necessary to navigate the Swiftsure to England,

> by taking advantage of every wind in moderate weather and sparing her as much as possible when blowing strong. I hope your Lordship will not deem this statement disrespectful or improper; but as I think ten weeks at this time of year a very good passage for a single ship from Alexandria to Spithead I have thought it my duty to make this representation while there is a probability of her reaching England and by getting a thorough repair becoming again a serviceable ship to the country.

The message here is that Hallowell wished to sail independently to avoid convoy escort duty. This would have been obvious to Keith. On the next day he dashed that prospect in a letter telling Hallowell that he could sail as soon as his landed sailors and marines had been re-embarked 'and the convoy in Aboukir Bay ready to sail, your orders for proceeding to Britain will be delivered to you.'

Hallowell did not give up. In his same-day reply to Keith he again emphasized that if the *Swiftsure* sailed with a convoy she would be subject to unavoidable delays that would extend the voyage into September and the equinoctial gales. Furthermore, in every storm Hallowell would be so busy worrying about his own ship that he could not look after the convoy properly. For the good of the service and the crew serving under him he once more pleaded to be allowed to sail independently, but 'Having made this report I shall cheerfully obey whatever orders your Lordship may think proper to give.'

Keith had already issued Hallowell's sailing orders, directing him to proceed via Malta, Minorca, Gibraltar, and Lisbon to Spithead, collecting ships for his convoy as he went. The voyage would obviously be prolonged into the season of bad weather. 'As the *Swiftsure* has been reported to be in an imperfect state' he authorized Hallowell to have the ship re-surveyed at any of the ports en route and remain there if he judged it necessary. He was also allowed to land some of his guns if he believed it would help to ease the ship. Keith did not acknowledge that landing guns would reduce the *Swiftsure*'s effectiveness as an escort.

These orders forced Hallowell to escort a convoy, yet they took just enough account of the *Swiftsure*'s unseaworthiness to get Keith off the hook if the ship should suffer a disaster. It was a no-win situation for Hallowell, but he would certainly have obeyed without question had it not been for one phrase in the orders. Keith had reduced Hallowell's detailed concerns about the dangerous state of his ship to an innocuous phrase: 'As the Swiftsure has been reported to be in an imperfect state'

If Keith had tried to provoke his subordinate he had certainly succeeded. Up to now Hallowell had been firm but respectful, but in the face of such gross misrepresentation he could not prevent himself from reacting as he had done over the shoes:

> As your Lordship has in one part of your Instructions mentioned 'that the Swiftsure has been reported to be in an imperfect state' I must inform your Lordship that no such report has ever been made to me; but the report of the last survey says 'that the Swiftsure is in a very dangerous state, that she should be sent home immediately, and if she continues in this country any longer it is a matter of doubt if she could reach England or not.'

So far, blunt but not quite calling his superior officer a liar. But he went on:

> Knowing this statement to be correct I shall feel it my duty to warn the Masters of trading ships under my convoy of the state of the ship and shall inform the Underwriters of the same, that no responsibility shall be attached to me if I am obliged to abandon the ships placed under my protection.

Such actions would have reverberated among the shipowners, merchants, and insurers of the City of London, whose commerce provided the resources to sustain Britain's war effort. Had Hallowell made good on this challenge he no doubt would have been court-martialled and disgraced. Perhaps he received some wise advice or even a verbal order from Admiral Bickerton, who was just on the point of shifting his flag. In any event Hallowell accepted the inevitable without a public challenge and prepared to sail. Typical of the ingrained sense of duty of the navy, he and Keith exchanged several last minute administrative communications in punctilious style. An uninformed reader would be quite unable to deduce from them that the authors were in a state of bitter enmity.

At this precise time Samuel Hood Inglefield was serving as flag-lieutenant to Admiral Keith. He must have known at least some of what was going on, but the slightest attempt to support his brother-in-law would of course have been out of the question.

Hallowell's convoy sailed from Aboukir on 3 June 1801. By Keith's orders eighty of his best men had been drafted to other ships, and fifty-nine sick men being repatriated were sent on board in lieu. The last time he had left the Bay of Aboukir the enthusiasm of Nelson's command and the Battle of the Nile was still fresh in his memory. Now angry and frustrated, he recognized that his quarrel with Keith could never be settled to his advantage.

As he had predicted, the convoy made slow progress against the contrary winds. Unbeknownst to Hallowell, it passed within sight of Admiral Ganteaume, who mistook the numerous sails on the distant horizon for Keith's fleet and ran for the safety of Toulon. On June 10 Keith became aware of Ganteaume's presence on the African coast and confessed that he was uneasy about the safety of Hallowell's convoy.

In total ignorance, Hallowell continued on a course that would have kept him well clear of Ganteaume had not a chance encounter changed everything. On 19 June the *Swiftsure* exchanged recognition signals with the cutter *Pygmy*, who flew the signal for 'Intelligence to Communicate.' Summoned on board the *Swiftsure*, her commanding officer Lieutenant Sheppard informed the surprised Hallowell that a French squadron was in the area.

Sheppard also presented a letter from Admiral Keith to the senior officer at Malta, which Hallowell opened to learn that it directed Admiral Warren to intercept the French squadron on its return to France. Hallowell feared that if Warren was at sea he might be taken unawares by Ganteaume's superior force before he received Keith's warning. He quickly decided that the safety of Malta and of Warren's force was more important than that of the convoy. On 22 June he parted company and hurried on in search of Warren.

Hallowell's decision was based on the insight that the *Swiftsure* alone could not protect her convoy if Ganteaume intercepted it, but that the addition of another 74 might be decisive if Warren's squadron were to encounter the French. But another factor may have been at work in his subconscious. He was with the convoy only under protest, and psychologically receptive to any plausible pretext for leaving it and acting independently, as he had begged to do from the beginning. Whatever the outcome, he would at some point have to justify his decision to his commander-in-chief, the same Lord Keith, with whom he had just quarrelled.

At three o'clock on the morning of 24 June, with the wind at northwest, Lieutenant Greenway, the officer of the watch, reported five sail in sight to leeward. Even in the half-light Hallowell had little doubt that this was the French squadron. At dawn his suspicions were confirmed; the enemy consisted of four line of battle ships and one frigate.

The *Swiftsure* and the French squadron were both on the port tack, but at 5:30 two of the line of battle ships tacked and stood on until they got into the *Swiftsure*'s wake, when they tacked again and followed in direct pursuit. Meanwhile the other three vessels gradually overhauled and passed the *Swiftsure* thanks to their superior sailing qualities. By eight o'clock they were able to tack toward the *Swiftsure* and arrive within gunshot of her lee quarter, where they resumed the same course as their quarry. Meanwhile the two ships astern were gaining fast.

Hallowell took his only chance by altering downwind to pass astern of the ships on his lee quarter in hopes of disabling one of them and escaping before the others could come up. In his own words:

> *I bore up and steered to pass astern of the sternmost ship with all our steering sails set on the starboard side, when the enemy tacked and stood toward us. At half past three the Indivisible of 80 guns bearing Rear Admiral Ganteaume's flag, and the Dix Août of 74 being in close order and within half a gunshot of us opened their fire, which was instantly answered and a warm action ensued. Their great superiority in point of sailing gave them every advantage of position and baffled all our attempts to get to leeward of then. At 37 minutes past four the Jean Bart and Constitution of 74 guns, being*

within gunshot and closing up on our starboard quarter very fast, the Indivisible almost on board of us on our larboard bow, and the Dix Août on our larboard quarter, our fore yards and fore topsail yard shot away, all our running and part of our standing rigging cut to pieces, the fore mast, mizzen mast and main yard badly wounded, the carronades on the poop dismounted, our deck lumbered with wreck and sails, all hope of making our escape and falling in with any succour being cut off, and only one of the enemy's ships apparently much damaged, I thought further resistance in our crippled state would be exposing the lives of valuable men without any advantage to their country resulting from it. With pain, therefore, I ordered His Majesty's colours to be struck, after an action of one hour and seven minutes.

9

TAKING STOCK
1801–1802

Altho it is my fate to experience your silence and neglect for some unknown and unwilled cause, still I feel a brotherly participation in your misfortunes and rejoice whenever fortune advances your fame.

Ward Boylston to his brother Benjamin Hallowell,
14 December 1801

Intending to capture rather than sink the *Swiftsure*, the French had aimed at masts and rigging rather than at her hull. In consequence casualties were remarkably light — only four killed and five wounded — but the ship was so crippled that she had to be taken in tow. Ganteaume sent four hundred seamen and skilled artificers on board, but with all their efforts it was six days before she could make sail and proceed on her own.

Ganteaume treated his prisoner with great consideration. On board *L'Orient* at Aboukir he had been under the fire of Hallowell's guns, escaping by boat just before the fatal explosion. Hallowell was welcomed aboard Ganteaume's ship with a guard of honour and was permitted to organize the distribution of his captive crew among the French ships. He was even permitted to continue to exercise discipline over them. One can imagine the erstwhile enemies at the Admiral's dining table, sharing stories over the wine, with the ship's officers listening in fascination.

The French squadron — with French colours flying over British in the captured ship — did not anchor in Toulon Road until 22 July. Napoleon's official gazette, the *Moniteur of Paris*, proclaimed the success on 23 July. The *Moniteur* put the French casualties in the action as ten killed and twenty-three wounded, and called the *Swiftsure* 'one of the finest vessels in Lord Keith's squadron.' Once, this would have been an accurate description, but to so characterize the unseaworthy and ill-manned prize was ludicrous propaganda.

Remarkably, a private letter from the captive Hallowell reached London on 27 July. Ganteaume had either arranged for Hallowell's letter to be posted ashore as the French squadron made its slow progress up the Italian coast or had forwarded it by dubious means in the same dispatch as the *Moniteur* report. He no doubt had Hallowell's word that the missive contained nothing but personal matters. By far the most likely recipient of the letter was his cousin Anne Gee. She passed the news to a London businessman, who in turn reassured Ward in Boston that his brother was well and that the *Swiftsure* had given a good account of herself.

Hallowell was impatient to undergo his inevitable court martial, and to either resume his career or be disgraced forever, according to its verdict. First it was his painful duty to report the capture to his superior officer. Under any circumstances this would have been a distasteful task. It was particularly humiliating to announce his failure to Admiral Keith. His letter began, 'My Lord, it is with infinite concern I have to inform you of the capture of His Majesty's late ship Swiftsure.' Masterful understatement, the word 'concern.'

The account quoted in Chapter 8 formed the core of Hallowell's report. He was also forced to admit that the French had captured some out-of-date night signals and the current recognition signals. These were of great importance, since they allowed two British ships encountering each other to verify their respective identities and prevented enemy vessels from posing as British. There were procedures to destroy such material if there was danger of it falling into enemy hands, but in the heat of the action the steps were not taken. In this case no harm resulted because peace ensued before the French could make use of the intelligence.

Viscount Keith

Hallowell also gently reminded the admiral that his ship was eighty-six short of its full complement, many fit men having been removed at Keith's orders before she sailed. He also had a sick list of fifty-nine, many from other ships, who had embarked just before the *Swiftsure* left Alexandria. Hallowell could justly claim that the undermanned and unseaworthy *Swiftsure* had put up a remarkable fight thanks to 'the steady and gallant conduct of the officers and men I had the honour to command on this occasion, and with whom I have been acting nearly four years on various services, I have no doubt of what would have been the issue of a contest on more equal terms.'

Hallowell's report was composed by 24 July, but there was no way of sending it. Meanwhile he gathered important intelligence of the strength and condition of the French fleet — what he could see for himself plus surreptitiously gathered information on detached squadrons and building programmes. Without comment but not without pain he listed the *Swiftsure* among the other enemy ships lying in the outer harbour of Toulon.

Having been paroled, on 8 August he sailed from Toulon in a cartel, one of the neutral vessels through which the very active exchange of prisoners was conducted. By a stroke of good fortune the cartel was intercepted the same day by Admiral Warren's squadron and Hallowell was taken on board the flagship *Renown*. Warren forwarded Hallowell's reports to Keith, but Hallowell remained in the *Renown*.

This chance encounter was a stroke of luck. Now, instead of Admiral Lord Keith, the nearest superior officer to whom Hallowell could apply for court martial was a man on whose neutrality and fairness he could rely. The trial was held as soon as the squadron reached Minorca. The president was John Aylmer, captain of the *Dragon*, third in command in the Mediterranean. Among the nine other captains sitting in judgment was Welters Berkeley, Hallowell's commanding officer in the *Falcon* on the West Indies station nearly fifteen years before. The court decided first to try Hallowell as an individual for leaving his convoy, and then to try him and the other surviving officers and men collectively for the loss of their ship. There was no prosecutor, and Hallowell conducted his own defence and that of his officers and men.

This was the second time he had been court-martialled for losing a ship under his command, and as an old hand he presented a succinct but effective defence. On the first charge he read out his narrative of events up to the time he left the convoy. He then called his purser Mr. Gamble and Lieutenants Waters, Davis, and Mudge to testify to the truth of the encounter with the *Pygmy* and the intelligence he had received from her captain.

The court retired to deliberate on the first charge but soon reconvened and without announcing its verdict proceeded to the second charge. Hallowell continued his narrative, carrying the story forward through his sighting the enemy, his attempts to escape, and the action that resulted in his surrender.

The president asked him if he had any complaint to make against any of his officers or men. He answered that on the contrary he felt himself very much in their debt for their exemplary conduct. The president then asked the assembled officers and men of the *Swiftsure* whether they had any complaints against Hallowell's own conduct. In a single voice the ship's company answered 'None.' Hallowell then called in succession his four lieutenants and Mr. Luckey, the master. Each was asked if Hallowell had done everything he could to evade the enemy and whether he had continued the action as long as there was a possibility of escaping or of inflicting proportionate damage. Each of the five answered in the affirmative to all the questions.

The court did not take long to completely vindicate the *Swiftsures*:

> Captain Hallowell's determination to leave the said convoy and join Sir John Warren was dictated by sound judgement and zeal for the service of his King and Country. And the Court was further of opinion that the

> *loss of His Majesty's ship the Swiftsure was unavoidable, and that the conduct of Captain Hallowell, his Officers and Ship's Company in defence of the Swiftsure was highly meritorious, and that Captain Hallowell displayed great judgment in the mode he adopted to avoid so superior a force and equal gallantry in execution of the plan so formed, they did therefore judge that they should be honourably acquitted.*

In the nearly twenty years of war between 1793 and 1815 the navy lost twenty-nine ships of the line, the vast majority to storm or accident. Hallowell's *Courageux* was one of the victims of the elements, and his *Swiftsure* was one of only three to be captured. Statistically, he must have been the navy's most disaster-prone captain, but in light of the verdicts of his two courts martial he would not worry overmuch about this dubious distinction.

Hallowell's exact movements after his acquittal are uncertain. The ship in which he travelled called at Gibraltar where he may or may not have been briefly reunited with the wife he had not seen for more than a year and have met for the first time his infant son Charles, born in January 1801, while Hallowell was at Malta with the expeditionary force. John Inglefield was leaving his post, and Ann may have sailed with him. Hallowell arrived in England in early October 1801, but it was not until December that his family was established at Hackney. By March 1802 Ann was pregnant with their second child.

For Hallowell, it was a time for taking stock on several levels. The state of international relations was always of supreme interest to a professional naval officer, especially to one on half pay. Long out of touch on family matters, he needed to catch up with his siblings and with his wife and growing family. Finally there was his career, and especially the immediate question of employment, threatened, he knew, by his quarrel with Admiral Keith.

The Treaty of Amiens brought peace between England and France for the first time in eight years. Both nations desperately needed a respite. The defeat of Austria had advanced the French frontier to the River Rhine, and the Czar Paul had switched sides and allied Russia with Napoleon. Britain had been fighting alone for the last two years.

Inflation was rampant, and after two poor harvests in a row the indigent were driven to riot by the outrageous price of food.

Ireland was seething with discontent after a near invasion by the French in 1796, an actual invasion in 1797 that achieved some success before it was defeated, and finally in 1798 an unsuccessful rising of the Catholic peasantry led by their priests. William Pitt, the British Prime Minister, proposed to end all prohibitions against the Catholic religion throughout Britain, but the intermittently mad and stubbornly Protestant King George III forced him to resign. Addington, who succeeded Pitt, strongly favoured peace and opposed Catholic emancipation.

France was experiencing its own difficulties. Nelson's victory at Copenhagen and the assassination of Czar Paul had put an end to Napoleon's hopes for a new alliance. Especially among the commercial classes suffering from the British blockade, French public opinion was against the war. Menou's defeat in Egypt was the last straw. Napoleon heard the news before the British and hastened to conclude the treaty on favourable terms.

The British agreed to recognize his gains in Holland, Switzerland, and the Rhineland, and to evacuate Malta and Egypt; the French were to withdraw from Naples and the rest of Italy. Neither country regarded the Treaty of Amiens as more than a breathing space before the inevitable renewal of hostilities.

Jefferson, hoping to win the next American presidential election, threatened to go to war with England over the perennial grievances arising from the British blockade of France and recovery of deserters from American ships. But the cessation of European hostilities in October 1801 persuaded Jefferson that the time for war with Britain had passed.

It must have been during the operations on the Italian coast that Hallowell learned of his father's death in March 1799. They had last seen each other just before Hallowell sailed for the Mediterranean in the *Camel* six years before. Neither could have imagined that the parting would be final. Hallowell had always been much closer to his father than to his mother, and without his father's influence and financial assistance his naval career could neither have begun nor have prospered. Hallowell's sorrow would be mitigated by the knowledge that news of

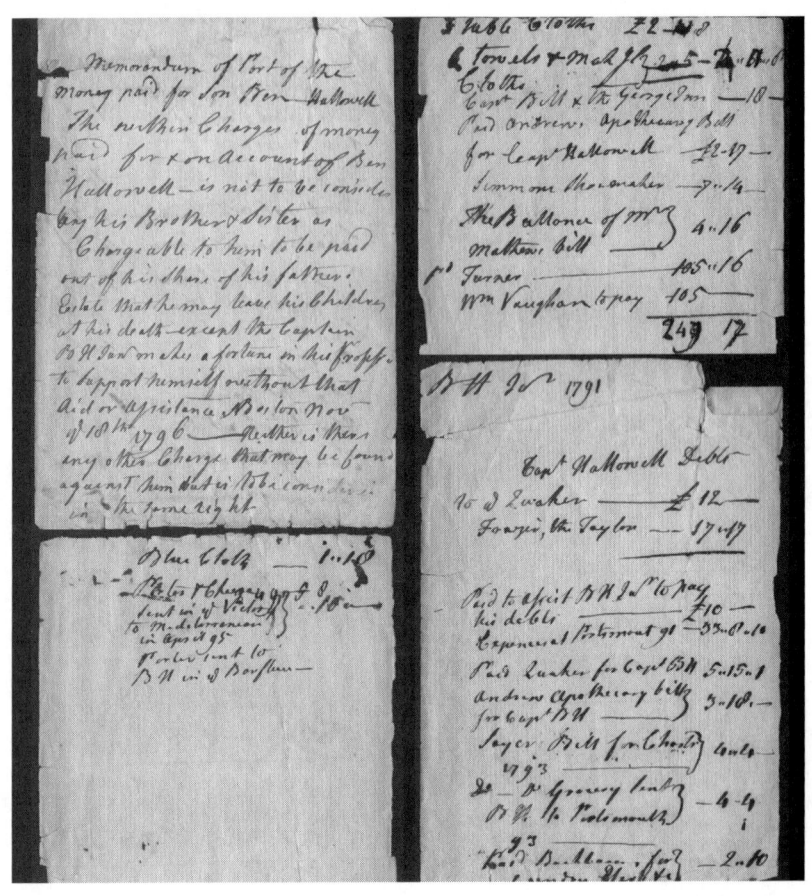

By this codicil Hallowell Senior ensured that his naval son would inherit equally with his brother and sister, despite his outstanding debt

the Battle of the Nile had reached York just before his father's death and that the old man had lived to take pride in his son's distinguished part in the famous victory.

Benjamin Sr.'s will had been drawn up and signed at Boston 18 November 1796, while he was en route to Canada. At his death it was deposited in the Surrogate Court of York County, 'The last Will and Testament of Benjamin Hallowell Esq. of the town of York in the Province of Upper Canada.' It divided his property equally among his three children; the property included the Nova Scotia lands, investments in British bonds, and anything that might emerge from the holdings in Boston and

Maine. By their marriage settlement Mary's share devolved on her husband. Ward Boylston and John Elmsley were appointed co-executors.

From beyond the grave Hallowell Sr. was to make one final gesture of regard for his younger son. Attached to the will was 'A Memorandum of Part of the Money paid for his son Benjamin Hallowell.' The charges date from the critical period of Hallowell's first command, the *Scorpion*, and consist of a carefully itemized list of expenses ranging from greens and fish for his cabin to outlays for transportation to and from London. Most are comparatively minor but the list includes two items over £100 with no amplifying detail. The total of nearly £250 was half Benjamin Sr.'s then annual income. Generous assistance indeed, probably only made possible because of the timely settlement of the Loyalist claim.

At the time the senior Benjamin made these outlays, they were fully repayable loans. Four years later he no longer required repayment, and he took pains to make sure the sum would not be deducted from his sailor son's share of the estate unless he no longer needed it:

> *The within charges paid for the account of Benjamin Hallowell is not to be considered by his Brother and Sister as chargeable to him to be paid out of his share of his father's estate ... except the Captain Benjamin Hallowell can make a fortune in his profession to support himself without that aid or assistance. Neither is there any other charge that may be found against him but is to be considered in the same light.*

On 17 March 1799, as he lay dying in the house of the chief justice, Benjamin Hallowell added several codicils to this testament. One of them provided that the properties in Upper Canada were to be included with the lands to be divided among his children, with the exception of his town lot in York which was left outright to John Elmsley. The hundred-acre so-called park lot in the town of York was sold at once for £100 equally divided among the three heirs.

Ward sent word to Hallowell of their father's death by nine different routes but received no acknowledgement. He did not hear from his brother at all between the autumn of 1798 and March 1802, when

Benjamin was back in England after the peace. Many of Ward's letters did not catch up to him until then. Despairing of the mails, Ward thought it useless to reply even after his brother finally answered. Thereafter, Ward occasionally wrote directly to Benjamin in England, but Benjamin always replied through his agent William Vaughan. Ward's sorrow and puzzlement are very evident. He speculates that a letter from sister Mary may have included some family matter that displeased Benjamin, but what this might have been he does not say. Benjamin may have resented Ward's return to Boston as the ultimate betrayal of his Loyalist family, although there is ample evidence that it was prompted solely by the need to settle the family affairs in America, an outcome which would benefit Benjamin just as much as it would his siblings.

Benjamin's continued silence is difficult to explain or justify, since at least at this time Ward seems to have done his best to be fair. There was one curious indirect communication between the two. Ward had shipped a cargo of gunpowder that was found to be spoiled on arrival in London, and he was demanding indemnification from the carrier. Through Vaughan he consulted his brother on the proper method of stowing powder. Benjamin replied through Vaughan that he always took the precaution of frequently turning the casks to ensure proper mixing, otherwise the saltpetre would filter to the bottom and the powder would lose its explosive force. There is no record of Ward's subsequent legal proceedings.

On their arrival in England, Hallowell had installed his wife and growing family in the Hackney area of London. Now one of the poorer inner London boroughs, at that time it was a countrified suburb, very near the wealthy village of Wanstead, the home of his surrogate parents William and Sarah Vaughan.

A dozen miles or a day's journey away on the south bank of the Thames was the magnificent Beddington Manor, the residence of Hallowell's cousin, the former Anne Gould, and her husband William Gee. The couple had been married on 27 February 1792, in the London church of St. Marylebone, as Hallowell patrolled the coast of Africa. William's brother Richard Gee-Carew, the owner of the property, usually dwelt elsewhere. William had grown corpulent and lazy and had relinquished all details of estate management to his wife. Twice a week her existence was enlivened when the vicar of the adjacent church came to dine and was obliged to remain until his host fell asleep over the port.

Hallowell seems to have kept in much closer touch with his cousin than with his brother, but the nature of their relationship remains a mystery. At some point the Hallowells would have been invited to Beddington. If there was any awkwardness when Hallowell introduced Ann and Anne, his wife and his first love, it has not been recorded. The two women were later to spend a great deal of time together.

In autumn 1802 Hallowell became acquainted with Princess Caroline, consort of the Prince of Wales. Born a princess of the House of Brunswick, she was betrothed at twenty-six to her cousin George, eldest son of King George III. Her appearance and manners were not prepossessing. It is recorded that on their being introduced the prince's first reaction was to call for a glass of brandy. After the wedding the Prince of Wales continued his liaison with his mistress, Mrs. Fitzherbert, whom many believed he had secretly married. The new Princess of Wales bore the prince a daughter, Charlotte, but the royal couple became completely estranged. Banished from the court, in 1802 she was presiding over her own increasingly indiscreet establishment at Blackheath.

Hallowell had been appointed captain of the *Argo*, fitting out at Woolwich. He roomed near the dockyard and thus became a neighbour of the discarded princess. She had exhibited excessive interest in the opposite sex before coming to England; it was said her father had not allowed her even to pass from one room to another without her governess. Now that her brief co-habitation with the prince had ended, she was free to entertain frequently, her usual guests being young and handsome men of outstanding physique.

Among them were numerous naval officers including Hallowell. Sir Sydney Smith was probably her first lover, succeeded by Captain Manby of the frigate *Africaine*, also outfitting at Woolwich. Her lady-in-waiting recorded that 'She had a Chinese figure in one of her rooms at Blackheath that was wound up like a clock, and used to perform the most extraordinary obscene movements. How the captains used to colour up when she danced about exposing herself like an opera girl!'

Robert Hallowell Gardiner was the son of Hallowell's uncle Robert, who had returned to Boston to settle the family estates. Having just graduated from Harvard the twenty-year-old made an extended tour of Europe. In London he met his first cousin Benjamin, whom he greatly admired as possessing 'all the finest qualities of an officer of the Royal Navy.' Hallowell spoke openly of his acquaintance with the rejected Caroline, whom Robert says 'had not yet become notorious.' Hallowell may have been among those captains who 'coloured up,' but almost certainly was not on the list of lovers. Had the relationship been an intimate one, it would not have been mentioned. Adultery with the consort of the heir to the throne constituted high treason, and could bring both parties to the scaffold.

At this time Hallowell was among the most effective and respected of British captains. Jervis had numbered him with Troubridge for his work in the Toulon blockade, and in 1800, when it had appeared necessary to defend the Channel against a possible French invasion, he advised the First Lord that 'Sir Edward Pellew, Sir Thomas Troubridge, the captains Hood and Hallowell are the only characters I could place entire reliance on in such a case.' Nelson had singled Hallowell out at Calvi and as one of his chief supporters after the Battle of the Nile and had praised him as a rare man of resource. He was one of four captains to have been honoured when King Ferdinand expressed his gratitude to those who had done most to restore his kingdom. Nelson had been awarded the rank of Grand Cross of the Order of St. Ferdinand and of Merit, and Captains Hallowell, Troubridge, Ball, and Hood had been made Commanders.

Thus his reputation was high, but that made no difference when it came to promotion. His position on the captains list had been determined by his late entry to the navy, which meant that he was still only a lieutenant at the beginning of the ten years of slow peacetime advancement after the American war. Of Nelson's fourteen captains at the Nile, he was older than seven but ahead of only two on the captains list. No matter how outstanding his ability the dead hand of seniority would always control his progress.

At about this time St. Vincent commented to Lord Spencer, 'The promotion to the flag has happily removed a number of officers from the command of ships of the line who at no period of their lives were capable of commanding them; and I am sorry to have the occasion to observe that the present state of the upper part of the list of captains is not much better than it stood before.' By this time Hallowell was slightly below the middle of the list. He was well aware of his superior merit compared with much of the deadwood above him, and his frustration and resentment must have been all the more corrosive because they could not be openly expressed.

Having married Ann Inglefield, Hallowell unknowingly became involved in his father-in-law's career problems. With peace on the horizon, the First Lord planned a shuffle of dockyard commissioners that would put the right men in the right jobs for a long-overdue reform of yard administration. John Inglefield at Gibraltar was one of the men in the mix. In answer to Spencer's query as to his abilities, St. Vincent replied, 'Commissioner Inglefield is an honest man and sufficiently intelligent, but pompous, flowery, indolent and wrapped up in official forms, stay tape and buckram. He has however corrected many abominable abuses and peculations practised under his predecessor.'

St. Vincent had a hidden agenda. However, Spencer took his somewhat ambiguous assessment at face value. Inglefield was offered and accepted the commissionership at Halifax. However, he already had an agreement with his opposite number at the Sheerness Dockyard to exchange positions, an action that would have reunited his family with the new Mrs. Hallowell.

When St. Vincent succeeded Spencer as First Lord he made it his top priority to stamp out the rampant corruption and inefficiency in the home dockyards. Within this larger aim he continued to pursue his own agenda. He treated Inglefield with great consideration, but behind his back he was manoeuvring to keep him out of England.

Publicly, St. Vincent exhibited a lifelong antipathy toward nepotism, but he had his own influential connections and favourites. His private goal was to make his good friend Captain Grey commissioner at Sheerness. Grey could not be appointed immediately, so the position had to be kept warm until the time was ripe. In 1799 Inglefield had become a superannuated captain. He had thus 'passed his flag,' that is he had taken himself out of the automatic promotion system. Once ensconced at Sheerness he would be a permanent impediment since he would never become an admiral and move on. It was therefore necessary to fill the Sheerness position with someone whose tenure would be only temporary.

Fortunately, such a person was already at hand. Ironically, it was Isaac Coffin, Hallowell's fellow-Loyalist and near contemporary who had raced ahead of him during the Revolutionary War, thanks to his earlier entry into the navy. Coffin's career had suffered setbacks. In 1788 while in command of the frigate *Thistle*, he was court-martialled for falsifying his ship's books. Probably the disputed entries were simply the not uncommon subterfuge through which the son of a friend could gain paper sea time. Nevertheless, Coffin was convicted and dismissed from his ship. Two years later he was hurt rescuing a man overboard and was never afterwards physically fit. He embarked on a new career as a dockyard commissioner and after postings in Corsica, Lisbon, and Minorca he was sent to Halifax in 1799. After only six months he went on leave to England.

In St. Vincent's eyes Coffin had two very desirable qualifications for the Sheerness position. Unlike Inglefield he had not passed his flag. At some point he would be promoted to rear admiral and open the position for Grey. This motive could not be revealed, but a plausible public reason was available. During Coffin's brief tenure in Halifax he had succeeded in antagonizing both the squadron he was supposed to be supporting and his subordinates in the navy yard. What could be more logical than to pacify the colonials by appointing Coffin to Sheerness and sending Inglefield to Halifax in his stead?

To soften the blow St. Vincent gave Inglefield everything but an absolute promise of a commissioner's appointment in the United Kingdom as soon as a yard became available. Knowing nothing of St. Vincent's ulterior motives, Inglefield took up his position in Halifax under the impression that his stay was to be a short one. He would serve there for ten years.

With his patron as First Lord and his friend Captain Troubridge a key member of the Board, Hallowell need have little fear that he would be on half pay for long. He could even hope to exercise a degree of choice over the details of his employment. St. Vincent had a reputation as a vengeful enemy who destroyed those who crossed his bows, but nothing in their professional or personal relationship had given Hallowell reason to believe that St. Vincent was anything less than his own staunch ally. Unknowingly, he was now to be drawn into the admiral's web of deceit over the commissioners.

St. Vincent offered Hallowell command of a frigate on the North American station, based at Halifax. Given Hallowell's property interest in Nova Scotia and with his father-in-law's position as Commissioner of Halifax Dockyard, the offer appeared to be an act of great consideration. In reality St. Vincent's gift was all about Inglefield. As the admiral explained in private, 'Hallowell has married his daughter, I will give him a frigate and send him to that station, where they will all take root together, and I shall hear nothing more of the Commissioner wishing to come home.'

Hallowell saw drawbacks in the superficially attractive offer. St. Vincent had led Inglefield to believe that his Halifax posting would be only temporary. Why would Hallowell move his pregnant wife and young children to a distant outpost when her family support there might vanish at any time? Moreover, very recently a squadron had been outfitted for a particular station only to be given a last-moment change to the unpopular West Indies. Some of the crews had briefly mutinied rather than sail and St. Vincent had insisted that the ringleaders be executed even in time of peace. Hallowell was unwilling to risk being similarly deceived. He declined the Halifax job, unknowingly derailing the First Lord's scheme.

Hallowell was taking a big risk. In peacetime there were many claimants for the few seagoing positions. Having turned down his patron's first offer, he had to accept the next one, no matter how unattractive.

He fell on his feet. On 12 August 1802, he was appointed to the *Argo*, a fifth-rate of forty-four guns. Thanks to his experience in the *Scorpion*, he was to assume Inglefield's former role as senior officer of the West Africa patrol. Certainly there was a downside: he would be separated from his family in a notoriously unhealthy and uncomfortable climate. On the other hand, the patrols were short, and there was an excellent chance that there would only be time for one of them before Anglo-French tension led to a new war. While on the station he would fly his own pennant as commodore.

All seemed well, but in the background lurked the ever-present threat of the powerful Admiral Keith. Hallowell's rash letter had challenged the Admiral's dishonest statement about the *Swiftsure*'s seaworthiness, 'that she was in an imperfect state.' Keith had forwarded it to the Admiralty, and the Board had only one option. Hallowell could not have been surprised by their reproof, received on his arrival in England after the loss of the *Swiftsure:* 'they consider the style in which it is written to your Commander in Chief to be highly improper and that they expect you will be more guarded in your correspondence in future.' They made no comment on the merits of the dispute.

Keith had to be content with this mild censure on the affair of the survey. But as Hallowell soon discovered, his enemy was not prepared to let the matter of the shoes fade away so easily. Hallowell had forwarded the initial correspondence to the Navy Board, and Keith had made a complaint to the Admiralty on 18 May 1801. He followed up with an elaborate investigation using long questionnaires to be answered by his agent, the consul at Palermo, and others with knowledge of the case, all this while commanding the naval support to a major land operation. In November 1801 he sent the voluminous evidence to the Admiralty, despite or perhaps because of Hallowell's recent honourable acquittal for the loss of the *Swiftsure*.

As early as November 1801 the Navy Board had given the Admiralty an interim report. They saw nothing wrong with the purchase of the shoes, but made no criticism of Hallowell. This report was neither acted upon nor passed on to Keith, and the matter languished until the admiral returned from the Mediterranean on conclusion of peace.

In July 1802 he complained from his house in Harley Street that the Admiralty had not even given him a receipt for his letters, still less any explanation or censure of Hallowell. Silence continued to reign. He then wrote to Martin, ex-captain of the *Northumberland*, asking him what he knew about the matter. Martin was a key figure since it was from him that Hallowell had obtained the information that started the whole mess. Keith might well have made this inquiry sixteen months earlier while all parties were together off Alexandria.

Martin advised Hallowell of Keith's inquiry. Blinded by his antipathy, on 4 October 1802, Hallowell wrote another rash letter, informing the admiral that the *Argo* was sailing in eight to ten days, but that before his departure he would gladly appear with Keith in front of either the Navy Board or the Admiralty in order to settle the matter!

This breathtaking communication ran directly counter to their Lordships' exhortation to be more guarded in his correspondence. In so far as he was not blinded by his dislike of Keith, Hallowell was standing firm on a principle, in this case that sailors in his ship should not be charged more than those in another ship for an article of clothing. Unless his sense of self-preservation had completely deserted him, he must have been extremely confident of St. Vincent's protection. With his ship under sailing orders he no doubt assumed that whatever happened, he would be well away before any serious consequences could arise.

He should have known his enemy better. Infuriated by Hallowell's letter and afraid that his *bête noire* was about to elude him, Keith immediately demanded that the Admiralty order a minute inquiry 'before Captain Hallowell is permitted to depart this country ... to determine how far the nature of his correspondence is entitled to their censure or support.' Two days later the Admiralty directed the Navy Board to update their report of November 1801, a copy of which they belatedly rendered to Keith.

Any First Lord except St. Vincent might well have suspended Hallowell's departure as Keith demanded. In that case Hallowell's opportunity for a peacetime command would certainly have evaporated whatever the board concluded. But — except for matters involving Inglefield — he continued to enjoy his patron's full support. Hallowell was not detained while the investigation unfolded. The *Argo* sailed for Africa as scheduled.

10

ARGO
1801–1804

A very important expedition is in contemplation, which it is my intention to name you to the command of....

Admiral St. Vincent to Benjamin Hallowell,
November 1803

The matter of the shoes was unresolved, but once the *Argo* was at sea it would have receded into the background for Hallowell, like everything else not directly concerned with his mission. The *Argo* with her consort, Commander Burrowes's 16-gun sloop the *Pylades*, proceeded down the gradually deepening Channel before a favourable wind. As they neared the limit of soundings the deep-sea lead was set going. The leadsman's report, 'No bottom with this line,' marked the point at which Hallowell officially left the limits of the Channel station and could hoist his commodore's broad pennant.

Commanding even a tiny squadron represented an increase in responsibility and a shift in perspective. Now the daily gunnery and seamanship exercises enhanced the combat readiness of the ships not just individually, but as an integrated unit that Hallowell could bring into action as a team.

Inevitably, the squadron's first port of call was Madeira, first seen by Hallowell as a callow midshipman twenty-five years earlier. Minor repairs were made good and fresh provisions obtained. Equally inevitably, the love affair with the wine of the island was renewed and a suitable quantity carefully stowed in the captain's stores for the long voyage. After four days in port the squadron weighed anchor for Sierra Leone.

When Hallowell had left Freetown back in 1792, the little settlement was looking forward to the arrival of 1,100 Black Loyalists from Nova Scotia. The local Temne tribe had virtually destroyed the first attempt at establishing a home for freed slaves, and the newcomers represented the last slim hope for a revival. As in Nova Scotia the new arrivals did not receive the whole of their promised grants. Nevertheless, they set to work establishing their farms and making a new life. But contrary to their expectations of self-government, the Nova Scotians found themselves under strict control by the white officers of the Sierra Leone Company, representing British abolitionists. In 1800 they rebelled with initial success, but the governing council restored order after some bloodshed. Many of the ringleaders fled to the hinterland and joined a local chief known as King Tom.

Now new actors appeared. The Maroons of Trelawney Town had long terrorized the white planters of Jamaica. In 1796 they were finally overcome when a hundred bloodhounds and their handlers were brought in from Cuba. One of the peace terms was that they should not be removed from the island. But in June 1796 some Maroons were alleged to have breached the treaty. Five hundred men, women, and children were removed to Nova Scotia, where they were granted land at Preston, near Halifax.

Their warlike attributes made them a real asset at a time when a French attack was possible. They were organized in military units and received uniforms and an insignia of an alligator holding a wheat sheaf and an olive branch. Wentworth would have been content for them to settle permanently in the province. But the climate did not agree with them and their background did not fit them well for pioneering in the temperate forests of Nova Scotia. It was decided that they should go to Sierra Leone. Thus, for the second time in a dozen years a group of blacks left for Freetown after a brief and unsatisfactory sojourn in Nova Scotia.

The Maroons arrived on 1 October 1800, at a critical moment. In

November King Tom led his tribe in an attack on the Freetown settlement, assisted by some renegade Nova Scotians. The governor was wounded and the place would no doubt have been destroyed had it not been for the loyalty and martial ability of the Maroons, who repelled the attackers. With the aid of HMS *Wasp* the colonial forces captured King Tom's town. They declared it conquered territory, but withdrew and left the place a sort of no man's land.

A truce was achieved in March 1802, but King Tom launched a second unsuccessful attack in April. The inhabitants were virtually confined in Freetown, even after a company of the Africa Corps arrived to bolster the defences.

The Africa Corps had been raised to protect British possessions in West Africa during the just concluded war with France. It was a 'condemned battalion' made up of pardoned deserters, criminals from the prison hulks, and a few local blacks. Despite their unpromising origins they behaved well and would be honoured as the 'Royal African Corps' in 1804.

Influential circles in Britain were pressing for an end to the slave trade. If this were to occur, Freetown would become even more important as a haven for liberated captives. The directors of the Sierra Leone Company and the Board of Trade well knew that the settlement was in a sorry state, but lacked the up-to-date and accurate knowledge to plan remedial action. A credible emissary was needed. Almost certainly Hallowell was picked to command the Africa squadron at this juncture because his previous experience and known intelligence and probity fitted him perfectly for the role of investigator.

Before he left England he was provided with a questionnaire requiring written answers from the governing council. He may have had a hand in framing the questions and certainly had some flexibility to alter them. The queries focused on the economic and security aspects of the settlement's situation. The intent was that he should receive the council's response well before his departure from Sierra Leone and try to resolve any points of dispute. In fact he received no written answers until the *Argo* was actually underway upon her departure.

Deprived of an opportunity for face-to-face discussion, Hallowell appended his own observations to each answer given by the council. He supplemented his existing knowledge by taking every opportunity to observe things for himself and to obtain additional information from sources outside the council. He shared the home authorities' suspicions about the management of the settlement and suspected the council of timidity, incompetence, and hypocrisy.

His comments were typically blunt. The first question was, 'What is the extent of the colony of Sierra Leone which is at present cultivated, and inhabited by the settlers, and to which they can have free access without danger of being attacked by the natives?' After admitting that no cultivation of any sort had taken place in 1802, the response ended, 'The natives certainly are not in force within many miles of the town.' Hallowell commented, 'This answer is a very extraordinary one,' since

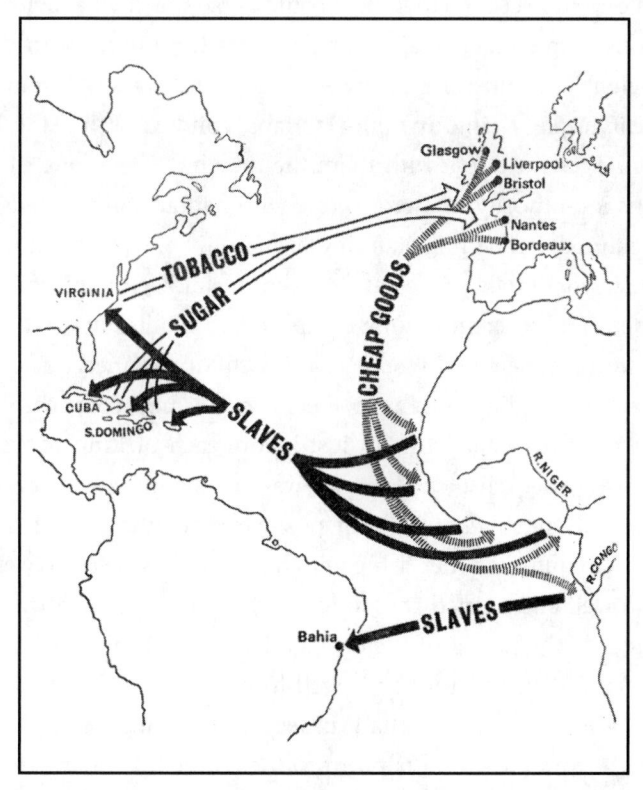

Taking advantage of the prevailing winds, the slave traders followed this three legged route, as did the ships of the navy's annual West Africa patrol.

he had just received a letter from the same council asking him to leave one of his ships behind for the protection of the settlement!

The council observed in another response that, 'Trade has not of late been a material object with the company.' Hallowell's comment was devastating:

> *It would be difficult then to pronounce what* has been *the material object, but it is perfectly clear that whatever it may have been, it has miserably failed. Has it been Agriculture? There is not one cultivated acre to be seen. Has it been Civilization? Not one convert has been made. And as to Commerce, the Governor and Council cannot conceal that it is all but annihilated.*

The one subject on which they could agree was the behaviour of the Maroons. The council praised 'their spirited exertions both offensive and defensive against the common enemy,' and Hallowell remarked, 'I can bear ample testimony to the laudable conduct of the Maroons.' He was on excellent terms with them; he may have been one of the few persons in authority in Sierra Leone who had actually visited Jamaica and acquired some understanding of their history and culture.

One incident tells us a great deal about Hallowell's political-military judgment and discretion. One of the council's allies in the hinterland was a Muslim merchant whose son Dallah Mohammed was permitted to operate a trading post near Freetown. He had conveniently been absent from his establishment just before each of King Tom's attacks and it was widely suspected that he was dealing in slaves. Nevertheless, the council argued that without positive proof they could not expel him, since continued friendship with his father was absolutely essential.

Hallowell entertained Dallah to lunch in the *Argo*, creating a useful reminder of the power of the navy and an opportunity for unguarded conversation. In the probably well-lubricated social setting, Dallah freely admitted that he had indeed traded in slaves. Hallowell refrained from passing this proof to the council, knowing that in the current dangerous situation it would trigger a series of events that might end in disaster. In his report he acquainted the government and the directors of the Sierra Leone Company with the facts.

To anticipate by a few years, Hallowell's report lit a slow fuse that was to prompt a major change in the status of Sierra Leone. The government had made annual payments to the Sierra Leone Company for constructing and maintaining the barracks and fortifications. Hallowell proved that the money had been almost entirely wasted, one of the consequences being rampant disease among the ill-housed Africa Corps. As a result the payments were suspended in 1803. The report also triggered a parliamentary inquiry into the whole situation, with inputs from numerous interested parties.

Mr. Zachary Macaulay, an early governor of the settlement, did his best to discredit nearly everything Hallowell had said, and Hallowell was personally examined by the inquiry. No doubt some of his comments were not fully informed, for he had been on the spot only two weeks. But, reinforced by other information, his report led Parliament to recommend that the settlement should be taken over from the Sierra Leone Company and made a direct crown colony. The change in status was made official in 1806, one year before British subjects were prohibited from trading in slaves. After the end of the Napoleonic Wars the prevention of slave trading by ships of any nationality became one of the Royal Navy's top priorities. Freetown at last began to fully deserve its name.

In parallel with his investigation Hallowell also had to deal with the immediate security threat. King Tom had joined forces with another chief called Mauricanou, and together they were known to be plotting a renewed attack.

The council's assessment of its ability to resist was not encouraging. The fixed defences were in terrible shape. Council admitted that Fort Thornton did not deserve the name. One of the four sides of the wall, or rather fence, was in complete disrepair and the only two blockhouses did not fully cover the other sides. A third blockhouse was still under construction. Some of the cannon supplied by the government had never been mounted on their carriages and were lying uselessly outside the perimeter. The fort could be defended only if it was manned by all the available fighting men, which would leave the 1,100 women and children in the town defenceless.

The heart of the defence should have been the company of the Africa Corps that had arrived in 1802. Unfortunately, a year in Freetown had turned them from a fighting unit into a handful of invalids. Forty-two of the original sixty-eight rank-and-file had already died and fourteen more were sick. None of the others were fit to do more than fire their muskets from the blockhouses.

The burden therefore fell on the Maroons and on the loyal Nova Scotians, who were now assisting fully in the defence of their settlement. Together they were capable of mobile operations, but the council feared to take the offensive because of the risk of an attack on the town while their only effective troops were absent.

Hallowell had nothing but contempt for the Sierra Leone Company and its local council, who between them had allowed this situation to arise. But he did not allow his emotions to blind him to the real possibility of the destruction of the settlement and the massacre of its inhabitants. That outcome would surely put an end forever to the noble dream of an African refuge for freed slaves. When the council officially requested him to leave the *Pylades* behind he at once agreed. The little vessel's sixteen six-pounders and two hundred men would in themselves be a useful addition to the defence, but the psychological effect of her continued presence was beyond estimation. Although Hallowell himself had spent a lot of time ashore, his policy had been not to let his sailors do so. The result was that there was not a single sick man in the two ships, in marked contrast to the decimated Africa Corps.

In mid-January the *Argo* sailed, exchanging farewells with the little *Pylades*. There followed the normal spring inspection of the Africa Company's forts and the always-challenging escape from the difficult Bight of Benin. As customary, the *Argo* followed the second leg of the triangular trade to the Leeward Islands and on 14 March 1803, she came to anchor in Man of War Bay, St. Thomas. Having entered the West Indies station under the command of Sir Samuel Hood, Hallowell ceased to be an independent commodore and hauled down his distinguishing pennant. Soon he would sail for home and the prospect of penalties for the shoe affair and potential half-pay status awaited him.

But in St. Thomas he found orders from Hood to join him immediately at Barbados. The *Argo* was needed to temporarily take the place of the *Blenheim*, 74, then being hove down at Antigua after running aground. Overjoyed, Hallowell sailed so quickly that he did not have time to send his African report or advise the Admiralty of the change of plan until he arrived at Carlisle Bay on 20 April. That he and Sir Samuel were old friends was an added bonus to the unexpected reprieve from returning to England.

For a fighting professional like Hallowell there was yet another bonus. France and Britain were rapidly moving toward a renewal of war. Each side accused the other of violating the Treaty of Amiens, but the underlying cause was Napoleon's insatiable ambition. Both sides were preparing for the inevitable, and Hallowell may well have taken part in the final planning for a quick mopping-up of the smaller French possessions in the West Indies. Britain declared war on 18 May 1803. The news must have travelled quickly, for by 21 June Hallowell was once again under fire, taking charge of landing British troops on the island of St. Lucia and leading the seamen and marines ashore in support. St. Lucia soon surrendered and the British then moved on to Tobago, which fell at the end of the month after little resistance. Hood was quick to express his appreciation to the Admiralty.

> *The Royal marines and a body of seamen were landed to cooperate with the army, under Captain Hallowell. To Captain Hallowell's merit it is impossible for me to add, as it is generally known, but I beg leave to say on this expedition his activity could not have been exceeded, and by his friendly advice I have obtained the most effectual aid to the service.*

At Toulon, at Bastia and Calvi, in Egypt, at Naples, and at Rome, and now in the West Indies, Hallowell had personally engaged in warfare on land. In Africa he had inspected forts and planned the defence of Freetown. Perhaps no naval officer then serving had more direct experience of the strange ways of soldiers and the milieu in which they fought. No wonder Sir Samuel Hood so valued his advice. Yet a time would come when Hallowell's military experience would lead him into a rash challenge to professional soldiers in the midst of a disastrous amphibious operation.

Hood ordered the *Argo* to sail immediately with his dispatches, the usual way of bringing a deserving officer to the attention of the Admiralty. Now that renewed war had dispelled any concerns about employment, the early return to England was welcome. Conditions on board would be even more unpleasant than usual, since the frigate carried about fifty soldiers of the 60th Regiment whose enlistments had expired but who had been kept until after the capture of St. Lucia and Tobago.

On the way Hallowell completed his reports on several experimental innovations that had been trialled in the *Argo*. The spirit of the Industrial Revolution was permeating British life, and the Admiralty was eager to embrace novel improvements if its hard-headed captains deemed them useful.

The *Argo* was fitted with a newly designed rudder and hoses made from leather rather than canvas, but perhaps the most interesting experiment involved a new means for measuring the ship's travel. Theoretically the device would be more accurate and more convenient than heaving the log. A cistern of water was connected to the sea through a small pipe. In accordance with the Bernoulli effect the level of water in the cistern would vary in proportion to the distance run. Hallowell took a keen interest in this device, and after he had adjusted the scale he found that in a voyage of 2,200 miles the cistern and the hand log were within five miles of one another.

He advised the adoption of all three innovations, along with numerous suggestions for their improvement. The whole voluminous report is a testimonial to his inquiring mind and technical practicality.

As soon as the *Argo* left the limits of the West Indies station on 11 July, Hallowell re-hoisted his commodore's pennant and again began to earn the extra pay of his temporary rank. It was the hurricane season; the fate of his father-in-law's *Centaur* ten years before must have crossed Hallowell's mind as he traversed the same waters. But the *Argo* was lucky with the weather, and on August 10 the deep-sea lead found bottom at the mouth of the Channel, and the pennant came down for the last time. No doubt Hallowell kept it as a memento. Four days later he anchored at Spithead.

As usual financial worries were never far from Hallowell's mind. He was paid his commodore's allowance, but only after a gentle reminder. He had heard that it was the custom to give a sum of money to an officer bringing news of the capture of an island. As soon as he reached Spithead he requested that traditional reward for having conveyed the news of Tobago. Someone at the Admiralty, perhaps St. Vincent himself, has simply written 'order' on this letter, so presumably he received something.

If Hallowell had hoped for some time at home he was to be disappointed. In all probability he never saw his sister Mary Elmsley and her family, then on leave in England, although they must certainly have visited his home and become acquainted with his wife Ann and his children. There was scarcely opportunity to land the disbanded soldiers and store the ship before the *Argo* was again at sea.

St. Vincent had misjudged the international situation. He had believed that the Peace of Amiens promised a long pause in hostilities. When war resumed sooner rather than later, he was criticized for overemphasizing the campaign against dockyard corruption to the detriment of building new ships and preparing for war. With great fanfare Napoleon was already massing troops on the Channel coast for an invasion of England, and every available British ship had to play its part.

On 12 September the *Argo* was on patrol four hundred nautical miles west of the entrance to the Channel. It was a miserable place during the season of equinoctial gales, and it was far from the potential scene of action in the Dover Strait. But it was an ideal position from which to provide warning if the cross-Channel threat was a bluff covering Napoleon's real intention of invading the ever-vulnerable Ireland. And here the *Argo* sighted and captured the privateer *L'Oiseau*, ten guns and sixty men under the command of Enseign de Vaisseau

Daubin. His second in command was killed by a shot from the *Argo* during the chase. *L'Oiseau* was nine days out of Rochefort and as yet had taken no prizes. Obviously, she was not part of an invasion fleet and her very presence in these waters might imply that they were not to be the scene of more important operations.

By 23 November the *Argo* was back at Spithead, but not for long.

The postwar political situation in Egypt was chaotic. British policy initially was to respect the sultan's sovereignty, which the Turks attempted to reassert with the aid of Albanian troops under Mehmet Ali. The Mameluke beys intrigued to maintain their position as the real rulers of the country, especially after a failed attempt by the Turkish governor to assassinate them all. When the Turks failed to meet their payroll, the Albanians effectively mutinied and began to act as an independent third force bargaining with both sides. All parties continued to oppress the Egyptian fellahin. One thing was clear: should war break out anew there would be no effective resistance to a French re-occupation.

Elphi Bey, who had been purchased as a boy slave for the unheard of sum of $1100, had risen to be one of the principal Mameluke chieftains, and had assisted the British army in its campaign to retake Egypt. When the army left in 1803 they took Elphi Bey and his suite with them. In London he succeeded in convincing the government that support of an independent Mameluke administration would be their best insurance against French invasion. With the renewal of war the moment had come to implement this policy, and it was decided to return Elphi Bey to his homeland as the catalyst.

It was only natural to choose Hallowell, the navy's acknowledged Egyptian expert, as the escort. As St. Vincent wrote, 'Captain Hallowell is well acquainted with the navigation up to Alexandria, and I believe much in the esteem of the Mamelukes and will perform the service better than any man I know.'

On 21 December 1803, Elphi Bey joined the *Argo*. Before boarding he toured Portsmouth dockyard and was captivated by his first sight of a steam engine in operation in the workshops. He witnessed a hand-operated fire engine in action and expressed an urgent desire to acquire one. Hallowell recommended by telegraph that his request should be granted, and the Admiralty approved it immediately. Elphi Bey was much gratified, but insisted that a portrait of King George III that he had also been given remained his most prized possession.

Hallowell was fully aware of the political importance of his passenger, but did not hesitate to subordinate Elphi's wishes to the requirements of the service. As the *Argo* passed down the coast of Spain she fell in with several stragglers from a convoy ahead of her. Hallowell took them under his escort and saw them safely into Gibraltar on 25 January 1804. Doing so significantly reduced his speed, infuriating Elphi Bey. Hallowell reported to the Admiralty, 'His Excellency was very angry with me for continuing six days with the convoy, and much displeased at my not complying with his request to quit them, but as we shall not anchor here [Gibraltar] and we have a fair wind I hope a short passage to Malta will reconcile us and put him again into good humour.'

As they passed Gibraltar, the *Argo* lost its mizzenmast in a gale that may have distracted Elphi Bey's attention from the delay and must have reminded Hallowell of the disaster to his *Courageux* in the same waters only a few years earlier.

Prolonged contact during the voyage had thoroughly aroused Hallowell's suspicions that his passenger might not be as committed to Britain as he professed. He repeatedly asked the bey whether or not he would cooperate with Hallowell in defending Alexandria if the French landed. If the Mamelukes agreed, Hallowell would land two hundred seamen to man the artillery in the port and would guarantee that the place could be defended until British reinforcements arrived. 'To this he answered with great warmth that if any enemy was to attempt to land he would devour the flesh from their bones, and enforced his expression by taking hold of his hand between his teeth and saying, "Thus would I treat them"'. Trying to pin down the wily Mameluke, Hallowell asked him point blank whether he considered the French as enemies or friends, only to receive the reply, 'They have been here once and are gone away again, nor do I think they will ever return.'

Hallowell concluded that Elphi Bey's real object was to seize power for himself and that meaningful alliance with him was a pipe dream. His judgment was confirmed when the *Argo* reached Malta on 31

January. A Turkish official called Selim Effendi visited the ship. He bore a letter from two of the most powerful Mameluke leaders, Osman Bey and Ibrahim Bey. Far from declaring their support of Elphi the leaders begged the British do their best to prevent his return, so much was their protégé detested and feared by his supposed colleagues. After reading the letter Hallowell called his passenger into his cabin and Selim explained the situation to Elphi Bey, 'His countenance altered very much and he indicated much inward agitation.'

Hallowell sailed for Egypt on 4 February. Elphi Bey was unwilling to be put ashore at Alexandria because it was garrisoned by the Turks, whom he now knew were alive to his intrigues. Hallowell therefore landed him and his small party (but not the fire engine) on the beach at Aboukir, and on 14 February Elphi disappeared into the desert. As Hallowell reported to St. Vincent, 'I think he stands a fair chance of being assassinated.' He was indeed pursued and nearly captured by the other beys and finally retreated far up the Nile with a few followers.

The entire political basis for Hallowell's mission had evaporated. He now had to assume that in the new situation the government would want him to co-operate fully with the Turks. Turkey and France were not at war, but that would not be an obstacle to a new French invasion.

The Turkish governor of Egypt, known as the Capitan Pasha, was at this time in Alexandria, where Hurshid Pasha was city governor. Hallowell called on them both as soon as he arrived on 19 February. He offered his full assistance in the event of a French attack, and suggested that as a precaution small vessels should be brought down into the outer harbour ready to be sunk to block the entrance. If the French could not get quick possession of the port a siege would be necessary, a full-scale invasion would be delayed, and of course, 'Our fleet will not fail to follow them up immediately and destroy them as they did before.' That fleet, he might have added, was again commanded by Horatio Nelson, the victor of the earlier battle.

The Turkish commanders appeared to accept his proposals. But when he called on Hurshid the next day to discuss details he was accused of trying to help the Mamelukes and Albanians by deflecting the pasha's attention on to an imaginary French threat. Incensed but polite, Hallowell left and drafted a powerful letter reiterating his offer to co-operate in the defence of Egypt and his suggestions for blocking the port entrance. He asked for an immediate written reply, adding not very subtly that he intended to forward all the correspondence to the Turkish and British governments, 'So that the two Courts may be able to judge where to attach censure if Alexandria and Egypt should again fall into the hands of the French.'

Hallowell's report was based on a deep understanding of Egyptian politics and astute judgments of the protagonists, although his long service there made him perhaps too emphatic in promoting the benefits of a British foothold. In his opinion the Egyptians themselves were heartily sick of Turks, Mamelukes, and Albanians alike and would welcome a British occupation. But if the British decided not to intervene, the Egyptians would reluctantly accept the French if it meant getting rid of their current oppressors. 'If some decisive steps are not immediately taken to preserve Egypt from another French invasion it will be lost to us forever.'

On his first arrival at Malta, Admiral Nelson had sent Hallowell orders taking the *Argo* under command and directing Hallowell to join him for instructions after landing Elphi Bey and before leaving the Mediterranean. After the negative response from the Turks there was nothing to be gained by remaining in Egypt, and Nelson's order became operative. Summaries from the log of the *Argo* on its voyage from Alexandria give some impression of the challenges of day-to-day life at sea.

March 19: Off Sicily. Daily expenditure of fresh water: one and one half tons. Winds fresh SW by W, course NW by W, speed 4–7 knots. Five or six guns exercised every day. 'Punished John Ford (Seaman) with 12 lashes for theft.'

March 25: Mustered at Divisions and read the Articles of War. Met and exchanged identities with Agincourt.

March 28: Exercised small arms firing at a target.

March 29: Split the mainsail, unbent and replaced it.

March 30: Fresh gales, down top-gallant yards and masts.

March 31: Split the main topsail coming to anchor in Gulf of Palma, latitude 29 degrees N, longitude 8 degrees 26 minutes E.

April 2: Watering and cutting wood. Received bullocks from the shore and provisions from the Agincourt. Drawing 17 feet 8 inches forward, 19 feet 3 inches aft. 'Punished Isaac Robinson (Cooper) and John Cross (Seaman) with 12 lashes each for striking a boatswain's mate.' Sailing toward Toulon.

Saturday 7th of April: fresh gales, carried away the fore topsail sheet.

Wednesday 11th April: At 1:10 taken aback, carried away the main topsail yard. Strong wind and squally with rain. Struck top gallant masts, ship under storm staysails. Strong gales with heavy squalls and hard rain. Crossed a new main topsail.

Friday 13th April: Repairing sails. 'Punished William Beckett (Bosn's Mate) with 12 lashes for disobedience of orders.'

There is no reference to the *Argo* trying to avoid damage by lying to while awaiting an improvement in the weather. Home beckoned, and Hallowell may have been driving her hard. Stress of more than a year at sea with scarcely a break was surely taking its toll on hull, masts, and rigging. Perhaps the human material was also overstressed. At this distance it is almost impossible to imagine the scene as men drenched to the skin lay out on the yards in the dark to capture a shredded sail or strike a topmast, 'one hand for the ship and one hand for yourself,' clinging for dear life as the ship reeled under the force of the gale. For days on end the captain seldom left the deck.

Hallowell's punishments of twelve lashes were the maximum a captain could award without the verdict of a court martial, and in practice twelve lashes was also usually the minimum. It must have been unusual for two petty officers — the cooper and a boatswain's mate — to be punished in such a short period. Apart from the flogging the two would probably be disrated and lose their privileges and the extra pay, but at the captain's discretion there was always the chance to earn their rank back through good performance and behaviour. In the meantime someone else would fill their shoes.

The Mediterranean fleet under Nelson had been blockading Toulon since the outbreak of war the year before and would continue to do so indefinitely. When Hallowell reported aboard the flagship, his boat also carried a quantity of wine as a present for his friend and commander. (Exactly where he obtained it is a mystery, neither Malta nor Egypt being renowned for their vintages.) The gift must have been typical, for it prompted Nelson's admonition, 'You will never be a rich man if you keep on giving away.'

Hallowell agreed to carry home presents for Lady Hamilton and promised to visit her at Merton, the admiral's estate near London. In Nelson's letter to his mistress there is a revealing glimpse of Hallowell as perceived by someone who probably knew him as well as anyone: 'His spirit is certainly more independent than almost any man's I know, but I believe he is attached to me.'

Nelson's orders to Hallowell were to take under his protection any merchant shipping at Gibraltar or Cadiz and convoy them to the United Kingdom. He was also to embark any private specie being remitted home by British merchants at the two ports. Specie meant coinage, often gold, that the navy agreed to transport to ensure its safety from privateers. For accepting the responsibility the captain of the transporting vessel personally received one or one and a half per cent of the value of the coinage. In the case of a large shipment, this 'freight money' might amount to a significant sum. Nelson was well aware that Hallowell was still struggling financially, and he certainly hoped that specific orders to embark specie would provide some sort of windfall.

In 1797, after the wreck of the *Courageux*, Nelson had made a similar gesture, sending the penniless Hallowell and the *Lively* to cruise for prizes off Santa Cruz. This time the action proved more rewarding. The *Argo* embarked specie to the value of 500,000 Spanish dollars, or about £112,000. Hallowell's freight money would be well over £1000, two years' pay for doing nothing more than his job.

The *Argo* anchored at Spithead 17 June 1804. Since December of 1803 she had inspected West Africa, crossed the Atlantic to the West Indies and back, patrolled the approaches to the Channel, and made a return voyage to the Mediterranean. Hallowell's only time at home throughout the period was a few days snatched before the Elphi Bey expedition. Nor was there to be any respite. He was greeted with new orders directing him to proceed without delay to the Downs anchorage off the mouth of the Thames and there to await further instructions.

He had been there for a week when he was ordered on a clandestine mission.

Most Secret

Government being in expectation of receiving from the coast of Holland information of the movements and intentions of the enemy in the Dutch ports, you are to bring to by firing a shot (in order to save appearances) any boat that approaches you from the shore, and to give every aid in your power to such of them as appear to be charged with letters for England, in order to facilitate their passage to the nearest part of our coast, taking care to communicate any intelligence of importance which you may receive from the person having such letters in his custody, to the Commander in Chief, as well as the officer commanding on that part of the coast to which such intelligence may particularly apply.

Intelligence was always important, but at this moment information from the continent was especially critical. Hundreds of landing craft were under construction and Napoleon was making frequent inspection tours and developing elaborate plans to gain temporary control of the Channel. In May Napoleon had insisted upon a practice embarkation despite warnings from his admirals. It had ended in disaster when many vessels were wrecked in rough seas and over 2,000 sailors and soldiers drowned.

During the Peace of Amiens the British had strengthened their network of agents in the French-occupied Channel ports. The coastal waters swarmed with fishing boats; if the pay was good a captain could usually be found to carry agents or letters to the nearest British ship and keep his mouth shut afterwards. What intelligence passed through Hallowell's hands at this time we do not know. It may have been significant, because later in the autumn the British fleet bombarded Boulogne in an attempt to disrupt Napoleon's preparations. This attempt and others were only partially successful, and countering the invasion threat remained Britain's top strategic priority.

On 4 May 1804, Napoleon had made himself Emperor of France with the right to nominate his successor. This and similar actions were confirmed by closely controlled plebiscites that inevitably produced huge majorities in favour of Napoleon's objectives. Revolutionary democracy was dead; within France there were no longer any effective challenges to Napoleon's power and boundless ambition. For the moment Britain was the only country in arms against him. William Pitt once again became leader of the government and Lord Melville succeeded St. Vincent as First Lord of the Admiralty.

Hallowell's clandestine operation ceased at the end of July. The *Argo* was about to be paid off into dockyard custody, but there would be no question of a return to half-pay status. With the navy straining every nerve to meet its worldwide responsibilities, ships were being returned to active service as fast as they could be outfitted and manned, and captains of Hallowell's calibre were urgently needed. He was directed to take command of the *Tigre* just two weeks after he left the *Argo*.

The affair of the shoes still hung over Hallowell's head. Despite Keith's demands, Hallowell had been allowed to sail for Africa while the investigation proceeded. An Admiralty letter sharply demanding a full explanation had caught up with him in Accra. All his records had been lost in the *Swiftsure*, but he worked as best he could on this tricky task on the two-week voyage to the West Indies. He had sent his spirited and unapologetic reply from St. Thomas in mid-March 1803, emphasizing that the whole controversy could have been prevented had Keith sought some facts from Captain Martin of the *Northumberland* while all the parties were together at Aboukir. Nevertheless Hallowell could have been under no illusion that his arguments would prevail against those of his vastly more senior opponent.

The Admiralty maintained silence until 7 July 1804, the date of its letter of reprimand. It only reached Hallowell when the *Argo* returned after the Dutch expedition at the end of July. Signed by the Secretary to the Admiralty, it read,

> I am commanded by my Lords Commissioners of the Admiralty, to acquaint you, that having perused the whole of the correspondence on the subject of the purchase of stores in Palermo by order of Lord Keith, my Lords are perfectly satisfied of the propriety of his Lordship's proceedings therein, and highly disapprove of your conduct on this occasion.

Tough language, but certainly no worse than what Hallowell must have anticipated. Moreover, the circumstances in which the reprimand was issued carried a more positive if unstated message. The investigation had probably been completed some time before the date of the letter, but with the *Argo* being driven so hard, the Admiralty may have wished to spare her captain the shock of censure until a more appropriate juncture. The timing made the upbeat subtext even clearer, since the reprimand and the prestigious appointment to the *Tigre* virtually coincided. In time-honoured naval practice Hallowell had had his wrist slapped, but his superiors' continued confidence in him had been reaffirmed in the same breath. In effect, 'Don't do it again, but get over the reprimand and get on with your job.'

It remained to be seen whether this second Admiralty censure would finally convince Hallowell to restrain his hasty outbursts against real or perceived injustice — or whether Lord Keith felt fully vindicated by this long-delayed and ambiguous response to his complaint.

In May Hallowell received from his brother Ward a seventeen-page status report on the settlement of family affairs in North America. Ward despaired at the delays in settling their grandfather's estate at Hallowell, Maine, and in Boston. Robert Hallowell had begun the task thirty-three years before, but resolution seemed as far off as ever! Reluctant to sue the old man, his uncle, whom he now regarded as incompetent rather than dishonest, Ward felt there was no alternative but to await his death and then turn the matter over to a good lawyer working on commission. Perhaps most frustrating of all, the Batterymarch shipyard was now worth at least £18,000 that could not be claimed by the descendants of the banished Loyalist.

As for the Nova Scotia lands, Ward took great care to remain on good terms with Governor Wentworth, corresponding frequently and sending him small delicacies not available in Halifax. Through William Vaughan, Ward had learned that Commissioner Inglefield had advised his son-in law to dispose of the Nova Scotia properties as soon as possible because they were at great risk of being escheated. In Ward's opinion this was poor advice. Inglefield may have been on the spot, but Ward was confident that if there was any real risk his friend the Governor would have given him ample warning.

John Elmsley was responsible for executing the Upper Canada portions of the will. For simplicity's sake the executors agreed that Mary would give up her share of the Nova Scotia property in exchange for the two brothers relinquishing their interests in Upper Canada. Although each of the brothers received considerably more land than their sister, they recognized that values in Upper Canada far exceeded those in Nova Scotia.

Ward had unwisely chosen to visit the Elmsleys in Canada during the winter of 1803–4, the most severe in memory. The family was happy and well, but the climate appalling. The temperature never rose above zero and one day fell to thirty-two degrees below zero Fahrenheit. 'I nearly lost my ears and nose on the 21st January and many others met a like misfortune that day. The only comfort in living there in winter is by a stoved room and fireside.' On his return journey he was 'obliged to lodge 12 nights in the woods or in hovels hardly fit for cattle, one night upon the ice in the River St. Lawrence in an open sleigh where I was very much frozen and have not yet quite recovered.'

This account led into a general lament:

> *My years must remind me of my claim upon time, tho at best uncertain cannot upon common calculation be much longer continued with usefulness to others or pleasure to myself — my last severe attack has left me with a degree of weakness in my breast that every cold I take convinces me the effect will be one day too deep to shake off.*

Ward was fifty-five when he wrote this; despite his fears he would live to seventy-eight, no doubt to his intense surprise.

While at York, Ward stood godfather to the family's second child, John Elmsley Jr. Benjamin Hallowell had earlier assumed the same role by proxy for the Elmsleys' first child. She was christened Anne-Gee as a compliment to the wealthy cousin and perhaps as a subtle reference to the link between the Christian name and the godfather.

Between leaving the *Argo* and joining the *Tigre*, Hallowell had two weeks to spend with his growing family. Charles had been born in 1801 at Gibraltar. Benjamin and Henrietta, born in 1802 and 1803 respectively, were conceived in the short intervals the *Argo* spent in England between her varied missions. Now in the summer of 1804 Ann was in the late stages of another pregnancy and may even have given birth during the father's brief visit. The next child, Mary, died before the end of 1804. In an age when infant death was common, she was the only one of the Hallowells' nine children not to survive to adulthood.

Nevertheless, Ann had the care of three children under the age of six and a husband whose return was unpredictable and even problematic. Money was always an issue. With her parents in Halifax her only support would be the Vaughans and her husband's cousin, the other Anne. As the daughter of a naval family she would know how to cope, but the responsibility and uncertainty would at times be nearly unbearable.

The *Tigre*, like the *Courageux*, had been captured from the French. As in the case of *Courageux/'Courageous,'* it is hard to believe that the sailors called their ship anything else but *'Tiger,'* even after a 12-gun brig of that name was commissioned a few years later. The *Tigre* mounted twenty-six 32-pounders on the gun deck, twenty-six 18-pounders on the upper deck, and twenty-eight 9- and 6-pounders on the quarterdeck and forecastle, besides carronades. Her eighty guns meant that she was among the most powerful third-rates and reckoned one of the finest two-deckers in the fleet. Hallowell's pay as her captain was significantly higher than in the fifth-rate *Argo*.

In the next few years Hallowell was to lose the patronage of the powerful St. Vincent, an advantage he had enjoyed since 1794. But in taking command of the *Tigre*, Hallowell unwittingly acquired a potential replacement even more influential than the recent First Lord of the Admiralty.

George John, 2nd Earl Spencer, stood at the pinnacle of the British aristocracy. His wife Lavinia was prominent in London society and his sister Georgiana was consort of the Duke of Devonshire. The earl had been First Lord of the Admiralty in the fateful years from 1794 to 1801, perhaps the most demanding and glorious period in the history of the Royal Navy. It was by his direction that the navy had re-entered the Mediterranean under Nelson and gained the decisive victory of the Nile. Politically a Whig, he was nevertheless a supporter of the Tory William Pitt and had lost his office when the King dismissed the latter.

In 1804 his thirteen-year-old son Robert was enrolled in the navy as a Volunteer 1st Class, first level in a hoped-for nautical career. In the past, younger sons of peers with military inclinations had usually chosen the army, but after Camperdown, Copenhagen, and the Nile service in the navy became perfectly acceptable even for the aristocracy.

The earl selected Hallowell to be his son's first mentor. Hallowell must have been consulted, but to refuse would have been social and professional suicide. The honour was immense, the potential benefits great, but he would be acting *in loco parentis* for the son of one the most powerful men in England, a son who was the apple of his mother's eye. Any reported shortcomings in the mentor, real or imagined, would certainly bring disgrace.

During his six years in office the earl had had ample opportunity to assess the character and competence of the senior officers of the service, albeit mostly by report and at a distance. But he had actually met

Hallowell in 1797, when Admiral Jervis entrusted him with the duplicate dispatches of the victory of St. Vincent. 'Captain Hallowell, who will have the honour to present you with this, has laid me under so great and lasting an obligation.... I shall esteem any kindness you are so good to shew him as the greatest favour you can confer on me.'

Seven years later the earl chose Hallowell as his son's captain over numerous captains of greater social standing and seniority. This was a singular testimony to his professional competence, his reputation for honesty and irreproachable moral fibre, and the impression he must have made at their meeting. Where Earl Spencer led other peers followed, and Robert Spencer was joined by several other noble youngsters beginning their careers in the *Tigre*.

One of these was Robert Spencer's older cousin, Midshipman Augustus Clifford. He was the illegitimate son of William Cavendish, Duke of Devonshire, and Lady Elizabeth Foster. Earl Spencer's sister Georgiana, Duchess of Devonshire, the Duke, and Lady Foster lived together very amiably for over twenty years, and young Clifford was openly acknowledged and protected by the Duke. (After Georgiana's death, the Duke and Lady Foster married, thus legitimizing Clifford.) In the *Tigre* he was no doubt intended to play the role of mentor and protector of his younger cousin. Within two years he passed his examination at the Admiralty and returned to the *Tigre* as one of Hallowell's lieutenants.

No doubt with some misgivings Hallowell also embarked his own nephew Nicky Boylston. Twenty years before, the eleven-year-old Nicky had been his uncle's servant on the West Indies station. This might have been the start of a respectable naval career, but Nicky had abandoned the sea as soon as the *Falcon* returned to England. From there it was all downhill. Nicky married a woman of good family in Charleston, but soon showed his true character. As Ward told his brother in April 1804:

> *I have long since given him up as lost beyond redemption; the last account I had of him was in Norfolk gaol in Virginia from which he was liberated by a friend of mine paying the debts which I*

immediately discharged. His wife he has robbed beaten and threatened and would have murdered had not assistance rescued her from his hands....Where her husband is I don't know nor is he worth inquiring after.

Ward undertook to support the abandoned woman and her child on condition she not come to Boston. Nicky returned to England and threw himself on the mercy of his Uncle Benjamin. Once again Hallowell took him to sea, but at thirty, with no naval credentials, it would have been difficult to fit him into the *Tigre's* establishment. Service on the lower deck would have been out of the question for the captain's nephew, nor could he have messed with the officers. In all likelihood he was borne as a schoolmaster or clerk, and lived in the cockpit with the sprigs of the nobility with whom he had almost nothing in common.

11
ENDURANCE
1804–1811

> *It is an easier matter to find men that will give themselves willingly to death, than such as will endure Labour with patience.*
>
> Admiral Sir George Monck,
> 1666

The *Tigre* had been captured 23 June 1795, and retained her original French name. Hallowell joined her in August 1804. After completing her stores in Cawsand Bay off Plymouth, she sailed on 3 September.

The voyage confirmed Hallowell's suspicions that all was not well with his new ship's company. In his anxiety to join Nelson he may have been too ready to settle for a barely adequate crew rather than wait for more experienced men to become available. As usual the complement had to be filled out with newly pressed merchant seamen and landsmen.

At least the pressed men were trained. Moreover, they were no strangers to discipline, just as necessary in a merchant vessel as in a warship. But many of the landsmen were quota men, the dregs of local society unloaded upon the navy. In the *Tigre's* case the situation was exacerbated in that a large proportion of the landsmen were Irish, acknowledged as formidable fighters but rightly or wrongly supposed to have little aptitude for either the sea or discipline.

There was then no introductory period of training ashore, no equivalent of the modern boot camp where basic knowledge, discipline, and teamwork are instilled in the classroom and on the parade ground before men join their first ship. Totally ignorant of their duties, landsmen had to be trained quickly on the job while at the same time learning the hard way to take orders and obey without question. Perhaps most were illiterate. At least at first they had to be driven rather than led.

While en route to the Mediterranean Hallowell met and could easily have captured several Spanish merchant vessels. But he was so eager to join his old friend Nelson in the best achievable state of manning that he refrained from taking them so as not to have to detach prize crews from his already barely adequate crew.

Since captains were directly responsible for manning their own ships, they would have resisted strongly if any admiral had tried to even out the quality and quantity of the different crews under his command. It was therefore very rare for this seemingly obvious action to be taken except when the ship being robbed was leaving the admiral's command. As late as 1810, six years after Hallowell took over, the manning of *Tigre* still reflected her unsatisfactory state on leaving Plymouth. As Lieutenant Crawford recorded in his reminiscences:

> *I found the Tigre what every British man-of-war ought to be — clean — in good fighting order — handy to work — sailing well and an admirable sea boat. The only thing in which she was deficient was a good crew; but that she did not possess. The proportion of able seamen to the rest of the ship's company was scantier than ever I knew to be in any other ship.*

Even if worse than usual, this sort of problem was nothing new, and in most circumstances Hallowell would have been confident of solving it expeditiously. But in the case of the *Tigre* the means of doing so were seriously compromised because of deep-seated problems among the ship's warrant officers. These veteran specialists ought to have been the heart of the ship's company, but in December Hallowell had to report to the Admiralty that none were up to their jobs.

'The Boatswain has been incapable of doing any duty for near two years from a violent blow he received on an old wound in his head.' It had been hoped that in the warmer climate of the Mediterranean his condition would improve, but 'he has not been able to do an hour's duty since we sailed.' Mr. Harriott the carpenter had been in the service since 1776 and had held his important post in eight different ships before the *Tigre*, but poor eyesight had made him 'incapable of performing any part of his duty without spectacles.' This circumstance meant he was unfit for sea. Mr. Stewart, the gunner, had an old leg wound and 'will be in danger of losing his leg or his life if he serves in a hot country.'

In acknowledgement of past service it was not unknown even up to recent times for incompetent or drunken officers and petty officers to be 'carried' until they reached pensionable age, rather than to be discharged. In the days before regular pensions there must have been even greater moral pressure to keep long-service warrant officers on the books, even when they were no longer capable of contributing.

Hallowell's warrant sea officers were all deserving men, but they could not stay in the *Tigre*. With great humanity he recommended in each case that the men be appointed to a special position where they could continue to be useful and continue to be paid. The boatswain could serve in a ship of the same rate where 'not so much exertion was required.' (This is a bit unclear; was service under Hallowell likely to require more exertion than under other commanding officers?) The carpenter could be employed in a dockyard rather than at sea, and the gunner could serve usefully in a vessel stationed in a northern climate. At the Admiralty, 'Recommended' has been scrawled on Hallowell's letter, so presumably the men left the *Tigre* but continued to serve elsewhere. In due course the Admiralty would have either confirmed Hallowell's choices for acting warrant officers or appointed replacements from outside the ship.

Shortcomings on the lower deck and among the warrant sea officers were bad enough. Worst of all, the *Tigre's* wardroom was less than fully supportive of the new captain. Some of Captain Dacres's former officers resented those whom Hallowell had brought with him, his 'followers' in common parlance, and discontent on this score simmered in the wardroom and cockpit. That situation would come to a head at the worst possible moment.

Responsible as he was for the professional development and personal well-being of Robert Spencer, Hallowell needed to report regularly to the boy's noble parent. Shortly after the *Tigre* entered the Mediterranean, Hallowell wrote that Robert was getting on well and was climbing to the masthead every day before breakfast, scrambling back downward up the futtock shrouds rather than climbing up through the safer but unseamanlike lubber's hole. The earl may not have passed this information to the doting Lady Spencer.

So far quite normal parental news, but the letter went on to discuss the movements of some French ships and a rumour that Admiral Nelson was asking for leave. These were professional and personal matters about which the earl was not strictly entitled to be informed. During his time as First Lord, Spencer had carried on an unofficial correspondence with Nelson, bypassing the chain of command. It seems to have been understood from the beginning that reports on Robert would also convey information and analysis on military, personnel, and political issues throughout Europe, as well as in the theatre in which Hallowell was serving. There were to be more than two hundred letters from Hallowell to Spencer, written over thirty-five years. Unfortunately, the return correspondence is not available, but its content can often be deduced.

Early in the correspondence Hallowell made it clear he was going to be objective about young Robert. He told the earl that his son showed great promise 'of being an ornament to the service, and in saying this I deliver my real sentiments without wishing to flatter your Lordship as his parent.' Some years later he did not hesitate to turn down the earl's request that his son be given special leave at a time when the *Tigre* was under sailing orders. Apart from the scions of the aristocracy, he found room for youngsters of lower social origin in his ship and treated all the aspiring officers in the same way, whatever their family status. He did not hesitate to subject a protégé of the Duke of Clarence, a future

George, 2nd Earl of Spencer

king, to particularly severe discipline for behaviour that fell short of Hallowell's high standards.

Napoleon personally planned naval operations as he did campaigns on land, moving his fleets like pieces on a chessboard. He never truly appreciated the special problems of sea warfare, including the low combat readiness of his long-blockaded ships, the difficulty of communications, and the over-riding importance of the weather.

The orders he gave to his admirals on 2 March 1805, were breathtaking in their sweep and scope. Villeneuve was to elude Nelson and join his fleet with the Spaniards at Cartagena and Cadiz, then sail for the vulnerable West Indies, thus forcing one or other British fleet to pursue him. Ganteaume was to get out of Brest and join Villeneuve, along with Missiesy's squadron from Ferrol.

After doing what damage he could in the Indies, Villeneuve was to return ahead of his pursuers and appear in the Channel with more than fifty ships of the line. Control of the narrow seas even for a few days would be sufficient for the emperor's numerous but very vulnerable transports to carry his army to England. Few believed Great Britain could withstand these veteran troops commanded by the supreme military genius of the age.

As 1804 merged into 1805 Nelson's fleet continued its blockade of Toulon. By the time the *Tigre* arrived the majority of the men in the fleet, including Nelson, had not set foot on shore for nearly a year and a half.

It was impossible to maintain an impenetrable barrier to a sortie. From the high ground the French could observe the British fleet many miles away, and mechanical telegraphs allowed rapid communication with the harbour. By choosing their moment of sailing according to wind conditions and the position of the blockading fleet, the French could usually avoid immediate interception, just as they had done in the invasion of Egypt in 1798.

Perfectly aware of these circumstances, Nelson did not rely on close blockade. Scouting frigates kept an inshore lookout, but the main fleet was kept well out of sight to tempt the French to sea, where Nelson was confident he could beat them if he could bring them to battle.

As the Egyptian campaign had demonstrated, scouting the blockaded enemy was the weak point in the strategy. Even on the clearest day enemy topsails might be sighted from the masthead only up to about forty miles away. At night or in fog the search radius was virtually zero. If the enemy destination was unknown, finding his fleet even in the relatively restricted confines of the Mediterranean was immensely difficult.

Villeneuve sailed on 18 January 1805. Nelson received the news at Maddalena in Sardinia the next day. In ignorance of Napoleon's grandiose plan, and always mindful of Egypt, Nelson at first sailed in the direction of Alexandria. In an eerie reprise of the events of 1798,

Hallowell in the *Tigre* was sent ahead to reconnoitre in a fever of anticipation that history would repeat itself. But it was not to be.

Alexandria looked the same, but this time there was no sign of the enemy, either there or at Aboukir, nor had any French troops been landed. Hallowell gathered information on the situation in Egypt — Elphi Bey had survived and was once again a factor in the country's violent politics — but of Villeneuve nothing could be learned. In fact, his fleet had suffered severely in bad weather and been forced to return to Toulon.

Villeneuve received peremptory orders to try again and sailed for the second time on 30 March, steering south with eleven sail of the line, seven frigates, and some smaller vessels. Informed on 4 April but still in total ignorance of their intended destination, Nelson steered to intercept the French to the westward of Sardinia. As in 1798 the British frigates lost touch and the French achieved their breakout. Forced to cover too many possibilities, Nelson naturally focused on his Mediterranean responsibilities. It was not until 16 April that he received reliable news that the French had been sighted off the southeast tip of Spain. Joined by the seven-ship Spanish squadron in Cartagena, Villeneuve had already passed Gibraltar on April 8. Nelson need no longer worry about Malta, Sicily, or Egypt, but everywhere in the North Atlantic from Ireland to the West Indies had become a possible French target.

Already ten days behind and frustrated by unfavourable winds, he set off in pursuit. He spent two days replenishing his provisions at Ceuta and did not enter the Strait of Gibraltar until 7 May, a full month behind Villeneuve. From Ceuta, Hallowell complained bitterly to Spencer about the failure of the British frigates to keep Nelson informed of the enemy movements. For the first time but not the last, this letter makes no mention of young Robert, the ostensible subject of the correspondence.

At Gibraltar Nelson should have received intelligence from Admiral Sir Robert Orde, who was blockading Cadiz, but none was forthcoming. Nelson appreciated that Villeneuve would join with the Spanish at Cadiz, but he thought the combined fleets would then proceed either to Ireland or to attack Cornwallis's Channel fleet blockading Brest. Nelson intended to sail for a position one hundred and fifty miles west of the entrance to the Channel, where he would be well placed to counter either possibility.

However, he learned from an American merchant vessel that the combined fleets had been off Cadiz on 9 May, apparently en route to the West Indies. Now only a matter of days behind, Nelson followed, having replenished his ships to five months' provisions. The fleets of both Villeneuve and Nelson now effectively vanished from the oceans as far as the Admiralty was concerned. It would be nearly a month before anyone in Britain knew where they were. Hallowell wrote that despite the horrors of the West Indies climate 'there is not a person here who would not be miserable at being separated from the Squadron.' Everyone in the fleet felt the exhilaration of being part of great events.

Nelson arrived at Barbados on 4 June. False information led him to suppose that the French objective was Trinidad, and he sailed south to the rescue. In fact Villeneuve was still to the north at Martinique, where he had arrived 29 May. Ganteaume had failed to break out of Brest and Missiesy had missed the rendezvous. But confident that he had lured Nelson away from the decisive theatre, Villeneuve and his twenty ships sailed for Europe on 5 June. Nelson learned the truth four days late and at once started in pursuit. He was little more than two hundred miles behind, and on one occasion saw several planks lost overboard from the enemy fleet. Hallowell wrote Spencer, 'If we do not cross the enemy on our way I think your Lordship may expect an action in the neighbourhood of Cadiz in the course of a fortnight.'

After a round trip of more than 6,500 miles, Nelson's fleet arrived at Gibraltar on 19 July without having intercepted the enemy. Hallowell wrote Spencer a long letter explaining that the failure to bring Villeneuve to action was not Nelson's fault but rather the incorrect intelligence that had led him to sail in the wrong direction from Barbados. The fleet had enjoyed only one day's issue of fresh meat since the beginning of April, 'for want of which the scurvy has made its appearance in all our ships, but with a few vegetables and bullocks to take to sea with us that disorder will soon be remedied.' Robert Spencer was well.

But Hallowell's prediction proved correct. Off northwest Spain the returning Villeneuve encountered a British force under Admiral Calder. After an indecisive action in poor visibility, Villeneuve at length led his fleet into Ferrol. Nelson's triumphs had spoiled the British people. Not having scored a decisive success, Calder was regarded as having failed, and an inquiry was initiated into his conduct.

Had Villeneuve sailed at once for the Channel instead of entering Ferrol, Napoleon's strategy might have succeeded. On learning that the enemy fleet was definitely in European waters, Nelson sailed north and joined Cornwallis off Brest, effectively guarding the door to the narrow seas. None of the British forces had been permanently lured from the decisive theatre, and they were in fact more concentrated than they had been before Napoleon's elaborate deception. Hearing of the British concentration, Villeneuve sailed to Cadiz where he was bottled up by a squadron under Collingwood.

On 3 August Napoleon was at Boulogne, confidently awaiting the arrival of his fleet while inspecting troops and his 2,000 landing craft. Constant practice had ensured that the transports could be fully loaded and ready for departure only an hour and a half after the order was given. He had said, 'It is necessary for us to be masters of the sea for six hours only, and England will have ceased to exist.' Until 23 August he remained optimistic, but on that date he learned that Villeneuve was not only not coming to the Channel, but had actually led the combined fleets in the opposite direction to Cadiz. Napoleon was never to enjoy those six vital hours. In an apoplectic rage he wrote, 'What a navy! What sacrifices all for nothing! All hope is gone!'

After uniting his squadron with that of Cornwallis, Nelson sailed home in the *Victory* for some much-needed leave. He received a hero's welcome. His dazzling victories set off by the eye and the arm lost in the service of his country made him an idol for all classes of the population. Even his now openly acknowledged relationship with Lady Hamilton did him no harm; perhaps for some of his admirers it even added a touch of common humanity to his image.

Adoring crowds collected whenever he appeared in public. The attention was by no means unwelcome to this complex personality, with his well-known vanity and thirst for fame. On one occasion Nelson was strolling in the capital with the former Midshipman Lee when the pressure of the crowd forced the two to take refuge in a bookshop. Nelson remarked, 'I still have the coffin which that good fellow Hallowell made for me in your ship; I always keep it in my cabin.' In fact, it was left behind in an upholsterer's shop the next time the *Victory* sailed; in his memoirs Lee reports that Nelson jokingly warned the proprietor to take good care of it since it might soon be needed.

It was obvious that the enemy could not remain long in blockaded Cadiz. Transport by mule, horse, and wagon over the atrocious roads could not feed the citizens plus the thousands of men in the fleet. On 15 September Nelson sailed the *Victory* to take command of the blockading force, his departure from Portsmouth witnessed by crowds cheering encouragement and anticipating a new and decisive victory.

Meanwhile Hallowell's *Tigre* and other ships joined Calder off Ferrol and later followed Villeneuve to Cadiz. The French and Spanish fleets together numbered thirty-five or thirty-six ships of the line. Calder and Collingwood together mustered thirty-two. In contrast to the situation at Toulon, it was possible to maintain a close blockade of Cadiz. There was good anchorage a few miles offshore where most of the blockaders could wait in some comfort, while an inshore squadron of the fastest ships maintained a close-in patrol.

The *Tigre* was part of this force under Admiral Louis. On 30 August Hallowell wrote Spencer that the wind was easterly, tending to blow the blockading force away from the harbour. Nevertheless, Villeneuve had not sailed, indicating to Hallowell that the enemy wished to proceed to the east, that is, back into the Mediterranean. Five days later Hallowell wrote in some bafflement that the enemy had not taken advantage of three days of westerly winds, which would have been ideal if the Mediterranean was the goal. In fact, Villeneuve did have orders to return to the Mediterranean but could not decide when to sail.

British intelligence at this time was excellent. It was mostly obtained from Spanish fishermen who were allowed to continue their daily work in exchange for selling some of their catch to the British inshore squadron. This barter provided cover under which messages could be passed from agents ashore. Hallowell knew and told Spencer that Villeneuve was in disgrace and that the Spanish admiral Gravina was so disgusted he wished to resign. The enemy were pressing untrained landsmen up and down the coast to bring their crews up to strength. Hallowell enclosed a copy of the enemy order of battle written in Spanish, listing every ship and the name of its commanding officer!

In mid-August Hallowell wrote Nelson, 'I look forward with pleasure to your resuming command of us, to lead your old Med. Squadron to victory.' He told Spencer on 13 September, 'We are in daily expectation of seeing Lord Nelson, and I assure you my Lord that his presence is wished for by every person.'

The *Victory* joined on 28 September, the same day that Villeneuve received peremptory orders to sail at the first opportunity. To conceal his arrival Nelson ordered that the customary gun salutes and flag courtesies should not be exchanged. Foregoing the close blockade, Nelson stationed the main fleet well to seaward to tempt the enemy out, using the same tactics he had employed off Toulon. Frigates maintained a watch inshore and formed a well-spaced line along which information could be signalled to the admiral.

The captains of the fleet were summoned on board the flagship where Nelson explained his plan for the battle that now seemed inevitable. It was based on two principles: concentration of his total force on a portion of Villeneuve's and the deliberate bringing on of a melee in which the superior morale and gunnery of the British would be decisive.

Assuming they 'held the weather gage,' i.e., maintained the advantage of being upwind of the enemy, the British were to close the French and Spanish line in two columns, one led by Nelson in the *Victory* and the second by Admiral Collingwood in the 100-gun *Royal Sovereign*. As they slowly approached nearly end on and unable to reply, the leading ships would be subjected to a terrible fire from the enemy line. But once they had penetrated that line the combined fleets would be cut into three, and the centre and rear segments would be engaged by ever-growing British forces as the following ships came into action. 'Rodney broke the line in one point; I will break it in two.' In addition to the two columns a separate squadron of the fastest ships was to form a sort of reserve. It could counter any attempt by the leading enemy ships to turn back to join the battle, or it could break the line at yet a third point and intervene in the dogfight, as seemed best to its commander.

Admiral Louis's squadron, including the *Tigre*, was selected as the mobile reserve whose actions might well decide the battle. On the list of enemy ships Hallowell had seen the name of his own lost command, the *Swiftsure*. Her presence in the enemy order of battle personalized the coming struggle, and the opportunity for revenge seemed at hand.

But luck was against him. Although the combined fleet would have to sail at some point, it might well hang on in Cadiz for a considerable period awaiting orders or a favourable opportunity. Nelson needed to re-provision his ships in rotation to ensure that he always had an adequately provisioned force available. On 3 October he summoned Admiral Louis and directed him to take his squadron to Gibraltar for supplies and to return as soon as possible. Louis protested at the prospect of missing the coming battle, but Nelson told him, 'My dear Louis, I have no other means of keeping my fleet in provisions and water but by sending them in detachments to Gibraltar. The enemy will come out and we shall fight them, but there will be time for you to get back first.... I send you first to insure your being here to beat them.' The squadron departed, none of its officers and men more downcast and frustrated than Hallowell.

Nelson may have believed what he told Louis. When the enemy sortie came it was not as a key element in some grand design but as the result of all-too-human conflict among the top French commanders. In his rage at Villeneuve's failure Napoleon had decided to replace him. His successor, Admiral Rosily, set off for Cadiz carrying the letter of dismissal. Villeneuve learned that he was to be the scapegoat and that Rosily was on his way. He also knew Nelson had been weakened by the detachment of Louis's six ships. Desperate to redeem himself, he led the combined fleets out of Cadiz toward the blockading British on October 19 and 20.

On 21 October the fleets met off Cape Trafalgar. The combined fleet numbered thirty-three ships of the line, eighteen French and fifteen

Spanish; the British had twenty-seven. Villeneuve and Gravina had actually anticipated Nelson's two-column attack, and the leading British ships were involved in desperate fighting before the allied line was broken. The absence of Louis's squadron was not a major factor because the leading enemy ships made only a token attempt to obey Villeneuve's order to come to his aid. Both sides fought with tenacity and courage, but at length the more rapid British gunnery at point-blank range turned the scale. An hour into the battle Nelson was shot through the spine by a French marksman in the rigging of the *Redoubtable*, but he survived in great pain for three and a quarter hours to learn that he had been completely victorious.

On the morning of 30 October Louis's squadron rejoined the fleet to find a scene of destruction. Almost every British ship showed signs of severe damage, but it was nothing compared to the nineteen enemy vessels that had surrendered and were now mostly under tow by their captors. A gale had blown up on the night of 21 October, and many of the prizes had sunk or gone aground. Hallowell and his colleagues with Louis were devastated at having missed what all recognized as the defining battle of the war, and above all at the death of their incomparable leader in his moment of triumph. Like Hallowell, many also mourned him as a friend.

For Hallowell there was one redeeming factor. After he had been forced to surrender the *Swiftsure* the British had immediately built a new ship of the same name. She happened to be in Nelson's fleet, so that at Trafalgar each side had a *Swiftsure*. Hallowell's old *Swiftsure* was recaptured — Collingwood said she had been 'knocked to tatters' — and although she never again saw active service, she would survive until 1813 as a prison ship, under the name *Irresistible*.

Apart from tactical innovation, a number of factors contributed to the British success. In contrast to the blockaded French, they had spent long and arduous periods at sea, honing their seamanship both as individual ships and as a fleet. Frequent weapon drill at sea was bound to produce more rapid and more accurate gunnery than the training the French could carry out in harbour. The British crews had unbounded confidence in their leader, the hero of St. Vincent and the victor of the

Benjamin Hallowell, circa 1805

Nile and Copenhagen; Villeneuve had been unable to earn or at least to retain similar stature. The presence of two different nationalities in his combined fleet was an additional complication. The perception in both fleets that the French and Spanish had been avoiding battle while the British had been seeking it had a profound psychological effect, adding to the overwhelming self-confidence of the British ships' companies.

One of Nelson's last requests was that his body not be thrown overboard, as was the usual practice. It was placed in a cask of spirits and carried to Greenwich in the *Victory*. In the meantime Hallowell's coffin had been ordered down from London and Nelson's surprisingly well-preserved body was placed inside it, with a second coffin of lead installed around Hallowell's. In the yacht of Commissioner George

Grey it was then landed to the Painted Hall at Greenwich Hospital, where it lay on view for three days before the admiral's own barge crew rowed it up the Thames to the sound of minute guns. At the Admiralty it rested until the next day.

On 9 January 1806, the state funeral was held. The procession was impressive in the extreme. The inner and outer coffins were placed in an elaborate funeral car supposed to resemble a ship of the line. The mourners were led by Admirals Peter Parker and Lord Hood. Nearly 10,000 soldiers marched in the procession to the beat of the dead march. Otherwise silence was so complete that the sound of the spectators removing their hats as the bier approached could be distinctly heard.

The favourites of the crowd were the forty-eight seamen of the *Victory*, carrying the ensign flown at Trafalgar, and unfurling it from time to time to reveal the holes torn in it by enemy shot. After a four-hour service in St. Paul's Cathedral the coffins were taken to the crypt and lowered into a marble sarcophagus. At this point the sailors of *Victory* were supposed to fold the ensign and lay it on the coffin, but they spontaneously ripped away a sheet of cloth and tore it into forty-eight pieces, one for each man. The crypt was sealed, and England's greatest hero rests there in the mainmast of *L'Orient*, fulfilling Hallowell's wish 'that when you have finished your military career in this world you may be buried in one of your trophies.'

Like everyone else in the fleet Hallowell had experienced the anxieties and frustrations of Nelson's long chase to the West Indies and back. At the same time he had had to deal with problems in his own ship, the rot at the top of the *Tigre's* command structure. We have already seen him requesting the removal of the carpenter, boatswain, and gunner for incapacity. The situation among the commissioned officers was even more troubling and culminated in two courts martial, including one against Hallowell himself. They had been held in Gibraltar on 12 and 13 November 1805.

The records tell the story. They give the impression that Hallowell's predecessor, Captain Dacres, had not insisted upon a high standard of discipline for his officers. Lieutenant Sir Norborne Thompson in particular chose to thumb his nose at Hallowell's orders, a most unwise course of action. In the background was the almost unavoidable tension between the young officers who had accompanied Hallowell and those who had been sponsored by Dacres.

Some of the wardroom officers had been in the habit of dining in the cockpit with the midshipmen. On one such occasion Thompson deliberately made one of the young men drunk. A fight had ensued and another mid had been stabbed fourteen times with a fork, but survived. Hallowell put a stop to the officers' visits, warned the midshipmen against some of the lieutenants, and placed Thompson under arrest in his cabin. Thompson requested to be allowed to take the air for an hour a day for health reasons. Hallowell consulted the surgeon who assured him Thompson was perfectly healthy. Hallowell refused his request. Later Thompson was allowed on the poop for an hour a day, and when the ship entered European waters and action became probable he was returned to duty.

At some point Thompson raised a bone of contention of the sort that could only happen at sea. The captain's and officers' servants were quartered just forward of the wardroom. There was no screen between their berths and the officers' mess. Thompson thought there should be. He therefore alleged to Hallowell that the captain's steward was repeatedly beating one of the other servants, causing him to cry out and disturb the officers' rest. At the same time he wrote privately to the steward that he did not wish to get him into trouble, but that he simply wanted to make sure a screen was put in place.

Apparently having learned nothing from his period of arrest, Thompson grew more and more provocative. On October 2, the day before the *Tigre* and her squadron were detached to Gibraltar, Thompson returned drunk from visiting a friend in the *Victory*. As soon as they had sailed Hallowell had improved the sailing trim of the *Tigre* by having some guns and shot moved forward. While officer of the watch that night, Thompson caused the watch to move shot from forward to aft, in direct reverse. This could only be construed as a deliberate aspersion on Hallowell's professional competence.

From 8 to 10 October the *Tigre* was at anchor in Gibraltar. Hallowell's standing orders stated that never fewer than three lieutenants, or two and the master, were to be on board. On two of the nights on which Thompson should have been one of the three, he nevertheless went ashore.

Hallowell had been astonishingly forbearing, but matters came to a head in Tetuan on 12 October. Hallowell had directed that there was to be no leave. Thompson sent him a message asking permission to go ashore. Hallowell called him to his cabin and said that he had abused his privileges in Gibraltar and did not deserve leave. Thompson insolently replied that any officer had a right to go ashore in any port and that this privilege could not be rescinded by the captain. No doubt it was at this time that Hallowell decided to request the commander-in-chief to convene a court martial, but the actual trial would have to wait until the fleet was reunited and the minimum number of captains and above were available.

After Trafalgar was fought and won, Thompson was tried on 12 November in the Earl of Northesk's flag ship *Britannia*, he being president and twelve captains the members. Hallowell called several of his officers as witnesses to Thompson's delinquency; the accused did not try to refute their testimony but instead threw himself on the mercy of the court. It was not forthcoming. He was found guilty and sentenced to be dismissed from the service and rendered incapable of ever serving again.

But it wasn't over. As was his right, Thompson had preferred charges against Hallowell, including twenty-three separate allegations of oppression, tyranny, browbeating of officers, courting popularity with the ship's company, false musters, and embezzlement of stores. Hallowell was tried the next day before the same court. One of the charges related to Hallowell's reprimanding the ship's chaplain for reading the Sunday lesson sitting down. Another alleged that Hallowell had slapped the cook. How this fitted with the sin of courting popularity with the ship's company is unclear, unless of course slapping the cook's face was a means of doing just that. Unfortunately for Sir Norborne, the prosecution's own witnesses tended to discredit his allegations. Given his opportunity to rebut the charges, Hallowell simply stated that he rested his defence on the testimony the court had already heard.

This was Hallowell's third court-martial. The trials for losing the *Courageux* and the *Swiftsure* involved issues of his professional competence and physical courage. In contrast this trial was about his character and probity, and therefore touched him in a more personal way. Knowing himself to be innocent, he could have had little doubt about the verdict. But entering the court and seeing the hilt of his sword pointed toward him as a sign of acquittal must have tested his ability to hear the decision in disciplined silence. 'The charges are malicious, scandalous and ill-founded ... the conduct of Captain Hallowell was in every point of view thereon attended to highly meritorious and becoming the character of a zealous and experienced officer, adjudged to be honourably acquitted.'

It is difficult to measure the intense strain on Hallowell as the *Tigre* crossed and re-crossed the Atlantic and participated in the blockade of Cadiz. He shared in the general anticipation of a battle on an almost day-to-day basis and in the frustration when it did not occur. He also bore the added burden of knowing that the ship he would lead into action was not the integrated fighting machine it should have been, thanks to the dissension and turmoil among his officers. Also very much on his mind was his responsibility for the young gentlemen entrusted to his care, including above all Robert Spencer. At least one of his officers seemed all too ready to corrupt the youngsters. Reprimanding a chaplain and slapping a cook may have been unconscious safety valves to relieve the intolerable tension. The pressures he had to face bring a new dimension to the idea of loneliness of command.

Sir Norborne Thompson's behaviour suggests he may not have been entirely sane. But there is another possibility, namely that Thompson enjoyed the patronage of someone of such influence that he could imagine that his gross indiscipline would be overlooked and that his fabrications against his captain would be given credence. With unfortunate consequences, Hallowell came to believe that something like this was indeed the case.

Ward's disgraced son Nicky Boylston had left the *Tigre* and his Uncle Benjamin in Gibraltar en route to the Mediterranean. Hallowell probably saw his departure as a blessing. Unlimited complications could easily have arisen from the presence of the captain's ne'er-do-well nephew in a ship carrying the likes of Sir Norborne Thompson.

Since arriving in the Mediterranean, the *Tigre* had been caught up in great events making huge demands on her captain's expertise and character. Morale issues culminating in the two courts martial added further pressure. Any matter not directly connected with his ship would have faded into insignificance. But at intervals Hallowell was temporarily reminded of the wider world.

Ward had written from Boston in February of 1805, remonstrating bitterly with his brother for not having written a line in reply to any of his own numerous letters, which certainly must have caught up with him by then. Inglefield at Halifax had muddied the waters by warning that the Manchester grant was at risk of escheatment. To the contrary, as Governor Wentworth informed Ward in December 1805, 'Your property at Manchester is daily rising in value from the settlement of Scotch emigrants in its vicinity and the completion of a good road directly from Manchester to Halifax.' Wentworth had just received news of Trafalgar, 'Of such blessed magnitude to Great Britain and so important to the cause of civil and religious safety throughout the world that I cannot venture to express sentiments to which language is inappropriate.'

Hallowell may have believed his father-in-law's erroneous information and suspected that Ward was bungling his duties as executor or even manipulating affairs for his own benefit. That would provide a possible explanation for his refusal to deal with Ward except through a lawyer. In the absence of some such rationale his continued silent treatment of his brother remains unexplained.

John Elmsley had been promoted to chief justice of Lower Canada in May of 1802 and moved from York to Quebec City. He suffered from cancer of both the liver and the lungs and in February of 1805 he travelled to Montreal for treatment. For a time he improved, but suffered a relapse and died on 29 April. Two days earlier at Quebec City, Mary Elmsley had given birth to their third child, another daughter. Ward Boylston travelled to Quebec in early 1806 to help her settle her Canadian affairs and arrange her passage to England with her young family.

Hallowell had lost one brother-in-law but gained another before the year was out. In late July a storm-damaged British ship was towed into Halifax Harbour. She was the 74-gun *Centaur*, successor to the *Centaur* whose loss in the hurricane of 1782 had led to Captain John Inglefield's epic journey of survival. Not surprisingly, the first man to board the stricken vessel and greet her captain was now-Commissioner John Inglefield. The navy yard took the *Centaur* in hand for repairs and Captain Henry Whitby was welcomed into the commissioner's comfortable residence. The post of Commissioner in a colonial port offered real advantages for a none-too-wealthy father with three daughters to marry off. Ann had married Benjamin Hallowell four years earlier, and on 16 November 1805, the *Halifax Chronicle* recorded the marriage of Captain Henry Whitby, RN, and Catherine Dorothy, youngest daughter of Commissioner John Inglefield.

The struggle between Napoleon and the British after Trafalgar has been likened to a contest between the elephant and the whale. Each was master of its element, but was unable to seriously injure its opponent in the latter's own sphere. For Britain, ultimate victory depended on maintaining the struggle until some combination of European powers was able to defeat the elephant on land. Similarly, Napoleon continued to build ships and a fleet, in hope of eventually combining with the Russian and the Scandinavian fleets in a force capable of overthrowing the whale. The war became as much an economic as a military test of strength.

The outlines of the future standoff became apparent soon after Trafalgar. Lubricated by British subsidies, in August 1805 the Third Coalition had come together, consisting of Austria, Russia, and England, plus Naples and Sweden. Even before Trafalgar Napoleon had recognized that his grand plan to seize control of the Channel had failed with Villeneuve's retreat into Cadiz. He broke up his camp at Boulogne in great secrecy and marched the Grand Army of more than 300,000 men into southern Germany.

Never before had such large numbers of troops been manoeuvred on such a scale in accord with a strategic master plan. The Austrian General Mack was slow to recognize the approaching threat. Before his

Russian allies could come to his aid, Mack was surrounded at Ulm in Bavaria, and forced to surrender with 50,000 men. The date was 20 October 1805, one day before Trafalgar. A little over two months later Napoleon won perhaps his most brilliant victory ever over the Russians and Austrians at Austerlitz near Vienna, and the Third Coalition fell apart like its predecessors.

For Hallowell and the Royal Navy the coming years were to be a test of endurance. There were no major battles and only rarely did any opportunity for action occur. The first came in early 1806, when five French ships of the line were captured or burnt off Santo Domingo in the West Indies. The British force consisted in large part of the squadron that had missed Trafalgar. Unfortunately for Hallowell, the *Tigre* had left Louis's command, and with his customary ill-luck Hallowell was cruising unsuccessfully off Cadiz when his former colleagues had their own moment of glory.

To Spencer, Hallowell wrote saying he was happy for them to have gained both honour and riches, 'but cannot help lamenting most seriously my unfortunate lot.' The bad fortune was accumulating: separation from his family in childhood, their impoverished exile, the late entry to the navy with its devastating effect on promotion, two unsuccessful love affairs, the loss of the *Courageux* and the *Swiftsure*, missing Trafalgar and Santo Domingo. Was fate for some reason against him?

His essential nature nevertheless remained unchanged. About this time a French ship was sunk and her captain brought to Gibraltar. He arrived bereft of everything but the clothes he wore, in precisely the same situation as Hallowell after the wreck of the *Courageux*. Empathizing completely, Hallowell sent him a trunkful of wearing apparel and a cheque for £100 to help the unfortunate man fight through his own seemingly final disaster.

His letters to Spencer continued to describe political and military developments in the Mediterranean. With an almost pathetic eagerness he seized on every scrap of intelligence that might point to a sortie by the French fleet and the opportunity for a new Trafalgar. It never happened, but only because the navy doggedly persisted in its never-ending watch, by turns soul-destroying in its boredom and all too exciting in the frequent gales. Maintaining its watch was an enormous burden: in 1808 the Royal Navy had eighty-eight ships in the Mediterranean, one-third of them ships of the line.

Most of the 28,000 seamen in this fleet did not set foot ashore for years on end. Each ship became a world unto itself, where minor irritants among six hundred men crowded into a tiny space could grow wildly out of proportion without firm but balanced discipline. Maintaining health and morale required strenuous effort: fresh provisions at every opportunity, frequent gunnery and small arms practice, encouragement of bands and hornpipes, swimming over the side when conditions permitted.

But most important was the traditional daily routine of the Royal Navy, the passage of time marked by the ship's bell, the changing of the watch, the daily issue of grog or wine, church and the reading of the Articles of War on Sundays, the hearty if unappetizing meals at regular times: a familiar and comforting framework that brought order and security to the lives of men detached from everything else they had known, perhaps forever.

By early 1807 the kaleidoscopic politics of the Ottoman Empire had brought the Turks into an alliance with their former enemies, the French. Admiral Duckworth was dispatched to Istanbul with a squadron to encourage the Turks not to actually go to war with Britain. There was an acute danger that a new French army would be landed in Egypt and the threat to the Middle East and India renewed. To forestall the enemy it was decided to send a British force to Alexandria. Major General Frazer commanded the army and the naval contribution was entrusted to Hallowell, the navy's acknowledged Egypt expert. This was a rare distinction for a captain still well down the seniority list.

The Turks had hired an army of Albanians, brave and hardy men whom Mehmet Ali had moulded into a well-trained and effective fighting force. He co-operated closely with the French consul Drouette. Meanwhile the Mamelukes leaned toward the British but awaited events.

The troops, both British and Sicilian, left Messina on 6 March. As they approached Alexandria, a number of the troop transports lost touch, and Hallowell ordered the others to remain out of sight of land while he and the general approached the port in the *Tigre*. They rendezvoused at sea with Major Missett, the British resident in Alexandria, who assured them that the governor was ready to surrender the place. But when a formal surrender demand was made to him under a flag of truce he unexpectedly declined.

On the evening of 17 March seven hundred British troops landed through heavy surf and moved to block the Albanians who were advancing to the city's relief from Rosetta. The next day the surf was so bad no more could be landed, but the Albanians were repelled. On 19 March the missing transports rejoined and anchored in Aboukir Bay, place of memories for Hallowell. This reinforcement convinced the governor that resistance was futile and Alexandria was surrendered to the British.

Hallowell had planned the naval side of the expedition in great secrecy and had carried it out with such efficiency that it achieved complete strategic surprise. As Collingwood wrote: 'I cannot sufficiently express to you the very great satisfaction I have felt at the promptitude with which this service has been done, and as its success is in a degree dependent on its sudden execution, I doubt not that its termination will be as fortunate as the beginning.'

At the general's request Hallowell joined army headquarters ashore from the beginning, advising Frazer on political and military as well as naval matters. Frazer's instructions were simply to occupy and hold Alexandria, but unfortunately he decided to go further. According to Hallowell the fault again lay with Major Missett. He had misled Frazer and Hallowell about how easy it would be to take Alexandria and had infuriated Hallowell by staying aboard a merchant ship until the danger was passed and the city had capitulated.

Hallowell believed that the Albanians could have been bought off, but Missett convinced Frazer that Alexandria would be starved out unless Rosetta was captured to ensure the supply of provisions. Two successive attacks failed, the Albanians fighting from loopholed houses against which only artillery had any effect. The Sicilian troops did not perform well and the expected Mameluke reinforcements did not turn up. Losses were severe and about five hundred British were taken prisoner, while the remainder of the assaulting force retreated to Alexandria.

Hallowell wrote to Spencer that he had not taken off his clothes or slept in a bed for eighteen days. In contrast, he was keeping young Robert Spencer on board until he was fully adapted to the climate.

With his sailors and marines Hallowell had been in the forefront of the advance to Rosetta, frequently accompanying the skirmishers at the head of the army. The British needed to send a force across the Nile to neutralize an Albanian battery on the far bank. No vessels were available until the resourceful Hallowell spotted some river craft that had been deliberately sunk by the retreating enemy. He had them hoisted out by night and determined that they were badly but not irreparably damaged. He ordered them resunk. At the next nightfall, they were retrieved and repaired in time to carry a British force across the river to a successful dawn attack.

More than twenty-five years later, on Hallowell's death, a general who had been a lieutenant during the campaign wrote to the *United Services Journal*, remembering how the admiral had been:

> the life and soul of that expedition, and he was admired and beloved as much for his dauntless exertions in flood and field as for the benevolence and kindness he extended to all whom it was in his power to be useful to. One survives that gratefully remembers what is due to the memory of the indefatigable Hallowell, who for nearly a month under the burning sun and cold wind of an Egyptian April shared with him his cloak and bivouac at night and fought alongside of him each succeeding day.

The attack on Rosetta had failed, but despite Misset's dire predictions Alexandria continued to be well supplied. The defenders were outnumbered 9,000 to 3,400, but were assisted by twelve gunboats that Hallowell had deployed on Lakes Mariotis and Mahdi on the city's outskirts. He was certain Alexandria could be held, although several thousand more troops would be needed if any further advance were to be made. Many of his sailors were working ashore but slept on board at night and were not allowed to get drunk. In consequence there were no health problems in the ships.

At heart the army did not want to be in Egypt, and in Hallowell's view it was not doing its best to extend and improve the city's fortifications: not all the guns had been landed, and each new engineer came up with a different plan of defence. Egypt was almost a personal issue with Hallowell, and he was scathing in his reports to Spencer about the apathy of the soldiers who did not share his commitment.

Meanwhile, Duckworth's mission to Istanbul had failed, the Turkish Sultan Selim had been assassinated, and the British government decided to evacuate Egypt. Hallowell managed this always-difficult task with complete success. Before sailing he negotiated the liberation of the British prisoners of war, dispatched an overland letter to India advising the authorities there of the situation, and partially blocked the harbour of Alexandria. During the recent invasion, Hallowell's former passenger Elphi Bey had been poisoned by persons unknown, and shortly after the British departed Mehmet Ali treacherously massacred most of the remaining Mamelukes. The sultan in Turkey had no choice but to

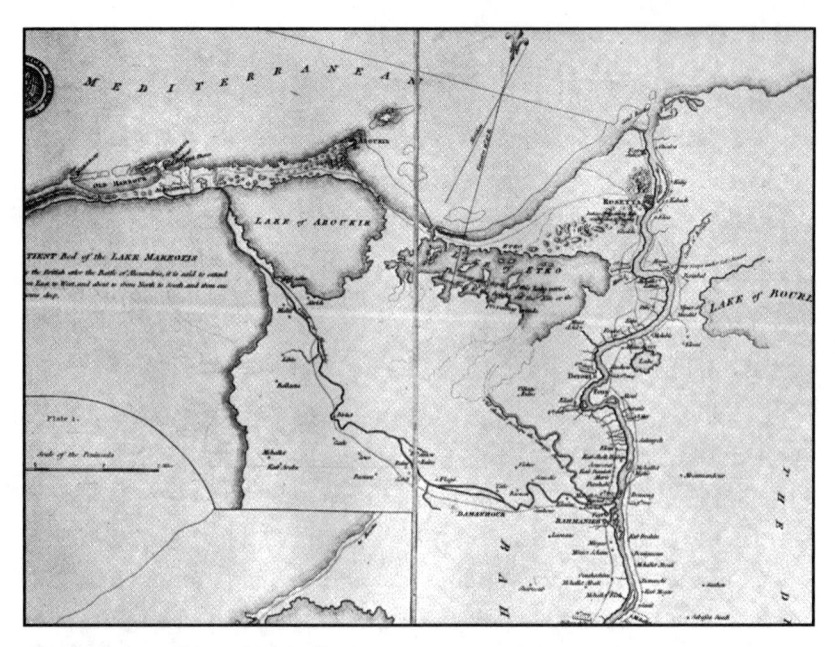

Contemporary Map, Lower Egypt

appoint Mehmet Ali as pasha, and he thus became the unchallenged ruler of Egypt.

General Frazer praised Hallowell and the navy lavishly. Admiral Collingwood wrote complimenting Hallowell on 'your ability, your resolution in looking dangers in the face and your skill in surmounting them,' and told Admiral Louis, 'the laborious part he has taken ever since the army landed and the advantages derived from his intelligent mind cannot but obtain for him the highest approbation of the Lords Commissioners of the Admiralty.' And indeed the Lords were quick to express 'in the strongest possible terms their high approbation of the zeal and intelligence with which the enterprise was carried out.'

Gratifying praise, but as nothing in the face of Hallowell's crushing disappointment. As a schoolboy he had listened to Ward's tales of his journey through that mysterious country. He had fought with Nelson at the Nile and operated afterwards on the coast for several months. He had been there again in 1801 with Keith, ill-starred as that operation was for him. He had carried out the potentially important but eventually abortive mission with Elphi Bey, and had just been deeply involved in the contest for the country for the fourth time.

He now had to face the fact that his superhuman efforts to make the latest expedition a success had been in vain. What could have been a resounding triumph for British arms had ended in what he saw as an unnecessary evacuation. His performance became a footnote to a footnote of history instead of the highlight of a famous victory. Unkind fate again, and this latest contact with the British army might have led to a perhaps unconscious resentment that would in time prove unfortunate.

His devotion to duty faltered briefly. In a letter to Spencer he reported, 'Tigre's copper is growing foul and in so many places is coming off that I hope she will be ordered home ... and although I would never apply to have my ship ordered from a foreign station when there was certainty of active employment, yet I cannot help expressing a wish to see my family from whom I have been absent three years, if it can be done with propriety.' The appeal for Spencer's intervention could hardly have been more apparent.

And yet when, in October 1807, Collingwood arrived in Syracuse with the fleet and asked Hallowell to stay he was glad to do so and got busy repairing the *Tigre's* copper, merely complaining that not a letter had been received from England for some months. At this time Hallowell was Collingwood's most trusted colleague, and the *Tigre* would lead the larboard column in the event of a fleet action.

In the end, either Collingwood or Spencer succeeded in getting *Tigre* ordered home. She arrived at Spithead 28 January 1808, three years and five months since her departure. On arrival Hallowell was obliged to give Spencer some bad news. While riding in Malta on the way down the Mediterranean, young Robert had fallen from his horse and broken his leg. Of course Hallowell could have sent word of the accident from Malta. He was not one to shirk this unpleasant duty, but probably reasoned that there was no point in alarming the parents when in any case there would be no opportunity of keeping them advised until the ship arrived home. He took a chance, but was able to provide a happy ending with the news that the boy was recovering well and had been walking for the last two weeks.

A few months later he found it necessary to advise the earl of a very different matter. Robert had been carrying on an intense correspondence with an unnamed married lady who had numerous admirers. Her husband was extremely jealous and had actually forbidden Augustus Clifford, Robert's cousin, to call at his house in London. Hallowell had cautioned Robert and directed him in future to enclose all his letters to the lady in an envelope addressed to her husband 'to prevent him saying anything ridiculous.' He was sure Robert would have forgotten the whole thing by the end of the *Tigre's* next voyage. However, he was instead forced to caution young Robert again, still hoping that it would not be necessary for the earl himself to deal with the matter.

More than twenty years earlier Ward Boylston had returned from his journey to Egypt with a mummy. Brother Benjamin Hallowell topped this by arriving with an ancient six-ton sarcophagus that he presented to Earl Spencer, expressing the hope that it would not be too big for either of his patron's houses! A coffin to Nelson, a sarcophagus to Spencer — what eccentricity hidden beneath the demeanour of the consummate naval officer! Like Nelson, Spencer was apparently not offended, for a few weeks later young Robert delivered a silver-plated dinner set for Hallowell, 'the most valuable article I ever possessed.'

While his ship reprovisioned at Portsmouth, Hallowell enjoyed a brief leave with his family. The eldest child, Charles, was now eight years old; Benjamin, seven; and Henrietta, five. He had been gone for over three years; even Charles and Benjamin would hardly remember him. Many years later the children's nurse would receive a generous bequest in Hallowell's will, but we do not know what he thought at the time of how the children were being brought up. Whatever his opinion, he probably kept it to himself, realizing that his prolonged absences disqualified him from playing the master of the house. The family were now living at Eltham, a semi-rural London suburb not unlike Hackney. It was situated near enough to Greenwich to remind Hallowell of his former friendship with the disgraced Queen Caroline. Eltham was also several miles closer to the Gees at Beddington Manor and on the same side of the Thames, so Hallowell's frequent visits either alone or with his family, were made easier.

In early April the *Tigre* was ordered to the Downs, and Earl Spencer made the short passage from Portsmouth as Hallowell's guest. If his visit was in part an inspection, he was apparently satisfied, for he not only continued to entrust Robert to Hallowell's care, but also sent a second son to the *Tigre* a short time later.

Hallowell hoped to be part of a squadron under Admiral Saumarez being readied for service in the Baltic, but when he turned down the job of Captain of the Fleet he was told to remain in the Downs anchorage under the command of Commodore Owen. He took advantage of the hiatus by having his wife live on board, very much a second honeymoon after his three years in the Mediterranean.

The idyll was briefly interrupted when the Duke of Clarence, a naval officer and second in line to the throne, insisted on visiting various ships, including the *Tigre*, and a whole day was wasted in useless ceremonial. Hallowell had met the duke many years before when in the *Falcon* in the West Indies, and was certainly on better terms with him than with his brother the Prince Regent, but the intrusion was frustrating.

Commodore Edward Owen was responsible for the Royal Navy's surveillance of the French-occupied Channel ports. Napoleon's camp at Boulogne was long gone, but the French were building warships very energetically, especially in the Dutch yards on the River Scheldt, which after Toulon was Napoleon's largest naval arsenal. The Dutch site was capable of building and sheltering a large fleet that could reach British shores in twenty-four hours.

It was almost impossible to maintain a close blockade of the Dutch naval yards because of weather and the intricate passages and shoals of the low-lying coast. The possibility of a sudden concentration of troops and a renewed attempt at invasion was very real.

One day just before the Baltic squadron sailed, Hallowell and Owen were walking on the strand. Hallowell told his companion that he wished he were going with them on 'real service.' Owens's enigmatic reply was that if they had indeed been going on real service Hallowell would certainly have been with them, and that in a short time he would have no reason to complain at being left behind.

12

LOST FRIENDS
1808–1811

I am astonished that his Lordship would for one moment suppose me capable of submitting to receive any favour from him in future.

Benjamin Hallowell to Sir Samuel Hood,
referring to the Earl of St. Vincent

On 5 May 1808, Hallowell received 'Most Secret' orders. His mission was to determine whether blocking the Scheldt with sunken vessels would prevent ships of the line from deploying from Napoleon's Dutch naval arsenal. Ann Hallowell hurriedly disembarked and the ships sailed the next day for a preliminary reconnaissance.

A detailed knowledge of the tides and currents and the depths in the channels was essential before the operation could even be planned, but it had to be gained in such a way as not to alert the enemy. At Hallowell's request he was given a considerable force, consisting, besides the *Tigre*, the *Edgar*, *Triumph*, and *Minotaur*, all 74s, and a gunboat, a schooner, and two cutters. The ships of the line were present to create the illusion that the British were actually implementing a blockade of the River Scheldt while the survey work, the true mission, was accomplished by the smaller vessels, which alone could be risked inshore.

Hallowell was amazed at the navy's lack of knowledge of these strategically important waters after more than ten years of war. For eight to ten days he embarked in one or other of the smaller vessels and reconnoitred the Durloo and Weilingen channels, the main exits from the Scheldt and the port of Flushing on Walcheren Island. The ships came under frequent fire from the shore batteries that they pretended to be observing. He learned that eight enemy ships of the line were ready for sea. He measured the precise widths and depths of the channels at various stages of the tide, and determined that under the right conditions enemy ships of the line could pass through either the Durloo or the Weilingen.

Hallowell established close contact with both Dutch and British smugglers plying between Britain and the continent. The implicit bargain was a blind eye — sometimes — toward the illicit trade in exchange for intelligence, especially information concerning the Scheldt. These dealings had to be handled with great discretion and subtlety. Hallowell was well aware that many of his informants were actually double agents equally prepared to pass to the enemy any information he might let slip.

He concluded that blocking the Durloo would merely divert the tidal stream into the Weilingen, making it more easily navigable.

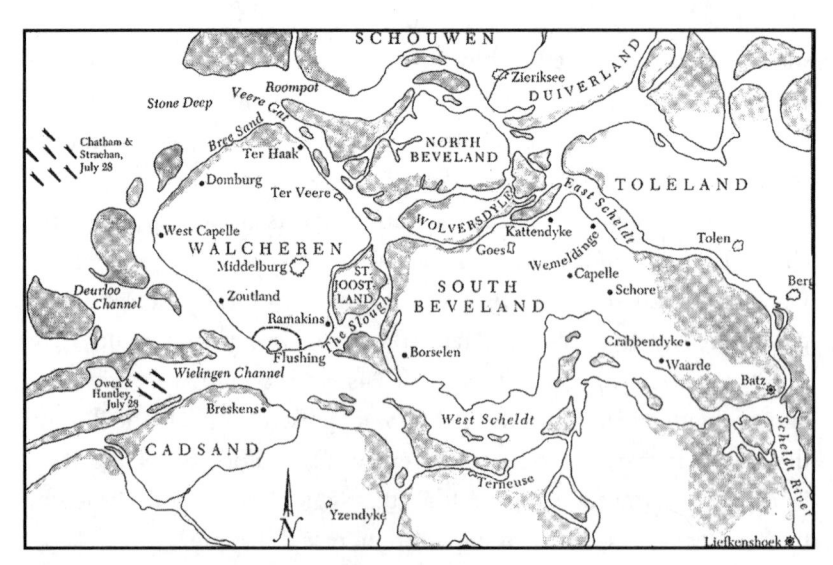

Hallowell's reconnaissance led to the unsuccessful amphibious expedition of 1809 (the ships are those participating in that attack).

Sinking blockships in the narrowest part of both channels would be extremely expensive, since each was more than a mile wide. Even if successful, such a blocking operation would prevent a sortie only temporarily — once the obstacles had been located and marked with buoys it would be possible for ships of the line to work out with favourable wind and tide conditions. In sum, he did not consider a blocking operation feasible.

He made three recommendations: that the smugglers should be tapped for regular intelligence, that a closer watch should be placed over the Scheldt, and that consideration should be given to an amphibious attack on Walcheren.

After Hallowell's return to the Mediterranean, this last recommendation was to lead to one of the most costly British failures of the war. A major amphibious attack under General Lord Chatham and Admiral Sir Richard Strachan made slow progress in the waterlogged terrain of the lower Scheldt. The French resisted strongly, but sickness more than the enemy decimated the British army. Walcheren was captured but abandoned, and the force eventually withdrew without having achieved its aim. (In 1944 Canadian troops fought through the same conditions in the same area in one of the most difficult campaigns of the Second World War.)

However, for the moment, Hallowell's mission had been a complete success, providing the government with all the information it needed to make a decision. It was not his fault that the chosen course of action later failed disastrously in execution. His intelligence, professional knowledge, and personal courage had again met the challenge.

His commander in the first Egyptian expedition, Admiral Sir Richard Bickerton, was now one of the Lords Commissioners of the Admiralty. As a special mark of favour Bickerton asked Hallowell where he would like to go next. Hallowell consulted Earl Spencer. Personally, he would never lobby for a particular station: 'As long as I live I shall consider my life devoted to the service, it will always be a matter of indifference to me in what climate I serve.' However, if the earl wanted his son to be in any particular location then Hallowell would ask Bickerton to send the *Tigre* there.

In the meantime, the ship was temporarily attached to Admiral Russell's squadron, which had the duty of watching both the Scheldt and the main Dutch naval station at the Texel. Hallowell had no respect for Russell's professional abilities. Hallowell believed that each area should have been a separate command and criticized Russell for basing his force at Yarmouth, too far from the Scheldt to be effective. He had been unable to convince the obstinate admiral that there was no need to maintain a close watch at the Texel except at periods of spring tides, the only times when the depth of water was sufficient for ships of the line to depart. Hallowell asked Bickerton to remove him from the squadron, no matter where, as long as it was not under Russell.

At the end of July 1808 he was writing to Spencer that he had been confined to bed by a cold that had fallen on his lungs. His ship's surgeon predicted that he would recover within ten days, and he remained aboard while his first lieutenant sailed the *Tigre* to Spithead, Bickerton having arranged the ship's transfer to the Channel fleet. But a few days later Hallowell's condition worsened. A new doctor removed forty ounces of his blood — 'which has relieved me wonderfully' — and ordered him ashore to recuperate. Captain Kerr came on board in temporary command, but Bickerton assured Hallowell that he would be reinstated as soon as he recovered.

His illness occasioned a remarkable letter from Lady Spencer, relaying young Robert's deep concern for his mentor's health and her own anxiety for the man who had been entrusted with her beloved son's safety and upbringing. He was urged to persuade Bickerton to give the *Tigre* a better surgeon than the one who had so underestimated the severity of his illness. He was not to think of returning to duty until he was fully recovered, and above all when he did return to sea he was 'to take all possible care of yourself and not start out of bed in the middle of the night, and run out on deck stark naked when a penetrating fog surrounded you, upon every trifling noise happening twenty times an hour.'

This last injunction must have originated in some incident related by young Robert. After long experience in command many captains speak of a sort of sixth sense that spontaneously brings them on deck just as some critical situation is about to arise. After more than fifteen years Hallowell would surely have developed such an instinct. But if Lady Spencer's words reflect reality, it seems that he was beginning to sense non-existent emergencies.

Perhaps the awesome responsibilities of command, accepted without a break for so long, were at length beginning to tell on his nervous system. Such jumpiness may also have been related to a lack of confidence in his watch-keeping officers, that may have been unjustified now that they had been under his guidance for four years. Already in the loss of the *Courageux* we have seen a failure of officers to rise to the occasion in the absence of their captain, and here is a second, albeit inconclusive, indication that developing his lieutenants might not have been one of Hallowell's strengths, whatever his success with the youngsters such as Robert.

Hallowell's recovery took much longer than expected. In early September he was riding horseback, but not until the end of October did he rejoin his ship. None of the correspondence gives a specific diagnosis. In Corsica in 1794 he had contracted what may have been malaria, a recurrent disease. In 1807 he had spent three weeks in the Nile delta, home to numerous endemic maladies. His contacts with the Scheldt smugglers may have exposed him to the fever that was to take the lives of so many British soldiers in 1809. Remarkably, in all his numerous actions he had never been wounded except for grazes at Les Saintes and the Nile, but from this period onward his health becomes increasingly problematic. At some point he developed gout, legacy of his lifelong love affair with the wines of Madeira and the endless consumption of the Royal Navy's beloved salt beef.

Charles was nearly ten, quite old enough to be sent to sea under his father as the first step in a naval career. The two rejoined the *Tigre* at a fateful moment. After the battle of Austerlitz in 1805 the Austrians had once again withdrawn from the coalition. The Prussians, neutral up to now, had chosen this inopportune moment to confront Bonaparte. They were soon forced to conclude a humiliating peace after the emperor crushed their army in the twin battles of Jena and Auerstadt.

Napoleon now concentrated against the Russians, and after a series of hard-fought encounters they were induced to negotiate an end to the war. Meeting on a raft in the River Niemen, Napoleon and Czar Alexander concluded the Peace of Tilsit on 25 June 1807.

This event and the subsequent Congress of Erfurt probably marked the apex of Napoleon's power. The three great continental nations had repeatedly been defeated. Large areas of Germany, Italy, and the Adriatic coast had been incorporated into France. One of Napoleon's brothers was King of Holland, another King of Westphalia, and a third King of Spain; and other relations ruled principalities in Italy and elsewhere. To legitimize his meteoric rise from nothing the emperor divorced the barren Josephine and secured the hand of the Princess Marie Louise of Austria in marriage. Any descendants would carry the royal blood of one of the most illustrious ruling families in Europe as well as that of the Corsican adventurer.

Napoleon's alliance with Russia deprived Britain of a large portion of the hemp, tar, and timber essential to the maintenance of her fleet. With virtually the entire coast of Europe under his control, Napoleon reinforced his Continental Policy: no goods of British origin were to enter the continent. His aim was to weaken his enemy by destroying the trade that was her lifeblood. This strategy began to inflict real hardship.

But the emperor had perhaps not fully considered the effects on the people within his empire. Their seaborne trade was paralyzed and they were loath to be deprived of the British manufactures and colonial produce upon which they had come to depend. Napoleon had long ago incurred the hatred of the ruling dynasties he had humiliated. Now discontent began to stir among the ordinary people who were paying the price of his boundless ambition.

Napoleon believed that if he could increase the combined fleets of the nations under his control to a total of one hundred and fifty ships of the line, he would finally overwhelm the hundred such vessels in the British fleet, a number that could not be increased for lack of manpower. In pursuit of ships he invaded Portugal in November 1807, but the Portuguese fleet escaped just before Lisbon was captured and then a

British expedition forced a French withdrawal.

The abortive Portuguese adventure offered France a pretext for occupying Spain with a large French army. Napoleon forced King Ferdinand to abdicate and replaced him with Joseph Bonaparte, the emperor's brother. In May 1808 the populace, led by their priests, rebelled spontaneously against the godless regime of the puppet king. The French regained control of most of the main cities,

Viscount Collingwood

but their communications remained under constant threat as the Spanish waged a guerrilla campaign characterized by ferocity and cruelty on both sides.

In support of the rebels the British sent an army under General Sir John Moore. The *Tigre's* next mission was to carry a large quantity of money to the general to finance his advance into Spain. The ship also carried specie for the merchants of Oporto, Lisbon, and Cadiz that would earn Hallowell £1000 in freight money. Perhaps this windfall marked the end of the years of financial hardship that had been Hallowell's lot since boyhood. With this errand completed the ship sailed on to Mahón on Minorca to join Collingwood's Mediterranean fleet.

Hallowell had a realistic appreciation of the Spanish struggle. 'There is great spirit among the lower class of people but there wants energy and exertion on the part of the leaders.' He predicted that the nobles in the regional juntas directing the Spanish forces would be incapable of organizing effective co-operation, and so it proved. After an initial advance Moore's army found itself alone and almost surrounded by the French. It was forced to withdraw to Corunna on the north coast.

Moore was killed and the troops were re-embarked after suffering heavy casualties.

Nevertheless, the policy of aiding the rebels was maintained and General Arthur Wellesley, later Duke of Wellington, took command of a force at Lisbon. The struggle seesawed, but Wellesley would gradually drive the French from Portugal and advance into Spain. A running sore had opened that Napoleon was never able to heal.

Hallowell strongly advocated the creation of a standing amphibious strike force consisting of a few warships and transports and about 2,000 British troops capable of descending anywhere along the coast to support Spanish operations and cut French communications. Naturally he hoped to command the squadron himself.

For purely political reasons the sort of force Hallowell envisioned nearly came into being under someone else. The famous Captain Lord Cochrane was the hero of numerous small ship engagements, in which he had triumphed through courage and daring tactical innovation while earning a fortune in prize money. His latest exploit had been to lead an attack by fire ships and explosion vessels against a French squadron at anchor in the Basque Roads in southwestern France. The attack had been only partially successful because Cochrane's superior, Admiral Gambier, had failed to render him timely assistance.

Cochrane was a Member of Parliament. Mulgrave, the First Lord of the Admiralty, proposed that the House of Commons should honour Gambier with a vote of thanks for what was being touted as a major success. The disgruntled Cochrane not only refused as a Member of Parliament to support the vote, but also threatened to expose the admiral's delinquency on the floor of the house. Mulgrave tried to buy him off or get him out of London, eventually offering him command of a flying squadron of three frigates with a regiment of soldiers embarked and a free hand to harass the enemy throughout the Mediterranean. What would Hallowell not have given for such a mandate! The unstable Cochrane turned the offer down, jeopardizing his whole career, and no such interdiction squadron ever came into being.

Again the dreary routine they had briefly escaped enveloped Hallowell and the *Tigre*. Again the blockade of Toulon, counting the enemy ships, which often outnumbered the British but never ventured far beyond the harbour mouth; the *Tigre* occasionally exchanged distant broadsides with them before they ran for safety. Hallowell kept the *Tigre* at sea beyond its fair share, frequently declining opportunities to return to Mahón.

Again the frustration and disgust at the lack of energy and the political intrigues of the British allies in Naples and Spain. The Spanish sent so many French prisoners of war to Minorca that they could conceivably have overcome their ill-disciplined guards and captured the essential base at Mahón. Collingwood refused to permit the prisoners to be landed except to the isolated island of Cabrera, where he kept them well supplied for nearly a year. Nevertheless, they remained a threat if a surprise raid were to succeed in providing them with arms.

And all this was apparently destined to last forever, as Napoleon moved from strength to strength and nothing but the British fleet seemed able to set a limit to his progress, albeit at the water's edge.

What excitement there was came from the Italian coast, where inshore boat operations obtained intelligence and interdicted the coastal shipping. When pursued, the little coasters invariably sought shelter in the many small coves, and their crews landed and took up positions in the rocks and trees ready to fire upon the British as they entered. Sometimes the *Tigre's* boats anchored by night in secluded bays, meeting agents and climbing the cliffs to observe the countryside by the light of dawn. For Robert Spencer and the other young officers such independent action provided invaluable experience in positions of independent responsibility.

Hallowell learned from his reconnaissance that Napoleon had withdrawn many of the occupying troops. He recommended to the British commander in Sicily that he make a landing on the coast of Tuscany. His recommendation was not accepted.

The British base at Mahón on the Spanish island of Minorca was a commodious harbour about two miles long and half a mile wide, capable of sheltering an entire fleet. Some two hundred nautical miles from Toulon, it was strategically well placed to support the blockade, sheltering ships from the winter gales and providing a secure anchorage for the transports, as well as offering the capacity to careen ships of the line. Mahón was defended by a fort at its mouth and contained a barracks for about 5,000 soldiers and a large hospital. Its main handicap was that in easterly winds it was very difficult to exit from the harbour.

At carnival time the little place was lively, and when permitted ashore the younger officers participated in nightly masked balls at which they were introduced to the waltz, the new dance that was sweeping Europe, as well as to Spanish dances. The island was flat, treeless, brown, and arid, but it was possible to go on picnics in the hinterland, and there was an excellent restaurant operated by Admiral Brueys's former personal chef in *L'Orient*, one of the flagship's few survivors. Possibly he had been among those rescued by the *Swiftsure*.

In Admiral Sir Cuthbert Collingwood, Hallowell had a commander whom he respected and with whom he was on terms of real friendship perhaps even closer than his relationship with the departed Nelson. Their association, if at first indirect, was of very long standing. Collingwood had been a lieutenant in Graves's flagship in Boston in the months leading up to the evacuation of 1776 and had fought on shore at the Battle of Bunker Hill. He must have been well aware of the sensational quarrel between Graves and Hallowell's father the Customs Commissioner. When Midshipman Hallowell joined the *Asia* in 1778, his mentor had been Cuthbert's younger brother Wilfred, who probably introduced the two men in the West Indies when all three were serving there in the mid-1780s.

Of humble origins, the unpretentious Collingwood despised those of his colleagues who lusted too much after prize money. He had led one of the British lines at Trafalgar and was the obvious and indeed the only choice to take over as commander-in-chief in the Mediterranean after Nelson's death. He and Nelson had been great friends, but apart from Hallowell he appears to have had few other friends. When serving under St. Vincent in the Channel fleet, he had made no secret of his dislike of his commander's administrative micromanagement.

Collingwood's responsibilities as commander-in-chief were impossibly extensive. From Gibraltar to the Dardanelles the Mediterranean is 2,000 miles long. Maintaining a continuous blockade of Toulon against an often-superior enemy and co-operating with the difficult Spanish, while at the same time directing and administering his own scattered fleet of eighty vessels, would have been challenging enough. But he had also to be aware of developments in Turkey, Egypt, Italy, and the Adriatic, and ensure that his forces were distributed to meet emergencies in any quarter. The fleet and the fortress of Gibraltar were both heavily dependent for supplies upon the Barbary States, which therefore had to be treated diplomatically and kept in a state of amity despite their piratical conduct.

A stratagem devised by Collingwood and Hallowell produced the only notable action of this dreary period. A retired officer of the pre-revolutionary French navy sometimes came offshore in the vicinity of Toulon to pass to the British information which often proved correct about the French fleet. But Collingwood believed the man to be a double agent whose real loyalty was to Napoleon. On this occasion he brought news that a relief convoy was preparing to sail from Toulon to Barcelona, information Collingwood already had. Collingwood believed the spy's real mission was to ascertain the readiness of the British fleet.

Anticipating his arrival in Mahón, Collingwood struck the topmasts on some of his ships, careened others, and generally created the impression that a full-scale refit was in progress and that it would be some time before the fleet would be combat ready.

The agent made his report and duly observed the activity in the navy yard. Within an hour of his arrival he was on his way back to Toulon in the frigate that had brought him. No sooner was he out of sight than the flagship signalled for 'All Captains' and 'Prepare for Sea.' According to an eyewitness,

> *The boatswain's pipe is heard, and in an instant the men's occupations are changed. Tar, paint and blacking brushes are laid aside. Caulkers are knocked off and scaffolding and stages got on board. Top and top-gallant masts are swayed aloft, yards crossed and sails bent, in an incredible short space of time, and, before sunset, the studding-sail gear is rove, boats are upon the booms, everything in its place, the decks clean swept, and the men at their grog; and the*

whole fleet, which a few hours before seemed half dismantled, and all bustle and confusion, is now in perfect order, and only awaits the land breeze in the morning to lift their anchors and proceed to sea.

The next morning the fleet was underway. With battle imminent, Hallowell had to consider the naval future of ten-year-old Charles should his father not survive. In a private note to Robert Spencer he solicited his help:

Well, I do think these people will at last put to sea, and then of course we shall have an action: and if anything should happen to me in it, Spencer, I shall leave you my little boy here as a legacy; he will want protection and care, and I know you will have the will, and I hope you will have the power to give him both, and to bring him forward in the profession.

On his return to Toulon the completely deceived agent assured Hallowell's one-time captor Admiral Ganteaume that the time was ripe to resupply Barcelona. On 23 October 1809, he dispatched a convoy and escort. Since 17 October Collingwood had been waiting off Cape St. Sebastian. On the night of the twenty-third the British frigate *Voluntaire* was seen approaching from the direction of Toulon, displaying the night signal 'Enemy Fleet at Sea.' Collingwood ordered his ships to prepare for action.

As dawn rose after an anxious night on full alert, the enemy were perceived to windward — three sail of the line and two frigates, with a convoy of seventeen or eighteen merchant vessels. The *Tigre* and *Bulwark*, two of the fastest ships, were detached to intercept. The enemy convoy then altered course toward the Bay of Rosas at the mouth of the Rhône, while the naval escort fled to the southeast, with the *Tigre*, the *Bulwark*, and five others under Admiral Martin in pursuit. Two of the British became separated, but the rest searched through the night.

At the next dawn the French were not in sight. The *Canopus*, Martin's flagship, had sprung her mainmast and he wished to call off the search.

But Hallowell and another senior captain offered their opinion that the French could not yet have reached any port, that they were probably making for the mouth of the Rhône, and that the British should stand into the land with a view to making an interception later in the evening. Accordingly, the squadron continued to approach the intricate shoreline in poor visibility with no land in sight, but discoloured water showing that they were nearing the mouth of the river. Martin had hoisted but not executed the signal to wear away from the shore, when the *Tigre* sighted four ships to the north.

The signal was cancelled and the squadron stood on to intercept. The French were well inshore and came to anchor when they sighted their pursuers. With night coming on and unable to fix his position, Martin did not think it prudent to proceed further into shoal water. The British stood off, keeping as close in as they safely could to prevent the enemy from escaping in the dark.

Dawn found the French ships under way, but it was clear that they could not escape. The *Robuste*, 80, and the *Lion*, 74, immediately grounded themselves between two sandbanks and began disembarking their stores and men. The *Tigre* and *Bulwark* pursued the *Borée*, 74, and the frigate *Pauline*. Hallowell got off a few shots before the fugitives under full sail literally ran themselves over the bar of the little harbour of Sète. The *Tigre* and *Bulwark* now rejoined the other ships and Admiral Martin summoned his captains for a council of war. The issue was whether the British could safely approach the grounded Frenchmen closely enough to destroy them with gunfire. Hallowell volunteered to find out, and dispatched one of the *Tigre's* boats under Lieutenant Edward Boxer to take soundings.

Boxer's boat approached closer and closer to the enemy, signalling the changing depths as she went. The French ships opened fire but the intrepid lieutenant did not interrupt his work. When the French launched their own boats to drive him off, Boxer was forced to give way. His soundings showed that the water was too shallow for the British to come within range. But the matter soon became moot. Before dark the mizzenmasts of the grounded ships toppled over their sides, making it obvious that the vessels would soon break up under the relentless pounding of the sea.

The French left nothing to chance. That night they set both enemy vessels afire. Lieutenant Crawford's eloquent account brings the scene to vivid life, at the same time illustrating why a fire at sea was the greatest terror of every seaman in the days of sail:

> In less than ten minutes both ships were in flames fore and aft. The haze, which prevailed all day, had now dispersed, and the night was beautifully fine, with just enough wind to blow aside the smoke and fan the fire, which rapidly spread to every part of the upper works, and raged and burned with the fierceness and intensity of a furnace. It was a grand and sublime spectacle, the sight of these two burning ships, and one which might be viewed without anxiety for the fate of the crews.

The French ashore and the British afloat gazed in awe as the fire reached the magazines and one ship, then the other, erupted in enormous explosions. Hallowell must have been forcibly reminded of the Egyptian night a dozen years before when the tar melted in the *Swiftsure's* seams, as *L'Orient* and her 1,000 men vanished in an instant of time.

The store ships had taken refuge under the protection of the batteries in the Bay of Rosas. As soon as the fast squadron rejoined Collingwood, he ordered the *Tigre* to return and complete the work of interdiction. Hallowell had the *Cumberland*, 74, and the frigates *Voluntaire*, *Apollo*, and *Topaze*. The boats of the squadron attacked under the command of Lieutenant John Tailour, first lieutenant of the *Tigre*. The bay was well protected by shore batteries, and four of the convoy were armed and resisted strongly, especially the *Lamproie*, a naval frigate armed *en flute* and converted to a store ship, mounting sixteen 8-pounders. The British suffered significant casualties, Tailour himself being wounded, but all eleven of the enemy were burned or brought out as prizes. This was the sort of operation Hallowell had always envisaged, but opportunities had rarely occurred. In recognition of his success, Tailour was promoted to commander.

Hallowell informed Spencer that Robert 'was in the first boat in the attack on the convoy; he possesses such a store of manly courage that you may be assured that he will be an ornament to his profession.'

In the early spring of 1810, off Toulon, the Physician of the Fleet warned the ailing Admiral Collingwood that his life could be saved only if he relinquished command at sea and returned to Mahón to recover. At Collingwood's request, Hallowell accompanied him in the *Ville de Paris*, temporarily turning the *Tigre* over to Captain Abel Ferris.

Although suffering from a blockage of the pylorus, Collingwood could not refrain from trying to carry out his duties, and far from improving, his health continued to worsen. At length Hallowell and the doctors persuaded Collingwood that he must return to England without waiting for a successor. For a few days contrary winds prevented the *Ville de Paris* from sailing. When she at last cleared the harbour, Hallowell and Collingwood made their final farewells and Hallowell disembarked. Both were well aware that they would never meet again. Less than two days later Collingwood died, without having seen his wife and children for nearly seven years.

In January 1810 there was a spectacular rupture between Hallowell and his one-time patron John Jervis, Earl of St. Vincent. The cause went back as far as Inglefield's problems as a commissioner in 1801 and St. Vincent's intrigues to get Hallowell to serve on the Halifax station: 'Hallowell has married [Inglefield's] daughter, I will give him a frigate and send him to that station where they will all take root together and we will hear no more of the Commissioner coming home.' Several years afterwards an unknown gossip repeated these words to Hallowell, and from then onward his trust in St. Vincent was shaken, although he kept his disappointment to himself.

Another circumstance may have entered into St. Vincent's changing perception of Hallowell. We have already seen that Benjamin Hallowell Sr. had been instrumental in winning the Westminster election in 1796 for the Tory Member of Parliament Admiral Sir Alan Gardner. In 1800 Gardner became the Whig St. Vincent's second in command in the Channel fleet, and the two quarrelled incessantly. How much of this was due to personal and professional factors and how much to political antagonism is unknowable. But association of the Hallowell name with the hated Gardner may perhaps have affected St. Vincent's judgment.

Sir Norborne Thompson was the indirect cause of the open break. The result of the two courts martial in Gibraltar had been that Thompson was dismissed from the service and Hallowell vindicated. In April 1806 Hallowell learned that St. Vincent had been persuaded to intervene on Thompson's behalf to get him reinstated in the navy. Convinced that the admiral would not have done so if he knew the facts, Hallowell wrote, 'Knowing your sense of discipline and of the service I cannot imagine your lordship could be induced to exert yourself in his favour if you were acquainted with the particulars of the trial.' To make sure St. Vincent knew the particulars, Hallowell enclosed copies of the charges and verdicts from both courts martial. He ended by urging that reinstating Thompson 'would be doing an injury to the service and holding out to others that character is of no importance when put in competition with powerful interest.'

Contrary to its author's intentions, St. Vincent took this very badly. From his flagship the *Hibernia* St. Vincent replied, 'I cannot help expressing my surprise and indignation that you of all men living should have for a moment entertained the unworthy suspicion contained in your letter, my conduct regarding Sir Norborne Thompson being the very reverse of that you have attributed to it.' Hallowell was surprised and hurt at the admiral's tone, the more so when he later heard that St. Vincent had in fact intervened, although not very energetically. Since the exchange of letters there had been no intercourse between the two men.

All this was recapitulated in a letter from Hallowell to Spencer. It went on to inform Spencer of the latest development. In December 1809 the Tory government was in severe political straits because of the disastrous failure of General Sir John Moore's Spanish expedition. St. Vincent made one of his rare speeches in the House of Lords, a vitriolic attack on government policy. The potential change of government raised the possibility that either St. Vincent or his friend Lord Grey would become First Lord. St. Vincent himself apparently thought so, because Sir Samuel Hood approached Hallowell as the admiral's go-between to offer him the position of Comptroller of the Navy.

The Comptroller was the senior official of the Navy Board, which in its own sphere of logistics and finance had an authority comparable to that of the Admiralty in regard to operations, discipline, and officers' careers. This important position was one of the very few full-pay shore positions for captains and would have allowed Hallowell to recapture some of the family time so lacking since the war broke out again in 1803.

Hallowell's reply to Sir Samuel was vitriolic:

> *I have to request you to state to his Lordship that honourable as I consider the situation, and gratifying as it would have been to me to have received such a proposal from any other person, yet when I consider the various instances of his lordship's unhandsome conduct toward me in the last three or four years, and particularly the insulting letter he wrote me from the Hibernia ... in answer to one I addressed to him in the most respectful terms, I am astonished that his Lordship would for one moment suppose me capable of submitting to receive any favour from him in future.*

When his friend Hood would not promise to forward Hallowell's letter to St. Vincent in the original Hallowell did so himself, '.... so that your Lordship may not be ignorant of my sentiments.' The break was of course final and complete. Hallowell's status as one of the very few officers who enjoyed the admiral's full confidence had been transformed into bitter enmity. How stark the contrast with the scene after the victory of St. Vincent, when 'so sensible was Sir John Jervis of Hallowell's advice and services on that memorable day, that as soon as the battle was over he could not refrain from telling him so, publicly on the quarter deck, embracing him at the same time, in testimony of the great emotions which he felt.'

Hallowell had reason to fear St. Vincent would use his position to spread false information. Anxious to retain Spencer's good opinion, he provided the earl with the full background, at the same time making it clear that he was not asking for the earl's support or interference. Nonetheless, both Spencer and St. Vincent were Whigs, so Spencer was well placed to counter any unfriendly rumours in the political circles in which they both moved.

This incident illustrates the distinction then existing between the professional relationship of officers of different ranks, on one hand, and their common status as gentlemen, on the other. If assessed on the former basis, Hallowell's letter constituted gross insubordination. He intended it as a private response, one gentleman to another, and was fortunate that it was accepted as such and did not become a public issue. Conceivably, it might not even affect future strictly professional dealings between the two. In the event, Phillip Yorke, rather than St. Vincent or Lord Grey, went to the Admiralty, and no more was heard of the matter.

Again Hallowell had taken a stand against a senior officer and expressed himself with remarkable freedom at great professional risk. As in the quarrel with Keith, Hallowell's readiness to risk everything on the basis of questionable information stands out. His shoe complaint rested on second-hand knowledge and so did his reaction to St. Vincent's conduct in the Inglefield affair and with regard to Thompson. He must have trusted his informants implicitly, whoever they were, but one certainly wonders whether that trust was altogether justified.

It is also worth noting that at the time of the Thompson dispute St. Vincent was very ill. He had in fact resigned for that reason in April 1807. Always short-tempered, perhaps the tone of his letter to Hallowell was even less moderate than usual because of his physical condition.

With the war apparently destined to last forever, Hallowell could see only one escape from the drudgery of the *Tigre's* role in the Mediterranean, a paradoxical combination of boredom and constant readiness. Promotion to rear admiral would open up new opportunities and offer a respite from the relentless pressure that was the lot of every captain. Had merit been a factor, he knew he would have been an admiral long ago, but the iron rule of seniority continued to penalize him for his late entry to the service. Like all those in his position, he anxiously awaited the annual promotions. As he neared the top there was always the tantalizing possibility that the next selection would delve down to his name and bitter disappointment when it did not.

At this time the Royal Navy had about sixty rear admirals. Each year about fifteen captains would be promoted and a similar number of rear admirals would be pushed up to vice admiral. Seniority-based promotion often resulted in incompetents reaching and progressing through post and flag ranks, but the Admiralty usually retired them or kept them in half-pay status while their more competent colleagues filled the sea appointments.

In January 1809 Hallowell was thirty-seventh on the list; the promotion of that year moved him up to twenty-seventh. The 'youngest' seniority promoted that year were those made captains in 1790, the year the Nootka Sound scare had broken the long drought following the American Revolution. Hallowell and his future brother-in-law Henry Whitby had both been among the thirty-five new captains made in 1793, a year of renewed war with France. In 1810 nineteen captains made rear admiral, including many with seniority of 1793, leaving Hallowell in seventh position. But because some of those above him were medically unfit for service he was one of the very top men not to have been promoted. This time the disappointment was crushing and personal. Those promoted included a madman and a known homosexual, and the line had been very pointedly drawn just above him. According to one of his subordinates with wide experience, 'As an officer and a seaman, few, if any, surpassed him in the service, to which every faculty of his mind seemed entirely devoted.' No matter: the iron hand of seniority continued to restrain him.

There was some consolation when he was made an Honorary Colonel of Marines, a rank that did not require the performance of any duties but brought with it a salary of £500 per year. This sinecure was sometimes awarded to particularly deserving captains nearing the top of the list, but in no way was it seen as a substitute for hoisting one's own flag.

There are signs that from about 1808 on Hallowell's attitude underwent a significant change. He was nearing fifty, still a captain when many considerably younger men of less merit had gained their flags. His achievements in Egypt had exhausted him but counted for nothing. 'My mind and body have been employed to the utmost during my stay in Egypt, and my health has suffered material injury.' For more than three years he had neither set foot in Britain nor seen his family, and he had made a slow recovery from what must have been a serious illness. The violent break with St. Vincent, to whom he had been so close, must have left deep psychological scars.

His letters to Spencer began to contain criticism of his superiors, beginning with Russell at Yarmouth. In the Mediterranean he criticized Admiral Martin for remaining at Palermo doing nothing but claiming his share of prize money. He soon became equally disgusted with Admiral Sir Charles Cotton, who relieved the respected Collingwood but who in Hallowell's eyes could never replace him either professionally or personally.

Cotton arrived with an Admiralty commission making Hallowell Captain of the Fleet or chief of staff. The commission was accompanied by a very flattering personal letter from Lord Mulgrave, the First Lord. At their initial interview Cotton casually mentioned to Hallowell that he had first asked for Captain Rowley and then for Captain Halsted, but both had turned the position down. Hardly flattering to the third choice.

Hallowell conveyed his refusal of the position in language as flowery as Mulgrave's own:

> *The handsome manner in which your Lordship has been pleased to express yourself of me is highly flattering, but I fear the partiality of my friends has induced them to overstate my abilities, for could I view them in the same light your Lordship has described them I should feel it my duty to sacrifice every consideration ... by immediately accepting the appointment of First Captain, but as I am sensible that there are many others more equal than myself to perform the duties of that office I must beg leave with deference to decline the honour proposed to me.*

Writing to Spencer in May 1810 he was more frank. He was sorry Mulgrave had not consulted him in advance, because the First Lord well knew that Hallowell had turned down the same position under Admiral Saumarez in the Baltic. Indeed, he had also declined to take it under Sir John Jervis immediately after the Battle of Cape St. Vincent. It was essential that a commander-in-chief and his captain of the fleet see eye to eye on professional matters. Hallowell was sure that he would never have the proper relationship with Cotton, who had the reputation of being indecisive and lacking in self confidence, yet very averse to accepting advice. Rowley had previously been Cotton's Captain of the Fleet on another station and had turned down a second opportunity to work under him. No one could accuse Hallowell of not having done his duty, 'for ever since I embarked in 1793 I have only been 10 months on shore and that was during the short interval of peace — the remainder of the time I have been actively employed on foreign service, sacrificing every domestic comfort to my public duty.'

A Captain of the Fleet had to possess great organizational and administrative skills and be capable of working smoothly with the ships' commanding officers. Although he did not fly his flag or wear the uniform, the pay was that of a rear admiral, a financial inducement to which Hallowell could never be indifferent. Three times Hallowell had been nominated for Captain of the Fleet, a sure sign that he was seen as an unusually competent staff officer, as well as a superb fighting captain, a rare combination. That conclusion is supported by St. Vincent's abortive offer to appoint him to the very important administrative post of Comptroller of the Navy.

Conscientious senior officers such as Hallowell were beginning to note a gradual degradation in the combat readiness of the fleet. At sea a certain operational sloppiness was becoming evident, most noticeably in the lack of the frequent gun practice that had been so necessary when the enemy was a real threat. Perhaps only one-quarter of captains actually fired their guns and they often looked for reasons to return to or remain in harbour when they ought to have been at sea; and they began to leave too much responsibility to their first lieutenants. In conscious or unconscious compensation for slackness at sea, there was a heightened concentration on ceremonial and spit-and-polish in harbour. Thus, at Mahón:

> *The morning and evening gun, accompanied by a volley of musketry from each ship, produced a grand effect, when echoed from the surrounding heights. Besides the reveille played by drums and fifes at daylight, there was a military symphony every evening after sunset: this performed in reciprocal responses by the different ships, and associated with the serene sky, and the stillness of the sea, really seemed to partake of magical illusion.*

Port Mahon. This almost landlocked harbour on the island of Minorca was the main Royal Navy base inside the Mediterranean.

No doubt such spectacles kept people busy and amused, but it was by no means certain that such precision and teamwork in port would necessarily carry over to the reality of an action at sea. From retirement the Earl of St. Vincent thundered, 'I hear the exercise of the great guns is laid aside, and is succeeded by a foolish frippery and useless ornament.' In this matter, at least, the views of Hallowell and his one-time mentor continued to coincide.

Wintering at Mahón, the officers lived ashore in hotels and indulged in billiards, gambling, and balls. But Hallowell felt that idleness was the root of all evil, kept the hands hard at work, and ensured that his lieutenants, including the lords and honourables, did duty all day on board ship or in command of the boats. Hallowell felt that the professionalism of his officers was being eroded, and eventually directed that the *Tigre's* officers were to be on board by the evening gun, no matter what leave was granted by other captains. In all probability he was mainly worried about young Spencer, but saw no way of shielding him from trouble without restricting all the officers.

In fact, much of Hallowell's time was occupied in lobbying for the advancement of Spencer, Clifford, and the other young officers serving in the *Tigre*. There was now an Admiralty priority list for commissions as lieutenant and promotions to commander, running in parallel with the traditional personal discretion of individual commanders-in-chief.

The navy was on the way to centralized control of promotion, but for the moment the situation was chaotic. Hallowell's local efforts on behalf of his 'youngsters' met with little success, perhaps because his attempts to be helpful had incurred Cotton's displeasure. However, as soon as young Spencer passed his midshipman's examination he received an Admiralty commission to return to the *Tigre* as one of the ship's lieutenants. Hallowell assured the proud earl, 'He is justly entitled to promotion from his own merit, and you may rely on his becoming a very distinguished character in his profession.'

Hallowell endured the despised Cotton until his friend Sir Samuel Hood left the position of second in command in the Mediterranean. With the buffer removed Hallowell contemplated asking to leave the station:

> *I have never before applied to be removed from any station, nor should I have done so now if I had the smallest confidence in the skill of the man who is to conduct the fleet, but entertaining the opinion I do of his imbecility ... I would sooner resign my command and return to England immediately if it were not for the youngsters under my care, whose interest I cannot abandon.*

Hallowell's unflattering opinion of his commander was widely shared, and no doubt reached the Admiralty through numerous channels, including probably the Hallowell-Spencer voice pipe. In July 1811 Cotton was relieved by Admiral Sir Edward Pellew, who would also earn Hallowell's criticism, but was a definite improvement on Cotton.

The promotion of 7 August 1811, finally made Hallowell a rear admiral of the blue, second on the year's list. To his great joy he would not spend any time on half pay in his new rank. He was to go home briefly to hoist his flag and then return to the Mediterranean in command of the British squadron supporting the Spanish land forces operating against the French invaders on the east coast of Spain.

The *Tigre* arrived at Spithead 1 August 1811. Characteristically, Hallowell called all the officers together in his cabin and told them that he was to hoist his flag as a rear admiral and that any who wished were welcome to accompany him to his flagship. He promised to further their careers according to their merit, in so far as it would be possible for him to do so as a junior admiral. Should anyone not wish to accompany him, he would do his best to secure for him whatever posting he desired, and did so for the one officer who so chose.

In mid-August he was reunited with his family. There were now four children, including three-year-old William Henry, the child of the second honeymoon in the *Tigre* in April 1808. As always, Hallowell's rare and brief visit had resulted in another addition to the family: daughter Mary-Anne would be born in 1812.

In February 1811 the Prince of Wales was officially appointed Regent, his father George III having been certified insane after a series of mental breakdowns going back to 1788. Hallowell disapproved of the Prince's extravagant lifestyle and questionable morals. As one of those who had been on good terms with Princess Caroline immediately after the breakdown of the royal marriage, he may have come to the unfavourable notice of the Prince. There is no direct evidence of any adverse effect on his career. But Hallowell was on a much firmer basis with the Prince Regent's brother and eventual successor, the sailor Duke of Clarence. It would not be until Clarence ascended the throne as William IV more than twenty years in the future that some long-overdue honours would come Hallowell's way.

Of Hallowell's political leanings we know virtually nothing. Party labels were much looser than those of today. Broadly speaking, the Tories were the party of the country gentlemen and the agricultural interest, strenuously monarchical. The Whigs were supported by many of the great lords and the commercial interests and promoted the powers of Parliament while remaining loyal to the Hanoverian dynasty. Outside the major parties was a small but noisy group known as the Radicals, many of whom supported the aims if not the methods of the French Revolution and remained sympathetic to Napoleon for that reason.

Benjamin Hallowell Sr.'s sympathies had been staunchly Tory, but Hallowell's patrons Hood, St. Vincent, and Earl Spencer were all Whigs, even though Spencer served as First Lord of the Admiralty under the Tory Pitt. Interestingly, the Comptroller of the Navy was the only position on the Navy Board whose incumbent was allowed to stand for Parliament. Hallowell had of course refused to accept that position at the hands of St. Vincent, but if he had ever had any interest in a political career he might have thought twice before turning it down.

The only physical description we have by one who served with Hallowell dates from this period:

> *In person he was the exact cut of a sailor, five feet eight or nine inches high, stout and muscular, but not at all corpulent. His countenance was open, manly and benevolent, with bright, clear grey eyes, which, if turned inquiringly upon you, seemed to read your most secret thoughts. His mouth was pleasing and remarkably handsome, but indicative of decision and strength of character; and his thinly scattered hair, powdered, and tied in a cue [queue] after the old fashion, displayed, in all its breadth, his high and massive forehead, upon which unflinching probity and sterling good sense seemed to have taken their stand. His usual manner was thoughtful and reserved; but that was often laid aside, when his conversation became lively and entertaining, mixed with anecdotes of old times and old scenes, and occasionally even sportive and playful.*

This description does not accord well with several accounts that picture Hallowell as being tall and physically imposing to a very unusual degree. At five feet eight or nine inches he would have been considerably above average, for the time, but by no means a giant. His only full-length portrait does not really help to settle the matter. Perhaps his manner and personal presence made him appear larger than life to his acquaintances.

John Inglefield's career problems continued. In 1807 he had disposed of many of his domestic effects and returned to England under the impression that St. Vincent's supposed promise of a commissionership at a British yard was about to be fulfilled. What he was actually offered was a seat on the Navy Board. He declined on the grounds that his eyesight was no longer good enough for that type of work. The Admiralty chose to regard this disability as also rendering him unfit for a home dockyard. He could, however, return to Halifax, and if the change of climate should restore his sight 'their Lordships will give favourable consideration to your claim to a similar appointment at home when an opportunity offers.'

So once again it was back to Halifax. Four years later he was still there. He was sixty-three years old, had been in the navy for over fifty years, and the prospect of a home yard was no closer than before. His thoughts turned to retirement, and in June 1811 he entered into negotiations with the Admiralty over his pension.

Rather generously he was offered £750 per year and since government would no longer be employing him he could begin to draw his captain's half pay as well. He accepted, and was relieved as Halifax commissioner by Captain Wodehouse on 9 September 1811. In early 1812 he and his family returned to England.

Regrettably, they were not to be reunited with daughter Caroline. The *Naval Chronicle* of 1810 announced the passing 'Lately, at Lymington, Mrs. Whitby, wife of Captain Whitby, late of the Leander, and second daughter of Commissioner Inglefield, of the naval yard at Halifax.' Captain Whitby was left a widower, although not for long, since he himself was to die in 1812 after a short illness.

Inglefield's letter had begun with a plea to the Admiralty to assist his son, Captain Samuel Hood Inglefield, unexpectedly on half pay despite the fact a world war was raging. His advancement had been entirely due to his merit, since neither father nor son had any weight of interest. The timing of John Inglefield's plea could not have been better. The new Admiral Hallowell was seeking a flag captain, and the obvious choice was his brother-in-law. This family-based patronage would not raise an eyebrow; indeed it would have caused general astonishment if Hallowell had chosen anyone else.

13

REAR ADMIRAL OF THE BLUE
1809–1814

We are lately returned from Catalonia shamefully disgraced.

Benjamin Hallowell at the evacuation
of Tarragona, 1813

At length the *Malta* was settled upon as the new admiral's flagship. She had a personal significance for Hallowell, being the former *Guillaume Tell*, one of the two French ships of the line to have escaped from the Battle of the Nile only to be captured later. She was not ready, so Hallowell hoisted his blue flag at the mizzen of the *Royal George*, a first-rate of 100 guns, and proceeded to the Mediterranean.

Hallowell shifted his flag to the *Malta* when she caught up at Mahón on Minorca in early spring of 1812. Anxious to know the *Malta's* sailing qualities, he received permission to make an independent cruise and proceeded to the Toulon station. Thanks to his long experience on that coast he was able to place the ship just out of range of the shore batteries, but able to observe the inner and outer harbours and determine the enemy's state of readiness.

Having formed an opinion of his ship, Hallowell returned to Mahón and set the crew to work. In only four days the ship was unrigged and re-rigged, a larger rudder installed, four hundred tons of water emptied overboard and every cask rinsed out and refilled, one hundred fifty tons of gravel ballast landed in the ship's boats, all the iron ballast shifted to change the ship's trim, and the hold completely re-stowed.

This feat was accomplished as an evolution involving every officer and man on board, but when it was concluded Hallowell allowed the officers leave to enjoy themselves ashore. As Lieutenant Crawford commented, 'Idle indeed we were, and fond of amusement when in harbour, and duly admitted of relaxation, — but yielding to none in zeal and true devotion whenever the service called for our exertions.'

Although only a two-decker, the *Malta* was classified a second-rate by virtue of her eighty-four guns; in addition she mounted twelve carronades up to 68-pounders. She could easily accommodate a flag officer and his retinue, although admiral and captain had to share the latter's quarters under the poop. Commodious as they were, during long periods at sea this could easily lead to friction between incompatible personalities. But in this case friction was unlikely thanks to the family relationship, and indeed the brothers-in-law got on extremely well.

The *Malta* had its share of characters. Hallowell's secretary and also purser of the flagship was Archibald Murray, with whom he had sailed previously and for whom he had particularly asked on hoisting his flag. A gentle man of broad education, Murray introduced an unusual element of the intellectual into the *Malta*. In marked contrast was Lieutenant Sutton, who had spent five years as a prisoner of war in France. His detention had done nothing to improve his professional ability, but he had acquired French army slang and could imitate an officer or drum major to perfection.

The master was Ben Hunter, a seaman of the old school, quiet and reserved, but a fine navigator and a fount of knowledge on all matters nautical. His one failing became apparent when he did not return from a night's leave in Alicante. Two midshipmen finally found him, severely hung over and penniless, among the denizens of the local underworld in an underground slum outside the city walls. He was too valuable to be punished, but he endured a severe upbraiding by Captain Inglefield, after which he was heard to mutter, 'I wish there wasn't a bit of bloody land in the world!'

Midshipman Henry Coffin was among the young officers in the

flagship, proof that despite Hallowell's rejection of the Coffin daughter the two families retained their affinities as fellow Loyalists.

The fathers of most of Hallowell's youngsters were men of rank and influence, but however powerful they were, their sons were treated alike: strictly but fairly. Fox was the son of Lord Holland, but that did not save him. 'Young Fox is excessively indolent — he detests the profession, and he has no more sense of religion than a broomstick.' His father asked for leave for his son, and to this favour Hallowell instantly agreed, glad to get Fox out of the youngsters' mess in the gunroom because of his conversation, drinking, and lack of religion.

Earl Spencer approved so highly of Hallowell's mentorship of Robert Spencer that he confided another offspring, his third son Frederick, to Hallowell's care. Hallowell described the boy as 'excessively sensible, engaging, interesting in conversation, and better informed on all subjects (not related to his profession) than most boys his age.' Perhaps this was due to his just having finished three years at Eton.

But in Hallowell's opinion Frederick did not appear to have the same aptitude for the navy as his elder brother, nor a strong enough physical constitution. He recommended to the earl that he choose another career for his son, perhaps the diplomatic service. The young man wanted a transfer to the army so that it would not be thought he was leaving the navy out of cowardice. But neither alternative was necessary, because within a few months Hallowell was able to tell the earl that Frederick had begun to show great promise and 'is everything you would wish him to be.' He was to remain in the navy until he succeeded to the earldom with the deaths of both his elder brothers. Lady Diana Spencer, late Princess of Wales, was his great-great-granddaughter.

Always conscious of his youngsters' morals and education, Hallowell had gone to a great deal of trouble to secure the services of a Mr. Suffield as chaplain and schoolmaster. He came highly recommended from the position of chaplain at the Royal Naval College.

By 1811 Napoleon's Continental System was beginning to break down. Under Czar Alexander, Russia especially had virtually ceased to enforce it. If that country were allowed to defect others would soon follow and Napoleon's one economic weapon would be lost. Ignoring many warnings, in June 1812 Napoleon invaded Russia to enforce obedience. This fateful event showed that Britain was winning the economic struggle, despite being almost equally damaged.

But in the same month she acquired a new enemy, when the United States declared war over the long-standing grievances of blockade and the Royal Navy's impressment of seamen they believed to be British from American merchant vessels. In a professional sense Hallowell took no part in the conflict, but there was one intriguing personal note.

In 1805, as Nelson's fleet passed Gibraltar in pursuit of Villeneuve, it had been observed by the captain of the anchored American brig *Syren*, 16, under Master Commandant Charles Stewart. His ship was part of the American squadron waging its long struggle against the Barbary pirates. The ships used Gibraltar frequently, and Stewart had often associated with British officers. It is quite possible he had met Hallowell. He almost certainly knew of him because of the noteworthy surrender of the *Swiftsure* in 1801, and he may have known that he was in command of one of Nelson's ships as they passed before him into the Atlantic.

In November 1813, in the midst of war between Britain and the United States, the two officers became connected by marriage when Stewart married Delia Tudor of Boston. Her sister Emma Jane was the wife of Robert Hallowell Gardiner, Benjamin Hallowell's first cousin. There is no record of Stewart and Hallowell having corresponded, but they must have remained at least dimly aware of each other out of professional interest and through the common connection with the Gardiners. Moreover, on at least one occasion Stewart dined with Hallowell's brother Ward Boylston.

As captain of the famous USS *Constitution*, Stewart enjoyed great success in several of the frigate actions that characterized the early part of the War of 1812. The British had become accustomed to winning one-on-one encounters with the French and Spanish even when heavily outgunned. Since Trafalgar, officers such as Hallowell had deplored the complacency of many captains who managed their ships more as yachts than as men-of-war. The results of such overconfidence became apparent when the Royal Navy was faced with an enemy of at least equal professional competence in single-ship actions.

Hallowell's return to the Mediterranean in 1812 coincided with unfolding strategic developments in the Spanish peninsula. Arthur Wellesley, now ennobled as Lord Wellington, was besieging the fortress of Badajoz on the Portuguese-Spanish frontier. When it fell he would be able to lead his Anglo-Portuguese army into Spain. There it would join with the Spanish to exert increasing pressure on Napoleon's southern flank as it struck toward France itself.

It was critical that the French armies opposing Wellington in the west not receive reinforcements from eastern Spain. Thus, Wellington insisted that a British force should be readied for service in that theatre. That army would have to come from the forces of Lord William Bentinck, British commander in Sicily. He sent General Maitland in command of three British regiments, a unit called the German Legion, plus Sicilians and Spanish, amounting in all to 6,400 infantry, plus artillery.

Rounding out the allied forces were about 14,000 Spanish regular troops in eastern Spain, apart from guerrilla bands whose effectiveness varied greatly and whose co-operation could never be relied upon.

It was obvious due to Spain's long Mediterranean coast that the Royal Navy would play a key role in the new campaign, convoying

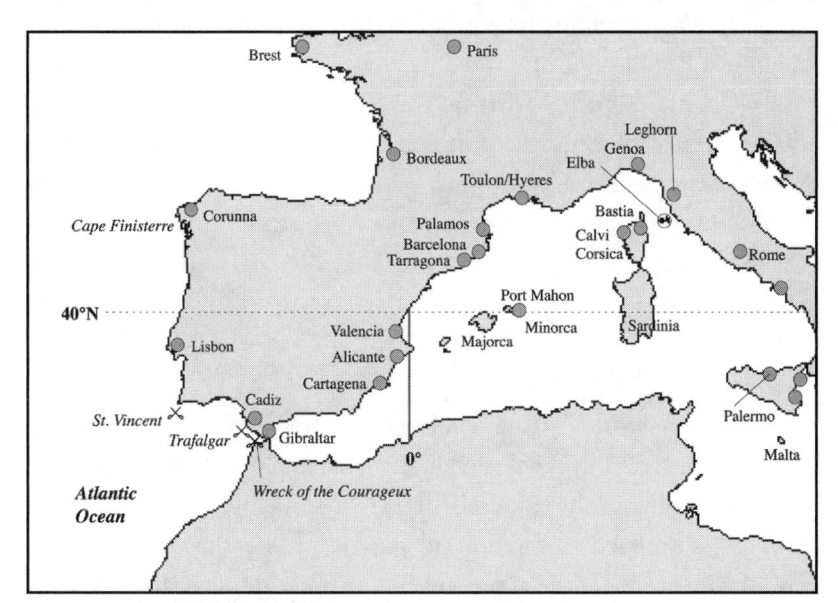

Map of Western Mediterranean

troops and supplies, interdicting French communications along the coastal roads, and supporting the army in amphibious operations. Hallowell was given command of the squadron assigned to this role. His first task was to embark the reinforcements in Italy and escort them to the Spanish coast.

Hallowell quickly familiarized himself with the situation of the Spanish forces with whom he was to co-operate. He found a distinct lack of enthusiasm for the rebellion among the upper classes, and that many of the soldiers were deserting for lack of proper clothing.

A key strategic objective for the Anglo-Spanish forces was the port of Tarragona, situated on the main route between Barcelona and French headquarters at Valencia. The capital of the province of the same name, Tarragona dated from Roman times. In 1813 it was a sleepy provincial town, most of its trade having vanished thanks to the British blockade by sea and the guerrillas' interdiction of the roads. It was now in the hands of the French, but prior to its capture it had been an important entry point for supporting the regional guerrillas with arms and money. Its recapture would increase the effectiveness of these forces while cutting the critical French supply route.

Hallowell convinced General Maitland to threaten an amphibious landing at Palamós, one hundred twenty-five miles north of Tarragona, and when the French had concentrated there, to sail by night and attack the real objective. Unfortunately, the general was hobbled by orders from Bentinck warning him not to over commit his force because he might at any time be required to return to Italy. The plan was therefore called off, and the entire force was landed at Alicante, where it occupied the surrounding countryside against some French opposition, and spent the winter of 1812–3 awaiting the spring campaigning season.

Wellington wrote asking Hallowell if the troops could be re-embarked successfully if defeated in the field. Hallowell answered in the affirmative, but admitted the possibility of some difficulty for the last lift. He then offered an opinion outside his professional capacity: 'but with the troops you have at present [i.e., in Alicante] and the assistance that can be afforded by the navy I see no necessity for the measure.'

What Wellington thought of this military judgment by a sailor is not recorded. After his numerous operations with the army, Hallowell had come to believe he was capable of rendering high-level military opinions. He may well have been correct, but it was by no means certain that all senior army officers would agree.

Before the soldiers did, Hallowell foresaw that there would be an increasing need for fodder for the horses and collected ample supplies from Morocco. Meanwhile he kept his transports ready to embark the allied troops at a moment's notice and constructed a wharf that permitted horses and mules to be walked down straight into the boats rather than hoisted aboard in slings.

Hired transports were a constant source of difficulty and frustration for senior naval officers. Their crews were ill disciplined but could not be pressed or regulated. Chartering costs were very high, yet many of the vessels were scarcely seaworthy. Beginning in 1810 the navy had converted a number of warships to troop transports armed *en flute*, but there were never enough. Hallowell's squadron included one, the *Brune*, but later the chartered vessels under his command also achieved everything he asked of them.

General Maitland suffered a nervous breakdown. His relief, General Sir John Murray, had commanded a brigade under Wellington, who had said of him: 'I entertain a very high opinion of his talents, but he always appeared to me to want what is better than abilities, viz. sound common sense. There is always some mistaken principle in what he does.' Murray's handling of operations at Alicante soon demonstrated to the whole army that he was incapable of reaching and adhering to a firm decision. General Rufane Donkin was Maitland's quartermaster general or chief of staff. He was a man of pleasing manners who made a good first impression, could be very convincing, and gradually came to exercise undue influence over his commander.

The *Malta* lay at anchor at Alicante all through the fall and winter of 1812–3, and his officers observed 'an unwonted degree of fidgetiness and irritation in the Admiral.' Quite likely he also became alarmed at the nightly entertainments on shore to which the *Malta's* officers, including his special charges, the Spencer brothers, were becoming unduly addicted. Strictly speaking, it should have been Captain Inglefield who curtailed any unwarranted behaviour, but no doubt a word from his brother-in-law was sufficient. Just as in Mahón a few years earlier, all officers were required to be on board by the evening gun, and no one doubted that this ruling came from their admiral. Some officers staged a silent protest by refusing to go ashore on leave at all, a gesture which, if noticed, was ignored.

As spring 1813 approached, rumours began to spread that an amphibious operation was being contemplated. The admiral's 'countenance had resumed its open cheerfulness, and his keen, penetrating eye kindled from time to time as the hope of more active and busy times flashed across his mind.' On 29 May Sir John Murray's army began to enter Alicante. Thanks to Hallowell's preparations, by the afternoon of 31 May 16,000 men, 1,700 horses and mules, and the army's field and siege artillery had all been embarked in the transports and the whole force had sailed northward.

At noon of 2 June they arrived off the promontory of the Col de Balaguer, and a brigade was landed to assault the fort, which commanded the only road over which artillery could conveniently pass from Valencia to Tarragona. By five o'clock the same afternoon the remainder had anchored in the Bay of Tarragona, once again the focus of allied operations.

It had been intended to land the advance guard on the first night, but Hallowell judged the surf to be too heavy, so the landing began the next morning, 3 June, following an elaborate plan prepared by Hallowell and Inglefield. The boats of the fleet formed the first two lines, with the assault troops and field pieces in the first line and cutters in the second line, ready to provide assistance if a boat was hit. The third line was formed of boats from the transports carrying the second wave of troops. Inglefield led from a cutter equipped with signal flags for passing instructions. (The illustration on page 319 of the landing in Egypt in 1801 gives a good idea of the formation adopted.)

Landing troops and equipment was a purely naval responsibility. The solders had only to embark from their transports into the boats assigned to their units and perhaps endure the fire of the enemy during their final approach. Once ashore their officers formed them up and moved inland. On this occasion the landing was unopposed.

No sailors were to land except by Inglefield's express permission; unsupervised British seamen could find the means of getting drunk anywhere.

By afternoon Tarragona was surrounded. In just three days a complete army with all its *matériel* had been embarked, transported, and landed; and had laid siege to a city over two hundred miles from the place of embarkation. There could hardly have been a better demonstration of the benefits of surprise, mobility, and flexibility inherent in amphibious operations made possible by control of the sea. Wellington might complain about the lack of naval enterprise on the west coast of Spain, but under Hallowell the eastern squadron had nothing to apologize for.

But now the fruits of Hallowell's planning and the professionalism of the naval forces were to be wasted by General Murray. The French Marshal Suchet had watched the fleet pass his headquarters at Valencia, but could not follow until 7 June. A smaller French formation under General Maurice Mathieu was seventy miles north of Tarragona, several days' march away. Murray had recognized from the beginning that Suchet would move to the relief of Tarragona as soon as he heard of the

An amphibious landing, similar to Hallowell's attack at Tarragona.

landing, but he was a hundred seventy miles distant. The British and their allies had plenty of time.

Suchet's advance would give Murray two good alternatives. He had overwhelming numerical superiority and about ten days in which to capture and prepare to defend Tarragona, supplied by and with the gunnery support of the navy. Or he could choose his moment to re-embark his army and sail to capture Valencia, from which most of Suchet's force would have departed.

From the moment he set his foot ashore General Murray began to worry that he had undertaken more than he could accomplish. Hallowell and others believed that he should have stormed the place at once, but he decided to commence a formal siege. Not until the evening of 3 June was the order given to land entrenching tools. On 4 June nearly twenty siege guns and mortars, each weighing more than a ton, were landed through the surf along with their ammunition, a feat accomplished by the navy as a matter of course. Two days later the general's forces, including the bomb vessels and gunboats of the squadron, at last commenced a bombardment against the key bastion of the Fuerte Real.

Hallowell's energy and decision were evident to the whole army, a vivid contrast to the behaviour of some of the senior soldiers. The colonel of a regiment of German hussars assured Inglefield that 'the military esteemed Hallowell to be as good a general as any they had there.' The admiral was constantly on shore to ensure that the landing and re-supply went forward as smoothly as possible in the changing weather and sea conditions. He even had a small tent set up on the beach in which he could snatch a few hours' sleep while remaining at hand should the general need him.

But Hallowell saw the signs of coming trouble and urged Admiral Pellew to expedite the arrival of Lord William Bentinck from Sicily. 'Until he comes we cannot be sure of the fate of the army — such indecision and such occasional panic I never witnessed in my life.'

On the morning of 7 June the fort at the Col de Balaguer surrendered after a tough resistance; the only direct road on which Suchet could have moved artillery toward Tarragona had been cut. Success appeared to stimulate General Murray. On the night of 9 June he ordered two more batteries of guns and mortars to be mounted within four hundred fifty yards of the walls of Fuerte Real. Four hundred seamen and marines dragged the heavy pieces and their ammunition into the positions prepared by the engineers. This noisy operation attracted the notice of the enemy, who illuminated the area with flares and directed a heavy fire against the working parties.

As usual, Hallowell was on the spot. The circumstances must have carried him back in memory more than fifteen years, to the days under the Corsican sun when Nelson lost his eye as the two friends fought the batteries before the walls of Calvi.

On 10 June all batteries were in action, a total of nineteen heavy guns ashore and twenty-three in the bomb vessels and gunboats. A practicable breach was opened, and at dawn the next morning Murray ordered General Clinton to prepare to storm Fuerte Real that night. Meanwhile Murray rode to the north to reconnoitre the ground in case Mathieu advanced from Villa Franca. At eight in the evening he returned and half an hour later General Mackenzie's brigade received the order to attack at ten that night, when three rockets were to be fired as a signal. In the meantime the assaulting troops under General Mackenzie lay concealed in a dry river bed.

At 11:00 Hallowell was waiting in one of the gun batteries when word arrived that the operation was cancelled. Accompanied by Major Thackeray of the engineers, Hallowell went to Murray's tent and found the general in conference with General Mackenzie and Major Williamson of the artillery. To the astonishment of everyone Murray announced that he had decided to raise the siege.

Mastering his emotions, Hallowell made no comment, although like most of the army officers he considered the decision wrong-headed, given the balance of forces in Murray's favour. The general ordered Williamson to get as many of the heavy guns as he could out of the batteries before daylight. Hallowell's job now was to prepare to embark the guns and later the troops, thus keeping open the option of an attack on Valencia.

The officers of the *Malta* had gathered on the quarterdeck anxiously awaiting the moment of the assault. As the appointed time passed and the delay lengthened it became clear there had been a change of plans. But nothing prepared them for the astonishing news they would soon receive. About midnight the admiral returned on board looking very grim and proceeded to his cabin, his only words being to order the captain and the first lieutenant to join him. A short time later the first lieutenant emerged, and the officers crowded around him to learn not only that General Murray had cancelled the assault on Fuerte Real, but also that he had decided to give up the siege and re-embark the army forthwith.

Within minutes officers had been dispatched to the transports and men-of-war ordering all boats to be on the beach by daylight to embark the men, animals, and artillery of the army. At dawn the re-embarkation began, but the keenness and alacrity exhibited by both soldiers and seamen when success seemed at hand had been replaced by downcast looks and muttered comments.

Whatever the merits of Murray's decision, the stage was now set for an orderly evacuation and reversion to the idea of a surprise attack on Valencia. But later in the morning of 12 June another surprising change of orders threw everything into confusion. Major Williamson was on the beach superintending the loading of the artillery. At nine o'clock General Donkin rode up and ordered him in the name of General Murray to desist. Instead of embarking the heavy guns, he was told to spike them and burn their carriages. Devoid of siege artillery, the army would be incapable of attacking Valencia.

Lieutenant Cole, Agent of Transports, had been on the beach since dawn. To him the army appeared to be in the greatest confusion. To his astonishment, at about eight General Murray rode up unaccompanied by any staff and asked for a boat to take him to the *Malta* to see the admiral. Cole procured one, sent the general off, and returned to his duties.

As was his custom, Hallowell had been breakfasting with the officers of the morning watch. General Murray advised his colleague that, despite his promise of the night before, the field and siege artillery and the cavalry were to be abandoned because of the difficulty of embarking them. He left as suddenly as he had arrived.

The remainder of the meal passed in melancholy silence, until

Hallowell exclaimed, 'I fear all is over, but I will make one effort more. I will try and get all the generals together and go and represent to [General Murray] their opinion of the measures he is pursuing.' At the same time he called for his secretary and dictated a note to the General recommending that the cavalry and artillery immediately march toward the Col de Balaguer, from which place Hallowell pledged to take them off safely. As soon as the note was dispatched Hallowell went ashore to rally the senior officers in protest. (His advice with regard to the cavalry and field artillery was taken and they were duly re-embarked.)

Meanwhile the bemused Lieutenant Cole had more bizarre visitations. Close behind Murray, General Donkin galloped up and told Cole to stop embarking the guns and embark troops instead, stating that the French were only two and a half hours away. Busy as he was, Cole noted that at about ten o'clock Murray appeared again, still without any staff, appearing quite at a loss and asking several trivial questions of the sailors.

Riding on to another part of the beach, Donkin gave the same orders to Principle Agent Withers, actually telling him to lower one gun that was already hoisted for transfer to a boat. Much disturbed, Withers hurried to inform Captain Inglefield, who said that he was going to continue loading artillery until his orders were changed by Hallowell personally. Soon afterwards Donkin rode up with his aide Captain Bowen. Inglefield commented on how famously things were going with the guns. Donkin made no direct response, but asked Inglefield to order the boats to the west, where the troops were to be embarked as far from the town as possible. He claimed excitedly that the enemy were nearby in great force, delivering this disturbing information before the whole working party. Inglefield nevertheless continued to embark guns until all that had reached the beach were off at about one in the afternoon.

At about 11:00 Cole had heard Major Williamson give some directions about spiking the guns and mortars — the order Williamson had received from General Donkin in the name of General Murray. 'At the same time Admiral Hallowell appeared looking very much hurt and disappointed at the haste our army was about to retreat in, saying there was no occasion for it, and some warm language passed between him and General Donkin.' Donkin told Hallowell that Murray had said that the boats were to be used for men only — except of course for a few favourite horses of the generals. Hallowell ordered Cole to carry on embarking the guns and to obey no one's orders but his own. Hallowell also intercepted Major Williamson preparing the guns for destruction and persuaded him to delay putting the destruction fully into effect until Hallowell had talked to General Murray. This the major was very willing to do.

Hallowell found Murray in a house near the beach. Colonel Adam was waiting in an outside room. Needing a witness, Hallowell asked Adam to join him in the general's office. In formal tones he said,

> *I have come to represent to you the shameful manner in which things are going on the beach. General Donkin has just now given direction in your name to spike all the guns in the batteries and destroy the carriages. We are bringing disgrace on the British character by running away so precipitately, leaving our guns behind, merely from a report of eight thousand men advancing toward us. If you are determined on raising the siege for God's sake do so in a soldier-like manner and not in the disgraceful manner we are now doing it. If you remain till night I pledge myself to bring everything off.*

Murray said he had never given such an order, but Hallowell insisted that Donkin had directed Williamson in Murray's name. Reiterating his pledge, Hallowell convinced Murray to rescind the order and Hallowell immediately informed Williamson.

Returning to the beach, they met Donkin and told him that Murray had denied giving the destruction order in the first place and in any case had rescinded it. The general replied, 'He gave me that order, it was verbal, but I shall have it always in writing in future. Do you suppose I fabricated that order?' Hallowell could only answer, 'I have nothing to say on that subject, I only repeat to you what Sir John Murray has said.'

Donkin then began to plead with Hallowell to give priority to embarking the soldiers rather than the guns. He noted that each lift of the boats could only take about 5,000 men, so that after two lifts fewer than 5,000 British would be left facing 8,000 French. Hallowell said it would indeed be unpleasant, but that a better alternative was to use the entire army to repel the French in the first place, 14,000 against 8,000. Knowing that the excited Donkin had told Inglefield that the French would be in Tarragona at one, Hallowell glanced pointedly at his watch and observed to Donkin that it was quarter past twelve and that the enemy would be there in just three-quarters of an hour. This was manifestly impossible since they were nowhere in sight.

Disgusted with the impasse, Hallowell agreed to return with Chief of Staff Donkin to Murray's headquarters to obtain a final decision. Murray was not there but an aide-de-camp to the Spanish general Capon had just ridden up. He reported that two hours earlier the French had been at Villa Franca, twenty-five miles away, and at that time were not advancing. 'General Donkin, do you hear that?' asked Hallowell. The general prevaricated, but the Spaniard stuck by his report.

A short time later Hallowell and Donkin met Murray and Colonel Adam on the road nearby. All were mounted. In his smooth fashion General Donkin told Murray that Hallowell agreed with him about the need for an early embarkation. Hallowell made him admit that Hallowell had merely said that the situation of the last lift would be unpleasant and that the problem could be solved by simply repelling the French. Murray said that it was still his intention to bring off the heavy guns that night as Hallowell had recommended.

Murray and Donkin then rode on ahead. Hallowell followed closely, telling Adam that if he left the two alone together Donkin would certainly change Murray's mind. Sure enough, as the two overtook the generals Murray turned in his saddle and said that he had decided to embark immediately and leave the guns. Stunned, Hallowell asked him to confirm the decision, which Murray immediately did.

Hallowell gave orders accordingly. About 3:30 p.m. the troops began to embark, no enemy in sight. All were back in their transports a little after midnight. But no stores or heavy guns were saved except the guns embarked earlier in the day contrary to Donkin's orders, and a quantity of engineer's stores picked up by Inglefield late that night 'without the least molestation from the enemy.'

The mortar and gun carriages were set alight at mid-day. Hallowell

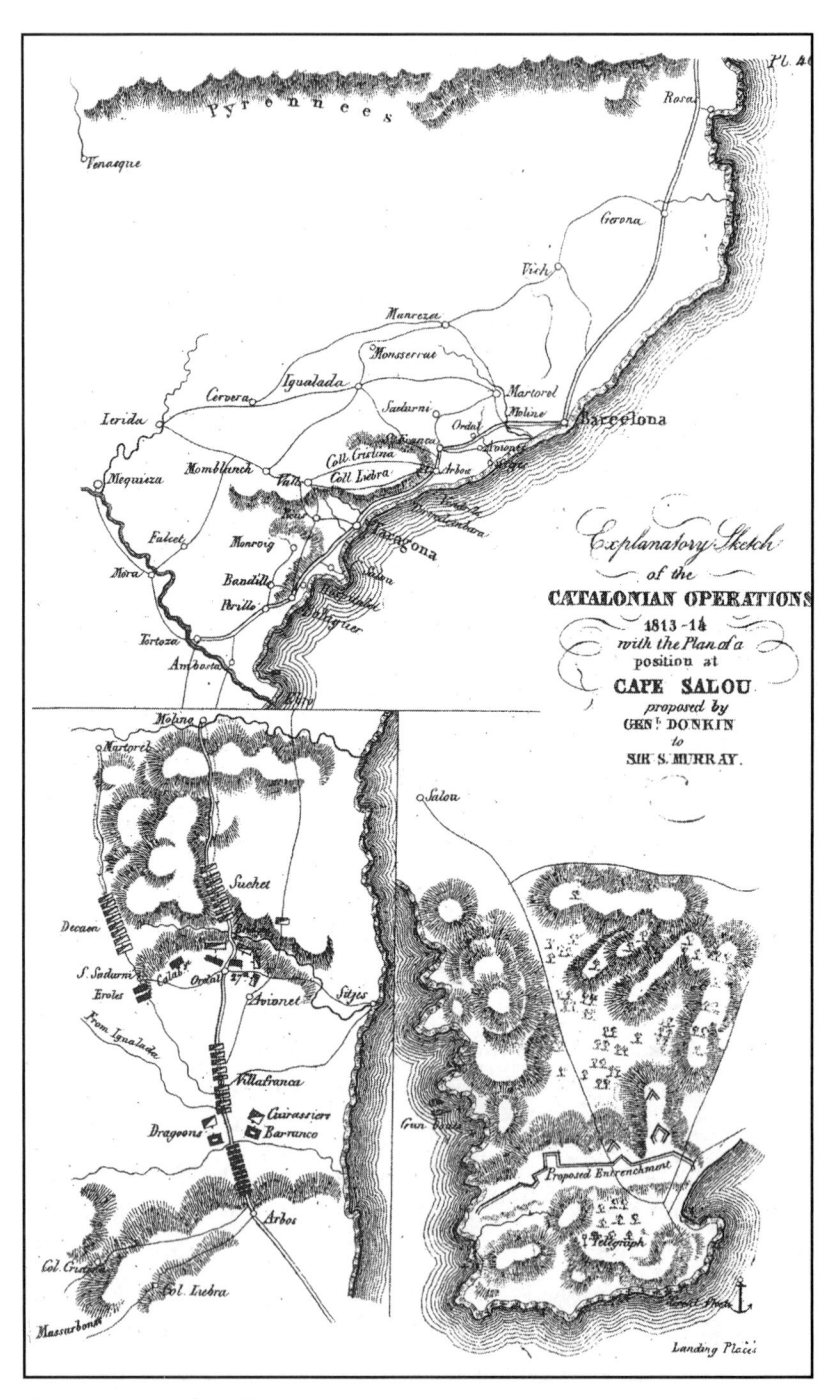

Contemporary plan, Tarragona

exclaimed, 'My God, what a sight, set fire to our carriages at noon, in sight of the enemy.' He would have been even angrier had he known of the element of farce that had entered the proceedings. Several of the guns were ready to be spiked, and their carriages arranged for burning, but if Murray had changed his mind again they might have been saved. But in the process of withdrawing his troops General Clinton was personally fired on by a French battery. Apparently forgetting his own orders, in an archaic act of defiant courtesy he removed his plumed hat and waved it at the enemy. This was the agreed signal for destruction of the guns, which were duly spiked and their carriages burnt. Later the gleeful French were observed moving the salvaged barrels inside their fortifications.

Murray went on board the *Malta* at eight o'clock on the night of the embarkation. The atmosphere in the senior officers' quarters must have been sulphurous. The general left early the next morning with a division of transports to the Col de Balaguer, and the *Malta* followed once Hallowell had assured himself that the last of the troops had been taken aboard the remaining transports.

General Murray's indecision at Tarragona was if anything exceeded by his unsteady conduct of the pointless operations around the Col de Balaguer. Hallowell had washed his hands of the proceedings ashore while continuing to provide naval assistance to the best of his ability. Troops and supplies were landed, re-embarked, re-landed and re-embarked in response to a succession of orders the naval officers could hardly keep up with: 'every mast-head was covered with his signals and four fast-moving gigs were hardly sufficient to convey his orders.' The acting first lieutenant of the *Malta* complained that for six days the men were never unemployed and the officers never had more than an hour or two of rest before being called upon to respond to some new demand.

Unbelievably, in the midst of this chaos, Murray suggested to Hallowell that 5,000 men be re-embarked and re-landed at Tarragona in hope of taking the place by surprise. Hallowell commented drily that he did not think it likely that the operation would succeed, given that Murray had not felt equal to it when his entire army, including its now-abandoned siege batteries, had been arrayed before the city. Of course the useless delay at Balaguer completely ruled out the possibility of attacking Valencia.

After the evacuation was completed on 12 June, Hallowell found time to write his report. Commander Carrol of the bomb vessel *Volcano* was sent overland with dispatches carrying news of the withdrawal to Lord Wellington. Carrol then continued to Britain with a copy of Hallowell's dispatch to Pellew, that Hallowell had most unwisely sent directly to the Board of Admiralty.

He was as angry and disgusted as ever when he put pen to paper. As in Egypt five years before, he had done everything possible as the senior naval officer to make an amphibious operation a success. Again he had exhausted himself both mentally and physically. Both times his efforts had been nullified by senior army officers. Egypt had been bad enough, but the shambles at Tarragona was a disgrace to British arms. His report included such phrases as: 'He [Murray] is impossible to depend on for an hour — he never has a plan,' and 'tarnishing the British character and striking a death blow I fear to the cause of Spain.' The hasty retreat had caused the unnecessary abandonment of four to eight 24-pounders, five 10-inch mortars and five 10-inch howitzers, he reported, 'although it was my decided opinion and advice to wait until night, when I promised to embark the whole.' The French garrison of Tarragona was only 1,600 men, and although Donkin had persuaded Murray they were within an hour's march, no mobile enemy had come nearer than Villa Franca twenty-five miles away.

Hallowell's language seriously alarmed the Admiralty. No doubt fearing a clash with their sister service, they regretted in a letter to Pellew 'that any such circumstances should have occurred as in the opinion of Rear Admiral Hallowell were sufficient to justify the strong expressions he has used in regard to the events at Tarragona, and the conduct of Lieutenant General Sir John Murray.' This was not exactly a reprimand, but was certainly intended to influence Hallowell to be more circumspect.

It arrived too late to prevent one last outburst. On June 18 Pellew's fleet arrived carrying Lord William Bentinck to assume command of the army. On being apprised by signal, Hallowell replied, 'we are all delighted,' perhaps a personal welcome to Bentinck, but interpreted by many as an insult to General Murray with whom he was supposed to have been collaborating. Few in either the army or navy would have quarrelled with Hallowell's sentiments.

Privately, Hallowell confided in Spencer that 'I may say to you my Lord that personal fear made Sir John Murray fail, and I do not think a more worthless coward ever existed.' Made public, such a charge would have had explosive repercussions, but it remained a secret between the two men.

Hallowell's opinion may have altered after further reflection. When Murray left the theatre some weeks later, Hallowell saw him off, and with typical openness told him, 'I have written fully as strongly to Pellew as I have expressed myself at any time on the subject.' Sir John replied, 'I have been aware of that, and had reason to expect so from the manner in which you have always spoken.' Hallowell added, 'I feel it but justice to you to state also that I firmly believe that if you had been allowed to exercise your own judgment you would have allowed the guns to be embarked, and my reason for having this opinion is because you told me you would, and as long as I live I shall say that General Donkin prevailed on you to leave the guns behind.' Murray did not reply, but immediately entered the boat that was to take him to his waiting ship.

Hallowell's intemperate language certainly worked against him, but the scandalous affair could not be overlooked. General Wellington directed that General Sir John Murray be tried by court martial as soon as the strategic situation permitted.

Despite his overwhelming disappointment, within a few days Hallowell took the trouble to write to the commanding officer of each of his ships. He passed on the appreciation of Admiral Pellew for the good work the squadron had done, to which even Murray had testified, and asked the captains to thank their ship's companies on Hallowell's behalf:

> *That greater advantages to the public cause did not result is to be lamented, but ought not, and will not, I trust, discourage in the smallest degree further exertions. It is yet early in the campaign; and further operations are projected, wherein the same unwearied perseverance, the*

same alacrity, and cordial cooperation with the army will have happier effects, I hope, and be crowned with complete success.

Here Hallowell shows the qualities of a true leader dealing with disaster. He acknowledges that the operations were not a success, but reassures his men that they had done all they could. He holds out the hope that there are better things to come. He preserves discipline by not publicly blaming those he considers to be the villains of the piece. The tone is much more constructive than that of his vituperative letter to Pellew and the Admiralty written only a few days before. Perhaps his temper had cooled. More likely he was simply addressing a different audience and his real feelings remained unchanged.

General Bentinck decided that the army needed to be reorganized and refreshed after its crushing disappointments, inexplicable as they were to everyone. The troops were therefore withdrawn to Alicante from whence they had set off with such high hopes only a few short weeks before.

As soon as morale had been restored, General Bentinck advanced by land toward Valencia, Tarragona, and Barcelona. Hallowell succeeded in acquiring two horses and marched with the general, while his flagship, the transports, and the rest of the squadron followed the coast, landing supplies and rendering gunfire support whenever opportunity arose.

Hallowell and Bentinck became firm colleagues, and the admiral in effect became part of the general's staff. This relationship continued when Bentinck was obliged to return to Sicily and General Clinton took command of the army. That Hallowell enjoyed good relations with Bentinck and Clinton is additional evidence that he worked well with most senior army officers, and that his difficulties with General Murray were mainly attributable to that officer's own shortcomings.

The wily Marshal Suchet still commanded a powerful force and conducted a skilful withdrawal in conformity with the main French army that was retreating before Wellington in western Spain. Valencia fell on 14 July and Tarragona in mid-August, and the allied army marched on up the coast to the siege of Barcelona. Here it paused for the autumn and winter.

Decisive events were taking place elsewhere. As we have seen, while retreating in Spain, Napoleon had invaded Russia in June 1812. The Russians were encouraged by the news of Wellington's successes, and it was only after very severe fighting that the Grand Army reached Moscow on 14 September. A great fire broke out that night, deliberately set by the Russians, and it destroyed much of the city. Mistakenly confident that the Czar would have to sue for peace, Napoleon hung on amid the ruins. In October, conscious of the approaching winter, Napoleon was forced to begin the famous retreat from Moscow during which the Russians and the weather combined to virtually wipe out the Grand Army.

Encouraged by the disaster, in July 1813 Austria had joined Russia, Prussia, and Sweden in a new coalition. Their combined armies defeated Napoleon at the Battle of the Nations near Leipzig 16–18 October. In the same month Wellington crossed the Pyrenees into France, having won a decisive battle at Vittoria in June. The eastern army in Spain took Barcelona and also crossed the Pyrenees. Napoleon demonstrated some of the best generalship of his career in delaying the advance of the continental armies through the winter, but the net was closing. In March 1814 Wellington took Bordeaux, the allies entered Paris, and on 11 April Napoleon was forced to abdicate. The allies made the defeated emperor ruler of the tiny island of Elba off the Italian coast as the Bourbons returned to the throne of France and peace negotiations began at Vienna.

While Napoleon's forces were suffering setbacks in Russia and central Europe, the British and Italian troops in Spain were dispatched to Italy, escorted by the *Malta*. Suchet's main army had retreated into France and was in any case being broken up as Napoleon milked it for reinforcements. As the *Malta* crossed the Gulf of Genoa, unaware of the end of the struggle, the lookouts spotted a strange sail that proved to be the frigate *Undaunted*. She telegraphed a message of such importance that it was read out on the *Malta's* quarterdeck to the astonishment of the whole ship's company: 'I have got the Emperor Napoleon on board, going to the Isle of Elba.'

At Toulon, just over twenty years earlier, Napoleon had taken his first step on the way to the domination of Europe, and the newly promoted Captain Hallowell had helped evacuate the terrified refugees fleeing before his revolutionary army. Since then all but a year of Hallowell's life had been spent at sea in the seemingly endless struggle against the tyrant. As the *Undaunted's* news was absorbed in the *Malta*, Lieutenant Crawford observed the overwhelming joy and pride of the men of the Royal Navy, who had done perhaps more than any other force to secure the ultimate victory. It would have been natural for the admiral to order the *Malta* and *Undaunted* to close each other so that his men could view at last the genius whose ambitions had for so long controlled their lives. But Hallowell sailed contemptuously on in execution of his orders.

14

AT ANCHOR
1814–1824

The Admiral ... is afraid the Admiralty will not listen to his applications for further employment.

John Elmsley, letter to Ward Boylston,
22 February 1827

For the first time in eleven years Britain was at peace, and no threats were on the horizon. The total tonnage of British men-of-war equalled or exceeded the combined tonnage of the next four largest European navies. The Royal Navy had achieved a command of the sea not to be challenged for nearly a century.

But there would be no more opportunities for distinction, and promotion would grind to a halt. Typically, Hallowell's first thought was for those under him. In May 1814 he wrote directly to Melville, First Lord of the Admiralty, asking him to take a personal interest in furthering the career of Edward Boxer, first lieutenant of the *Malta*, 'than whom there is no more deserving officer in the king's service.' Lieutenant Boxer was made commander in March 1815.

Advancing the careers of subordinates was a measure of a senior officer's influence and standing. Conspicuous failure might be taken as a sign that the officer had powerful enemies. Hallowell pointed out to Melville that after two and a half years on the station not one of the officers or petty officers he had recommended had obtained preferment. In his communications Admiral Pellew had been almost embarrassingly complimentary, but he had failed to express his admiration in concrete form.

Hallowell could not help but suspect that the reason lay in the failure of the Tarragona landing, in no way the navy's fault but nevertheless a failure and not conducive to recognition and rewards — a repetition of the Egyptian expedition of 1807. Even more insidious, vicious rumours were spreading in England concerning Hallowell's conduct at Tarragona. General Napier, who participated in the war against Napoleon in Spain, described the rumours in his history:

> *The warmth of temper displayed by the principal prosecutor, Admiral Hallowell, together with his signal on Lord William Bentinck's arrival, whereby, to the detriment of discipline, he manifested his contempt for the general with whom he was acting, gave Murray an advantage which he improved skilfully, for he was a man sufficiently acute and prompt when he was not at the head of an army. He charged the admiral with deceit, factious dealings, and disregard of the service; described him as being of a passionate overweening busy disposition, troubled with excess of vanity, meddling with everything and thinking himself competent to manage both troops and ships.*

Hallowell heard of the rumours about him from many sources in the interval before the court martial. He disdained to respond despite his frustration at having his squadron's excellent work subjected to insults and innuendo. But there was no denying that the verdict would have a very personal significance for him. In late July he sailed for Tarragona where it was expected that the trial would begin shortly. Having lingered there for a month, he was shocked to learn that Wellington had ordered the court to assemble in England, although this meant that none of the Spanish officers could testify and that there would be no opportunity for the members to examine the scene of action. On these grounds Murray himself had protested against the change of venue, but was overruled.

The timing could not have been worse. With the peace, Sir Edward Pellew had sailed for England with the fleet, leaving Hallowell as senior officer in the Mediterranean with a squadron of five ships of the line, three frigates, and three brig/sloops. To be commander-in-chief in that sea, even in peacetime, even with a small squadron, was to have achieved the height of his ambition. And action was not entirely out of the question. The always troublesome Algerian corsairs were in growing need of a lesson in international law of the sea, an attack on their base that would finally put an end to Mediterranean piracy.

Moreover, Hallowell had also discerned an even more dangerous threat. Writing to Bentinck, he observed,

> *Bonaparte is not idle in Elba, and if he is not watched he will give us the slip from that island. He is in the habit of going afloat to visit ships — this I conceive to be a finesse of his to familiarize us to such occasional embarkations, and when his plans are ripe for execution he will push across, and be landed on the continent before they have an idea on the island of his intentions to quit them. I should be very much disposed to lay my hands on him if I caught him at any distance from Portoferraio [Elba] — it is impossible to be too much on our guard against such a fellow.*

Within a year he was proven right. By that time Hallowell had left the Mediterranean. Perhaps under his command the naval watch on the exiled emperor would have been more vigilant and Europe would have been spared the last spasm of Napoleonic ambition.

Early in November 1814 Hallowell was taken aback by the totally unexpected arrival of Admiral Penrose with orders to assume command. The reason given was that Hallowell was required to proceed at once to England to be a witness in Murray's court martial. Whatever the validity of the rationale, to relieve a senior officer in this peremptory manner was discourteous in the extreme, another intimation that the rumours about Tarragona had brought Hallowell into disrepute.

Hallowell arrived in England in December 1814. After a short time in quarantine he left for London, taking Frederick Spencer and the other youngsters with him, 'as I have always considered a seaport to be a very improper place for them to be left without a person to look after and pay particular attention to them.' Vacancies for midshipmen were going to become extremely scarce with the end of the war, but Hallowell would keep one open for Frederick.

This time he had been away from home for two and a half years. Before entering the Naval College, Charles had been with his father for part of the time, but now there were four other children with whom to become re-acquainted. Certainly he looked forward to spending some time with his family before the trial. But he also looked forward to a quick return to the Mediterranean as soon as a verdict was reached. With the peace it might well have been possible to take his family with him. Unexpectedly, on his arrival he was ordered to strike his flag and go on half pay, but he could put this down to Admiralty penny-pinching and not to a change in his career prospects.

This seemed all the more true when he received an honour directly from the Prince of Wales, who had been acting as regent for his mentally incompetent father since February 1811. Medieval in origin, the Order of the Bath was so named because of the ritual cleansing and prayer that originally had preceded induction. The order had come to be the primary means of recognizing noteworthy achievement just short of the rare high standard that would warrant elevation to the peerage.

With the end of the Napoleonic war there were so many senior officers deserving recognition that the Prince Regent reorganized the order into three classes, including 115 Knights Grand Cross (GCB), 328 Knights Commanders (KCB), and 1815 Companions (CB). At the same time the ancient rites of induction were discontinued. Hallowell was made a KCB, entitled thereby to the appellation Sir Benjamin Hallowell. His wife became Lady Ann Hallowell. No doubt she saw the title as indirect but well-deserved recognition of her single-handed struggle to maintain a household and raise a family in the absence of a father. Membership in the Order of the Bath was not hereditary; the title 'Sir' would die with its recipient.

Before being inducted Hallowell had to defray the costs of 'recording the pedigree of your family, your coat armour, and statement of military services, in the Books appropriated to the Knights Commanders.' One thing rankled: dress regulations forced him to wear the badge of the order instead of his precious Nile Medal, the decoration of which he was most proud.

Sir John Murray's trial at Winchester began 16 January 1815, and concluded on 7 February. There were three charges. The first related to Murray's decision to attack Tarragona when he believed that a superior force of the enemy would arrive before he could accomplish his aim. The second alleged neglect of duty in having re-landed his army at the Col de Balaguer rather than returning at once to Alicante after leaving Tarragona.

Hallowell was not involved in these charges, but very unexpectedly he was directed by the Admiralty 'to substantiate by your evidence what you have stated in your letters on the subject,' and thus become prosecutor on the third charge against Murray:

> *For neglect of duty in hastily re-embarking the forces under his command without any previous preparations or arrangements and thus precipitously and unnecessarily abandoning a considerable quantity of artillery, stores and ammunition ... when he was so far from being compelled to this degrading measure by the immediate approach of any superior force or by any other sufficient cause, that by due zeal, firmness and exertion the greater part, if not the whole, might have been embarked in safety — Admiral Hallowell who was at that time on duty on the station engaging to effect the same — such conduct being highly to the prejudice of the service, and detrimental to the British military character.*

Murray was acquitted on the first two charges. On the third, he was found 'guilty only of so much of that charge as states "that he unnecessarily abandoned a considerable quantity of artillery and stores which he might have embarked in safety"'. The court considered Murray's failure to have proceeded from an error of judgment and recommended that his sentence be limited to an admonishment. On 15 February the Prince Regent confirmed the finding and sentence in his capacity as commander-in-chief, but took no action to make it effective. With the war at an end leniency was in the air, but Napier leaves little doubt that the results of the trial were generally regarded as a travesty.

If he had been convicted of such negligence, Hallowell believed he would at the very least have been dismissed from his ship and might even have been shot. Nevertheless, he felt vindicated by the outcome. The charge on which he had prosecuted was the only one judged to have been proven.

Just as importantly, he was sure that public misconceptions about his actions had been corrected. 'I went down with strong prejudices established against me, from the misrepresentation of Sir John Murray and General Donkin — in a short time the whole were removed and I left with the public opinion as strongly in my favour as it had been against me on my arrival.' Less than two weeks after the Prince Regent's ruling Hallowell's rehabilitation was signalled by a dinner in his honour given by Lord North. The guests included Lord Bathurst, the Minister of War. Whatever the Regent's decision, the army could hardly have signalled its disapprobation of Murray in a more obvious way.

With the legal proceedings at an end a long-suppressed and private aspect of the Tarragona fiasco came to the fore. Two days after the evacuation Hallowell had by chance encountered General Donkin at the Col de Balaguer. He accused the general of having claimed that the French would arrive at Tarragona by one o'clock on 12 June, when in reality they were not even advancing and in fact did not appear until the evening of 13 June. Donkin denied it, but Hallowell vehemently insisted. He was clearly angry, but in a later signed statement several of the army staff officers who witnessed the confrontation certified that words such as 'liar' and 'scandal' were not used on this occasion, despite Donkin's later accusation to that effect.

The next night the two met once again while waiting outside Murray's tent. The following dialogue ensued.

> *Donkin: How dare you look me in the face after attacking me in the manner you have done?*
>
> *Hallowell: I have nothing to say to you; you know what I stated yesterday respecting your public conduct, and until that is cleared up I*

shall have nothing to say to you.

Donkin: You must be a dammed scoundrel and a damned rascal.

Hallowell: I will take no notice of anything you say until there has been a public investigation of the events before Tarragona. I have a pretty good memory, and when the investigation is over I shall not forget what you now say.

Donkin: You are a damned scoundrel and an infernal rascal.

Hallowell: There is nothing that you can say that will provoke me to take notice of it until the investigation is over, when you may rely on my reminding you of this conversation, and till then I do not care what you may say of me, for you are such a damned lying rascal that no person in the army will believe a word of what you say.

Hallowell later admitted to Spencer that he was sorry he had finally allowed himself to be provoked into the kind of language Donkin had been using from the beginning of the conversation. With the possible exceptions of General Murray and General Whittingham no one overheard the exchange.

Two weeks after the encounter, General Donkin wrote to Hallowell challenging him to a duel because of 'the gross and unjustified insults you have offered me as an officer and a gentleman.' Duels being prohibited, he asked Hallowell to keep the challenge secret.

Hallowell replied the same day that his public accusations were not personal but related to Donkin's advice to Murray to abandon and destroy the siege guns. He would therefore not meet Donkin until that issue had been resolved. However, he remembered very clearly Donkin's insults outside Murray's tent. After a further exchange of letters in the same vein silence ensued, but it was clear that a challenge had been delivered and accepted.

In 1799 John Jervis, Earl of St. Vincent, had been challenged to a duel by Rear Admiral Sir John Orde on a service issue, but had refused to fight over a public as opposed to a private disagreement. In declining Donkin's challenge until the Tarragona court martial was concluded, Hallowell may have consciously patterned his behaviour on that of his one-time mentor.

A year and a half later, as the court martial neared its end, Hallowell wrote to Donkin suggesting that as soon as the verdict was announced they should repair to a spot near Winchester selected by their seconds, 'where I shall be prepared with pistols to give you that satisfaction you have demanded, and to call on you for redress for that language you made use of to me at Balaguer.' He signed himself 'Your obedient servant' in conformity with the arcane courtesies expected of men who would shortly attempt to kill each other. Donkin's second was Lord Frederick Bentinck; Hallowell's, his brother-in-law Samuel Hood Inglefield. (Incongruously, Lord Frederick had written Hallowell before the court martial offering to give evidence against Murray.)

There were real problems with Hallowell's suggestion, as Donkin was quick to point out. Duelling was illegal in England. One of the principals was almost certain to be killed, and the other principal and the two seconds could be tried for their lives. He therefore suggested that they all meet in France to settle the matter. Hallowell felt that if he asked the Admiralty for permission to leave the country, suspicions would be aroused and he would not be allowed to travel, so he continued to advocate a meeting at Winchester immediately after the trial. Since it was the two seconds who were most at risk, the principals agreed to let them decide.

This was on 20 January 1815. The next day Hallowell received an unexpected visitor, Colonel Sir Andrew Bernard. He carried a letter from the Minister of War, Lord Bathurst. It warned that 'you will incur [the Prince Regent's] highest displeasure if you shall either give a challenge to Major General Donkin or accept one from him after the receipt of this letter, or if you act upon any challenge previously given, or arrangements made to that effect.' Colonel Bernard was authorized 'to receive from you any such assurances as will I trust supersede the necessity for any further proceedings.' Donkin received a similar communication.

Of course the rumour of a duel had become generally known;

Hallowell had already received two warnings from the Admiralty. But the Prince Regent's wishes could not be disregarded. Hallowell gave the necessary assurances, as did Donkin, and what would have been a sensational encounter did not come to pass. There is no reason to doubt that both men were prepared to fight had their sovereign not intervened.

The consciousness of having done his duty had always been more important to Hallowell than the fame that motivated Nelson or the prize money that drove men like Keith. After serving under him for several years Lieutenant Crawford had declared,

> *In my experience I never knew an officer imbued with a more fervent and untiring zeal for his profession and his country's service. His whole soul, indeed, and every faculty of his mind seemed to be directed to the single object of advancing their interests. He was a man of the nicest honour and strictest probity and truth, and his indifference — I had almost said contempt — for money, could only be equalled by his love for his country's glory and happiness, and an honourable thirst for well-earned fame.*

Most of the then-famous officers whose names are vaguely familiar to this day — the Fremantles, Cochranes, and Pellews — won distinction in spectacular but relatively unimportant single-ship actions. Hallowell had almost always been part of one fleet or another, fleets that had in fact been the principal factors in winning the war through relentless blockade and occasional decisive battle. His contributions to the team, however valuable, had rarely put him in the spotlight.

Nevertheless, he was acutely conscious of his own merit, to a large extent unnoticed because of the ill fortune that had dogged him. In Egypt and in Spain he had led amphibious operations, either of which might have made him famous had they succeeded. It was not his fault that both failed. With the end of the war it seemed there would be no more opportunities for distinction. Worse, continued silence from the Admiralty made him wonder if he was indeed to return to the Mediterranean as he had expected.

Hallowell became acutely sensitive to any sign that he was being treated unfairly. Others were receiving greater recognition for services far less valuable than his own. Shortly after the impending duel had come to nothing, Hallowell poured out his frustrations to the First Lord in a letter from Anne Gee's Beddington Park. He made the point that he had won a conviction against Sir John Murray on the charge he had prosecuted. In his eyes that proved that his intemperate dispatch after the evacuation had indeed been written from a sense of duty, and not as a matter of personal pique, as some had alleged.

With that out of the way, he moved to his present difficult situation. Everyone had expected that he would return to the Mediterranean after the trial. If instead he were placed on half pay that would be seen as a public censure. He wondered if the KCB was simply intended to be a trade-off for that humiliation. In support of this suspicion he brought up several cases in which, in addition to other rewards, officers had been made KCB or even GCB for services far less distinguished than his own. He requested the First Lord to erase any possible stigma by some public gesture of support, such as a prestigious appointment.

How the First Lord would have responded is unknown. The issue was temporarily overtaken by events. Four days after the letter was dispatched Napoleon Bonaparte escaped from Elba, exactly as Hallowell had predicted. He landed in France with a few hundred men of his Old Guard. The troops sent to arrest him went over to his side, King Louis XVIII fled, and on March 20 the restored emperor was once again in Paris, with France at his feet and Europe in an uproar. The Peace Congress in Vienna had been informed of the escape early on March 7, and orders to mobilize the allied forces were on their way in less than an hour. A few days later the Congress declared Bonaparte an international outlaw.

On the 28 April Hallowell was ordered to join the Channel Fleet and hoist his flag in the *Royal Sovereign*, the Trafalgar flagship of his dead friend Cuthbert Collingwood. Napoleon had no navy, so the Channel Fleet was limited to supporting the royalist rebels who had taken up arms in the west of France. In command was Admiral Lord Keith, fated once again to play a major part in Hallowell's professional life. None of the few opportunities for action came Hallowell's way, since at Keith's orders his flagship did nothing more than swing to her anchors in Plymouth Sound. The fleet itself was so small Hallowell thought it was beneath Keith's rank and that the admiral only hung on in command in hope of prize money. The bitterness lingered.

Rumours circulated that Napoleon was embarking some of his personal possessions in American merchant vessels, with a view to making his escape to the New World. Keith considered instituting a stop-and-search policy for American ships. It was Hallowell who pointed out that the whole thing might be a Napoleonic stratagem. Britain was not at war with France, so any form of blockade would be illegal and might embroil Britain with the United States by once again raising the issues that remained unsettled after the War of 1812.

By now Hallowell knew there was a chance that he would be appointed commander-in-chief of the Irish station. If so, his future flagship would be the *Tonnant*, currently being refitted; but as she was in a terrible state there would be a considerable delay. To combat boredom Hallowell concentrated even more on the development of his youngsters. His cabin became a schoolroom, and he moored a frigate

Defeated at Waterloo, Napoleon surrendered to the Royal Navy.

close by in which the volunteers spent every afternoon familiarizing themselves with the rigging. They were, he said, 'too much occupied to think of going on shore.' One young gentleman, Lord Henry Thynose, was allowed ashore as a major concession, but failed to return on time and was put on stoppage of leave for the rest of the ship's time in Plymouth. Frederick Spencer was due for leave but Hallowell delayed him to give him the rare opportunity of observing the fitting of water tanks and the loading of ballast in the *Tonnant's* hold.

On 24 June 1815, momentous news reached Plymouth. A week earlier, allied troops under Wellington and the Prussian Marshal Blucher had decisively defeated Napoleon in two days of bloody battle near the Belgian village of Waterloo. His army was in full retreat and disintegrating fast. The possibility that he might attempt to escape by sea suddenly became strong, and British ships patrolling the French coast were put on high alert.

On 15 July Napoleon and his immediate staff surrendered themselves on board the *Bellerophon* off the Île d'Aix, throwing himself on the hospitality of the British people, as he chose to put it. His latest attempt at conquest had cost numerous lives and more than £6 million in subsidies alone, all this on top of the horrendous human and financial cost of the previous twenty-year struggle. It has been estimated that on a proportionate basis total casualties in his wars exceeded those of the Second World War. Yet Napoleon seemed to believe that all would again be forgiven.

The *Bellerophon* anchored in Torbay on the morning of 24 July. Despite efforts to prevent a leak, the word soon got out that Napoleon was on board, and the bay soon became crowded with sightseers who were with difficulty kept away from the ship's side, where Napoleon often appeared. Plymouth was deemed to be a safer anchorage and the *Bellerophon* re-anchored there on 26 July while the allied governments deliberated what to do with Napoleon.

When Hallowell learned the name of the ship on board which Napoleon had surrendered his thoughts must have gone back to that August night at the Nile, almost exactly seventeen years before. By not firing upon the unknown shape emerging from the darkness and smoke of battle, Hallowell had perhaps preserved the *Bellerophon* for this moment in history. Plymouth Sound was crowded with boats of sightseers, and those who could contrive to be invited on board hurried to view the famous captive. Hallowell stayed away.

In our enlightened times Napoleon might have been tried as a war criminal, and even in the early nineteenth century some argued he should be put on trial. On the other hand, despite twenty years of conquest and tyranny there was considerable sympathy for Napoleon on the part of those who still saw in him a symbol of the reformist ideals of the French Revolution. His supporters began a campaign to prevent his exile to a more secure place of captivity.

Napoleon's legal status was in fact unclear. The King of France could legally have tried him as a rebel, but he did not dare to take this unpopular step. Since England was not at war with France, it was argued that Bonaparte could not be considered a prisoner of war. His British supporters devised a scheme by which Napoleon was to be called as a witness in an obscure trial. This led to the issue of a writ of habeas corpus requiring Napoleon's presence in a London court, threatening a significant delay in resolving his status.

On 31 July Keith went on board the *Bellerophon* and advised Napoleon that he was to be exiled to the south Atlantic island of St. Helena. Napoleon complained but acquiesced, but insisted on going in the *Bellerophon* instead of the *Northumberland*, which had been especially provisioned for six months to carry him. He and his suite proclaimed that they would not be taken out of the *Bellerophon* alive. Meanwhile attempts were being made to serve writs of habeas corpus upon Keith, as well as on Captain Maitland of the *Bellerophon*. The ship was sent to cruise off Start Point, out of reach of servers of writs.

At this juncture Keith ordered Hallowell to supervise the transfer of Napoleon from the *Bellerophon* to the *Northumberland*, which was under the command of his Tenerife comrade, now Rear Admiral Cockburn. To Hallowell his duty was clear:

> *I will be answerable for putting him on board the Northumberland ... and if the [court] officer gets on board I will not deliver the person of*

> Bonaparte to him, as I consider him a prisoner of war. If I act improperly in keeping that monster on board they may send me to prison afterward — it will be much better for me to be imprisoned for life than that fellow should be suffered to escape and set all Europe again in flames.

Legally correct or not, these sentiments were shared by the vast majority of Hallowell's countrymen and by the government. On 4 August the transfer was successfully made and on 9 August Napoleon began his voyage to the speck on the map where he would live out his life.

Hallowell and Bonaparte never met, but as a newly made captain Hallowell had been at Toulon in 1793 when Napoleon began his meteoric rise. He had seen the *Undaunted* transporting him to Elba in 1814, and now as an admiral in 1815 he was overseeing the tyrant's final departure from the European stage. Throughout those eighteen years, Napoleon's ambitions had determined the course of Hallowell's life, and even now Hallowell had not heard the last of him.

Finally in late summer it was confirmed that the *Tonnant* was to be Hallowell's flagship and that he was to become commander-in-chief of the Irish station. The *Malta*, the ex-*Guillaume Tell*, his flagship in the Mediterranean, had been important to him as a reminder of the Nile. Even more significant was the *Tonnant*, next astern of *L'Orient*, and the *Swiftsure's* opponent after *L'Orient* had blown up. The *Tonnant* was almost identical to the *Malta*, but carried eighty rather than eighty-four guns. Her captain was Edward Pelham Brenton, a Nova Scotian from a well-known Halifax family. Unfortunately, he soon incurred Hallowell's displeasure over his slowness in getting her to sea and his handling of the youngsters.

Hallowell arranged to have Brenton relieved by Captain Tailour, one-time first lieutenant of the *Malta*. At Hallowell's request the Admiralty allowed his son Charles to leave the Royal Naval College and join him in the *Tonnant* as a midshipman, but on condition that he would not be allowed to resume his studies. Frederick Spencer also returned, but within a year he was to move to the *Glasgow* upon promotion to lieutenant. Even when both Earl Spencer's sons had left Hallowell's ship the long-standing correspondence between them continued.

Napoleon's final defeat had had a drastic effect on the Royal Navy. Within two years of Waterloo the fleet had shrunk from ninety-nine ships of the line to only thirteen, and from 140,000 seamen to 19,000. For most of the displaced men this reduction meant simply transferring to the merchant service, but for the officers it was devastating. Promotion was paralyzed. There were more than two hundred and forty admirals on the list compared with just over sixty at the beginning of the war. Captains often went ten years between commissions and only eight or nine hundred of 3,000 lieutenants could be employed at any given time.

When Hallowell was commanding in Ireland he was one of only ten rear admirals out of seventy-five who were actually employed. A few years later at the Nore, he would be one of only three vice admirals out of sixty-four to have an appointment. Positions at sea and promotions were desperately sought. Always too important, for a time influence and interest became almost the only factor in preferment.

A case in point was very close to home. Hallowell had mentored Robert Spencer as a midshipman and as a lieutenant. As a favour, the Admiralty attached his brig the *Ganymede*, 16, to the Irish squadron. Out of respect and affection for his former captain the young commander kept a midshipman's vacancy open for Charles Hallowell, who duly transferred from the *Tonnant*. This sort of reciprocal rotation was by no means uncommon and it made the navy a virtual closed shop. Gradually, it would become clear that this grossly unfair state of affairs had to give way to a more efficient and equitable policy, but in Hallowell's time advancement required tireless lobbying and shameless pulling of strings and calling in of favours owed.

Charles Hallowell's service in the *Ganymede* later led to an amusing echo of his father's own behaviour as a midshipman. For reasons probably having to do with the below-decks layout, the *Ganymede's* midshipmen were berthed in two messes rather than one. The consequence was a social divide based on money, the affluent inhabitants of the port mess, including Charles, indulging themselves in expensive delicacies, fine wines, and even servants hired off the ship's books, while their poorer colleagues subsisted on little more than the ordinary ship's fare. Charles's exuberant behaviour led to his being billed for such excessive breakages of mess utensils that his already heady mess bills became insupportable. Forty years earlier Charles' grandfather had still been paying mess bills a year after his son left the *Asia*. Now Robert Spencer had to seek that former delinquent's approval to put his son Charles on a strict allowance and to keep in reserve the weapon of transferring Charles to the plebeian starboard mess.

Robert Spencer had a justification for permitting such high living on the part of his midshipmen: by allowing them to 'live as well on board as any lieutenants in the service,' he believed that 'when they go on shore on leave, the temptations to tavern dinners and all their mischievous consequences are not so irresistible.' Then as now, one suspects that few young men would spurn the taverns and mischievous consequences of a good run ashore, no matter how splendid their mess.

Hallowell had only been in his new station for a few months when the First Lord sent him a personal letter offering him a new command, 'the most important and confidential the Admiralty can offer at present.' He was asked to relieve Admiral Sir George Cockburn as commander-in-chief at the Cape of Good Hope. Despite the title, the real duty of the position was to maintain the naval watch on St. Helena to ensure that Bonaparte never again escaped. The admiral's official residence would be at St. Helena, not at Cape Town.

Perhaps Melville had come to hear of Hallowell's forewarnings of Napoleon's escape from Elba. Certainly the command was one that would only be entrusted to someone who enjoyed the Admiralty's full confidence. But Hallowell turned it down on the grounds that if he were tied to St Helena there would be no prospect of any active service. Even the Irish station would be livelier. Lady Hallowell would have rebelled at the idea of trading the admittedly provincial society of Cork for the prison atmosphere and very limited official circle at St. Helena. Hallowell also mentioned that he had just been to considerable expense and trouble moving his family to Cork. But he had to be careful here, because as he told Melville he would be quite willing to uproot everything if it was a question of returning to the chief command in the Mediterranean. Deep in his subconscious he may have shrunk from the possibility of actually meeting Napoleon, a courtesy that would have been inevitable in the circumstances.

The expenses of raising and educating his ever-increasing family were heavy, and it was still very important for Hallowell to be employed. As a captain he had never been fortunate in the matter of prize money. On hoisting his flag in the *Malta* he had become entitled to share in the admirals' one-eighth portion of the value of all prizes taken in the Mediterranean. In earlier times this privilege had made many senior officers fabulously wealthy, but by 1811 enemy trade had been so curtailed that very few prizes were taken. Out of principle he had refused altogether to accept an admiral's share of freight money. At the very end of the war he became embroiled in a controversy with Pellew over the shareout of prize money from captures in Italy, and the matter was still unsettled in 1816.

At St. Helena he would have received the pay and allowances of a full admiral, two steps above his current rank. In choosing to remain at Cork, Hallowell was making a financial sacrifice only partly redeemed by his share in his squadron's customs seizures.

Late in his tenure there was a revealing sequel. Hallowell was detached in the *Tonnant* to lead fleet manoeuvres in the Channel and Sir James Rowley took temporary command in Ireland. The latter very generously offered to let Hallowell continue to receive the commander-in-chief's share of customs seizures during his absence. Tempting as the offer must have been Hallowell quickly declined. His declared reason was that he did not wish to set a precedent for others, but the decision was fully in keeping with his long-standing aversion to the more mercenary aspects of his profession.

There was great unrest in Ireland at this time, with large sections of the population chafing under the corrupt and repressive policies of the regime. County Tipperary was under martial law. Hallowell viewed the Irish scene with all the prejudices of his religion and his class. He was incapable of understanding the fundamental detestation of British rule that permeated much of society, blaming it on the priests who had taught the Irish to hate the Protestant ascendancy. At the same time Hallowell was infuriated by the corruption and incompetence that characterized much of the ruling bureaucracy. As he conceived his duty, it was to act impartially within the limits of his authority.

What those limits were was not always clear. In June 1817 there was serious rioting in Cork over the price of food. The *Tonnant* was moored within pistol shot of the town market where the mob frequently gathered. One day they seized a vessel loaded with potatoes and tied her up to the wharf. A magistrate applied to Hallowell for help and he sent two boatloads of unarmed seamen, led by Captain Tailour, to recover the ship. As they approached the shore they were met with a shower of cobblestones. Tailour sustained two broken ribs and two lieutenants received head wounds that rendered them unfit for duty, but the potato ship was duly brought off and secured to the *Tonnant*.

The legitimacy of this particular action was clear, but Hallowell was forced to ask the Attorney General of Ireland for clarification of his authority in a number of hypothetical instances. For instance, could he land armed sailors and marines to disperse a mob if requested to by a magistrate? If the mob attempted to break into the naval victualling stores opposite the *Tonnant*, could the ship open fire, or if the workmen repairing the naval depot on Haulbowline Island attempted to seize the arms therein, could he stop them by force? Within two days he had his answers: affirmative in every case. He was of course unnecessarily cautioned to use armed force only in the last resort and after due warning.

The navy's role in enforcing customs regulations was important, Ireland being a hotbed of smuggling. Hallowell believed that every man in Ireland was ready to assist a smuggler and that the revenue authorities needed to be supplemented by military detachments to enforce the laws. They had not been enforced for a very long time. Hallowell must have been keenly aware of the parallel between his circumstances and those of his father in Boston forty years before. Both were struggling against a pervasive culture of law-breaking, and in both cases an underlying spirit of rebellion fed upon and abetted the traffic in illegal merchandise.

Brothers named Morley and Roger O'Sullivan were influential in the area of Bearhaven, to the west of Cork. Morley was the local magistrate. In a fashion that was perhaps typically Irish, their activities mingled a certain charm with serious crime. In December 1817 Morley posed as an agent of Lloyd's insurance and succeeded in landing five hundred bales of tobacco without paying duty. The customs officials asked Hallowell to send a ship to the area and undertake a search of the properties of O'Sullivan's very numerous relations and tenants. By the time Lieutenant Townshend commanding the *Beresford* reached the scene, the tobacco was nowhere to be found and nothing could be done about it.

This was not the first time the O'Sullivans had come to Hallowell's notice. Throughout the war the Royal Navy had maintained a chain of signal stations all around the British coasts. From a high mast the stations were capable of displaying warning signals to merchant vessels when privateers were in the vicinity and could exchange messages with passing warships. A lieutenant, a midshipman, and a small party of sailors manned each station. With the end of the war the now unnecessary network was being closed down.

One such station was located on Dursey Island in Bearhaven Harbour. As was typical, the officer in charge, Moriarty, was an elderly lieutenant who lived in the signal tower with his wife and four children. In early 1816 he received orders to close the station and wrote to Hallowell asking that a ship be sent to take himself, his family, and the naval stores to Cork. Weather and navigational problems led to some delay, and before transport arrived the signal mast and yard and some naval stores had been stolen by the local inhabitants. Moriarty planned a search of the island using a small party of soldiers stationed there. He also dispatched his midshipman by boat to seek assistance from the militia commander on the mainland.

The midshipman was a locally recruited member of the O'Sullivan clan. He, like Moriarty, was on the point of being discharged, a fate he averted by deserting. He warned his relatives of the search and most of the loot was quickly removed from the island. Moriarty did locate a portion of the yard and arrested the woman in whose house it was found, her husband being absent. This was the signal for all the boats on the island to be stove in, thus marooning Moriarty and his family. Fortunately, the schooner *Picton* arrived and took a message to Commander Mould of the *Mutine* and Colonel Parry of the militia. They decided on a thorough investigation, to be carried out by Lieutenant

King of the militia and Lieutenant Morgan of the *Picton*, under the supervision of the local magistrate — none other than Morley O'Sullivan.

Not surprisingly, their report exonerated the locals and laid the blame for the thefts on Moriarty himself. Morgan behaved with extreme rudeness to Moriarty, his social and professional inferior. It was only with great difficulty that Moriarty persuaded him to embark his wife and family, who by this time feared for their lives. Morley O'Sullivan then applied to Hallowell to have Moriarty court-martialled or tried in civilian court. After interviewing Moriarty, Hallowell concluded that his version of events was nearer the truth and sent a curt letter of refusal to O'Sullivan. We don't know whether Hallowell chastised Morgan for his high-handed treatment of Moriarty, though it would have been in character for him to do so, but Morgan was not among the officers Hallowell later recommended for preferment.

Still full of energy, Hallowell was unable to relax and enjoy life at his comfortable official residence. At every turn he discovered some nefarious practice crying out for improvement. First it was the untendered award of the contract for his squadron's beef at a price higher than a competing contractor would have charged. Then the standard of living of the jailkeeper, far above what his wages could cover, paid for by irregularities in jail provision contracts and by illegally selling whiskey to his prisoners. Both must be investigated. 'There is nothing but corruption in every department in this country. I have put a stop to it in every branch where I have the slightest control, and I am very sorry I have not the power of using it in others.'

Cork was the departure point for vessels carrying convicts to the new British penal colony in Australia. Some were hardened criminals, others guilty only of petty crimes, and in Ireland some at least were transported solely because of their political views. The vessels would sometimes lie at anchor for long periods awaiting a full load. Among them was a ship called the *Canada* that was to carry a significant number of female prisoners. No direction had been given regarding the children of these unfortunate women. On his own responsibility Hallowell ordered that if the mothers so wished, their children could accompany them. Further, he directed that children under five years old were to be victualled at half the woman's allowance and the rest at full woman's allowance.

It would not have been a typical Hallowell appointment without a challenge to someone in high authority. In this case it was no less a being than the Lord Lieutenant, Charles Chetwynd, second Earl Talbot, the crown's representative in Ireland. In September 1818 Talbot announced his intention to visit the *Tonnant*. Very little notice was given, but Hallowell nevertheless laid on a dinner for 110 guests on the poop, followed by dancing to the music if the ship's band. Staging such on-board entertainment was old hat to him and was something he did well, and the Lord Lieutenant left the ship 'very much pleased by his excursion.'

The problem arose over ceremonial, always a touchy subject. The earl's aide had requested Captain Tailour to fire a 21-gun salute and hoist the royal standard at the main when His Excellency boarded the ship. These marks of respect were the prerogative of the reigning monarch and in Hallowell's opinion were not due to his representative. But with no time to clarify the matter he authorized Tailour to provide the requested honours. Immediately thereafter, he queried the Admiralty, and after much high-level discussion the Lord Lieutenant was politely informed that he was entitled to vice-regal honours only. Unusually for him, Hallowell had defused a possible confrontation and made his point without antagonizing a superior, for he continued to be on good terms with the earl.

In the autumn of 1818 the only major warships in commission in the British Isles were eight scattered ships of the line and five frigates. Since 1815 there had been no opportunity to practice the close station-keeping and precise manoeuvring that had helped to make British fleets so effective in battle and had honed the individual crews to exceptional standards of professionalism and teamwork. Lord Melville ordered a yearly gathering of these vessels for combined manoeuvres, and Hallowell was given command of the first ad hoc fleet that was to undertake six weeks of exercise in the western approaches. Earl Spencer at first accepted Hallowell's invitation to join him in the *Tonnant*, but had to back out because of an attack of gout.

Small as his squadron was, Hallowell laid down a full set of standing tactical instructions that would have been appropriate to a large-scale fleet. There followed a rigorous period of exercises designed to challenge the crews in seamanship and gunnery and to improve the officers' station-keeping and manoeuvring skills. There was a limit to what could be achieved in the time available, but the results fully justified the experiment, and the annual concentration became a matter of policy, a fitting finale to Hallowell's Irish posting.

Due to the scarcity of postings Hallowell was rotated out of the Irish station after three years. By the end of 1818 the Hallowell family was back in Eltham, the admiral of course on half pay. He hoped to have another active commission within three years. He must have been very confident of his standing at the Admiralty. In fact, ever since his vindication at the Murray court martial his influence and reputation had stood very high both professionally and among the general public.

It was rumoured that he was to be given the appointment to the Newfoundland station. Typically, the incumbents spent only the summer months on post, returning home in the autumn. The commander-in-chief also held the civilian governorship of the island. Hallowell was manoeuvred out of the posting on the flimsy grounds that the incumbent must hold at least the rank of vice admiral in order to uphold the dignity of the governor's position.

But he did receive one more appointment, that of commander-in-chief at the Nore, the sprawling naval complex in the Thames estuary. Ireland's unique challenges had added interest to an otherwise routine peacetime posting. The same could not be said of the Nore, where little of note is on record for his tenure from July 1821 to July 1824. (By coincidence Napoleon died 5 May 1821, and the news must have reached England very near the date Hallowell assumed command.)

Three events stand out. On 23 May 1823, a small vessel named the *Comet* was launched at Deptford Yard. She weighed under a hundred fifty tons and carried no guns. But she heralded a revolution, for she was the first steam vessel built for the Royal Navy. As commander-in-chief on the station Hallowell would have played a prominent part. With his keen interest in the practical application of scientific knowledge, he may have been among the first to grasp the potential of the new mode of propulsion. The navy adopted steam power only gradually, at first as an auxiliary, and it would be many years before sails ceased altogether to be employed.

With the end of the long war what was left of the Royal Navy took on new roles, among them the interdiction of the slave trade and a greatly expanded interest in exploration. The most significant prize would be the discovery of a navigable sea route around the Arctic coast of North America, the long-sought northwest passage. By virtue of his job Hallowell oversaw the conversion of the bomb vessel *Hecla* for northern service, and during Hallowell's tenure she twice sailed from the Nore on her errands of discovery. Grateful for his assistance and out of professional esteem, the ship's officers named a promontory on Baffin Island Cape Hallowell, and so it still appears on modern maps, at the western mouth of Fury and Hecla Strait, at latitude 69 degrees 59 minutes N, longitude 85 degrees 13 minutes W.

In 1820 the mentally ill King George III died, and the Prince Regent succeeded as George IV. The long-estranged Queen Caroline returned from a scandalous life on the continent to claim her place at his side. The King attempted to have Parliament pass a Bill of Pains and Penalties to banish the Queen and divest her of her titles, an outcome that would have permitted him to divorce her. However, public opinion favoured the Queen, who somehow succeeded in portraying herself as a grievously wronged wife. The bill passed narrowly in the House of Lords but probably would have failed in the Commons, so the government dropped it.

The new King was crowned in Westminster Abbey 19 July 1821, in a costume costing nearly £25,000. The stubborn Queen unsuccessfully tried to force her away into the ceremony. Two weeks later she died of undetermined causes and her body was returned for burial to her native Brunswick in the frigate *Glasgow*. Perhaps Hallowell observed the *Glasgow's* departure and thought again of those long-past days at Greenwich when the honest naval officers 'coloured up' at the antics of their royal hostess.

Shortly afterwards Hallowell was called upon to exercise his diplomatic skills when the American ambassador Richard Rush visited Chatham dockyard. At this time Rush and the British Foreign Minister

Canning were concerned with the situation in South America. Both countries had an interest in promoting the independence of Spain's colonies there, and co-operation between the recent enemies was a distinct possibility. If so the two navies might need to work together, and Rush no doubt wished to learn more about the British fleet.

The ship that had carried him to England in 1817 was the USS *Franklin*, commanded by Commodore Charles Stewart, brother-in-law of Hallowell's first cousin Robert Hallowell Gardiner. Rush and Stewart were old friends, and the ambassador could hardly have been ignorant of the cousinly connection. Moreover, Hallowell's cousin William Vaughan also knew Rush, who dined at Vaughan's Wanstead home. Ambassador Rush maintained a detailed journal, *A Residence at the Court of London*, but, unfortunately, it does not cover the period of the dockyard visit. Nevertheless, it is easy to imagine that on greeting his host Rush would mention these connections as a conversational icebreaker. Tension there must have been between the scion of a banished Loyalist and the intensely patriotic ambassador, but whatever the admiral's emotions we can be sure that Rush would have received every courtesy and assistance, unimpaired by events already fading from memory.

As yet only the officers of the navy had a standard uniform. But since most ships carried similar items of clothing for resale, some degree of standardization developed among the seamen also. Hallowell's reputation for interest in and humane treatment of his men prompted the Admiralty to appoint him head of a committee to standardize and improve the inventory of slops. Some lingering corporate memory of his quarrel with Keith over the price of shoes might have had something to do with the choice. Certain items were eliminated and better substitutes provided. For the first time the black silk handkerchiefs that had long been in informal use were added to the official holdings and were later incorporated as 'silks' in the Royal Navy's standard seamen's uniform. Variations to the basic outfit were established for ships on foreign stations. Every item was assessed for its practicality and above all for its affordability.

Hallowell retained a keen interest in new technical developments, and his advice was frequently sought on everything from water tanks to gun sights and carriages and the first tentative steps toward mounting guns in rotating turrets.

Old shipmates solicited him to use his influence on behalf of their sons. As one of the last survivors of the battle at Les Saintes, he was asked by the son of Captain Douglas to confirm that it had been his father and not Admiral Rodney who had conceived the idea of breaking the French line. Hallowell politely declined to become involved in the forty-year-old controversy.

Within a month of delivering Napoleon, the *Bellerophon* had sailed to Sheerness, where she was converted to a civilian prison ship. She accommodated about four hundred prisoners. Most of them were landed daily to perform heavy labour in the dockyard. The *Bellerophon* remained there throughout Hallowell's command at the Nore, not under his jurisdiction, but a reminder of a glorious but never-to-be-repeated occasion.

In June 1824, at the very end of his three-year appointment, Hallowell shifted his flag to the newly built three-decker *Prince Regent*, 120. She was among the first ships of that armament to enter the navy, having spent six years seasoning on the stocks. From time to time he received secret Admiralty summaries of French naval strength, a tantalizing reminder of the days when such knowledge might be all-important. But he never went to sea in his magnificent flagship, and he was never again to face an enemy. As his nephew John Elmsley wrote a few years later:

> *The Admiral is longing for a portion of the active employment these eventful times are affording his brother officers, who have the good fortune to procure commands, but as he had the command of two Stations since the peace, he is afraid the Admiralty will not listen to his applications for further employment.*

And so it proved.

15

THE LEGACY
1824–1834

Twenty years ago it would indeed have been a blessing, but now I am old and crank.

Admiral Sir Benjamin Hallowell, on inheriting the Manor of Beddington, 1828

Hallowell had put his senior appointments to good use in the interest of his sons and nephew. Having been a midshipman under Robert Spencer in the *Ganymede*, Charles was commissioned lieutenant on 30 August 1820, thirty years to the day of his father's making post. In 1821 he served as his father's Flag Lieutenant at the Nore. He was promoted to commander on 3 August 1824, and in 1826 took command of the sloop *Cadmus*. Just one year later he was made a post captain and went immediately on half pay of just under £200 a year. He had never seen action and never served at sea again.

Hallowell's third son, William, served as a midshipman on the South American station in the flagship of Thomas Hardy, captain of the *Victory* at Trafalgar. In 1827 he was a lieutenant in the *Asia*, 84, successor of the vessel in which his father had learned his trade, and fought under Hallowell's friend Codrington in the Battle of Navarino, when a combined British and French fleet shattered the Ottoman navy in support of Greek independence. After the naval battle a contingent of

French troops was landed to assist the rebels, and the freedom of Greece was eventually proclaimed.

This episode prompted a letter from Hallowell to Earl Spencer in which he warned that the French had never ceased to covet Egypt and that their involvement in the Greek rebellion was a merely a stepping stone to another attempt to seize Egypt. He believed the French had a secret agreement with Russia whereby, at the expense of the Turks, Russia would finally gain access to the Mediterranean from the Black Sea while France enjoyed a free hand in Egypt. He backed up his thesis with good arguments, but he may have over-emphasized the danger to Egypt; protecting Egypt from the French having figured so significantly in his career.

Hallowell's sister Mary's son, John Elmsley Jr., had also risen under the patronage of his uncle. He was a volunteer and later a midshipman in the *Tonnant* at Cork. When Hallowell left Ireland he arranged for young Elmsley to transfer to the *Newcastle*, 60, on the Halifax station. When Hallowell became commander-in-chief at the Nore, John returned and was borne as a master's mate in all three of Hallowell's flagships. On 3 August 1824, Elmsley was commissioned lieutenant and two weeks later retired on half pay of about £90 a year, professing a strong dislike for an occupation whose purpose was to kill his fellow man. He soon returned to Canada, although while his mother lived he often revisited England.

Charles Hallowell's promotion to commander and John Elmsley's commission as lieutenant were both dated 3 August 1824. Hallowell's three-year appointment as commander-in-chief at the Nore had come to an end just days before, on 31 July. The conjunction of dates is highly significant. Even a commander-in-chief was no longer in a position to make these promotions on his own authority and technically they did not in fact become effective during his tenure. But at the Admiralty Viscount Melville was still First Lord and one of the members was Hallowell's old friend Cockburn, colleague in the cutting-out expedition at Tenerife. Patronage and interest perhaps, but Hallowell's friends no doubt saw the promotions as a well-earned compliment to a hero of his country in his declining years.

The majority of Loyalist families never felt at home in England and either returned to the United States or moved to a British colony. Many of those who remained settled for mutual support in the vicinity of Croydon; Hutchinson, the last royal governor of Massachusetts, was buried there. By 1827 the surviving Hallowells had congregated in the area. After her husband's death Mary Elmsley and her family had returned to England, where they lived in the nearby village of Waddon, and after his appointment at the Nore, her brother Benjamin and his family moved to Addiscombe, also in the immediate vicinity of Croydon.

The hub of the little colony was Beddington Manor. In the early years of the nineteenth century the miserly Richard Gee-Carew had owned the estate, but he rarely dwelt there. The manor was occupied by his brother William Gee and the former Anne Gould. Gee's illegitimate son William Pritchard lived in the mansion during school vacations. He later attended Oxford University and became a clergyman and vicar of the parish of Walton, which was in the gift of the owner of Beddington.

William Gee died in 1815. He left almost his entire personal estate to his wife and only a minor bequest to Pritchard. One year later Richard Gee-Carew also died, and bequeathed Beddington Manor and a fortune to his brother's widow, again without providing for Pritchard.

The would-be heir now launched a long campaign to convince Anne to allow him a significant income, claiming that she had always treated him like a son, that she had led him to believe that she would ensure that he received his due share of the estate, and that for that reason his father had seen no need to make him a major direct beneficiary. Anne made him an additional allowance and paid off some significant debts. But Pritchard remained unsatisfied and in 1818 published a long memoir called *The Adopted Son*, in which he alleged that from the beginning Anne had schemed to get possession of Beddington and to deny Pritchard his moral rights. Anne had to obtain a court injunction to prevent the publication of the letters between the two.

Pritchard blamed Anne's legal advisors for the injustice and her relatives as well. He specifically exempted two relatives: Mary Elmsley, 'the only connection you have with an independent mind and feeling heart,' and Admiral Sir B. Hallowell, 'who is a man of the greatest honour, integrity and independence.' The bitter tone of his memoirs strongly suggests that if Pritchard had even an inkling of anything questionable in the relationship between Hallowell and Anne he would have used it to his advantage.

Anne made up for her benefactor's stinginess by her generosity to her tenants, to the citizens of the neighbourhood, and to her own relatives. She fell seriously ill in 1826, but by early 1827 she was thought to be recovering. The entire Hallowell family spent the Christmas of that year as her guests at Beddington. It came as a shock when she died 28 March 1828. She was apparently sincerely mourned by all who had known her, including the tenants of the estate she had managed for so many years.

Sir Benjamin Hallowell-Carew

Her death may have been the greatest personal blow of Hallowell's life. Forty years earlier the two had been forbidden to marry, but she had never ceased to be his confidante and friend through both their marriages and in her widowhood. It may well have been platonic to the end.

On doctor's advice, Hallowell did not attend the funeral. He bitterly regretted this decision, but Robert Spencer reassured him that he owed it to his family to take care of himself, whatever his personal feelings.

In her 1825 will Anne left the whole of the Beddington property to her cousin, on condition that he assume the name Carew in order to maintain that ancient family's connection with the land. And so he became Admiral Sir Benjamin Hallowell-Carew and commissioned a new coat of arms incorporating symbols of both families.

Anne's bequest had probably not come as a surprise. The unpredictable factor was whether Hallowell would live to inherit. At times it must have seemed more likely that he rather than Anne would be the first to die. To whom Anne would have left Beddington in that event can only be a matter of speculation: perhaps to Mary Elmsley and Ward Boylston, perhaps to Mary alone. To Ann Hallowell?

In the end Hallowell had fortuitously acquired the wealth and position that ability alone would have won him in a profession based more on merit than on interest. Despite his numerous quarrels with people in authority, his good fortune was welcomed by all those who knew him. As Robert Spencer wrote, 'It is certainly no exaggeration to say that every individual who has ever been with you or has seen you most cordially join with your nearer friends in their feelings, and this is a source of lasting satisfaction to us all, and I hope will prove so to you.'

The Beddington estate had been in the Carew family since the days of Henry VIII. The house contained a splendid hall dating back to the sixteenth century and was flanked by a church and a pigeon cote. Nautical associations were not lacking. There was an orangery, originally planted with seeds brought from America by Sir Walter Raleigh, whose wife had been born in the mansion. It is said that the pirate Bluebeard was once entertained in the great hall.

One feature of the grounds was a deer park through which the graceful animals grazed in complete security. Winding its way through the estate was the Wandle River, well known as an excellent trout stream, and there was first-class shooting over the extensive grounds. This rural paradise was within an easy journey of London even before the advent of the railway. It was reckoned to produce an annual income of over £12,000, dwarfing the £750 half pay Hallowell received as a full admiral after his last appointment.

But opulence had come at the cost of his closest personal relationship, and his deteriorating health meant that it had come too late to be fully enjoyed. His gout had long ruled out taking advantage of the outdoor amenities. To one of the first to congratulate him he said, 'Twenty years ago it would indeed have been a blessing, but now I am old and crank.' Grief and ill health both worked against the happiness and contentment that should have been his at last, but he would also have to contend with an even greater disappointment.

THE LEGACY

A view of the manor house at Beddington inherited by Anne Gee and bequeathed to Benjamin Hallowell. His grandson gambled the estate away.

Anne Gee's death was of course the most devastating event of 1828, but two other close family ties were broken in the same year. On 28 January his brother Ward Boylston died on the family property at Roxbury, leaving a widow his second wife and their son. At his death Hallowell received the £1217 principal of a bond that had paid him interest of £60 per annum since 1795, in accordance with an agreement winding up all their financial affairs in North America. The Boylston family papers contain a letter of condolence to Ward's son John from John Elmsley Jr. at York. There are no similar letters from either of Ward's siblings.

In the same year John Inglefield died at eighty. To the end his personal affairs were in a tangle, Hallowell having had to assist him in obtaining a pension for his wife, for whom he had never thought to apply. His father-in-law's problems had indirectly led to the traumatic breach with St. Vincent, but Hallowell retained his affection for his commander of thirty years before, the parent of his loyal wife, and grandfather to his children.

Each of the three deaths severed a significant strand in Hallowell's life. But in June of the same year there came a sign of new beginnings, when his eldest son, Charles, married Mary, daughter of Admiral Sir Murray Maxwell. The union held out the hope that there would soon be a grandchild to solidify the family succession in the new estate.

In 1831 untimely death cut short the promising career of Robert Spencer, who owed much to his early training under Hallowell. In his memory Earl Spencer presented his son's mentor with Bob's ornate snuffbox, which Hallowell promised would be added to the accumulated heirlooms of the Carews.

Many of the significant actors in Hallowell's life were gone. Admiral Hood had died in 1816 as Governor of Greenwich Hospital. Uncle Robert Hallowell Gardiner had passed away at Gardiner, Maine, in 1818. Both St. Vincent and Keith died in 1823. General Sir John Murray died in 1825, a patron of the arts, but never having been made a member of the Order of the Bath. Hallowell was perhaps human enough to take some satisfaction in having outlived these one-time enemies. He would be aware that Rufane Donkin had become a lieutenant general and a Member of Parliament, but did not live long enough to learn that the man who had once challenged him to a duel hanged himself at the age of sixty-eight.

Mary Elmsley retained a large portion of the Upper Canadian grants. When York was captured and plundered by the Americans in 1814 a quantity of furnishings disappeared. Nevertheless, after the war her property became the temporary home of the Governor of Upper Canada, the original official residence having been burned down during the occupation. She too was caught up in the delay in settling her grandfather Benjamin's affairs. Cousin Robert Hallowell Gardiner made repeated promises to dispatch funds, but as late as 1827 she was financially embarrassed by their non-arrival. Fortunately, her cousin Anne left her a generous annuity to be paid out of the revenues of the Beddington estate, and she continued to dwell at nearby Waddon.

In these final years Hallowell would have taken satisfaction in his family's circumstances had it not been for the disastrous conduct of his second son and namesake. Benjamin had been enrolled in the prestigious Charter House School in 1811, thanks again to the influence of Earl Spencer. He went on to Trinity College, Cambridge, in preparation for a career in the Church of England. At £350–£400 per year Cambridge would have been a serious expense, but the prospect of a clergyman son was highly attractive to a man of Hallowell's strong religious convictions.

Benjamin duly matriculated in 1822 at the age of twenty, but in September of 1823 the old man was forced to confess to Earl Spencer his bitter disappointment in his son:

> *His extravagant and ill-regulated conduct in other respects has convinced me that he is not a proper character for the sacred profession. I could not conscientiously recommend him to your lordship's notice or solicit your patronage in the Church for a character as unfit for the profession as he appears to be.*

Now he had a son whose career prospects were nil. The irony must have been apparent: a reprise of his father's situation fifty-seven years before, when he had made his own humiliating exit from school.

His son's predicament was actually worse than his had been. The student of divinity had fallen in love with a Cambridge girl named Kezia, last name not recorded, deemed by his family to be an entirely unsuitable match. What was needed was an occupation that would get young Benjamin out of his entanglement and leave him some prospect of an honourable and rewarding career. So the navy must have appeared to his own father so long ago when he had sent then midshipman but now Admiral Hallowell to the *Sandwich*. But in this case the navy was out of the question. The boy was far too old, and there was too much risk that his character faults would bring disgrace on his naval brothers and father.

Once again Earl Spencer's enormous influence came to the rescue. Through him young Benjamin obtained a cadetship with the East India Company. It would sever his connection with the unfortunate Kezia and open the prospect of rehabilitation and even riches. The young man was also favoured with Spencer's private recommendation to a wealthy family in Calcutta.

Benjamin had promised never to see Kezia again and he had actually embarked in the ship that was to carry him to the Far East. All seemed settled, but again Benjamin broke his father's heart. 'He came on shore, brought the girl up to town from Cambridge, and they were married at St. Giles Church by a license on 2 January. The new wife kept the secret until a child was born in March — a girl.'

Meanwhile the baby's father had sailed. Honour had not totally deserted him — he had made his pregnant mistress an honest woman and legitimized his daughter — but his cruelly disappointed father focused entirely on the broken promise. In his anger and disappointment he advised the earl to warn his Calcutta friends not to have anything to do with the young man he had previously recommended to them. There is no sign whatsoever that he interested himself in his unwanted daughter-in-law or granddaughter.

He received more recognition. In 1830 a new King came to the throne as William IV. Formerly the Duke of Clarence and a naval officer, he was personally acquainted with Hallowell from West Indies days and thus disposed to listen to the urgings of Earl Spencer in Hallowell's favour. On 6 June 1831, the old man received a private letter directly from the First Lord, Sir James Graham, beginning, 'I have received His Majesty's commands to inform you of his intention of conferring on you the honour of a Knight Grand Cross of the Bath.' Sir James's letter concluded with a personal tribute going beyond conventional congratulations. 'It gives me the most heartfelt satisfaction to pay this tribute of gratitude and of respect to the merits of an officer whose services can never be forgotten, while the naval glory of England is cherished and remembered.'

Hallowell took to his bed for a week to forestall a new session of gout and was thus able to attend the royal levee at which he was honoured with the red riband of the GCB. To Spencer he wrote, 'His majesty has been pleased to state … that independent of my services he has great satisfaction in gratifying the feelings and wishes of the individual who was at the head of the Admiralty at the time if the battle of the Nile…. I cannot express my gratitude in words adequate to my feelings.' With his appointment the number of naval Knights Grand Cross exceeded the established ceiling, but in light of the recipient's ill health and advancing years the new King had made this highly unusual exception.

The GCB must have seemed the culmination of his long search for recognition. Nothing more could realistically be expected. But in fact there was more to come. In early 1833 he was asked in confidence if he would accept the greater honour of a baronetcy. Instead of being Sir Benjamin Hallowell-Carew, Knight, he would be Sir Benjamin Hallowell-Carew, Baronet. The minor terminological difference was of enormous practical significance, because his title would thus become hereditary rather than dying with him.

Officers had been elevated to the peerage for truly outstanding services in wartime. Jervis and Nelson were created viscounts, and others barons or baronets. But it was very unusual for an officer to be distinguished by civil honours in peacetime for his exploits in past conflicts. The King's friendship and the Spencer influence were important, as was the fact that the Carews had long been baronets before the estate passed through the Gees to Hallowell. Lord Grey, the Prime Minister, had been First Lord of the Admiralty in 1806–7 and Chief Secretary of Ireland during Hallowell's tenure at Cork, so he certainly knew Hallowell by repute if not personally. Codrington became Member of Parliament for Devonport in 1832 and may also have had some influence on the monarch.

But the baronetcy must have been offered in the realization that even the KCB conferred in 1815 had not fully discharged the debt the nation owed to the last survivor of the Band of Brothers that Admiral Nelson had forged in the Mediterranean. It would certainly not have been proposed unless it was known that the gesture would be popular in naval and military circles and in the country as a whole.

Here was recognition indeed, long overdue, but perhaps even more gratifying for that reason. And not just he but his descendants would carry the honour. For many in his position, acceptance would have been automatic. But Hallowell was haunted by the shadow of his second son and namesake who had so bitterly disappointed him.

On inheriting Beddington, Hallowell had purposely retained on his new coat of arms the motto of the Carew family, 'To have a conscience free from guilt,' a motto that also happened to be that of the family of his great friend Collingwood. These words perfectly matched his own beliefs. In accepting the GCB Hallowell had assured the first Lord of the Admiralty that 'every part of my future conduct will convince him (the King) how sensible I am of the distinguished honour he has conferred upon me.'

Thus, the offer of a baronetcy presented Hallowell with perhaps the greatest moral dilemma of his life. Young Benjamin had been disowned, but even from the other side of the world his character flaws had the potential to dishonour both his family and the title itself. However remote that possibility, Hallowell could not in conscience run the risk. The offer was declined, no reason being given. No doubt Earl Spencer divined or was told the truth.

There was to be one last cruel twist of fate. In India young Benjamin had found his way into the army and by 1825 he was a lieutenant in the 35th Regiment of Bengal Native Infantry and perhaps on the path to rehabilitation. But on 7 May 1832, he had died of unrecorded causes. Communications between the Far East and Britain were notoriously slow. At the time the baronetcy was offered and declined the old admiral still believed his disgraced namesake to be alive. The unexpected news probably arrived quite soon afterwards. Hallowell may have briefly considered asking the King to renew the rejected honour, but pride and self-respect made such a step inconceivable.

In early 1834 Hallowell's third son, William, was promoted to commander. The old man wrote in thanks to the First Lord, 'As soon as I am able I shall take the opportunity of paying my respects to you at the Admiralty, which nothing but extreme debility prevents me from doing now.' Perhaps William's success compensated, however inadequately, for the baronetcy forever lost because of his brother's faults. Dated 15 February 1834, the letter is the last document in Hallowell's hand to have been preserved. When he wrote it he had not been out of bed since December of the previous year.

Admiral Sir Benjamin Hallowell-Carew, Knight, died at Beddington Park on 2 September 1834, at seventy-four, the same age at which his father had died.

His chief executor was his brother-in-law Samuel Hood Inglefield. His wife Ann received £1000 at his death, all the furnishings in a rental property at Orpington, Kent, all his silver plate, all the furnishings in the

Breakfast Room at Beddington, and all his wines. She was to receive an annual sum of £600 from the income of the estate for the rest of her life.

The entailed estate passed to his male heir, Charles. Of Hallowell's personal possessions Charles received all the furniture not given to his mother. Specially mentioned were two silver snuffboxes, the one presented to Hallowell by Earl Spencer as a memento of his son Robert and one given to Anne Gee's father, General Paston Gould, signifying the freedom of the City of Cork.

So far, nothing out of the ordinary. But the will also included two most unusual provisions.

Beneath St. Mary's Church next to the Beddington manor house is a vault in which generations of the Carew family are buried. It would have been assumed that the new lord of the manor would be interred there. But the following instruction is inserted at the very beginning of his will, 'If I should die at any place distant more than ten miles from Beddington (except in London) I desire that my body be buried in the church or churchyard of the parish wherein I may die and a tablet which I have ordered to be prepared to be fixed in the Chancel of Beddington [St. Mary's] Church.'

Hallowell was not fond of London. But the proviso also implies that even Beddington meant little to him. Otherwise, why make a stipulation that might prevent him from resting forever on the lands of his family, the outward symbol of his success? Exiled as a child, denied a normal domestic existence by the history of his time, did he feel rootless to the end, despite his cousin's legacy? He has made a statement, but its meaning is a mystery, unless to the very end he never felt truly at home anywhere but at sea.

A second stipulation is perhaps even more mysterious. Hallowell treasured a number of books given to him by his cousin Anne. The will referred to them specifically. 'I likewise give to my said wife all my books except those bequeathed to me by Mrs. Gee, and I give to my said wife all such of the books bequeathed to me by Mrs. Gee as shall have my wife's name written in them at the time of my death.'

We do not know the titles of these books or anything else about them. Why must some be withheld from his wife? Was it because of their content or because of annotations made by Anne? In any case, why not just destroy them, instead of drawing attention to them in a way that had to be hurtful to his wife, unless he had given her some explanation in advance? And what was to become of those that he had not certified by the time he died? By inference that would be a problem for Ann's brother the executor. One more ambiguous circumstance, raising more questions than answers about the enigma that was Hallowell's lifelong relationship with his first love.

We know many things about Hallowell the professional. He was courageous, enterprising, intelligent, and a master of his profession. Liked and respected by those who knew him, he nevertheless made powerful enemies when standing obstinately upon a principle. Nelson said, 'Duty is the great business of the sea officer.' He may have departed from that ideal during his Neapolitan interlude, but Hallowell most certainly exemplified the maxim. He served his country loyally at great personal cost. He treated his enemies with respect, but conceived an antipathy toward the tyrant Napoleon that bordered on the personal. Although a commoner, he was a confidant and friend of two generations of one of the most illustrious families of the British aristocracy.

Generous, perhaps to a fault, Hallowell raised a large family under great financial difficulties, using his influence unashamedly to advance his sailor sons' careers. His moral courage, strengthened by a sincere religious belief, helped him recover from a litany of disappointments that might have crushed his spirit.

Hallowell could hardly have been unconscious of his own merit, but it is hard to believe that he died contented. His last wishes regarding his place of burial and the books of Anne Gee strongly suggest what a psychologist might call unresolved internal conflicts. His treatment of his second son may have been all the harsher because of a suspicion, perhaps unacknowledged, that his own prolonged absences had in some way contributed to the young man's scandalous behaviour. Despite his motto, his conscience may not have been entirely free of guilt.

EPILOGUE

On succeeding to the manor of Beddington Charles Hallowell-Carew did what his father had chosen not to do — ask the Prime Minister to re-offer the baronetcy. His grounds were that the reason for the original rejection was a purely domestic circumstance that had now disappeared. This referred indirectly to the death of his brother Benjamin. But Charles's timing was bad. In the political turbulence of the early 1830s his appeal went unnoticed, and he received no reply from Melbourne or Peel, the two leaders who rotated as Prime Minister in the course of two general elections.

The Beddington estate experienced financial trouble as early as 1835, when a beech grove was sold for timber. But disaster struck when Charles's eldest son Charles Hallowell-Carew succeeded to the manor in 1848 on the premature death of his father. A gambler, Charles had fallen into the hands of bookmakers at an early age. The deer from the park were sold off in 1852. In 1857 he risked his remaining resources on a losing horse, and was declared bankrupt with debts of £350,000, a sum equal to millions today.

The sole means of payment was to sell the estate, but so complicated were the provisions of various wills that in 1857 Parliament had to pass a special Carew Estate Act to allow disposal of the assets. The wastrel Charles was the last to be buried in the manor vault, which had become waterlogged and was forever sealed in cement.

The manor house and a few surrounding acres were bought by the Royal Female Orphanage Society for £14,500. Shortly afterwards part of the south wing was destroyed by fire. The centre wing of the great house had already fallen into disrepair under Charles' mismanagement, and the original graceful baroque edifice was reconstructed in a typical Victorian style. After the Second World War the orphanage became the Carew Manor School, dedicated to the instruction and development of children with learning difficulties. One feels that the man who invested so much of himself in the development of his own 'youngsters' would approve.

When the school is not in session a peaceful silence reigns. Much of the great park remains, now owned by the local authority. There are no deer. Occasionally an aircraft passes on its way to nearby Gatwick Airport and not far away run the express trains to the Channel Tunnel and the old enemy.

Hallowell was buried in the vault of St. Mary's Church at Beddington Manor, but his executors also installed on the west wall the stone memorial tablet that was to have been placed there only if he had been buried elsewhere. Measuring two hundred and twenty by one hundred and seventeen centimetres and designed by Hallowell himself, it displays a sarcophagus in relief, with above it a design of a broken ensign staff, a sword, and a wreath, linked by a ribbon inscribed with the one word 'NILE.' The executors no doubt felt that the tablet expressed his innermost feelings and should be displayed even in contravention of his testamentary wish. The symbolism is clear, except perhaps for the ensign staff — why must it be broken?

POSTSCRIPT

According to Prime Minister Winston Churchill, the only thing that really frightened him during the Second World War was the Battle of the Atlantic. Fought to protect the critical lifeline from North America to Great Britain against the deadly menace of Hitler's submarines, the Battle lasted from the first to the last day of the conflict.

Two warships named after the Hallowell family participated in this unspectacular but cruelly demanding struggle. Linking the navies of Britain, the United States and Canada, the two ships symbolized a new chapter in the historical record of the North Atlantic triangle.

In July 1943 the patrol frigate USS *Hallowell* was launched at Providence, Rhode Island. Named for the Maine town founded by Hallowell's grandfather more than 150 years earlier, she was immediately transferred to the Royal Navy under lend lease, and renamed HMS *Anguilla*. She served under the white ensign throughout the war, participated in the sinking of a U-boat, and was returned to the USN in 1946.

In the later stages of the war Canada built nearly 60 of a new class of frigates, a significant step up from the corvettes that had fought the battle up to then. All were named after Canadian towns, and it was proposed to name one of the newest after Picton, Ontario. However, a frigate called the *Pictou* was already in commission. The danger of confusion between the two very similar names caused the navy to substitute the name of the township in which Picton was located. One hundred

Above: Built as USS Hallowell, *she was lent to the Royal Navy and served in the North Atlantic as HMS* Anguilla *throughout WW II.*
Below: Christened HMCS Hallowell, *after the Ontario township named in honour of Benjamin Hallowell, Loyalist. Another veteran of the Battle of the Atlantic.*

and fifty years earlier Chief Justice John Elmsley had named that township after his father-in-law, the Loyalist Benjamin Hallowell. So it was that at Vickers Ltd. in Montreal, on 28 March 1944, the new frigate was christened HMCS *Hallowell*.

At the very end of the war two U-boats surrendered to her off southern Ireland. From an admittedly inaccurate poster of the time it can be seen that the townspeople recognized and celebrated the connection between their ship and the long ago hero. His war and that of the HMCS *Hallowell* were very different, but courage, endurance, and professionalism were as much a part of the struggle against Hitler as they had been against Napoleon. The ethos of Hallowell's navy lived on, albeit in a vastly different context. In many ways he would still have felt at home in the vessel that bore his family's name.

POSTSCRIPT

H.M.C.S. "HALLOWELL"

Built and Engined by

CANADIAN VICKERS LIMITED

MONTREAL, CANADA

Keel laid November 5, 1943   Launched March 28, 1944   Completed in July 1944

Hallowell — Prince Edward County — Province of Ontario — Canada, was visited for the time by loyalists in 1784 - founded in 1797. The name "Hallowell" was given in honour of Benjamin Hallowell, who was a prominent loyalist, and formerly from Boston. The first meeting of the municipality took place in 1798. Amongst the first pioneers were Major Peter Vanalstine and Lieutenant Paul Huff. The first house was inhabited by Colonel Archibald MacDonald and was built by shipbuilders. ℙ Picton, founded in 1830, is an important town in Hallowell Township. A Canal was constructed between Picton and Prescott the same year. In 1830, the "Hallowell Free Press" was put into operation. ℙ Benjamin Hallowell was knighted and subsequently became an Admiral in the Royal Navy. The name Carew was added to his own after his marriage to Mrs. Carew. Sir Benjamin fought as a Captain under Viscount Lord Nelson at the battle of the Nile. In the biographical memoirs of Nelson, published in 1806, it is recorded that Captain (later Admiral) Hallowell had been mentioned in despatches by Nelson. ℙ It may be said, therefore, that H.M.C.S. "Hallowell" has been named after one of Lord Nelson's Captains. Shown below is an authentic impression of the signature of Vice-Admiral Sir Benjamin Hallowell Carew, taken from the Carlton House Register in London, England, and dated September 11th, 1828.

The signature of Sir Benj. Hallowell Carew and certain of the above information was obtained through the courtesy of Mr. C.G. Hallowell of Paris, Ontario, a distant relative of Sir Benjamin.

Not entirely accurate historically, this WW II poster nevertheless illustrates the strong ties between the Hallowell and her namesake community.

APPENDIX

PEOPLE, SEAMANSHIP, AND TACTICS IN THE AGE OF SAIL

A sailing line of battle ship and its complement of sailors and marines formed probably the most complex man-made system in existence before the Industrial Revolution. For an aspiring midshipman his first sea-going ship was a critical step in achieving the mastery of this system upon which his career and even his life would depend. Hallowell was expected to absorb the most minute details of how his ship floated, moved, and fought. At the same time, he would need to develop a profound understanding of a disciplined way of life through which a disparate body of men was welded into a team capable of meeting the test of battle.

The Hierarchy

The complement of every vessel was fixed by Admiralty order, although it was very rare for any ship to be at full strength. As in any military body in any age the organizational keystone was a well-defined hierarchy. In the eighteenth century that hierarchy was based not only on professional expertise and level of responsibility, as it is today, but also on demarcations which reflected the class distinctions of British society as a whole. At the apex of society were the very few members of the peerage or hereditary aristocracy. Combined with a much larger educated and property-owning middle class, they constituted an upper class, the class of ladies and gentlemen. The upper class was sharply differentiated from the lower orders or lower class — predominantly illiterate, not necessarily impoverished but owning almost no property. As the son of an upper civil servant, Hallowell was from the class of professional men from which half the navy's officers were drawn.

In a ship social class, military rank, and competence were all reflected in a complex socio-professional matrix. The permanent heart of the navy consisted of its sea officers, made up of three groups: commissioned officers, superior warrant officers of officer status, and superior warrant officers not of officer status. All sea officers were distinguished from and in authority over the inferior warrant officers, petty officers, and the able and ordinary seamen who formed the vast majority of the crew.

At the pinnacle was the captain, the title signifying both his position as commanding officer of any vessel and also his rank, if the ship he commanded was a rated ship. The captain was a sea officer and also held the King's commission and, subject to regulations, had complete jurisdiction over the rest of the crew. Occupying his own relatively luxurious quarters under the poop deck at the after end of the quarterdeck, with a marine sentry at his door, he was a remote figure of awe to the denizens of the lower deck. Especially when on detached service in the days before radio, he was routinely called upon to make critical decisions in unforeseen circumstances with no possibility of seeking guidance from higher authority.

The lowest commissioned rank was lieutenant. There were at least six lieutenants in the three-decked ships of the first and second rates, at least four in third-rates, and so on down to the smallest bomb vessels where the only commissioned officer was the lieutenant in command. The lieutenants kept deck watches in rotation, taking complete charge of the ship when the captain was not personally directing operations. In action, two were stationed on each gun deck, directing the guns on opposite sides of the ship. The most senior lieutenant was the second in command, or first lieutenant, the executive officer in modern terminology. Then, as now, he was responsible to the captain for the organization and training of the crew for day-to-day operations and to fight the ship in battle.

In a third-rate, the lieutenants lived and messed in the wardroom at the after end of the upper deck, in small individual cabins between the guns, separated by screens that were removed in action, with a table down the centre of the space. Here also lived the officers of marines. They were commissioned, but they were not classed as sea officers.

Confusingly, the wardroom was also home to three men appointed by Navy Board warrant, sea officers, therefore, but not commissioned. First among them was the master, a relic of the days when seamen sailed the ship and gentlemen fought her. He was responsible for the ship's navigation and sailing efficiency and for the stowage of provisions and stores in the holds. As a warrant rather than a commissioned officer, he may have lacked social status, but the Admiralty recognized his unique importance by paying him at a higher rate than it paid the lieutenants. Nowadays, his position in the naval hierarchy is reflected in the rank of lieutenant commander.

The other warrant sea officers of officer status were the surgeon and the purser, the latter being responsible for the acquisition, custody, and issue of the ship's provisions and stores, the supply officer of later times. Both these men owed their wardroom status to educational qualifications obtained outside the navy. When the ship carried a chaplain, he joined the surgeon and the purser in the wardroom.

The vast majority of officers were from the upper middle classes, sons of landed gentry and professional men, with a few younger sons of peers. Commercial- or working-class entrants were also present but were much less likely than their social superiors to reach the higher ranks. Even so, the navy offered far better opportunities than did the British army, where promotion was by purchase.

Three superior warrant sea officers were key to the running of the ship. The most important and most highly paid was the carpenter. Before going to sea he had probably become a skilled craftsman as an apprentice shipwright in a dockyard. He was responsible for the ship's watertight integrity and the repair of weather or battle damage to the masts, spars, and hull. The boatswain took charge of the day-to-day activities of the crew, supervised evolutions such as weighing anchor and hoisting boats, and maintained the sails and rigging. Finally, the gunner maintained the ship's guns, had custody of the round shot and powder required in battle, and trained the gun crews.

The boatswain, carpenter, and gunner were termed the standing officers, because they were the only crew members who remained with the ship even when she was turned over to a dockyard for refit.

Standing officers were required to be literate and had to be certified by a qualifying board before taking up their posts. The ship's ability to float, to move, and to fight was heavily dependent on the hard-won professionalism of this trio. They did not live with the commissioned officers in the wardroom, but in sequestered messes on the lower deck. They would never have thought or ventured to call themselves gentlemen, but they were trusted and respected by all on board, not least by the captain and his commissioned officers. Their nearest modern equivalent in a professional rather than a social sense is that of chief petty officer, but in fact they occupied a niche between commissioned and non-commissioned status for which there is no exact counterpart in today's navies.

Below these warrant officers was a stratum of petty officers, holding their positions entirely at the discretion of the captain. This category included the midshipmen and master's mates, who aspired to wardroom status and for whom the petty officer level was usually just a way station. What we would regard as the real petty officers were men like the captain's clerk; the quartermasters and quartermasters' mates; the boatswain's, carpenter's, gunner's, and sailmaker's mates; yeomen of the sheets and of the powder room; and the quarter gunners, one for every four guns.

The heart of the ship's company was its complement of seamen, of whom there were three to four hundred in third-rates, and up to five hundred and fifty in a three-decked first-rate like the *Victory*. Newcomers without nautical experience were enlisted as boys or as untrained adults, known as landsmen. Those who progressed would be successively rated ordinary and then able seaman, with corresponding increases in pay. The aristocracy of the lower deck were the topmen, young and agile sailors who raced aloft in all weathers, swarming while hanging back downward over the futtock shrouds, laying out along the yards, and balancing precariously on the footropes a hundred feet above the deck to manhandle the stubborn sails.

A man was allotted thirty inches of space in which to sling his hammock. Between each pair of guns was a mess for eight to ten men, fitted with a table that could be lowered from the deckhead at mealtimes, each mess drawing its meal separately from the galley. Ten to twenty positions in each ship were designated 'widows' men'. No one ever filled these positions, but their pay was channelled to the widows of men killed in action or lost at sea, a rudimentary form of survivor's pension.

Sailing

In these days of steam power and the internal combustion engine, it is almost impossible to imagine the problems of seamanship in an era in which the mariner relied on the wind alone. If winds were favourable the ship might hold its course for days and nights on end, eating up the miles with little effort on the part of the crew. If the wind failed or blew from the wrong direction, voyages planned for a few weeks could stretch into months, as provisions ran short and disease broke out.

The theory of sailing a three-masted square-rigged ship was relatively straightforward. Each sail was designed and set to catch the wind so as to produce a force vector in the direction in which the ship was travelling. Complications arose because most sails also exerted a force vector at right angles to the vessel's course, unless the wind was from right astern. Because the mainmast was positioned at the centre of rotation its sails did not produce a turning movement. In contrast, by exerting leverage around the centre of rotation, sails set on the foremast and bowsprit tended to rotate the bows to leeward, while those on the mizzenmast tended to force the bow into the wind. The art of sailing a steady course at best speed consisted in trimming the sails so that the opposite turning moments were balanced. When this state was achieved it was hardly necessary to move the rudder except to adjust for minor fluctuations in wind direction.

The yards carrying the huge square sails were slung on the forward sides of their respective masts, so that the wind normally struck them from aft and the ship was effectively pulled through the water. But they could be backed so that the wind pushed the canvas against the mast, reversing the direction of force, and the ship could then be sailed astern. With some sails backed and some in their normal position the pull-push effects could be balanced to eliminate any ahead, astern or rotational movement, and the ship was then said to be lying to.

So much for theory. Putting the theory into practice was an art to be mastered only through study under expert ship handlers and above all through long experience. It was normal to set the maximum amount of canvas that could be safely carried, and great judgment was needed in

APPENDIX

deciding when to add or reduce sail as the wind speed or direction changed or if a rapidly falling barometer indicated an approaching storm. Directing such standard evolutions or altering the ship's course by tacking or wearing had to become second nature so that the manoeuvres could be accomplished as a matter of routine on even the blackest night in a howling gale.

Changing tack could be accomplished in one of two ways, depending on whether the ship's bow or stern was put through the wind. In the first case, the manoeuvre was known as coming about. If altering from the starboard to the larboard tack, a ship gained as much speed as possible before the order 'helm alee,' that is, to larboard, at which the rudder was put over to turn the ship's head to starboard. As the bow came into the wind the ship would slow or even stop and gather sternway, and was said to be 'in stays,' but by skilful handling of the sails it was usually possible to force the bow through the wind, so that it now began to blow from the larboard side. Gradually, the ship would again gather headway and pay off as desired on the new larboard tack.

In contrast, when changing from the starboard to the larboard tack by wearing, course was altered to larboard, and the ship followed a counterclockwise arc, so that relative to the ship the wind gradually moved aft on the starboard side, across the stern, and up the larboard side until the vessel was steadied on the larboard tack.

The ship was conned from the quarterdeck, which was under the immediate charge of the quartermaster, a petty officer who supervised the men at the wheel, caused the bells to be struck at the appropriate times, and once an hour heaved the log to determine the ship's speed. The master's mate and the midshipman of the watch assisted the officer of the watch by maintaining the traverse board, keeping a lookout, carrying messages to the captain, and generally making themselves as useful as their state of training would permit. As they progressed they would be allowed to take charge of increasingly difficult evolutions under close supervision, with growing skill and self-confidence.

The traverse board was a chalkboard on which speed and direction were recorded hourly. The captain or master used this record to calculate the ship's change in position since the previous calculation.

The hand log consisted of a wooden drogue called the log ship linked by a stray line to the specially laid log line itself. The length of the stray line varied to compensate for the height of a particular ship's gunwale above the waterline. The log line was calibrated by knots located at forty-eight-foot, i.e., eight-fathom, intervals. To measure the speed the quartermaster stood at the quarterdeck gunwale and lowered the log ship to the surface of the water. When ready he called out 'Turn,' the midshipman of the watch revolved a special sand glass, and the quartermaster allowed the log ship to be carried astern by the movement of the ship, counting the knots as they passed through his hands. After 28.5 seconds the sand glass had emptied and the midshipman called out 'Hold.' The ship's speed was equal to the number of knots that had paid out, fractions being expressed in fathoms, e.g., 'four knots and two fathoms' meant a speed of four and a quarter knots.

Navigation

When in pilotage waters within sight of a charted coast by day, it was usually possible to fix the ship's position by observing the bearings and estimating the distances of prominent marks ashore. Especially by night or in poor visibility care was taken to give any dangers a wide berth and in confined waters soundings were taken continuously. When approaching a coast from seaward a prudent captain adjusted his ship's progress so that landfall was made in daylight.

In the open ocean a ship's position was determined by estimation or calculation of its latitude (displacement north or south of the equator) and longitude (displacement east or west of a chosen meridian, that of the Greenwich Observatory for British vessels). Taking his departure from a known point based on his last sight of land, the navigator laid off his desired track on the chart. During each watch the courses actually steered were recorded on a traverse board together with the ship's speed through the water, determined once an hour by heaving the log. Given these courses and speeds, and making estimation for leeway, a deduced or dead reckoning position could be plotted at the end of the watch. The dead reckoning could be further refined by allowing for ocean currents as estimated by the navigator from his own experience.

The process was prone to errors of estimation and measurement of course, speed, leeway, and currents. The discrepancies could accumulate to cause missed rendezvous in the open sea and increase the dangers when the ship again approached land. In 1707 Admiral Sir Clowdisley Shovell ran a whole fleet ashore on the Scilly Isles at the mouth of the English Channel; 2,000 men, including the admiral, being drowned. Whenever weather permitted, therefore, opportunities were seized to correct estimated positions by observation of the heavenly bodies.

It was a relatively simple calculation to determine the ship's latitude from the sun's altitude at noon, as measured by the quadrant. In the northern hemisphere, latitude could also be calculated by observing the altitude of the pole star Polaris. An experienced observer with good instruments in favourable weather and sea conditions would often be within one minute or one nautical mile of the truth.

Calculation of latitude had been possible for centuries, but longitude could not be determined without an accurate means of keeping time at sea. In 1714 the British Parliament offered a significant prize for anyone who could produce a timepiece that could be set to Greenwich time and then remain accurate throughout a voyage, despite temperature changes and the motion of the ship. It was not until 1761 that John Harrison was able to claim success with the perfection of his chronometer. It then became possible to calculate the ship's longitude as well as its latitude, introducing a new precision in ocean sailing. However, these accurate timepieces were very expensive, and it was long before even ships of the Royal Navy carried them as a matter of course.

Fighting

The *raison d'être* of the line of battle ship was to achieve the strategic goal of control of the sea through successful engagements with their enemy counterparts. The main armament of a 74 such as the *Swiftsure* consisted of guns of several different sizes, identified by the weight of the solid shot they fired. For reasons of stability the heavier pieces were placed lower in the ship, the guns firing through ports that were closed by watertight hinged covers when not in action. On each side of a 74 were fourteen 32-pounders on the gun deck and fourteen 18-pounders on the upper deck. One level higher, the quarterdeck and forecastle mounted nine 9-pounders a side. Thus, the *Swiftsure*'s broadside consisted of thirty-seven guns firing a total weight of seven hundred eighty-one pounds of solid shot.

The 32-pounder was the heaviest calibre gun normally mounted in British ships of the line. Ten feet long, it weighed about three and a quarter tons and the bore had a diameter of about six and one-half inches. When propelled by a charge of ten and three-quarters pounds of gunpowder, its solid shot would theoretically penetrate three and a half feet of solid oak at the point-blank range of four hundred yards.

Apart from round shot, a number of special-purpose projectiles were available. Canister shot — a bag of musket balls which could be fired at short ranges as an anti-personnel munition — was often discharged to sweep the enemy's decks just prior to boarding. Bar shot and chain shot were designed to cut the enemy's rigging and bring down his sails or topmasts to deprive him of the power to manoeuvre.

With their muzzles run out through the ports, seamen using hand levers and tackles could manhandle the guns through a small arc, but basically they were positioned to fire on the beam. Essentially, therefore, a broadside was aimed by manoeuvring the whole ship to bring one side to bear on the target.

On firing, a gun recoiled until it was brought up by its breechings, a heavy rope looped through a metal eye at the rear of the barrel, with both ends firmly attached to the ship's side. The gun was then wormed and sponged out to ensure that no burning grains of powder were left in the chamber. A charge in a cloth bag was inserted in the muzzle and rammed home with a long rammer, with a wad rammed home on top to prevent the charge from falling out as the ship rolled. The charge was pierced through the touch-hole atop the breech, and powder poured in to fill the narrow tube leading to the chamber. The round shot was inserted through the muzzle and rammed home, again followed by a cloth wad. The gun's crew of six to ten men ran the muzzle of the gun out through its port by means of tackles on the carriage. When satisfied with his aim the gun captain ordered his men to stand clear, and fired the weapon by a flintlock trigger or by applying a slow burning match

APPENDIX

to the touch hole. At the same time, the captain leapt aside to avoid being crushed by the rebounding monster.

The loading and firing drill was then repeated as rapidly as possible; a well-trained crew could fire three broadsides in five minutes. Gunnery was highly inaccurate even with well practiced crews at point-blank range and became even more inaccurate as the distance increased.

On many occasions battles at sea ended with two ships, each more or less damaged by gunfire, running alongside each other and becoming firmly attached by grapnels or by their entangled rigging. The fight would then be settled by the crew of one ship boarding the other and engaging in brief but savage hand-to-hand combat. For this purpose a ship carried pistols, axes, short swords known as cutlasses, and needle-sharp boarding pikes. Each vessel also had a contingent of marines armed with flintlock muskets and bayonets. During the gun action marines stationed in the tops or along the ship's side would attempt to pick off individual members of the enemy's crew, and if it came to boarding, the marines formed the core of the attack or defence.

Until the seventeenth century a British fleet was organized for battle in three squadrons. The White squadron formed the van, the Blue squadron the rear, and the Red squadron the centre. Each squadron had its own admiral, vice admiral, and rear admiral, the admiral of the Red squadron being also the admiral of the whole fleet. After preliminary manoeuvring under his general direction, using rudimentary flag signals, the admiral signalled the order to engage, and the three squadrons went into action in separate groups. Once battle was joined, individual ships also operated more or less independently, and in practice a melee usually developed. In the smoke of battle signalling ceased, overall control of the fleet and squadrons was quickly lost, there was little mutual support, and it was all too easy for less enthusiastic captains to keep their units out of harm's way.

The solution to a system in which control was too loose was to adopt the concept of the line of battle. This was to have the unintended consequence of making control too tight. The whole fleet now fought in a single line. The commanding admiral's flagship, the strongest in the fleet, was positioned roughly in the middle of the centre squadron or main body, with two other powerful vessels stationed as his immediate seconds ahead and astern. When battle was joined this strong group of ships usually found itself opposite the enemy's flagship and its own seconds, leading to a personalized engagement between the contending admirals.

The admirals commanding the van and the rear were similarly placed within their own squadrons, and the remaining ships filled the intervals between. Normally a distance of two cables or four hundred and eighty yards was specified between adjacent ships, but the interval could be reduced if desired. With the enemy drawn up in the same way the two fleets would fight on parallel courses, admiral versus admiral, and each ship engaging its opposite number in the enemy line. When numbers were uneven the numerically superior fleet might even keep its weaker vessels out of the line to ensure one-on-one match-ups. For a captain to leave the line without permission was to invite court martial and the punishment of death if convicted.

If both fleets were equally willing the result was a stand-up slogging match, carried on at ranges of a few hundred yards or less. During the commercial wars between Holland and England in the seventeenth century the two sides met frequently in such encounters and inflicted terrible human casualties on each other. However, ships were rarely sunk, although they were often too badly damaged to fight again without repairs. Battles usually ended with the most damaged fleet discontinuing the action and drawing off to fight again another day. The enemy was usually too badly knocked about to pursue. In short, the tactic of the line made it almost impossible to lose a battle, but also impossible to achieve a decisive victory.

It was easy to bring about this type of battle if both sides meant to fight, the opposing admirals tacitly co-operating to make it happen. However, one of the fleets might wish to avoid action. In that case, the admiral who wished to fight had to manoeuvre to obtain the weather gage, that is, to get upwind of the enemy. From this advantageous position he was then able to bear down on his opponent and force a battle with both fleets in line ahead, the enemy line to leeward of his own. In these circumstances the enemy's usual response was to concentrate its fire on the masts and rigging of the attacking vessels. If successful in reducing their attackers' mobility, the reluctant admiral could disengage to leeward, leaving his opponent unable to follow. Once again, such encounters were unlikely to be decisive.

Gaining the weather gage to force the enemy to give battle was a double-edged sword, for it also meant giving up the advantage of fighting from leeward when the ship-against-ship action actually began. If the wind was strong, the windward vessel might be heeled over so far as to make it dangerous to open the lower-deck gun ports, and the elevation of the guns had to be watched very carefully to avoid firing into the surface of the sea. Engaging from the leeward position also had the advantage of limiting the enemy's opportunity to escape if the battle went against him. For long it seemed impossible to reconcile the need to gain the weather gage in order to force an action with the desirability of conducting the engagement from leeward.

On land, successful generals sought to surprise their opponents with the time, place, or weight of their attack, perhaps by making skilful use of the terrain to achieve a concentration of their whole force against a portion of the enemy's. At sea there were few opportunities for surprise: the opposing admirals could observe their enemy's movements and strength equally well, and the same forces of wind and wave constrained the movements of both fleets. Naval tacticians were of course aware of the principle of concentration of force, but it was not until Hallowell's time that the key was found to lie in isolating a portion of the enemy's fleet, which could then be overwhelmed by superior numbers. The battles of Les Saintes, 1 June 1794, and the Nile were milestones in a tactical development process culminating at Trafalgar.

At Trafalgar Nelson achieved a decisive concentration of force by closing from windward with his own fleet in two columns, breaking through the enemy line at two points. The allied fleet was thus divided into three isolated parts. Nelson recognized that he could not continue to exercise command once the *Victory* had come into close action, and wrote, 'No captain can do very wrong if he places his ship alongside one of the enemy.' Once he had brought on a melee the superior morale and professionalism of the British crews achieved the upper hand, as he had anticipated. But the fighting had been fierce; whatever their deficiencies in seamanship and gunnery the Franco-Spanish crews lacked nothing in courage. The advance in two single lines subjected the leading British ships to a concentrated fire that could easily have disabled them one by one as they approached the enemy line. If the wind had fallen in the final stages of their approach they might never have closed with their opponents and remained sitting ducks. By accident or design Villeneuve's line had been doubled at some points, and this alone could have prevented the breakthroughs on which Nelson counted for success. Had the enemy van reversed course as ordered and come into action energetically, the outcome might well have been different.

Ironically, except for one minor action later in the war, when the French used it unsuccessfully, the attack in two single lines was never repeated. Brilliant in the specific circumstances, it entailed too many risks to be embraced as a general tactical principle.

NOTES

1. Purchasing Power. Generally speaking the value of money has undergone an uneven but steady decline ever since the 18th century. Estimating relative purchasing power at different dates is bedevilled by the fact that the basket of goods available for purchase has changed enormously over time.

On its website at http://eh.net the Economic History Association provides a number of data series under the title of "How much is That?" Based on that information the following rough equivalents have been developed for the period 1790 to 1830.

a. Current Sterling: For an approximation of the current sterling amount required to yield the same purchasing power, multiply the historical sterling value by 60.

b. Current United States dollar: Over the period the exchange rate was about $4.50 to the pound, yielding a then current equivalency which must be adjusted for the 200 year decline in the purchasing power of the dollar. For an approximation of the current dollar amount required to yield the same purchasing power, multiply the historical sterling value by 85.

c. Canadian dollar: Over the period in question the different Canadian colonies used sterling, but the local currency did not usually exchange with the British equivalent on a one to one basis. As this was written the Canadian and American currencies were nearing parity, so Canadian current equivalents with historical sterling would be the same as American, within the limits of the calculations.

Thus, in 1828 the Beddington estate generated an annual income of £12,000. The amounts necessary to achieve the same purchasing power today would be approximately £720,000 and $1,020,000, but such estimates should not be considered as anything more than rough orders of magnitude.

2. Diet.

Regulations and Instructions relating to His Majesty's Service at Sea,

Sect. ix, Chap. i, 1806
Of the Provisions
Article I
There shall be allowed to every person serving in His Majesty's Ships a daily proportion of provisions, as expressed in the following table:

Day	Bisket Lbs.	Beer Gals.	Beef Lbs.	Pork Lbs.	Pease Pints	Oatmeal Pints	Butter Ozs.	Cheese Ozs.
SUN.	1	1		1	1/2			
MON.	1	1				1	2	4
TUE.	1	1	2					
WED.	1	1			1/2	1	2	4
THU.	1	1		1	1/2			
FRI.	1	1			1/2	1	2	4
SAT.	1	1	2					
WEEKLY	7	7	4	2	2	3	6	12

Note: Table format modified.

together with an allowance of vinegar, not exceeding half a pint to each man per week.

Article II
In case it should be found necessary to alter any of the foregoing particulars of provisions, and to issue other species as their substitutes, it is observed that, a pint of wine, or half a pint of rum, brandy, or other spirits, holds proportion to a gallon of beer.

CHAPTER NOTES

CHAPTER 1.
The latest revision of the *Dictionary of National Biography* repeats the error with respect to place of birth. The same mistake occurs in the registry of the Church of Latter Day Saints and numerous secondary sources. The mistake, whether deliberate or not, first appears in an obituary by an unknown author in the *United Services Journal* of 1834. The true place of birth is confirmed by Birth Certificate No. 022731 issued by the Registry Division, City of Boston. The exploits of the *King George* are described in Smith; P.C.F. Details of the grant at Manchester, Nova Scotia, are from the Registry of Deeds, Guysborough. Danny D. Smith's *Yellow House Papers* is the authoritative work on the genealogy and history of the Hallowell family. I have also consulted the City of Boston Vital Records, and Webber and R.H. Gardiner provide vital amplification.

The Boylston family papers at the Library of the Massachusetts Historical Society, Boston, contain more than 40 years of letters and financial documents of the Hallowell family and their connections. (The out letters are in draft rather than final form, but it has been assumed that any differences are immaterial). Unless otherwise indicated, in this chapter and throughout the book all personal and family related information is from this source, abbreviated BOYLSTON, Boxes 3 to 9 for this Chapter. The reference to the death of Lucy Hallowell is from Benjamin Hallowell Sr.'s Memorial to the Loyalist Claims Commissioners. Events surrounding the siege of Boston and the subsequent evacuation are based on Ketchum, Clark, Ed., and Mika.

CHAPTER 2.
As usual family references are from BOYLSTON, Boxes 9 to 13. Official letters from Captain Vandeput are in ADM 1. Information on the French Shoal is from Finlay. The hand log consisted of a wooden

drogue called the log ship secured to an especially layed log line.

In the Royal Canadian Navy the daily rum issue lasted until 31 March 1972. Most men chose to mix their tot with Coca Cola. As a privilege Petty Officers were allowed to draw their tots neat, it being assumed that they could be trusted not to save several days issues in order to get drunk. In practice, the assumption about saving may not always have been strictly accurate but abuse of the privilege was extremely rare.

CHAPTER 3.
BOYLSTON, Boxes 14, 15, and 16 is the source for the senior Hallowell's letters to his son and various naval officers. The *Alcides's* Muster Book is in ADM 36. The Fighting Instructions was an Admiralty compendium of battle maneuvers and their associated signals, first issued in 1673 and gradually modified over the centuries. On taking command of a new station, an Admiral issued his own set of Additional Fighting Instructions that then became binding on his subordinates. Normally, the additional instructions closely followed those promulgated by the Admiralty, with a few modifications reflecting the new admiral's personal preferences and local circumstances. One of the difficulties facing Graves was that his own squadron was using a set of Additional Fighting Instructions that differed in some respects from those in effect in Hood's squadron, which had to adapt to Graves's version at short notice. Notably, Graves's version did not contain the option that on closing the enemy each ship was to steer initially for her opposite number, even if the signal for the line was kept flying.

It has been argued that Rodney's victory was entirely due to the wind shift, which in effect forced some of the French ships to break the British line rather than the other way around. Others claim that it was his First Captain Douglas who discerned the opportunity and convinced Rodney to take it. The controversy does not alter the fact that a decisive concentration was achieved and tactical thinking set on new lines. Rodney had amended the Fighting Instructions with signals that could place his flagship and her powerful supports at either the van or rear of his line rather than in the centre, thus bringing an overwhelming fire to bear against weaker opponents. In itself this provision is proof that Rodney had grasped the overriding importance of concentration, however achieved. The Fighting Instructions and their implications are exhaustively examined in Corbett's *Fighting Instructions*.

CHAPTER 4
Letters concerning the Nova Scotia grant and other family matters are in BOYLSTON, Boxes 16 to 30. General information on Governor Wentworth and his times is based on Brian Cuthbertson's *Wentworth, the Loyalist Governor*. The letter from Mrs. Adams is in Charles Adam's *Letters of Mrs Adams, the Wife of John Adams*. References to the future Admiral Nelson are from Vincent. The Antigua Dockyard has been reconstructed and is now a major tourist attraction, promoted rather inaccurately as 'Nelson's Dockyard.' He certainly visited the place frequently, but beyond recommending it as the preferred base in the area he had little to do with its development and operation.

CHAPTER 5
Descriptions of Stansted and its inhabitants are from the Earl of Bessborough. Apparently Hallowell's rejection of the Coffin girl did not cause a lasting breach between the two families. In 1807 a nephew of Isaac Coffin served with Hallowell in the *Tigre* as a volunteer, again in 1813 in the *Malta* as a midshipman, and in 1824 with Samuel Hood Inglefield in the *Ganges* as a lieutenant. Descriptions of the West African slave forts and the inspection process are from Captain Inglefield's letters in ADM 1. Events at Toulon are well described in Ireland, and Bonaparte's participation is from McLynn. References to Captain Elphinstone are based on McCrainie, who notes that Captain Elphinstone was extremely displeased at being superseded in the *Robust*, but seems unaware of his act of revenge. Hallowell's commendations from General Dundas and Admiral Hood are recorded in YALE. Nelson's comments are from Nicholas. Family matters are from BOYLSTON, Boxes 31 to 37.

CHAPTER 6

Hallowell's discovery of the truth about his supersession in the *Courageux* is in Hotham's 2 February 1795 letter in ADM 1. Although it is dated two days later, Hallowell's letter was enclosed with Hotham's, probably a secretarial error. All letters to and from the senior Hallowell are in BOYLSTON, Boxes 38 to 41, as are Hallowell's letter to his brother Ward, and the Admiralty Secretary's to Ward concerning intelligence gathering. Admiral Jervis's commendations arising from the Toulon blockade are in his letters of 3 September 1796 and 6 July 1797 (ADM 1/395). The story of the wreck of the *Courageux* comes from Jervis's letters of 15 and 19 December 1796 (ADM 1/395) and the record of the subsequent court martial (ADM 1/5338). The possibly apocryphal story of Hallowell's clapping Jervis on the back before the Battle of St. Vincent is from Fitchett. A copy of the captains' letter requesting that Hallowell share in the prize money is in BOYLSTON, Box 43.

CHAPTER 7.

Hallowell's communications with the Admiralty in 1797 are in ADM 1/1916. Nelson's desire to put financial rewards in the way of Hallowell and Cockburn is attested in Oman. The circumstances surrounding St. Vincent's refusal to duel are from Davidson. LEE and Willyams (chaplain of the *Swiftsure*) are the sources for all eyewitness accounts of events in the *Swiftsure* during the period of mutiny and later at the Battle of the Nile. Although Lee does not say so, the incident of the disobedient marine may be the source of the story that Hallowell once quelled a mutiny with his fists. Nelson's quote about desertion is from Vincent. The accounts of the supposedly typical demeanour of the British sailors before the battle are from Fraser and Nicol, a seaman with long service in both the royal and merchant navies. Clowes, Volume IV, contains the history of Nelson's search and a full account of the battle. More recent treatments are from Warner, *Nelson's Battles*; Lavery, *Nelson and the Nile*; and Fraser. The account of Hallowell's father's death is in Cameron.

NOTES

CHAPTER 8

The Beauchamp incident is recounted in Willyams. The report on the facilities at Rhodes is from the ship's Journal (ADM 1/1918). All other eye-witness descriptions are based on Willyams and LEE. According to Fitchett, one of the Turkish ships carried a gift from the sultan to Nelson: a clockwork operated jeweled aigrette that the monarch had torn from his own turban in ecstasy at hearing the news of the Aboukir victory. Hallowell's bravery at Naples, Nelson's approbation, and the negotiations with the French at Rome are from Clarke. Lord St. Vincent's opinion of the Scots in general and Keith in particular is from the Introduction to Volume IV of Corbett, *the Private Papers of George, 2nd Earl Spencer*. The quarrel over the price of shoes and Keith's dispatch of the *Swiftsure* is documented in McCrainie and in Lloyd and Perrin. The key letters, probably saved by Hallowell himself, are in SCIENCE. Some idea of the complexity of the issue may be gained from the fact that the calculation to determine the fair resale price involved the conversion of the total cost of 7,711 ouncos, 28 forins, and 8 grains Sicilian currency into pounds, shillings and pence, at different exchange rates. Hallowell's report of the action leading to the surrender of the *Swiftsure* is in ADM 1/5357, dated on board *l'Indivisible* in Toulon Road, 24 July 1801.

CHAPTER 9.

Dated 29 July 1801, the letter reassuring Ward of his brother's safety, from an unknown author, is in BOYLSTON, Box 49. Details of the *Swiftsure's* final action are from the *Minutes of Court Martial on Board His Majesty's Ship Genereux, in Port Mahon, 18 Aug. 1801* (ADM 1/5357). Statistics on British losses during the war are from Lewis. In noting that only one ship of the line was lost to enemy action, he apparently has not counted those such as the *Swiftsure* that were later recaptured. The manuscript will of Benjamin Hallowell Sr. is in the Archives of Ontario. Hallowell's involvement with the discarded Princess Caroline is based on Fraser and Gardiner. The Earl of St. Vincent's comments on the quality of the navy's senior officers are in

Corbett, *the Papers of George, 2nd Earl Spencer*. Hallowell's collected correspondence concerning his quarrel with Keith is in SCIENCE.

CHAPTER 10.
The early development of Freetown is based on Fyfe and Walker. The questionnaire and comments thereon are contained in Answers of the Governor and Council, BT6/70. The appeal for help to Hallowell from the Freetown authorities is in WO 1/35. Hallowell's reports to the Admiralty on his operations and on the trials of the innovations in the *Argo* are in ADM 1/1927. Sir Samuel Hood's commendation of Hallowell is included in his record of service, YALE. St. Vincent's comments on the importance of the Egyptian mission and Hallowell's qualifications for it are in Bonner-Smith, 10 November and 3 December 1803. The Admiralty mechanical telegraph between London and Portsmouth consisted of nine relay stations over which messages could be passed in as little as twelve minutes. Hallowell's dealings with Elphi Bey and with Rashid Pasha regarding the defence of Egypt are from his official report in ADM 1 /1929. Privately, he advised Nelson 'I can assure you nothing will give me so much pleasure as getting rid of him as I have never met with a person of so capricious a disposition; he is steady to nothing but his pipe, and his whims and caprices are more variable than the winds.' That comment and the extract from the log of the *Argo* are in NELSON. Nelson's comments on Hallowell's generosity and independence are from Ludovic Kennedy. Hallowell did call on Lady Hamilton at Merton, but no doubt owing to the dubious social position of Nelson's mistress his wife did not accompany him. In this they followed the example of Earl and Lady Spencer.

CHAPTER 11.
As usual information on the Hallowell family and their affairs is from BOYLSTON, Boxes 51 and 52. References to letters from Hallowell to Earl Spencer are from SPENCER. Napoleon at Boulogne awaiting Villeneuve's fleet is based on McLynn. Events in the British fleet immediately leading up to Trafalgar are mainly as recorded in Vincent. The

return of Nelson's body and the state funeral leading to its interment in Hallowell's coffin are vividly described by Pocock and Kennedy. The reciprocal court martial's of Thompson and Hallowell are exhaustively explained in SPENCER. Admiral Collingwood's congratulations on Hallowell's performance in the Egyptian Expedition are among the collected personal papers in SCIENCE.

CHAPTER 12.
References to letters from Hallowell to Earl Spencer are from SPENCER. The SCIENCE collection contains the Admiralty's instructions for the Scheldt reconnaissance, and Hallowell's copies of his extremely detailed reports. Lady Spencer's letter to Hallowell on his illness is in YALE. Harvey is the source of information on Cochrane. The post-Trafalgar naval struggle in the Mediterranean is mainly based on Mackesy and on Warner's *Life and Letters of Lord Collingwood*; events specific to the *Tigre* and her crew, including the physical description of Hallowell are from Crawford. During this period Hallowell learned of the death of his grandmother Rebecca, the miraculous survivor who had once been kept alive while unconscious through the ingestion of oysters. She died in London in June 1809, at the age of 94, cared for to the end by poor cousin Martha Hallowell, and having outlived her children. Her grave at St. George's Church, Hanover Square, was obliterated in the blitz of 1940. Hallowell's letter to the First Lord refusing the position of Captain of the Fleet is in SCIENCE. Commissioner Inglefield's appointment problems are discussed in Gwyn, *Ashore and Afloat*; Hallowell's personal involvement emerges from SPENCER.

CHAPTER 13.
Napier, Glover and Hall are the principle sources for the strategy and events of the Spanish War in general and the Tarragona campaign in particular, and for the assessment of key personalities. Wellington's assessment of General Murray is from Glover. Hallowell's own experiences and thoughts are revealed in SPENCER. Crawford sheds additional light from the perspective of one of Hallowell's subordinates.

CAIRD contains eyewitness accounts of the Tarragona evacuation from depositions collected by Hallowell in preparation for General Murray's court martial. Those deposing included Captain Inglefield of the Malta; Lieutenant J. Cole, Agent of Transports; Captain Thomas Withers, Principal Agent of Transports; Lieutenant John Bowie, commanding Gunboat 23; Lieutenant John Stoddart, commanding the *Stromboli*; Lieutenant R. Tweed, commanding the *Fame* beach party; and Lieutenant William Bathurst, *Malta* beach party.

CHAPTER 14.
So acute did the glut of officers become that it was even suggested that new enrolments should cease in order to prevent the average age on promotion to lieutenant from rising to thirty or even forty years. Giving the rank of commander to first lieutenants of ships of the line relieved some of the pressure at that level. Hallowell's letters to Lord William Bentinck and to Lord Melville regarding Lieutenant Boxer's promotion are in CAIRD. General Murray's court martial is in WO 91/9. Hallowell's own description of events at Tarragona and the proposed duel with General Donkin is in SPENCER, as are his description of the circumstances surrounding Napoleon's dispatch to St. Helena, and his rejection of the opportunity to mount guard over him. The long letter to Lord Melville regarding his reputation is in SCIENCE. DUKE is the source for most events during Hallowell's tenure as commander-in-chief in Ireland. The letter arranging the American ambassador's visit to Hallowell's command is in RUSH. John Elmsley's letter to Ward Boylston is in BOYLSTON, Box 73.

CHAPTER 15.
John Elmsley's letter of condolence to Ward's son Lane is in BOYLSTON, Box 74. After the initial break Benjamin had never again communicated with his brother except through agents. But the absence of condolences from Ward's siblings in the BOYLSTON collection may signify only that letters from Benjamin and Mary to the widow Boylston have not been preserved. Robert Spencer's letter is in YALE.

NOTES

The older Hallowell generation had included four brothers, but only Benjamin Hallowell Sr. and his brother Robert left known male descendants. Robert's only son assumed his mother's family name and lived and died as Robert Hallowell Gardiner. Ward Hallowell had changed his name to Boylston for inheritance purposes. Now for the same reason his younger brother became a Hallowell-Carew, and his children followed suit. The combined result of these independent events was that in this branch the Hallowell name ended in this generation, even though the three cousins had numerous descendants. The story of Hallowell's reaction to his unexpected legacy is in his obituary in the *United Services Journal*, 1834, Part III, p. 374. Internal evidence suggests that it was written by his brother-in-law Inglefield. Descriptions and history of Beddington Manor are based on Mitchell and on personal observation. William Pritchard's *The Adopted Son* (London, W. Anderson, 1818) is in the Local Studies section of the Sutton Library. Sir James Graham's letter on the GCB is in YALE. In the realm of honours and awards the monarch's word was final. It is tempting to perceive some hostility on the part of the Prince Regent, later George IV, evidenced by the way Hallowell was treated in the matter of honours. One reason might have been Hallowell's imprudent association with Queen Caroline shortly after she was rejected by the Prince, innocent as their acquaintance undoubtedly was. Another possible black mark was the threatened duel with General Donkin that the Prince Regent was called upon to forbid. This is speculation, but the fact remains that it was not until William IV ascended the throne that Hallowell received honours that many felt were long overdue. Charles Hallowell-Carew's attempt to revive the offer of a baronetcy is in PEEL.

BIBLIOGRAPHY

PRIMARY SOURCES
The capitalized abbreviations are for reference in the Chapter Notes.

CANADA
Archives of Ontario, Toronto
> Records of York County Surrogate Court
> Upper Canada Gazette
> Upper Canada Land Petitions

National Archives, Ottawa
> Loyalist Claims, MG-14, Audit Office 12 and 13
> Ontario Loyalist List

Nova Scotia Archives and Records Management, Halifax, N.S.
> Index to Deeds
> Crown Grants Index Sheets

Registry of Deeds, Guysborough, N.S.
> Land Grant, Antigonish Harbour, 5 September 1807
> Land Grant, Manchester, 22 October 1765

GREAT BRITAIN
The British Library, London
> Carewe Papers, 1585–1815 (CAREWE)
> Sir John Theophilus Lee, Memoir and Services (LEE)
> The Liverpool Papers, ADD MSS 38340 (LIVERPOOL)
> Nelson Papers, General Correspondence, ADD MSS 34922 and 34977 (NELSON)
> The Papers of the 2nd Earl Spencer, ADD MSS 75958, 75959, and 75960 (SPENCER)
> The Peel Papers, General Correspondence, ADD MSS 40411 (PEEL)

The East Sussex Records Centre, Chichester

The National Archives, Public Records Office, London
> Admiralty Captain's Letters (ADM 1 captains)
> Admiralty Ships Muster Books (ADM 36)
> Admiralty Court Martial Records (ADM 1 courts martial)
> Board of Trade (BT)
> War Office (WO)

The National Maritime Museum, Greenwich, Caird Library

Papers of Admiral Sir Benjamin Hallowell-Carew (CAIRD)

The Science Museum Library, London
Papers of Sir Benjamin Hallowell-Carew (SCIENCE)

The Sutton Library, Main Branch, Sutton, Surrey

UNITED STATES
Rare Book, Manuscript and Special Collections Library, Duke University, Durham, NC
Sir Benjamin Hallowell-Carew Papers (DUKE)

Massachusetts Historical Society Library, Boston, MA
The Boylston Papers (BOYLSTON)

Rare Books: Manuscripts Collection, Princeton University Library, Princeton, NJ
Rush Family Papers (RUSH)

James Marshall and Marie-Louise Osborn Collection, Beinecke Rare Book and Manuscript Library, Yale University, New Haven, CT
Account of the Naval Career of Admiral Sir Benjamin Hallowell-Carew (YALE)

SECONDARY SOURCES
Adams, Charles F., ed., *Letters of Mrs. Adams, the Wife of John Adams* (Boston; C.C. Little and J. Brown, 1848)
Admiralty, *The Navy List* (The Admiralty, London, 1816–1840)
Akins, Thomas, *A History of Halifax City* (Halifax, N.S., 1895)
Andre, John, *Infant Toronto* (Toronto; Ortoprint, 1971)
Baldry, W.Y, *Journal of the Society for Army Historical Research*, Volume xiv, Number 56, Winter 1935
Beatson, Robert, *Naval and Military Memoirs of Great Britain* (London; Longman, Hurst, Rees and Orme, 1804)
Benady, Tito, *The Royal Navy at Gibraltar* (Northampton, UK; Gibraltar Books, 1993)
Beresford, Rear-Admiral Lord Charles, *Nelson and His Times* (London; Harmsworth Brothers, 1898)
Berube, C., and Rodgaard, J., *A Call to the Sea* (Washington, DC; Potomac Books, 2005)
Bessborough, Earl of, with Clive Aslet, *Enchanted Forest, the Story of Stansted in Essex* (London; Weidenfeld and Nicholson, 1984)
Bond, Gordon, *The Grand Expedition* (Athens, GA; University of Georgia Press, 1979)

Bonner-Smith, D., *Letters of the Earl of St.Vincent* (London, Navy Records Society, 1921)

Bowen, Frank, *Wooden Walls in Action* (London; Haltom, 1951)

____, *Men of the Wooden Walls* (London; Staples, 1952)

Cameron, K.W., *The Papers of Loyalist Samuel Peters* (Hartford; Transcendental Press, 1978)

Cipolla, Carlo, *Guns, Sails and Empires* (Manhattan, KS; Sunflower University Press, 1985)

Clarke, Rev. James, *The Life and Services of Horatio Viscount Nelson* (London; Fisher, Son and Co., 1840)

Clark, Dora Mae, 'The American Board of Customs,' *American Historical Review*, 45, 1939/40, p. 777

Clark, William, ed., *Naval Documents of the American Revolution* (US Government Printing Office; Washington, DC, 1964–1986)

Clowes, Sir William, *The Royal Navy* (London; S. Low, Marston and Co., 1892–1913)

Colledge, J.J., *Ships of the Royal Navy* (London; Greenhill Books, Lionel Leventhal Ltd., 2003)

Corbett, Julian, *Fighting Instructions, 1530–1816* (London; Navy Records Society, 1905)

____, *The Private papers of George, 2nd Earl Spencer* (London; Navy Records Society, 1914)

Cordingly, David, *The Billy Ruffian* (London; Bloomsbury Publishing, 2004)

Crawford, Captain Abraham, *Reminiscences of a Naval Officer* (London; Chatham Publishing, 1999)

Cuthbertson, Brian, *The Loyalist Governor* (Halifax, N.S.; Pathetic Press, 1983)

Davidson, James, *Admiral Lord St. Vincent* (Barnsley, UK; Pen and Sword Maritime, 2006)

Dictionary of National Biography (Oxford; Oxford University Press, 2004)

Dictionary of Canadian Biography (Toronto; University of Toronto Press, 1966–2005)

Downer, Martyn, *Nelson's Purse* (London; Bantam Press, 2004)

Edgar, Matilda, ed., *Ten Years of Upper Canada in Peace and War* (London; T. Fisher Unwin, 1891)

Finlay, Alexander, FRGS, *South Atlantic Directory*. (London; Richard, Holmes, Lowrie, 1883)

Fitchett, William, *Nelson and His Captains* (London; Smith Elder, 1911)

Fraser, Edward, *The Sailors Whom Nelson Led* (London; Methuen, 1913)

Fraser, Flora, *The Unruly Queen*, (New York, Knopf, 1996)

Fremantle, Elizabeth, ed., *The Wynne Diaries* (London; Oxford University Press, 1952)

Fyfe, Christopher, *A History of Sierra Leone* (London; Oxford University Press, 1962)

Gardiner, Leslie, *The British Admiralty* (Edinburgh and London; William Blackwood and Sons, 1968)
Gardiner, Robert Hallowell, *Early Recollections* (Hallowell, ME; White and Horne Company, 1966)
Gentleman's Magazine 1834 Volume civ, part ii
Gill, Conrad, *The Naval Mutinies of 1797* (Manchester, UK; Manchester University Press, 1913)
Glover, Michael, *The Peninsular War, 1807–1814* (London; Penguin Books, 2001)
Greene, Jack, and Pole, J.R., eds., *Encyclopedia of the American Revolution* (Oxford; Blackwell Reference, 1991)
Gwyn, Julian, *Frigates and Foremasts* (Vancouver; University of British Columbia Press, 2003)
_____, *Ashore and Afloat* (Ottawa; University of Ottawa Press, 2004)
Hall, Christopher D., *Wellington's Navy* (London; Chatham Publishing, 2004)
Hamilton, Sir R.V. and Laughton, J.K., *Recollections of Commander James Anthony Gardner, 1775–1814* (London; Navy Records Society, 1906)
Hannay, David, ed., *Letters Written by Sir Samuel Hood in 1781–82–83* (London; Navy Records Society, 1895)
Harland, John, *Seamanship in the Days of Sail* (London; Conway Maritime, 1954)
Hart, Harriet, *History of Guysborough County* (Belleville, Ont.; Mika Publishing, 1975)
Harvey, Robert, *Cochrane* (New York; Carroll and Graf Publishers Inc., 2000)
Hood, Dorothy, *The Admirals Hood* (London; Hutchinson and Co., 1942)
Ireland, Bernard, *The Fall of Toulon* (London; Weidenfeld and Nicholson, 2005)
James, William, *The Naval History of Great Britain 1793–1820* (London; Harding, Lepard and Co., 1826)
Jenkins, E.H., *A History of the French Navy* (London; Macdonald and Janes, 1973)
Jonson, Merrill, *The Founding of a Nation: a History of the American Revolution* (New York; Oxford University Press, 1968)
Jones, E. Alfred, *The Loyalists of Massachusetts* (London; The Saint Catherines Press, 1930)
Kennedy, Ludovic, *Nelson and His Captains* (London; Collins, 1975)
Kennedy, P., *The Rise and Fall of British Naval Mastery* (London; Ashfield Press, 1983)
Ketchum, Richard, *Decisive Day: the Battle of Bunker Hill* (Garden City, NY; Doubleday, 1974)
Langford, Paul, *A Polite and Commercial People* (Oxford; Clarendon Press,

1989)

Lavery, Brian, *Nelson's Navy: the Ships, Men and Organization* (Annapolis, MD; Naval Institute Press, 1974)

———, *The Ship of the Line* (London; Conway Maritime Press, 1983)

———, *Nelson and the Nile* (London; Chatham Publishing, 1998)

Lewis, Michael, *A Social History of the Navy* (London; Allen and Unwin, 1960)

Lloyd, Christopher, *The British Seaman* (London; Allen and Unwin, 1960)

Lloyd, C., and Perrin, William, *The Keith Papers* (London; Navy Records Society, 1927–1955)

Lyon, David, *Sea Battles in Close-Up: the Age of Nelson* (Annapolis, MD; Naval Institute Press, 1996)

Mackesy, Piers, *The War in the Mediterranean, 1803–10* (London; Longmans Green, 1957)

Maffeo, Steven, *Most Secret and Confidential* (London; Chatham Publishing, 2000)

Marlowe, John, *Anglo-Egyptian Relations 1800–1953*, (London; Frank Cass, 1965)

Marshall, John, *Royal Naval Biography* (London; Longman, Hurst, Rees, Orme and Brown, 1827–1835)

McCrainie, Kevin, *Admiral Lord Keith and the Naval War against Napoleon* (Gainesville, FL; University Press of Florida, 2006)

McLynn, Frank, *Napoleon*, (London; Jonathan Cape, 1997)

Mika, Nick and Helma, *United Empire Loyalists* (Belleville, Ont.; Mika Publishing Co., 1976)

Mitchell, Ronald, *The Carews of Beddington* (Sutton, UK; Libraries and Arts Services, 1981)

Morriss, Roger, *Guide to British Naval Papers in North America* (London; National Maritime Museum)

Mundy, Godfrey, *The Life and Correspondence of the Late Admiral Lord Rodney* (Boston; Gregg Press, 1972)

Napier, Maj. Gen. W.F.P., *History of the War in the Peninsula* (London; Thomas and William Boone, 1856)

Natkiel, Richard, and Perkins, Antony, *Atlas of Maritime History* (New York; Facts on File, Inc., 1986)

Naval Chronicle, The, (London; J. Gould, 1799–1818)

Nicol, John, *Life and Memoirs* (Edinburgh, 1822)

Nicholas, Sir Nicholas Harris, ed., *Despatches and Letters of Lord Viscount Nelson* (London; H. Colburn, 1845–46)

O'Byrne, William, *A Naval Biographical Dictionary* (London; J. Murray, 1849)

Oman, Carola, *Nelson* (New York; Garden City, 1946)

Pocock, Tom, *Horatio Nelson* (London; Bodley Head, 1987)

Rodger, N.A.M., *The Wooden World, an Anatomy of the Georgian Navy* (London; Collins, 1986)
____, *The Command of the Ocean* (New York; W.W. Norton and Co. Ltd., 2004)
____, *Memoirs of a Seafaring Life by William Spavens* (Bath, UK, The Bath Press, 2001)
Rush, Richard, *A Residence at the Court of London* (Philadelphia; Lee and Blanchard, 1845)
Sabine, Lorenzo, *Biographical Sketches of Loyalists of the American Revolution* (Boston; Little, Brown and Co., 1864)
Schom, Alan, *Trafalgar: Countdown to Battle, 1803–1805*, (Harpenden; Queen Anne Press, 1990)
Smith, Danny D., *The Yellow House Papers* (Gardiner, ME; Gardiner Library Association, 1991)
Smith, P.C.F., 'King George, The Massachusetts Province Ship, 1757–1763,' *Publications of the Colonial Society of Massachusetts*, Vol. 52
Southey, Robert, *Life of Nelson* (London; Constable and Co., 1916)
Spencer, Charles, *The Spencers* (New York; St. Martin's Press, 2000)
Stark, James, *The Loyalists of Massachusetts* (Boston; J.H. Stark, 1907)
Steele, D., *List of the Royal Navy* (London; D. Steele, 1781–1815)
Spinney, David, *Rodney* (London; Allen and Unwin, 1969)
Stuart, Neil, *The Royal Navy in America 1760–1775* (Annapolis, MD; Naval Institute Press, 1973)
Trew, Peter, *Rodney and the Breaking of the Line* (Barnsley, South UK; Pen and Sword Books, 2006)
Tucker, Jedediah, *Memoirs of the Earl of St. Vincent* (London, Bentley, 1844)
United Services Journal, part iii, 1834 and part i, 1835
Vincent, Frank, *Nelson*, (New Haven and London; Yale University Press, 2003)
Walbron, Capt. John, *British Columbia Coast Names* (Seattle; University of Washington Press, 1972)
Walker, James W., *The Black Loyalists* (Toronto; University of Toronto Press, 1992)
Warner, Oliver, *Great Sea Battles* (London; Weidenfeld and Nicholson, 1963)
____, *Life and Letters of Vice-admiral Lord Collingwood* (London; Oxford University Press, 1968)
____, *Nelson's Battles* (London; Batsford, 1965)
Webber, Sandra, 'Proud Builders of Boston: The Hallowell Family Shipyard, 1635–1804,' *The American Neptune*, Spring 2001
Webster, J.C., *The Recapture of St. John's* (Shediac, N.B.; 1928)
Willyams, Rev. Cooper, *Voyage up the Mediterranean in His Majesty's Ship the Swiftsure* (London, 1803)

INDEX

Abercromby, General, 204, 206
Aboukir, 187, 193, 193, 194, 213, 216, 244, 250, 262
Acadians, 87, 89
Accra, 108, 249
Adam, Colonel, 324, 325
Adams, Governor, 141
Adams, John, 15, 85 – 86, 159
Addington, 221
Addiscombe, 360
Admiralty, 90, 95, 98, 110, 131 – 133, 141, 148, 162, 200, 208, 230, 231, 250, 258, 263, 270, 281, 301, 302, 303, 306, 309, 310, 328, 330, 353, 356
Adriatic, 290, 295
Africa Company, 111
Africa Corps (*see also* Royal African Corps) 234, 237, 238
Africa, 103, 110, 231
Africaine, 225
African slaves, 80, 93, 113
Agincourt, 246
Ainslie, Lieutenant, 146, 147, 149, 151
Albemarle, 91
Alcide, 63 – 65, 67, 69, 77, 144
Aldsworth House, 105
Aldsworth, Sussex, 96
Alexander the Great, 171
Alexander, 175, 177 – 79, 181
Alexander, Czar, 290, 313, 331
Alexander, Mr., 34, 50
Alexandria, 172, 173, 175, 188, 190, 199, 205, 206, 210, 211, 218, 231, 243 – 45, 261, 262, 277 – 80
Alfred, 67, 69, 70, 73, 77 – 83, 91, 94
Algeciras, 144, 146, 168

Algerian corsairs, 335
Ali, Mehmet, 242, 277, 280, 281
Alicante, 312, 316, 317, 318, 330, 337
Allen, Captain, 181
American Board of Customs, 16 – 17, 20, 30, 59, 84, 186
American Revolution, 55, 58, 61, 68, 87, 88, 102, 105, 111, 117, 159
Amiable, 78
Amsterdam, 204
Andromache, 148
Anguilla, 373
Annapolis Basin, 82
Annapolis Valley, 87
Antigonish County, 137
Antigonish Harbour, 137
Antigonish, 141
Antigua, 61, 62, 70, 90, 91, 93, 114
Antilles, 114
Antoinette, Marie, 115, 116, 123, 196
Ape's Hill, 147
Apollo, 298
Arabia, 171
Arawaks, 80
Arbuthnot, Admiral, 79
Argo, 225, 229, 230, 232 – 256
Arichat, 38
Army of Italy, 206
Articles of War, 277
Arundel, Earl of, 105
Asia, 41 – 43, 46, 47 – 57, 59, 60, 68, 69, 91, 110, 294, 348, 358
Aston Hall, 31
Atlantic Ocean, North and South, 46
Attorney General of Ireland, 350
Auerstadt, 289
Aurora, 167
Austerlitz, 276, 289
Australia, 352
Austria, 115, 185, 196, 197, 220, 275, 331
Aylmer, John, 218

Azores, 109
Badajoz, 315
Baffin Island, 355
Ball, Captain, 179, 226
Baltic, 283, 284, 304
Band of Brothers, 9, 174, 207, 367
Barbados, 69 – 70, 91, 92, 114, 239, 263
Barbary pirates, 314
Barbary States, 295
Barbor, Robert, 78, 80, 81
Barcelona 295, 296, 316, 330, 331
Barfleur, 61, 63, 67, 91, 97, 98, 100, 101, 166
Barnard's Inn, 86
Barras, Director, 137
Barwell, Mr. 105
Basque Roads, 292
Basseterre, 70, 71
Bastia, 123, 124, 166
Bastille, 115
Bathurst Street, 186
Bathurst, Lord, 338, 340
Batterymarch shipyard, 251
Batterymarch, Boston, 13
Battle of Cape St. Vincent. *See* Cape St. Vincent
Battle of Les Saintes. *See* Les Saintes
Battle of Martinique, 54
Battle of Navarino, 358
Battle of the Atlantic, 10, 373
Battle of the Nations, 331
Battle of the Nile. *See* Nile
Battle of the Pyramids, 173
Battle of Trafalgar. *See* Trafalgar
Bavaria, 276
Bay of Aboukir, 175, 205, 211, 213, 278
Bay of Biscay, 42, 167
Bay of Rosas, 296, 298
Bay of Tarragona, 318

INDEX

Bayne, Captain, 73, 77
Bearhaven Harbour, 351
Bearhaven, 350
Beauchamp, 190, 201
Beauharnais, Josephine, 137, 290
Beddington Manor, 224, 225, 283, 360 – 64, **363**, 367, 369, 371
Beddington Park, 342
Bedford, 63, 74
Belair, General, 201
Bellerophon, 168, 179, 180, 344, 345, 357
Bengal Native Infantry, 368
Bentinck, William, 315, 316, 320, 328, 330, 334, 335, 340
Bequires, 175 – 78
Berkeley, Commander V. C., 90, 91, 93
Berkeley, Welters, 219
Bernard, Andrew, 340
Berthelot, Lieutenant, 182
Bey, Elphi 242 – 45, 262, 280, 281
Bey, Ibrahim, 244
Bey, Osman, 244
Bickerton, Richard, 205 – 207, 209, 210, 212, 287, 288
Bight of Benin, 113, 114, 238
Bill of Pains and Penalties, 355
Bishop, Captain Thomas, 22, 26, 27, 29, 161
Bishop, Rebecca, 29,
Bishop, Rebecca, 29, 90
Black Loyalists, 233
Black Sea, 359
Blackheath, 225
Blackstakes, 116
Blenheim, 155, 239
Bligh, William, 99
Blucher, Marshal, 344
Bluebeard, 362
Board of Trade, 234
Bombay Castle, 140
Bombay, 41, 50 – 52, 56
Bonaparte, Jerome, 210
Bonaparte, Joseph, 291
Bonaparte, Napoleon, 56, 118, 119, 137, 139,
152, 170, 172, 173, 175, 185 – 88, 191, 201, 204, 206, 210, 221, 239, 241, 248, 249, 260, 261, 264, 267, 275, 284, 285, 289, 290, 291 – 93, 295, 313 – 15, 331, 334, 335, 342 – 49, **343**, 354, 357, 370, 374
Bordeaux, 331
Boreas, 92
Borée, 297
Boston Ports Bill, 21
Boston Tea Party, 21
Boston, 13 – 17, 20, 23, 25 – 30, 40, 41, 60, 63, 79, 82, 85, 86, 88, 103, 104, 105, 109, 120, 136, 140, 141, 143, 158, 159, 161, 217, 222 – 24, 226, 251, 255, 274, 294, 314
Boulogne, 249, 264, 275, 284
Bounty, 98
Bourbons, the, 115, 331
Bowen, Captain, 323
Boxer, Edward, 297, 333
Boylston grant, the, 136, 137, 141
Boylston, Mary. *See* Hallowell, Mary (mother)
Boylston, Nicholas (Nicky), 22, 85, 90, 254, 255, 273
Boylston, Nova Scotia, 95
Boylston, Rebecca, 86, 141, 159
Boylston, Thomas, 60, 86, 89, 94, 95, 96, 97, 98, 103, 141
Boylston, Ward Nicholas (*see also* Hallowell, Ward Nicholas), 98, 103, 105, 106, 114, 136, 140, 141, 149, 158, 160, 281, 282, 217, 223, 224, 250, 251, 252, 254, 255, 273, 274, 314, 362, 363
Brenton, Edward Pelham, 346
Brest, 162, 198, 200,
261, 263, 264
Brienne, 56, 119
Briggs, Rebecca, 85
Brimstone Hill, 70, 71
Bristol, 90, 96, 109
Britannia, 140, 144, 148, 272
British Customs, 25
Brown, Mr., 208, 209
Brueys, Admiral, 171, 175 – 78, 181, 198, 200, 202, 206, 207, 294
Bruix, Admiral, 198, 200, 202
Brune, 317
Brunswick, 355
Buckingham Gate, 84, 104
Buckingham, Marquis of, 206
Bulwark, 296, 297
Bunker Hill, 26, 27, 28, 161, 294
Burgoyne, 'Gentleman Johnny,' 40
Burrowes, Commander, 232
Burrows, Lieutenant, 144 – 47, 149 – 51
Byng, Admiral, 65
Cabrera, 293
Cabritta Point, 146
Cadiz, 152, 156, 162, 164, 167, **168**, 171, 198, 200, 203, 204, 247, 261 – 65, 267, 273, 275, 276, 291
Cadmus, 358
Cairo, 173
Calcutta, 365, 366
Calcutta, 41, 44, 49
Calder, Admiral, 264, 265
Calder, Captain, 11, 144, 153, 156
California, 101
Calvi, 123 – 25, 128, 129, 133, 140, 199, 226, 321
Cambridge, 166
Cambridge, 365, 366
Camel, 116, 117, 166, 221
Camperdown, 253
Canada, 352
Canary Islands, 110, 162

Canning, Foreign Minister, 356
Canopus, 296
Canopus, city of, 187
Canso, 38
Cape Charles, 64
Cape Finisterre, 42
Cape Hallowell, 355
Cape Henry, 62 – 64, 66
Cape of Good Hope, 41, 43, 47, 48, 52, 53, 170, 348
Cape St. Sebastian, 296
Cape St. Vincent, 11, 60, 148, 152, **153**, **155**, 159 – 160, 166, 304
Cape Town, 44, 50, 56, 121, 348
Cape Trafalgar, 267
Capon, General, 325
Captain, 139, 154, 155
Capua, 200
Carew Estate Act, 371
Carew Manor School, 372
Caribbean, 62, **70**, 116
Carleton, Sir Guy, 81
Carlisle Bay, 239
Carolinas, the, 55
Caroline, Princess, 225, 226, 308
Caroline, Queen, 123, 283, 355
Caron Iron Works, 102
Carrol, Commander, 328
Cartagena, 261, 262
Castle of Aboukir, 187, 192, 205
Castle William, 17, 21
Caton, 78
Caucasus, the, 170
Cavendish Square, 85
Cavendish, William (*see also* Devonshire, Duke of), 254
Cawsand Bay, 256
Centaur, 71, 109, 116, 240, 275
Ceres, 78
César, 109
Ceuta, 262
Channel fleet, 263, 288, 294, 299, 342
Channel Tunnel, 372
Chapman, Lieutenant, 146, 147

Charleston, 55, 67, 81, 117, 254
Charter House School, 364
Chatham dockyard, 82, 355
Chatham, Lord, 287
Chedabucto Bay, 14
Chelsea, 142
Chesapeake, 41, 62, 63, 65, 67, 75, 77, 79, 81, 109, 144
Cheshunt, 19, 23, 25
Chetwynd, Charles, 353
Christian, George, 59
Church of England, 364
Churchill, Winston, 373
Citoyen Marchand, 188
City of London, 212
Civitavecchia, 200, 201
Clam Harbour, Nova Scotia, 95
Clarence, Duke of (*see also* William IV, King), 259, 283, 308, 366
Clifford, Augustus, 254, 282, 306
Clinton, General, 62, 81, 321, 327, 330
Cochrane, Captain, 205, 207
Cochrane, Lord, 292
Cockburn, Captain, 162, 163, 359
Cockburn, George, 345, 348
Codrington, Admiral, 358, 367
Coffin, Henry, 312
Coffin, Isaac, 79, 105, 106, 228
Coffin, Nathaniel, 79, 105
Col de Balaguer, 318, 320, 323, 327, 328, 337 – 39
Cole, Lieutenant, 322 – 24
Colebrook, 41 – 42, 44, 47, 49
Collingwood, Cuthbert, 50, 68, 91, 116, 150, 154, 264, 266, 267, 278, 281, 282, **291**, 291, 293 – 96, 298, 299, 304, 342, 367

Collingwood, Wilfred, 50, 91, 92, 150, 294
Columbus, 80
Colville, Admiral, 14 – 15
Comet, 354
Commenda, 112
Committee of Public Safety, 137
Comptroller of Customs, Boston, 15, 16
Comptroller of the Navy, 300
Concord, 26
Congress of Erfurt, 290
Connecticut, 28
Constantinople, 170, 191
Constitution, 214, 314
Continental Policy, 290
Continental System, 313
Cook, James, 48
Coote, Sir Eyre, 49
Copenhagen, 207, 221, 253, 269
copper sheathing, 72, 78
Cordova, Admiral, 151, 152, 155, 156
Corfu, 172
Cork, 348 – 52, 359, 369
Cormin, General, 188
Cornwallis, General, 55, 61, 63, 65 – 67, 81
Cornwallis, Admiral 263, 264
Corsica, 123, **127**, 131, 139, 228, 289
Corunna, 291
Cotton, Charles, 304, 307
County Cork, 57
County Tipperary, 349
Courageux, 121, 123, 124, 129, 130 – 157, 159 – 61, 169, 206, 220, 243, 247, 252, 273, 289
Court of St. James, 85
Crawford, Lieutenant, 257, 298, 312, 332, 341
Crisk, Patrick, 166
Crookhaven, 57
crossing the Line, 44, **45**
Crown Courts of Vice-Admiralty, 17
Croydon, 360

INDEX

Cuba, 233
Culloden, 154, 168, 178, 197, 298
Cumberland, Duke of, 137
Cutler, Stuart and Wyatt, 95
Cutler, Thomas, 95
Cyprus, 172, 173
D'Estaing, Admiral, 41
Dacres, Captain, 258, 270, 271
Dalrymple, Colonel, 21
Danton, 116
Dardanelles, 294
Davis, Lieutenant, 219
de Grasse, Admiral, 58, 62 – 67, 70 – 75
de Vaisseau Daubin, Enseign, 241, 242
Declaratory Act, 16
Defence, 184
Deptford Yard, 354
Derna, 210
Devonshire, 13
Devonshire, Duke of (*see also* Cavendish, William), 253
Diadème, 74
Diana, 27
Digby, Admiral Robert, 81
Directorate (France) 170, 201
Dix Août, 214, 215
doldrums, 43, 57
Dolphin, 68
Dominica, 73
Donkin, Rufane, 317, 322, 323, 325, 328, 329, 338, 339, 340, 364
Dorchester Heights, 28
Dorchester, 158
Douglas, Captain Charles, 72, 75, 357
Dover Strait, 241
Downs, the, 59, 143, 248, 283
Dragon, 218
Drake, Admiral, 67
Drouette, 277
Dubardieu, General, 201
Dublin, 68
Duckworth, Admiral, 200, 201, 203, 277, 280

DuGommier, General, 119
Duke of Wellington, (*see also* Wellesley, Arthur), 292
Dumaresq, Peter, 81, 82
Dundas, General, 120
Duquesne, 133
Durloo Channel, 286
Dursey Island, 351
East India Company, 41, 46, 48 – 49, 105, 365
East Norfolk militia, 60
École Royale Militaire, 119
Edgar, 285
Edgware Road, 89, 104
Edward Augustus, Prince, 161
Effendi, Selim, 244
Egypt, 23, 170, 172, 173, 185, 186, 201, 204, 206, 221, 242, 244, 245, 261, 262, 277, 279, **280**, 281, 282, 295, 303, 328, 342, 359
Egyptian Club, the, 189
Elba, 172, 331, 335, 342, 346, 348
Elmsley, Ann-Gee, 252
Elmsley, John Jr., 252, 359, 363
Elmsley, John, 142, 143, 158 – 61, 223, 251, 274, 357, 374
Elmsley, Mary, 142, 241, 251, 274, 360, 362, 364
Elphinstone, George Keith, (*see also* Keith, Lord) 117, 118, 121, 129, 131, 133, 206
Eltham, 283, 354
Emsworth, Sussex, 105
English Channel, the, 54, 114, 161, 241, 261, 263, 264, 275, 349, 383
English Harbour, 93 – 94
equator, **45**, 57
Estates General, the, 115
Eton College, 19, 20, 313
Excellent, 154, 155
Executive Council of

Upper Canada, 160, 161
Exeter, 158
Fadden, William, 110
Faial, 110
Falcon, 90, 91, 93, 94, 116, 219, 254, 283
Falmouth, 161, 162
False Bay, 47
Fame, 78
Fanning, Colonel, 87, 94, 95
Ferdinand, King, 123, 196, 198, 226, 291
Ferguson, Niall, 52
Ferris, Abel, 299
Ferrol, 261, 264, 265
fighting in the Age of Sail, 384 – 388
firing mechanisms, 72
First Continental Congress, 26
Fitzherbert, Mrs., 225
Flushing, 286
Formidable, 74 –75
Fort Appolonia, 108
Fort l'Aiguillette, 119
Fort la Malgue, 117, 120
Fort Mulgrave, 119
Fort Thornton, 237
Fort Ticonderoga, 28
Fortitude, 123
Fortune, 188
Fortunée, 59, 61, 67
Foster, Lady Elizabeth, 254
Foudroyant, 199, 205, 206
France, 99, 101, 115 – 17, 137, 143, 167, 170, 174, 185, 196, 220, 221, 239, 244, 249, 290 – 92, 331, 340, 342, 343, 345, 359
Franklin, 179 – 81, 184, 356
Franklin, Benjamin, 22, 60
Frazer, General, 71, 277, 278, 281
Freetown, 112, 233, 234, 236 – 38
Frejus, 201
Fremantle, Captain, 139
French Revolution, 197, 345

French Shoal, 44
French West Indies fleet, 62
Fuerte Real, 320 – 22
Funchal, 42
Fury and Hecla Strait, 355
Gage, General, 21, 26, 28
Gallup's Island, 27
Gambier, Admiral, 292
Gamble, Mr., 219
Ganteaume, General, 206, 210, 213, 214, 216, 217, 261, 263, 296
Ganymede, 347, 358
Gardener, Captain Sir Alan, 142, 299
Gardiner, Maine, 364
Gardiner, Robert Hallowell, 96, 159, 226, 314, 356, 364
Gardner, Richard, 100
Gaspée, 21
Gatton, 46, 47, 49
Gatwick Airport, 372
Gee, Anne, 217, 361 – 64, 369, 370
Gee, William, 224, 225, 360
Gee-Carew, Richard, 224, 360
genealogical relationships, **99**
General Assembly, 159
Genereux, 184
Genoa, 133
George III, King, 221, 243, 308, 355
George IV, King, 355
Germaine, George, 54, 61
German Legion, the, 315
Germany, 275, 290
Gibraltar Navy Yard, 169
Gibraltar, 148
Gibraltar, 54, 117, 123, 138, 144, **145**, 150, 159, 168, 169, 171, 195, 200, 202, 203, 209 – 11, 220, 227, 243, 247, 252, 262, 263, 267, 270 – 73, 276, 294, 295, 314
Gill, Lieutenant Governor, 159
Gill, Moses, 29, 86, 135, 141

Glasgow, 346, 355
Glorieux, 74
Gold Coast, 108
Goliath, 177
Gould, Anne (*see also* Gee, Anne), 24, 90, 96, 104 – 105, 224, 225, 252, 360
Gould, James, 24
Gould, Paston, 22, 24, 369
Graham, James, 366
Grand Army, the, 275, 331
Grant, Alexander, 160, 161
Graves, David, 27
Graves, John, 27
Graves, Samuel Jr., 27
Graves, Samuel, 27 – 28, 31, 294
Graves, Thomas, 27, 62 – 68, 75
Gravina, Admiral, 266, 268
Greece, 173, 359
Greenway, Lieutenant, 214
Greenwich Hospital, 60, 270
Greenwich, 269, 283, 355
Grenada, 60
Grenville, Lord, 206
Greville, Charles, 196
Grey, Captain George 227, 269 – 270
Grey, Lord, 300, 302, 367
Guadeloupe, 73
Guanches, 110
Guerrier, 178
Guillaume Tell, 184, 311, 346
Gulf of Genoa, 331
Gulf of Guinea, 108, 113
Gulf of Marmorice, 191
Gulf of Palma, 246
Gulf of Simia, 191
Gulf Stream, 114, 116
gunnery, 72
Guysborough, Nova Scotia, 95, 136
Hackney, 220, 224, 283
Halifax Chronicle, 275

Halifax Dockyard, 229
Halifax Harbour, 275
Halifax, Earl of, 105
Halifax, Nova Scotia, 14, 17, 29 – 31, 40, 60, 68, 136, 137, 160, 186, 227, 228, 229, 233, 251, 252, 274, 299, 310, 346, 359
Hallowell, Anne (Aunt Gould), 22, 24
Hallowell, Benjamin (grandfather), 13, 22, 31, 86
Hallowell, Benjamin (son), 252, 283, 364, 365, 368, 371
Hallowell, Benjamin Sr. (father), 13 – 21, 25, 27 – 28, 29, 30, 31, 34, 40, 41, 55, 60, 63, 67, 68, 79, 84 – 89, 85, 94, 95, 103, 105, 109, 122, 134 – 37, 141 – 43, 159, 160, 186, 222, **222**, 223, 294, 299, 308
Hallowell, Charles, 220, 252, 283, 289, 296, 336, 346, 347, 348, 358, 359, 363, 369
Hallowell, Henrietta, 252, 283
Hallowell, Lucy, 18, 20
Hallowell, Maine, 13, 251
Hallowell, Martha, 85
Hallowell, Mary (daughter), 252
Hallowell, Mary (mother), 15, 18, 22, 26, 30, 86, 103, 104, 135, 140, 141, 223
Hallowell, Mary (sister), 16, 18, 59, 85, 89, 94, 96, 104, 105, 136, 224, 359
Hallowell, Mary-Anne, 308
Hallowell, Robert, 17, 20, 29, 40, 67, 68, 90, 96, 104, 135, 136, 159, 226, 251
Hallowell, Ward Nicholas (*see also* Boylston, Ward

INDEX

Nicholas), 15, 18, 22, 23 – 26, 30, 31, 60, 85, 86, 90, 94
Hallowell, William Henry, 308, 358, 368
Hallowell-Carew, Benjamin, 9, 361, **361**, 367, 368
Hallowell-Carew, Charles (son), 371
Hallowell-Carew, Charles Hallowell (grandson), 371, 372
Halsted, Captain, 304
Hamilton, Lady Emma, 11, 195, 196, 197, 199, 204, 247, 264
Hamilton, Sir William, 195, 196
Hancock, John, 17
Hannibal, 168
Hardy, Thomas, 162, 358
Harley Street, 230
Harness, Dr. 128
Harrison, Acklom, 17, 25 – 26, 140
Harrison, John, 383
Harrow, 19
Harvard University, 23, 88, 226
Hassan Bey, 190
Haulbowline Island, 350
Hecla, 355
Hellespont, 29
Henry the Navigator, Prince, 43
Hibernia, 300, 301
Hispaniola, 78
Hitler, Adolf, 373, 374
HMCS *Hallowell*, 374, **374**, **375**,
Holland, 116, 204, 221, 248, 290
Holland, Fox, 313
Holland, Lord, 313
Holy Land, the, 23
Hood, Samuel, 17, 40, 41, 58 – 67, **59**, 68 –71, 73, 74, 77 – 79, 90, 91, 96 – 97, 101, 109, 116, 117, 119, 121 – 124, 126, 128, 130, 134, 139, 159, 178, 192, 194, 199, 226, 238, 239, 240, 270, 300,
301, 307, 308, 364
Hope, 156, 158
Hotham, Admiral, 129, 131 – 134
House of Brunswick, 225
Howe, Richard, 58, 165, 174
Howe, William, 28, 58
Hudson River, 158
Hudson valley, 40
Hughes, Edward, 53
Hughes, Richard, 91, 92
Hunter, Ben, 312
Hutchinson, Governor, 16, 360
Hyères Bay, 128
Île d'Aix, 344
Île de France. *See* Mauritius
India, 41, 51, 53, 106, 171, 368
Indivisible, 214, 215
Inglefield, Ann, 169, 203, 220, 227
Inglefield, Ann, 225, 252, 285, 336, 348, 368
Inglefield, Catherine Dorothy, 169, 275, 310
Inglefield, John, 71, 109, 110, 112, 113, 115, 116, 169, 203, 220, 227, 228, 229, 230, 231, 251, 274, 275, 299, 302, 309, 310, 312, 318, 319, 320, 323, 325, 363
Inglefield, Lucretia, 169
Inglefield, Samuel Hood, 9, 110, 179, 205, 213, 310, 340, 368
Iran, 171
Ireland, 172, 221, 241, 262, 347, 349 – 54, 359
Irish squadron, the, 347
Irresistible, 268
Istanbul, 191, 277, 280
Italy, 23, 137, 139, 152, 196, 200, 221, 290, 295, 316, 331, 349
Jacobin government, 118
Jacobin minority, 115
Jacobins, 120, 137
Jamaica, 60, 62, 72 – 73, 77, 79 – 82, 233, 236
Jarvis, William, 186

Jason, 78
Jean Bart, 214
Jefferson, Thomas, 22, 86, 159, 221
Jena, 289
Jervis, John (*see also* St. Vincent, Earl of), 68, 132, 134, 135, 138, 139, 140, 143, 144, 148, 149, 151, 152, 153, **153**, 154, 156, **157**, 158, 159, 161, 162, 197, 226, 254, 299, 301, 304, 339, 367
John, George. *See* Earl Spencer
John, Georgiana, 253
John, Lavinia. See Spencer, Lady
Jones, John Paul, 38
Juan de Fuca, 100
Keith, Lord, (*see also* Elphinstone, George), 121, 138, 197, 198, 200, 204 – 214, 217, 218, **218**, 220, 230, 231, 249, 250, 281, 302, 341, 342 – 56, 364
Kennebec Proprietorship, 159
Kennebec River, 13
Kennebec, 86
Kerr, Captain, 288
King George, 14 – 15, 40, 68, 135
King Tom, 111, 233, 234, 236, 237
King, Lieutenant, 351 – 52
Kingston, 161
Knight Grand Cross of the Bath, 366
Knights of Malta, 172
Knightsbridge, 142
l'Artémise, 173, 175, 184
L'Oiseau, 241, 242
L'Orient, 122, 179, 180, **183**, 181, 182, 184, 188, 189, 194, 197, 198, 202, 205, 216, 270, 294, 298, 346
Lafayette, Marquis de, 41
Lake Champlain, 40
Lake Mahdi, 279
Lake Mariotis, 206, 279

Lamproie, 298
Langara, Admiral, 117, 120, 143, 144
League of Armed Neutrality, 207
Leander, 177, 181, 310
Lee, John, 166, 167, 169, 173, 181, 189 190, 193, 265
Leeward Islands, 62, 72, 90, 92, 93, 114, 115, 238
Leipzig, 331
Les Saintes, 73 – 77, **76**, 79, 109, 133, 289, 357, 388
Lexington, 26
Liberty, 17, 25, 109
Lind, James, 48
Lind, Lieutenant, 78
Lion, 297
Lisbon, 143, 148, 151, 161, 162, 164, 165, 211, 228, 290, 291, 292
Lively, 22, 26, 27, 29, 40, 156, 158, 161, 162, 164, 203, 247
Liverpool, 109
Livorno, 123, 133, 138, 139, 143
Lloyd's insurance, 350
Lodge, Mr., 94, 95
London Chronicle, 31
London Gazette, 124
London, 15, 31, 59, 86, 89, 90, 105, 158, 165, 196, 224, 335, 362
London, 66
Long Island, 104
Louis XVI, King, 115, 116, 117
Louis XVIII, King, 342
Louis, Admiral Captain, 201, 207, 265, 267, 268, 276, 281
Louisbourg, 14, 68
Lower Canada, 274
Lowestoffe, 130, 132, 133, 134, 151, 162
Loyalist Claims Commission, 20, 86, 89, 94, 104
Loyalists, 55, 61, 81, 82, 87, 88, 104, 111, 141, 142, 159, 360
Luckey, Mr., 219

Lumley, Earl of, 105
Macaulay, Zachary, 237
Mack, General, 196, 275, 276
Mackenzie, General, 321
Madagascar, 49, 53
Maddalena, 261
Madeira, 42, 44, 47, 52, 107, 110, 164, 232, 289
Madras, 52, 53, 54, 69
Mahe, 51
Mahón, 291, 293 – 95, 299, 305, 306, **306**, 311, 318
Maine, 159, 223
Maitland, Captain, 345
Maitland, General, 315, 316, 317
Malta, 172, 204, 210, 211, 213, 220, 221, 243, 245, 262, 282
Malta, 311, 312, 317, 321, 322, 327, 331, 332, 333, 346, 349
Man of War Bay, 238
Man, Admiral, 143
Manby, Captain, 225
Manchester grant, the, 274
Mandamus Councilors, 21
Maria Carolina, Queen, 196
Marie Louise, Princess, 290
Marlborough, 165
Marmeluke beys, the, 242
Marmelukes, the, 170, 173, 243, 244, 277, 278, 280
Marmorice, 204
Maroons, 80, 233, 234, 236, 238
Marseilles, 117, 171
Martin Vas, 46, 48
Martin, Admiral, 128, 178, 296, 297, 304
Martin, Captain, 207, 208, 209, 231, 250
Martinique, 60, 69, 72, 93, 263
Marysburgh, 161
Massachusetts General Court, 141
Mathieu, Maurice, 319,

321
Matra, Mr., 148
Mauricanou, 237
Mauritius, 49, 51
Maxwell, Mary, 363
Maxwell, Murray, 363
Mediator, 91, 116
Mediterranean fleet, the, 247
Mediterranean, 54, 116, 117, 121, 123, **124**, 134 – 36, 143, 152, 162, 170 – 72, **171**, 185, 188, 194, 198, 200, 202, 204, 209, 219, 245, 253, 257 – 59, 261, 262, 265, 273, 274, 276, 277, 282, 283, 287, 292, 294, 302, 304, 307, 311, 315, **315**, 335, 336, 341, 342, 346, 348, 349, 359
Medusa, 110, 113, 115
Melbourne, Prime Minister, 371
Melville, Lord, 249, 333, 348, 353, 359
Menou, General, 205, 206, 221
Merton, 247
Messina, 277
Milan, 138
Minerva, 162, 163
Minorca, 65, 200, 201, 209 – 211, 218, 228, 291, 293, **306**, 311
Minotaur, 285
Missett, Major, 278
Missiesy, Admiral, 261, 263
Mohammed, Dallam, 236
Molineaux, Anne, 22
Mona Passage, 78
Moniteur of Paris, 217
Montague, Admiral, 69, 79
Montreal, 40, 143, 160, 274, 374
Moore, John, 291, 292, 300
Morgan, Lieutenant, 352
Moriarty, Lieutenant, 351, 352
Morocco, 147, 317

INDEX

Morrice, John, 18 – 20, 24, 25, 34, 50
Morris, Charles, 87
Mortella, 123
Morton, John, 145 – 47, 150, 151
Moscow, 331
Mould, Commander, 351
Mount Etna, 172, 195
Mudge, Lieutenant, 219
Mulgrave, Lord, 292, 304
Murray, Archibald, 312
Murray, John, 317 – 328, 329, 334, 335, 337, 338, 339, 342, 354, 364
Musquodoboit, Nova Scotia, 136
Mutine, 162, 351
mutiny, Royal Navy, 164 –167
Nantasket, 27, 29
Napier, General, 334, 337
Naples Bay, 196
Naples, 23, 123, 143, 172, 185, 195, 197, 198, 200, 221, 275, 293
Nautic Legion, 187
Naval Chronicle, 310
Navigation Acts, 92
navigation in the Age of Sail, 382 – 384
Navy Board, 53, 208, 209, 230, 231, 300, 309
Nelson, Horatio, 9 – 11, 33, 91 – 93, 101, 123, 125 – 28, 131, 133, 140, 154 – 56, 162, 164, 167, 171 – 78, 181, 186 – 88, 194 – 200, **202**, 204, 207, 213, 221, 226, 245, 247, 253, 256, 257, 259, 260 – 262, 264 – 270, 281 – 83, 294, 314, 321, 341, 367, 370, 388
Netherlands, 99
New England, 89
New Hampshire, 88
New York City, 55
New York, 30, 40, 62, 65, 66, 67, 69, 81, 91, 95, 104

Newark, 143, 158
Newcastle, 359
Newfoundland fishery, 13
Newfoundland, 23, 30, 354
Niagara-on-the-Lake. *See* Newark
Niagara region, 158
Nichol, John, 176, 205
Niemen, River, 290
Niger, 148
Nile Medal, 337
Nile, **180**, **183**, 185, 196, 197, 199, 202, 203, 213, 222, 226, 244, 253, 269, 279, 281, 289, 311, 344, 346, 372, 388,
Nootka Sound Convention, 101
Nootka Sound, 101, 303
Nore, the, 165, 347, 354, 355, 357 – 60
Norfolk gaol, Virginia, 254
North, Lord, 15, 54, 88, 338
Northesk, Earl of, 272
Northumberland Strait, 137
Northumberland, 208, 209, 231, 250, 345
northwest passage, 355
Nova Scotia, 10, 29 – 30, 38, 81, 86 – 89, 92, 94, 103, 111, 136, 137, 141, 222, 229, 233, 251
Nunavut, 10
Nymph, 70
O'Brian, Patrick, 11
Old Guard, 342
Oliver, Andrew, 16
Ontario, 10, 373
Oporto, 291
Orde, Admiral, 166
Orde, John, 339
Orde, Robert, 262
Order of the Bath, 336
Orpington, 368
O'Sullivan, Morley, 350 – 52
O'Sullivan, Roger, 350
Ottoman Empire, 170, 185, 277
Ottoman navy, 358

Owen, Commodore Edward, 283, 284
Oxford University, 360
Painted Hall, 270
Palamós, 316
Palermo, 194, 195, 197, 208, 230, 250, 304
Paoli, the patriot, 123
Paris, 60, 115, 119, 137, 170, 201, 331, 342
Parker, Sir Peter Admiral, 79, 151, 270
Parr, Governor, 87, 88
Parr, Mr., 194
Parry, Colonel, 351
Parthenopean Republic, 197, 198
Pasha, Hurshid, 244
Paul, Czar, 220, 221
Peace Congress, 342
Peace of Amiens, 241, 249
Peace of Tilsit, 290
Pearl Rock, 148
Peel, Prime Minister, 371
Pegasus, 91, 92, 134
Pellew, Edward, 226, 307, 320, 328 – 30, 334, 349
Penrose, Admiral, 335
Persian Gulf, 49
Peuple Souverain, 181
Philadelphia, 26, 40, 55
Pickering, 160
Pico Rive, 42
Picton, 351, 352
Picton, Ontario, 161, 373
Pictou, 373
Pimlico, 142
Pitt, William, 221, 249, 253
Plains of Abraham, 134
Plymouth Sound, 343, 345
Plymouth, 82, 158, 256, 257, 344
Pommier, Xavier, 162, 164
Pondicherry, 51
Pope, Dudley, 11
Porcupine, 134
Port Information Book, 192
Port Royal, Jamaica, 73, 81, 82

Portland, Duke of, 88, 137, 142
Porto Agro, 125
Portsmouth Dockyard, 40, 58, 242
Portsmouth Harbour, 106
Portsmouth, 36, 38, 59, 105, 158, 161, 164, 265, 283
Portugal, 42, 162, 167, 292, 290
Preston, 27, 68
Preston, Nova Scotia, 136, 233
Prince Edward County, Ontario, 161
Prince Regent, 357
Prince Regent, the, 283, 337, 338, 340, 341, 355
Princeton, 159
Prior, Lieutenant, 146, 147
Pritchard, William, 360, 361
Proselyte, 124, 126
Protestant ascendancy, 349
Providence, Rhode Island, 373
Prussia, 115, 331
Puerto Rico, 78
Pygmy, 213, 219
Pylades, 232, 238
Pyrenees, 331
Quarter Bill, 77
Quebec City, 274
Quebec, 30, 81, 134
Quinte, 161
Radish, Thomas, 143, 158
Raleigh, Walter, 362
Ramsgate, 143
Rattler, 91, 92
Redoubtable, 268
Reign of Terror, 116, 117
Renown, 218
Revolutionary War. *See* American Revolution
Rhineland, the, 221
Rhode Island, 21, 54, 55, 62, 65
Rhodes, 190 – 92, 204
Rhône, River, 220, 296, 297

Ripon, 53
Robespierre, 116
Robust, 118, 120, 121, 129, 203, 206
Robuste, 297
Rochambeau, 62
Rochefort, 242
Rockingham, Marquis of, 88
Rodney, 357
Rodney, George, 54, 58, 60 – 62, 67, 68, 71 – 75, 78, 79, 90, 266
Rome, 197, 200, 201
Romney, 17, 109
Rosetta, 278, 279
Rosiers Bay, 144
Rosily, Admiral, 267
Rowley, Captain, 304, 305
Rowley, James, 349
Roxbury, 16, 28, **29**, 86, 363
Roy Thompson Hall, 160
Royal Admiral, 41, 47
Royal African Corps (*see also* Africa Corps) 234
Royal Canadian Navy, 10
Royal Female Orphanage Society, 372
Royal George, 311
Royal Henry, 41, 44
Royal Naval College, 313, 336, 346
Royal Navy, 11, 17, 54, 72, 88, 91, 112, 121, 132, 137, 164, 185, 201, 202, 237, 253, 277, 276, 302, 314, 315, 332, 333, 347, 351, 354, 355, 373
Royal Navy, hierarchy, 376 – 80
Royal Sovereign, 266, 342
Ruffo, Cardinal, 197
Rush, Richard, 355, 356
Russell, Admiral, 288, 304
Russia, 185, 197, 220, 275, 290, 313, 314, 331, 359
Sahara Desert, 112
sailing in the Age of Sail, 380 – 82
Salisbury, 158

Salvador del Mundi, 154
San Fiorenzo Bay, 123, 131
San Fiorenzo, 131, 139
San Isidore, 155
San Josef, 154, 155
San Nicolas, 155
Sandwich, 35 – 36, 38, 41, 365
Santa Cruz, 110, 162, 163, 199, 248
Santissima Trinidad, 151, 154
Santo Domingo, 276
São Tomé, 113, 114
Saratoga, 40
Sardinia, 172, 261, 262
Saumarez, Admiral, 283, 304
Savannah, 55, 67, 81
Scheldt Estuary, **286**,
Scheldt, River, 284 – 89
Scorpion, 102, 103, 106, 110, 113, 115, 223, 230
scurvy, 48
Seaman's Bill, 165
Second Coalition, 201
Second World War, 10, 373
Selim III, 170
Selim, Sultan, 280
Serocold, Commander, 124, 125, 129
Sète, 297
Seven Years War, 60, 65, 71, 170
Sheerness Dockyard, 227, 228
Sheppard, Lieutenant, 213
Shovell, Clowdisley, 383
Shrewsbury, 79
Sicily, 173, 188, 195, 197, 198, 262, 293, 315, 320, 330
Sierra Leone Company, 111, 112, 233, 234, 237, 238
Sierra Leone, 111, 112, 233 – 37
Simcoe Street, 160
Simon's Bay, 47
Slave Coast, 108, 111
slave trade, 108, 109, **235**
Smith, Sidney, 120, 204, 225

INDEX

Sons of Freedom, 21
Sophiasburgh, 161
Sotheby, Captain, 140
South Pacific, 98
Spain, 100, 101, 123, 138, 143, 243, 262, 264, 290 – 93, 307, 315, 328, 330, 331, 334, 342, 356
Spartiate, 194
Spencer, Earl, 134, 156, 170, 171, 200, 227, 253, 259, **260**, 262 – 66, 276, 279, 280 – 83, 287, 288, 298, 300, 301, 304, 308, 313, 329, 339, 346, 353, 359, 364 – 66, 368, 369
Spencer, Frederick, 313, 335, 336, 344, 346
Spencer, Lady Diana, 313
Spencer, Lady, 253, 259, 288, 289
Spencer, Robert, 253, 254, 259, 273, 279, 282, 283, 288, 289, 293, 296, 298, 306, 307, 313, 347, 348, 358, 361, 362, 364, 369
Spithead, 36, 38, 47, 59, 61, 98, 100, 117, 162, 165, 211, 241, 242, 248, 282, 288, 307
St. Elmo, 198
St. George, 139
St. Giles Church, Cambridge, 366
St. Helena, 56 – 57, 345, 348, 349
St. John's, 14, 68
St. Kitts, 70, 71
St. Lawrence River, 31, 134, 251
St. Lucia, 60, 73, 239
St. Mary's Church, Beddington, 369, 372
St. Marylebone Church, London, 224
St. Paul's Cathedral, 270
St. Thomas, 238, 239, 249
St. Vincent, Earl (see also Jervis, John), 156, **157**, 161, 162, 165, 167,

170, 171, 199, 200, 227 – 29, 231, 241, 242, 244, 249, 253, 268, 294, 299, 300 – 303, 305, 308, 309, 339, 363, 364
Stafford Row, 84, 104
Stafford, 49
Stamp Act, 15 – 16, 21, 88
Stansted House, 106, 107
Stansted Park, 105
Start Point, 345
steam power, 354
Stewart, Charles, 314, 356
Strachan, Richard, 287
Strait of Gibraltar, 144, 262
Strait of Messina, 172
Stuart, Charles, 123, 126, 128
Styles, Showell, 11
Suchet, Marshal, 319, 320, 330, 331
Suffield, Mr., 313
Sutton, Lieutenant, 312
Sweden, 275, 331
Swiftsure, 162, 166 – 71, 173, 175, 177 – 82, **183**, 184, 187 – 195, **189**, 197, 198, 201 – 211, 213, 214, 216 – 20, 230, 249, 267, 268, 273, 276, 294, 298, 314, 346, 384
Switzerland, 221
Sydney County, 137
Syracuse, 173, 281
Syren, 314
Tahiti, 98
Tailour, Captain John, 298, 346, 350, 353
Talbot, Earl, 353
Tangier, 148
Tarragona, 316, 318, 319, **319**, 320, 325, **326**, 327, 328, 330, 334, 335, 337, 338, 340
Tea Duties, 21
Temne tribe, 233
Tenerife, 110, 162, 164, 359
Terrible, 65
Tetuan, 272
Texel, 288

Thackeray, Major, 321
Thames, River, 59, 94, 116, 143, 165, 224, 248, 270, 283, 354
Theseus, 168, 179
Third Coalition, the, 275, 276
Thirteen Colonies, the, 18, 67, 72
Thistle, 228
Thompson, Admiral, 150, 165
Thompson, Boulden, 111
Thompson, Charles, 144
Thompson, Norborne, 270 – 74, 300, 302
Thynose, Henry, 344
Ticonderoga, 40
Tigre, 249, 250, 252 – 59, 261, 262, 267, 270, 271, 273, 274, 276, 281 – 83, 285, 287 – 89, 291 – 93, 296 – 99, 302, 306, 307, 308
Tobago, 239, 241
Tonnant, 181, 184, 194, 343, 344, 346, 347, 349, 350, 353, 359
Topaze, 298
Torbay, 344
Toronto, 160, 186
Toulon Road, 217
Toulon, 117 – 23, 128 – 30, 133, 137 – 39, 143, 162, 170 – 72, 201, 210, 213, 218, 226, 246, 247, 261, 262, 265, 266, 284, 292 – 96, 299, 311, 331, 346
Townshend Acts/Duties, 16, 21
Townshend, Lieutenant, 351
Trafalgar, 185, 268, 270, 274 – 76, 294, 358, 388
Treaty of Amiens, 220, 221, 239
Treaty of Versailles, 53
Trelawney Town, 233
Trincomalee, 52
Trinidad, 263
Trinity College, Cambridge, 364
Triumph, 285
Troubridge, Thomas,